The Holy Family
Model Not Exception

The Holy Family
Model Not Exception

Mary Shivanandan STD

KM Associates
P.O. Box 228
Glen Echo, MD 20812

ISBN: 1981948171
ISBN 13: 9781981948178

Nihil Obstat
Rev. Basil Cole, OP
Censor Deputatus

Imprimatur
Most Rev. Barry Knestout
Auxiliary Bishop of Washington.
Archdiocese of Washington
December 7, 2017

Dedicated to:
The Holy Family
And
My Family

Contents

Tables in Text

Preface

Today the need is great to develop a theology of marriage and family. The intuition already formulated by St. John Paul II that the family is the way of the Church (John Paul II FC no. 2) has been confirmed by the reflection of the Church for more than two years after the two synods called by Pope Francis. The Church has to spend its efforts in humanizing and evangelizing the family. From here arises a mission for theology, according to a twofold vision.

The family is the way *first* to enlighten modern man, helping him to escape his individualism, by communicating a relational experience of the person. Each member of the family arrives at an understanding of who he is and his identity only in the light of a communion of persons and never in isolation; since in the family we are sons and daughters, husbands and wives, fathers and mothers. . . The family is the way *secondly* for the evangelizing mission of the Church. One speaks of the "Gospel of the family," which is to say: in the family are learned the words which teach each to say the Good News of Jesus. Only through experiences in the family can we understand God as Father, that Jesus is the Son, that the Church gives birth to us, that in the Eucharist a body is given to us. . .

Mary Shivanandan's book is placed within the context of this great task: to offer a profound theological reflection on the family, upon which a spirituality of the family can be solidly founded. And it is from a concrete and original point of view that the book starts: the contemplation of the Holy Family. This choice seems to call forth an objection. Is not the chosen point of departure too "ideal"? Is not this family-- the Holy Family—a family too singular and inimitable; made unique by the presence of the Incarnation of the Word in Mary's womb, and by the virginal relationship of Mary and Joseph?

Faced with this apparent difficulty, Shivanandan fully succeeds in showing in this book that the Holy Family cannot be termed only the great exception to the life of the family, nor, indeed, only as a model for us to imitate. Rather, the Holy Family is the source from which springs the life of all Christian families; the Holy Family is the horizon for understanding in its depth the call to love of every man and woman, and the fact that every personal vocation passes in one way or another by the family.

In this undertaking Shivanandan does not journey alone, accompanied as she is by a great theological tradition. In fact the great medieval synthesis on marriage shows that the reflection on the Holy Family was decisive in setting out the points that were key to the Christian vision of marriage. So, for example, it was by starting from the reflection of the marriage between Mary and Joseph that it is the free consent of the Christian spouses that clearly establishes what constitutes the sacrament. Against the exaggerated patriarchal concepts of the ancient world, the Church could insist, then, that the marriage is founded on the free consent of the spouses, which, through a mutual gift of self, forms a community of life and love.

On the other hand, the Holy Family also allowed the Medieval to understand the importance of consummation in the flesh. In this light they came to see that the flesh does not diminish but strengthens marital love; that marriage only reaches its indissoluble perfection, (that is, is only a sign of the union of Christ and the Church) when it is consummated. And the point of departure for this conclusion was the Incarnation, which took place in the Holy Family. It is in Jesus' birth from Mary's flesh, that God sealed definitively his covenant with humankind. The Holy Family, allows us, then, to appreciate the importance of all the concrete and bodily aspects of conjugal life.

Mary Shivanandan's book follows, then, the path opened by the great Tradition, in order to discover the key to all family life in the Holy Family. Shivanandan, however, does not merely repeat the traditional reasoning but she places her argument in the context of the great question of modern man, who seeks to understand the world from the depth of his personal experience. Thus, the pages of this book confirm the fecundity of the teachings of St. John Paul II, the Pope of the Family, who took as the starting point of his approach the experience of love, an incarnate love that puts us in relation with the world and others and opens us to God, helping us to escape the isolation peculiar to the modern subject.

Shivanandan's study places in clear relief that the communion of persons is the central dynamic of the family. And it explains also the importance of the flesh, starting from the new measure of the language of the body, which Jesus, Incarnate Son of God, brought with him. This is in accord with Benedict XVI's vision, when, in celebration of the 30th anniversary of the Pontifical John Paul II Institute for marriage and family, he affirmed that the family is the place where the theology of the body and the theology of love come together.

Shivanandan thus succeeds in offering a concrete and incarnate vision of the Holy Family, which gives no place for any spiritualist reading. On the contrary it is capable of unveiling also the ways in which Modernity has initiated a process "of disincarnation," which has contributed to the separation in the family, between sexuality, love and life. In this respect the analysis of the cultural changes introduced by contraception is of much interest in the book. Another important contribution of Shivanandan's study are the pages dedicated to the figure and mission of St. Joseph, which medieval theology had not yet developed. It is an urgent necessity in our day, as it illuminates the person and mission of the father, who is witness of the mystery which transcends himself and becomes the carrier, of a name and of a destiny for his children.

This luminous study of Shivanandan confirms, then, the paradox, which we have already mentioned: it is precisely the Holy Family that helps us see that the Christian vision of the family is not merely an ideal, removed from concrete life, inaccessible to the majority of people. On the contrary, the fact that in the Holy Family the Incarnation of the Word took place; and the fact that the coming of Jesus in the flesh generated the relations between Jesus, Mary and Joseph; this very fact allows us to understand that the love which lives in each family has its source, not in a distant ideal, but in a fact, an event, of the encounter with a person who took flesh in our concrete space and time.

Certainly, it must be said, that the Holy Family holds a unique place in the history of salvation. However, this is not an isolated unique place but a place from which springs light and strength for all families. It is in the Holy Family that each family finds the logic of true love and fulfillment. The Holy Family helps to bring about, within each family, the transformative strength of the Gospel.

Let us take an example. The birth of Jesus was certainly unique, the virginal birth of the Son of God. And, nevertheless, it is this birth which helps us interpret and understand in a definitive manner what "being born" means, which is the ultimate truth of the original experience of every man generated by love. The presence of the Father in the birth of Jesus, his action in the womb of Mary, were without doubt unique, but they confirm that in every child born in the mother's womb the hand of God is present. Yet more, this birth of the Son of God in Mary's womb in turn becomes the key to understanding Baptism, a new birth in Jesus. It is possible, then, to understand that the Christian family does not only generate sons of Adam but that the parents' mission includes also to lead their children to their regeneration to eternal life in God, as Pope Francis said, recalling St. Augustine (cf. LF 43). The Holy Family, in its unrepeatable singularity, opens that universal place whence human love, by discovering its original vocation, is assumed and transformed into the new love of Christ. The life of the Holy Family is an invitation to families to discover the profound logic of the Gospel, which is the origin and goal of all family life; so that they understand their love is on route to a definitive transformation in the love of God in order to be assumed into the communion of the Trinity.

Mary Shivanandan has shown us, in a detailed and profound study, that the Holy Family reveals the unity of God's plan for human love: unity of the Old and New Testament; of generation in the flesh and the Spirit; of family experiences and the evangelical call; of marriage and virginity . . . We are, indeed, before a vision which displays the riches of the Christian life, in its different vocations, contributing greatly to the task which the last two synods on the family have put before us; to throw the light of God on the ways of the family, which are the ways of the Church, in order that those ways can bring us to a safe harbor.

Fr. José Granados, dcjm
Vice President of the Pontifical John Paul II Institute for Studies on Marriage and Family at the Lateran University, Rome.

Acknowledgments

My first appreciation goes to St. John Paul II, without whose lifetime work on the person and the communion of persons this book on the Holy Family would not have been possible. In his studies on the person the pope confronted the two major totalitarian regimes of his day Nazism and Communism. In the West he faced a different challenge. Drawing inspiration from Vatican Council II, especially *Gaudium et spes,* he saw, in his papacy, that only if marriage and family are viewed from the perspective of a communion of persons modeled on Trinitarian communion and the communion of Christ and the Church could they be restored to their true value, the value expressed in the Holy Family of Jesus, Mary and Joseph. It was his initiative also that founded the mother session of the John Paul II Institute for Studies on Marriage and Family in Rome, which gave flesh and blood to his ideas. Intrinsic to my own immersion in John Paul II's theological and philosophical anthropology is the Institute Session in Washington, DC, supported by the Knights of Columbus, especially its president, Carl Anderson. At this Session I owe special gratitude to Dr. Kenneth Schmitz, who inspired me by his own pioneering studies on John Paul II's thought and directed my S.T.D. dissertation, which was published under the title, *Crossing the Threshold of Love: A New Vision of Marriage in the Light of John Paul II's Anthropology.* Not to be forgotten is Stratford Caldecott, who was instrumental in its publication in the U.K.

I have drawn on the deep reflections on the family of many of the faculty at the Institute, whose names are mentioned in the text so they shall not be given here. I owe them a huge debt of gratitude. As a student and teacher at the Institute for 25 years I have had the privilege of learning much from the students who passed through and later established holy and happy families. In writing the book itself, I am particularly grateful for the support of the dean, Fr. Antonio Lopez, the graduate receptionist, Christina d'Averso-Collins and recent graduate, Payal Sarah Singh, the latter two putting together and formatting the bibliography and footnotes. In addition Sarah has provided insightful copy-editing. Elisabeth Cunningham, subsequent receptionist, has also provided invaluable assistance as has Alice Knaeble. Over the years, many of the ideas in the book have been presented in journal articles. A list of articles is given in the appendix of those that are integrated directly in the text.

Since the book incorporates the Church's rich teaching in *Humanae vitae*, I cannot pass over the many years I spent in the Natural Family Planning (NFP) field. Before becoming an academic I had the privilege of interviewing many NFP couples, who were always honest about their joys and struggles. Also inspiring were the professionals, especially physicians, who remained faithful to Church teaching in the face of great opposition in their profession. I am thinking not only of the Drs. Billings, and Thomas Hilgers but also those less well known such as Claude Lanctot, Robert Jackson, Konald Prem, Josef Roetzer, Edward Keefe, Hanna Klaus and others. I hope that one day their contributions will be much better recognized and appreciated.

Several colleagues were most helpful in reading first drafts of chapters. Among these are Fr. Jose Granados, Matthew Levering, Perry Cahall, John Kippley and Paul Vitz. Three persons did extensive editing: Fr. Basil Cole, OP and Dr. Jeanne Schindler, Senior Fellow at the Center for Cultural and Pastoral Research and Patrick Fagan, founder of Marripedia and now at the Catholic University of America. I could not have written the book without the prayerful support and encouragement of many friends. Especially notable are those who volunteer with me in Imago Dei, Inc. to bring John Paul II's *A New Language* on love and sexuality to those in the pew. Last but not least, I am grateful to my family: my son, who solved daunting computer problems; my daughter for her sure "sense of the faithful *(sensus fidelium)*"; and my recently deceased husband, who always supported my research, writing and academic pursuits, even when it inconvenienced him. As an astrophysicist he especially endorsed natural methods from a scientific perpective; in his autobiography he chose Pope Paul VI (for his encyclical, *Humanae vitae)* as one of four figures, who contributed the most to humanity in the 20th century. Our own inter-racial marriage was far from perfect but through a deep mutual commitment to each other and to the Church's wisdom and grace we enjoyed almost 50 years together. Here I must also pay tribute to our parish of Little Flower in Bethesda and its most recent pastor, Msgr. Peter Vaghi, who is himself an author.

Lastly it must be said that, although the book was inspired by courses that I took and gave at the John Paul II Institute, in Washington DC, as well as in Kerala, India and Melbourne, Australia, the book was written during my retirement and the Institute can in no way be held responsible for its content.

Abbreviations

CCC	Vatican City: Libreria Editrice Vaticana. Print. 1997. *Catechism of the Catholic Church: Revised in Accordance with the Official Latin Text Promulgated by Pope John Paul II.*
CDL	Zelie and Louis Martin. *A Call to a Deeper Love: The Family Correspondence of the Parents of Saint Therese of the Child Jesus.* 1864-1885.
DCE	Benedict XVI. *Encyclical Letter Deus Caritas Est of the Supreme Pontiff Benedict XVI on Christian Love.* 2005.
DD	John Paul II. *Apostolic Letter Dies Domini On Keeping the Lord's Day Holy.* 1998.
DV	Paul VI. *Dogmatic Constitution on Divine Revelation Dei Verbum Solemnly Promulgated by His Holiness Pope Paul VI.* 1965.
D et V	John Paul II. *Encyclical Letter Dominum et Vificicantem On the Holy Spirit in the Life of the Church and the World.* 1986.
EE	John Paul II. *Encyclical Letter Ecclesia de Eucharistica of His Holiness Pope John Paul II on the Eucharist in its Relationship to the Church.* 2003.

EG	Pope Francis. *Apostolic Exhortation Evangelii Gaudium of the Holy Father Francis On the Lay Faithful on the Proclamation of the Gospel in Today's World.* 2013.
FC	John Paul II. *On the Family: Apostolic Exhortation, Familiaris Consortio, of His Holiness Pope John Paul II Regarding the Role of the Christian Family in the Modern World.* United States Catholic Conference, 1982.
FR	John Paul II. *Encyclical Letter Fides et Ratio of the Supreme Pontiff John Paul II On the Relationship Between Faith and Reason.* 1998.
GS	Paul VI. Vatican II. *Pastoral Constitution On The Church In The Modern World — Gaudium et Spes.* 1965.
HV	Paul VI. *Encyclical Letter Humane Vitae of the Supreme Pontiff Paul VI on the Regulation of Birth.* 1968.
LE	John Paul II. Encyclical Letter *Laborem Exercens on Human Work on the Ninetieth Anniversary of Rerum Novarum.*
LF	John Paul II. *Letter to Families: Gratissimam Sane.* Libreria Editrice Vaticana. 1994.
LG	Paul VI. *Dogmatic Constitution on the Church Lumen Gentium Solemnly Promulgated by His Holliness Pope Paul VI.* 1964.
MD	John Paul II. *Apostolic Letter Mulieris Dignitatem of the Supreme Pontiff John Paul II on the Dignity and Vocation of Women on the Occasion of the Marian Year.* 1988.
MW	John Paul II. *Man and Woman He Created Them – A Theology of the Body.* Translated by Michael Waldstein. Boston: Pauline Books and Media, 2006.

MC	Paul VI. *Apostolic Exhortation Marialis Cultus for the Right Ordering and Development of Devotion to the Blessed Virgin Mary.* 1974.
NMI	John Paul II. *Apostolic Letter Novo Millennio Ineunte of His Holiness Pope John Paul II at the Close of the Great Jubilee of the Year 2000.* 2001.
NT	New Testament. *Holy Bible.*
NFP	Natural Family Planning.
OT	Old Testament. *Holy Bible.*
RC	John Paul II. *Apostolic Exhortation Redemptoris Custos of the Supreme Pontiff John Paul II on the Person and the Mission of Saint Joseph in the Life of Christ and of the Church.* 1989.
RH	John Paul II. Encyclical Letter Redemptoris Hominis – The Redeemer of Man. 1979.
RM	John Paul II. *Redemptoris Mater: On the Blessed Virgin Mary in the life of the Pilgrim Church.* 1987.
SD	John Paul II. *Apostolic Letter Salvifici Doloris on the Christian Meaning of Human Suffering.* 1984.
ST	Thomas Aquinas. *Summa Theologiae.*
TMA	*Apostolic Letter Tertio Millennio Adveniente on Preparation for the Jubilee of the Year 2000.* 1994.
VC	John Paul II. *Post-Synodal Apostolic Exhortation Vita Consecrata of the Holy Father John Paul II on the Consecrated Life and its Mission in the Church and in the World.*1996
VS	John Paul II. Encyclical Letter *Veritatis Splendor of the Catholic Church Regarding Certain Fundamental Questions of the Church's Moral Teaching.* 1993.

CHAPTER 1

Introduction

Background

Catholic tradition treats the Holy Family as both the model of every human family and also as the exception. Theologians, from the Fathers of the Church onwards, have stressed that the marriage of Mary and Joseph was a true marriage, since it possessed the three goods of marriage: offspring (Christ in his humanity), fidelity and indissolubility (sacrament). Indeed, the marriage of Mary and Joseph was cited in the canonical definition of marriage in the Middle Ages as formed by the consent of the couple and consummated by conjugal intercourse open to procreation. The fruit of the marriage of Mary and Joseph was the Child, Jesus, so that theirs was still a valid marriage although not consummated. At the same time, because conjugal intercourse distinguishes marriage from every other form of friendship, and because marriage from the time of St. Paul has been considered a remedy for concupiscence as a result of original sin, the virginal marriage of Mary and Joseph came to be seen as the exception.[1]

The historical lack of integration in living the three goods of marriage has had profound effects on the development of a theology of the family. Angelo Scola has given a cogent summary of the history of reflection on marriage in *The Nuptial Mystery,* pointing out the failure of Christian thought to provide "an organic, unified reflection on the person, marriage and family."[2] While the Fathers of the Church were steeped in Scripture, bringing forward the theme of the Christ-Church union from Ephesians (Eph. 5:21-33), their pastoral approach mostly stressed the moral requirements of the married state, indissolubility and monogamy, which were viewed in terms of the theology of creation. References to the family as such mainly concerned the education of children.[3] Scola goes on to say that in the Middle Ages, St. Thomas "orients the whole of Catholic theology toward a recognition of the sacramentality of marriage, favoring the spouses as imaging the Christ-Church union."[4] To counteract the downgrading of the sacraments in general by the Reformers, the Council of Trent conclusively defined marriage as a sacrament and indissoluble.[5] The rejection of marriage as a sacrament by the Reformers became particularly important with the secularization of marriage in the 19th century.[6] The emphasis in Trent is on the consent of the couple and the sacrament, and attention to the family is confined to children as one of the three blessings of marriage.[7]

This more juridical emphasis on the sacrament, necessary as it was, obscured the concept of the family as an image of the Trinity, and, therefore, an image of the Holy Family, regarded in the Middle Ages as an "earthly Trinity."[8] The thesis of this book is that both the recovery of the understanding of the family as the "domestic Church" and the new articulation by Vatican Council II of the family as an image of the Trinity in a communion of persons oriented to mutual self-gift, made it possible to see the Holy Family as not the "ontological exception" but a true model for the human family. This development has not come easily.

Scola points out that for two millennia in the Western world, marriage and family were, in actuality, lived as an organic unity encompassing sexuality (the person and sexual difference), love (marriage) and fruitfulness (family) so that the lack of an adequate synthesis in the theology of marriage among the three goods was not felt. With the advent of contraception on a mass scale in the 19th century, this lived unity crumbled. The resulting separation of the three factors, reduced to their purely biological components by the reigning secular ideology, meant, says Scola, that "Christians found themselves lacking adequate reasons to explain the marvelous unity of the nuptial mystery."[9]

The rise of a conjugal spirituality in various family movements heralded a new development before Vatican Council II. Catholic Action galvanized the Catholic laity in both France and Italy. Scola points to the advent of various family associations and movements, which promoted a conjugal spirituality. Christian families began to see themselves not just as passive recipients of the Faith but as active subjects in the Church. The idea of the family as an *Ecclesia domestica* or domestic church was revived from the patristic period in the Second Vatican Council.[10] The new spirituality developed specific formation around the themes of "marriage as a Christian 'state of life' in the full sense, the necessity of promoting a conjugal spirituality and the problem of the family or conjugal 'ministry'."[11] In spite of this promising development, Scola speaks of "a certain extrinsicism" informing these movements with regard to the relationship between marriage as a sacrament and as a created reality.[12] Consequently, not enough attention was given to the relationship of the mystery of Jesus Christ to marriage as a sphere of redemption. Furthermore, the emphasis on the consent of the couple as forming the marriage had accentuated the "ministry" of the spouses to the detriment of its Trinitarian and Christological identity.[13]

The flowering of this conjugal spirituality coincided with the spread of contraception and extravagant claims by its advocates like Margaret Sanger for an ecstatic conjugal union.[14] Here can be seen the damaging effects of a one-sided emphasis on the couple's relationship in a theology of the family; it left Christian couples prey to propaganda such as Sanger's. It is noteworthy that Pat and Patty Crowley, founders of the Christian Family Movement in the United States and one of the few married couples on Pope Paul VI's Birth Control Commission, were prominent dissenters from the encyclical, *Humanae Vitae.*[15] A leading international marriage movement, the Teams of Our Lady, while not espousing such a public position, nevertheless, quietly accepted the dissent of many of its member couples.[16] Rather than challenging couples to engage the good news of *Humanae Vitae*, their leaders and most chaplains preferred not to disturb their consciences, a pastoral practice that became all too common in the Church at large.[17]

Responding to these developments, another contemporary theologian, Marc Ouellet, also saw the pressing need for a true spirituality of the family.[18] Reiterating moral norms is not enough. What is needed is "a positive vision of domestic values, a 'personalist' family spirituality, which truly grounds conjugal and familial relations within Trinitarian communion, incarnated and revealed in Jesus Christ."[19] Ouellet speaks of a "theological turn," in which the members of the family cultivate "consciousness of a personal relationship with Christ." In fact a radical relationship with Christ is key to the transition of the family from "model" to "image."[20] He seeks to reintegrate the three traditional values of marriage—procreation, faithful love and sacramental signification—into the context of "fruitful conjugal love."

It is against this backdrop that this book proposes the Holy Family, with its union of both the created reality of marriage and the eschatological perspective of grace and the presence of Christ, as not just the model of family life but the path to transformation of the family from the inside. Central to the argument will be the concept of presence, both divine and human presence. Ouellet refers to the "'Presence' which gives to each person and to the communion of persons a sacred and inviolate character."[21] Again "the domestic Church is the 'sanctuary of life' (LF 11), the locus of that Presence which makes the communion of persons a sacred and sacramental reality."[22] The presence of the Trinity in the family is made manifest by its spiritual fruitfulness. Throughout history it has been a place of prayer, charity and evangelization.

As first a created reality, the family is, or ought to be, imbued with the human presence of its members. John Paul II has coined the phrase "discovers in the body the anticipatory signs…of the gift of self" (VS 48). The body is nuptial, orienting spouses to each other and to their children through specific bodily acts of conjugal embrace, gestation, birth and breastfeeding. The last, breastfeeding, is one key aspect of bodily communion in families that is commonly overlooked, even by scholars who promote the genuine procreation and education of children. To correct this oversight, this book will examine the detrimental effects of abandoning traditional theological and magisterial promotion of breastfeeding in favor of wet-nursing or bottle feeding, practices that could be permitted when necessary, as morally equivalent to the natural mother-child bond. Just as with contraception, the devaluation of breastfeeding came in part from an overemphasis on the life of the couple (particularly, the marital bed) to the detriment of a theology of the family. This book will show how a vibrant understanding of the Holy Family as exemplar for contemporary Catholic families includes meditation on Jesus at Mary's breast. Grace builds on nature, and without attention to the body's integrity and intrinsic orientation to communion, it becomes difficult to open the child to human love, let alone love of God.

The Communion of Persons

An important development of the 20th century that changed how we look at the Holy Family was the philosophy of personalism, which emphasized a new appreciation for the dignity of the person and the communion of persons. Of course, the notion of person had been developed in the early Christian centuries to explicate the mystery of the Trinity, but the concept of the dignity of the human person belongs to a century that perhaps violated the dignity of the person more than any other. Vatican Council II for the first time spoke of marriage as a communion of persons (GS, no. 12). Polish philosopher Cardinal Karol Wojtyla explored the nature of the human person and what he called "participation," the only form of being together that affirms the dignity of the person.[23] Later, as Pope John Paul II, he aligned it theologically with the concept of the communion of persons, which he developed more fully in his interpretation of the Genesis account of the creation of man and woman.[24] In the encyclical *Familiaris consortio* he writes:

> In matrimony and in the family a complex of interpersonal relationships is set up—married life, fatherhood and motherhood, filiation and fraternity—through which each human person is introduced into the "human family" and into the "family of God," which is the Church.[25]

The great pope's theology of the Holy Family was traditional but also innovative. A theology of the Holy Family as a communion of persons could develop in the 20th century because there was greater recognition of the role of Joseph in salvation than there was in the early church. In the early Christian centuries, although Mary was honored devotionally by the people, her place in theology remained limited until the doctrine of Theotokos was proclaimed at the Third Ecumenical Council at Ephesus in 431 AD. Something similar has happened with the role of Joseph in salvation over a much greater period of time. Devotion to St. Joseph had been widely promoted by such saints as Teresa of Avila and various popes, but it was not until the 19th century that the dignity of Joseph and his place in the Holy Family received recognition in Church documents, in response to new threats to the family.[26] In each case the delay in recognition of the role of Jesus' solely human family members in salvation served to preserve the integrity of the unity of Christ's divine and human nature in the Incarnation.[27] These two developments, the concept of the family as a communion of persons and the flowering of the theology of the Holy Family, now make it possible to see the Holy Family not as the "ontological exception," but rather as a model for all families.

> It is in the Holy Family, the original "Church in miniature (Ecclesia domestica)," that every Christian family must be reflected. "Through God's mysterious design, it was in that family that the Son of God spent long years of a hidden life. It is therefore the prototype and example for all Christian families" (FC, no. 15).

Using the lens of the Holy Family enriches our understanding of the theology of the communion of persons as explicated by Pope John Paul II, Hans Urs von Balthsar, and other contemporary scholars, but even more importantly, such a *Communio*-based understanding of the Holy Family enriches our understanding of family spirituality and morality. In particular, it enlightens one's understanding of the Church's controversial teachings on marital sexuality, including the difference between natural family planning and artificial contraception and the strong fit between breastfeeding and this Christian vision of family relationships.

Methodology

The methodology of this book is interdisciplinary. It will have as its goal to "hand on ever more effectively the prophetic truth" of *Humanae Vitae* in the light of John Paul II's own progressively deepened understanding of its implications for a Trinitarian vision of reality. Its newness will not lie in the originality of research--I shall be drawing mostly on John Paul II and members of the Institute he founded, the John Paul II Institute for Studies on Marriage & Family, among whom are Angelo Scola, Marc Ouellet, Joseph Atkinson, José Granados, and Livio Melina, who have made in-depth and original studies of the family. While it may seem confusing to bring so many voices to bear on the topic, it is hoped that each theologian illuminates a unique aspect of the theme. This book will focus on the integration of this research into an understanding of the Holy Family as a communion of persons and its implications for the human family as a communion of persons in both its human and salvific roles.

The John Paul II Institute has multiple, relatively independent but interconnected "sessions" throughout the world: Rome (the central session), Benin, Brazil, Spain, India, and the United States, as well as "affiliated" institutes in Australia, Lebanon, Korea, and the Phillipines., The Washington, D.C. Session was founded exactly 20 years after the encyclical, *Humanae vitae.* John Paul II made note of this in his message to Cardinal James Hickey August 22, 1988:

> I am pleased that the beginning of this undertaking coincides with the twentieth anniversary of Pope Paul VI's Encyclical Letter *Humanae vitae*, for I am certain that the Institute will give notable assistance to the Church's efforts to hand on ever more effectively the prophetic truth of that historic document.[28]

The mission statement of the catalog reads:

> The Institute's specialized ecclesiastical degree in the theology of marriage is unique. It is a degree in a specific topic of theology, not in a general area, such as moral theology. Its topic—marriage and family—is inter-disciplinary, and its program of studies draws from many disciplines what must be applied to elucidate the topic.[29]

Following the methodology of the Institute, my own doctoral dissertation was interdisciplinary, although not in an integrated way.[30] As the Institute developed, so did its understanding of its mission. The 2005-2007 catalog states:

> The distinguishing feature of the John Paul II Institute, in sum, lies in conceiving of marriage and the family, and all the moral problems associated with these, within an entire vision of reality. The uniqueness of the Institute lies further, in its anchoring of this vision of reality, and this marital-familial love, in God's self-revelation as a Trinitarian communion of persons (LF, 6: "The primordial model of the family is to be sought in God himself, in the Trinitarian mystery of his life.").[31]

The interdisciplinary focus remains but it is much more strongly grounded in a Trinitarian vision of reality, which David L. Schindler, Dean and Provost from 2000 to 2011, has expanded at the Institute. This book follows that same interdisciplinary but above all the Trinitarian pattern.

Organization of the Book

The book begins with an excursus on the family as both "domestic church" and as a communion of persons modeled on the love of the Trinitarian Persons. Our guides are John Paul II and his interpreters, Angelo Scola and Marc Ouellet. Beginning with Chapter Two it will be shown how the family has the vocation to image the Trinity and so be like the Holy Family, traditionally called an "earthly Trinity." Essential to the understanding of the communion of persons is the notion of person, so that the chapter will also take up the subjectivity of the person. In several documents John Paul II has highlighted Mary's subjectivity, particularly in her fiat at the Annunciation.[32] The nature of Mary's subjectivity sheds light on true subjectivity as opposed to the isolated autonomy of the Enlightenment and is essential for understanding the unity in difference of man and woman in marriage.

Without a clear vision of Joseph's role the Holy Family could not be seen as a true family. Chapters Three and Four trace the theological development of the Holy Family as a communion of persons from the Middle Ages to the 20th century with some reference also to the Church Fathers.[33] The two chapters consider the marriage of Mary and Joseph in the Tradition, focused mainly on the Middle Ages on the Western Church.[34] The papal documents from Leo XIII to John Paul II on St Joseph reveal a rising interest in the role of St. Joseph in salvation history and concomitantly devotion to the Holy Family, crowned by John Paul II's Apostolic Exhortation, *Redemptoris custos* (RC). Since John Paul II is known especially for his innovative theology of the body, considerable attention will be given on the way Mary's nursing was intrinsic to Jesus' human development, a practice that was increasingly neglected in the urban West with deleterious effects on mother and child as well as the spouses. In a sense, two aspects of the Holy Family, which contribute to a communion of persons, will be particularly drawn out, the closeness of mother and child through nursing and the chastity of Joseph, understood first and foremost as following God's will. This means the right use of the conjugal act and the true appreciation of masculine and feminine contributions to family well-being. Contrary to generally accepted views of the encyclical, *Humanae vitae*, this means full appreciation of the physical, psychological and spiritual dimensions of marriage and family life.

The communion of persons will then be explored in Chapters Five to Seven as it is expressed in the family through the spousal, maternal and paternal relations. The child plays a central role in this communion. Chapter Eight is a pivotal chapter, dealing with embodiment and Presence/presence, especially the role of bodily presence for communion. Bodily presence has perhaps suffered most in our culture from absence and distortion, especially in relation to the family and sexuality. The Holy Family epitomizes both human and divine presence in its fullness apart from conjugal intercourse. At the same time, it points to the perfect bodily subjectivity and inter-subjectivity of the resurrected state.

The question arises, how can sinful human beings in the family participate in the sublime communion of the Holy Family? Chapter Nine examines the encyclical *Humanae vitae,* proposing it as the good news of salvation as well as a path to healing the communion of persons of the family. The chapter situates the encyclical within the context of continuity with Tradition, giving examples of both faithful and dissenting views. It also affirms the full significance of marital chastity as the foundation of a communion of persons. Chapter Ten considers the universal call to holiness, which has particular relevance for living the truths of *Humanae vitae.* Every baptized Christian, whatever his state in life, is called to be "perfect." Through the sacramental life of the Church, every Christian is empowered to overcome sin and participate more and more not only in the life of the Trinity but in true human communion. In this vein, Chapter Eleven, addresses sin, mercy and conversion in Christ. When "structures of sin" in society make it difficult to live the truth, the Holy Spirit, through the Church, always accompanies the sinner with grace and mercy, leading to repentance and even holiness. The final chapter, by way of epilogue, concludes that the Holy Family, imbued by "fairest love" among its members through the Incarnation, is not the "ontological exception" but a true model of the family as a communion of persons. Some suggestions will be made for further research in the Epilogue.

This is, indeed, a large undertaking and only the exigencies of the times prompt an attempt to accomplish it. As I am a scholar who has specialized in the work of John Paul II, his thought will be paramount.

CHAPTER 2

The Holy Family and the Communion of Persons

§

THIS CHAPTER FOCUSES ON THE theology of the family as a communion of persons, modeled on the Trinity and fleshed out as the "domestic church," a cell of the bride of Christ. As John Paul II says: "He (Man) is, in fact, from the 'beginning' not only an image in which the solitude of one Person, who rules the world, mirrors itself but also and essentially the image of an inscrutable divine communion of Persons" (MW 9:3). He writes in the same homily:

> In the mystery of creation—on the basis of the original and constitutive "solitude" of his being—man has been endowed with a deep unity between what is, humanly and through the body, male in him and what is, equally humanly and through the body female in him. On all this right from the beginning, the blessing of fruitfulness descended, linked with human procreation (cf. Gen 1:28) (MW 9:3).

Beginning with this chapter, it will be seen how the family has the lofty vocation to be an interaction of fruitful reciprocal donation imaging the Trinity. In this way, the Holy Family is the supreme example as an "earthly Trinity." It is the thesis of this chapter that the Holy Family is not the "ontological exception" but a true model of the family.

This chapter is divided into two parts, Part I on the Trinitarian and Christological Foundations and Part II on the notion of "person" as the foundation of a communion of persons. We start with John Paul II himself, followed by reflections of two theologians deeply imbued with John Paul II's thought, Marc Cardinal Ouellet and Angelo Cardinal Scola. Both seek to restore the true nature of fecundity as an essential dimension of the communion of persons which was in some manner distorted as the history given in later chapters shows.[1] Ouellet cites John Paul II in *Letter to Families:* "The original model of the family must be found in God, himself, in the Trinitarian Mystery of His life" (LF no. 6). Scola takes as his starting point John Paul II's words in *Letter to Families* on the 'great mystery':

> St. Paul's magnificent synthesis concerning the great mystery appears as the compendium or *summa*, in some sense of the teaching about God and man which was brought to fulfillment by Christ.
>
> And the family itself is the great mystery of God. As the domestic church it is the bride of Christ (LF 19).

After considering their reflections on the Christological and Trinitarian roots of the family as a communion of persons, attention will be paid to the path John Paul II took in seeing the Holy Family, traditionally an "earthly Trinity," as the model of all families. Finally, the focus will be on the centrality of *person* in a communion of persons. John Paul II singles out Mary's consent at the Annunciation as emblematic of her personhood, which he shows to be foundational for a communion of persons in his encyclical letter, *Mother of the Redeemer*, his apostolic letter, *Mulieris Dignitatem*, and his philosophical analysis of "participation."

Part I: Trinitarian and Christological Foundations

John Paul II and Development of a Theology of the Holy Family as a Communion of Persons

At the beginning of his pontificate, John Paul II gave two encyclicals on the divine Persons, namely the Son, *Redeemer of Man* and the Father, *Dives in Misericordia.* By issuing an encyclical on Christ at the beginning of his pontificate with the first words, "The Redeemer of man, Jesus Christ, is the center of the universe and history" (RM 1), he made it clear that he was drawing on the Christocentric vision of Vatican Council II, especially *Gaudium et spes:* "Christ the new Adam, in the very revelation of the mystery of the Father and of his love, *fully reveals man to himself* and brings to light his true calling" (GS 22). While the focus of the encyclical was on man as the way of the Church, his attention to love later found expression in his concern for the family, explicating what he calls "the human dimension of the mystery of redemption" (RM 10). John Paul II connects man as the way of the Church with love precisely because "Man cannot live without love. He remains a being who is incomprehensible to himself, his life is senseless, if love is not revealed to him, if he does not experience it and make it his own, if he does not participate intimately in it" (RM 10).

God's love takes the form above all of mercy so that the second encyclical of his pontificate centered on the Father as the revelation of Mercy, which is especially revealed in sacrificing his only Son for the redemption of the world. He did not give the one on the Holy Spirit, *Dominum et Vivificantem* until 1986. Yet this is the one most devoted to love and communion in the Trinity and is particularly rich in Trinitarian themes.

> He is Person-Love. He is Person-Gift. Here we have an inexhaustible treasure of the reality and an inexpressible deepening of the concept of *person* in God, which only divine revelation makes known to us (D et V 10).

He is not only the gift to the person (the person of the Messiah), but *is a Person-gift* (D et V 22). The Holy Spirit reveals that the intimate life of the Trinity is an exchange of love between the divine Persons, and the Holy Spirit exists in the mode of gift. The Triune God whose mode of existence is interpersonal giving, gives the Holy Spirit to Man to transform him from within. Here John Paul II reflects on how Man, by following Christ as his model of self-giving love, is enabled to "find himself through a sincere gift of self," which is the "*whole of Christian anthropology"* put forward by the Council's Pastoral Constitution (D et V 59). It was in 1981 in the Apostolic Exhortation *The Role of the Christian Family in the Modern World* (FC 18) that John Paul II first applied the insight of the Council on divine and human communion to the family following the Synod of Bishops on the family.

It has already been noted by those familiar with his work and by his own frequent testimony that Vatican Council II was a major inspiration for the theological development of his thought on the Trinity and the family[2] and for his later philosophical writings, especially *The Acting Person. Gaudium et spes* was particularly salient theologically. No. 22 on Christ as the new Adam and no. 24 on Trinitarian communion and the *imago Dei* became a kind of mantra for him. The key passage for him, as already noted, in his ground-breaking homilies on the theology of the body is: "Man becomes an image of God not so much in the moment of solitude as in the moment of communion. He is, in fact, "from the beginning" not only an image in which the solitude of one Person, who rules the world, mirrors itself, but also and essentially the image of an inscrutable divine communion of Persons" (MW 9:3). The communion, while always keeping in mind the infinite distance between man and God and therefore the limits of any analogy, is linked to the creation of the dual unity of masculinity and femininity and their unity in one flesh. It is not the place here to draw all the implications for anthropology but it is pertinent to introduce two theologians who have considered this Christological and Trinitarian anthropology in relation to the family, before moving on to its implications for the Holy Family.

Marc Cardinal Ouellet

Marc Ouellet, former professor of dogmatic theology at the John Paul II Institute for Studies on Marriage and Family at the Lateran University, Rome, states: "The theology of the family is still in its infancy...No comprehensive overview of a systematic theology of the family exists as yet."[3] He goes on to say that "the theology of the family should follow the Christocentric and Trinitarian perspective that Vatican II opened up for contemporary theological reflection."[4] In spite of all the problems facing the family today, in *Familiaris consortio* John Paul II points to the positive developments of greater attention to human freedom, interpersonal relations and the dignity of woman. The task ahead is to integrate the traditional reflection on marriage from a more naturalistic and juridical perspective to seeing it in the context of *Gaudium et spes* as "a community of deep life and love."[5] Here Ouellet sees the Council's emphasis on an ecclesiology of communion as expressed in the union of Christ and the Church also to be pivotal. He asks: "Has the advent of the hypostatic union made possible any existential participation of family relations in the Trinitarian relations?"[6] Answering in the affirmative, he concludes that, to follow through on this Christological and Trinitarian perspective, analogy is a methodological presupposition and the movement will be from above—katalogical. What this signifies is that the meaning of human existence is revealed as first and foremost a participation in the exchange of love between the divine persons.

Ouellet begins by reviewing what the Tradition has to say on the familial analogy of the Trinity. It is well known that Augustine rejected the family as an analogy of the Trinity, but he also proposed the social analogy of love: the one who loves, the beloved and love itself. Although Augustine preferred not to pursue this approach, Ouellet shows how in Tractatus XXXIX he finds an analogy for the Trinity in the capacity of love "to create a common soul and a common heart among those who love one another."[7] Not only does Ouellet see this analogy in the Holy Trinity with the Holy Spirit as the bond of love, he also sees it in the Church where the Holy Spirit is the source of life in the community. Ouellet views this analogy of the capacity of love as the one that brings the most fruitful development. It was carried further by Richard of St. Victor and St. Bonaventure for a time but it was not until the contemporary development of personalism that the family analogy came to the fore again.

This fruitful development is premised on Scriptural exegesis of the *imago Dei* in Genesis 1:26-27,[8] and Ouellet refers to the interpretation of the imago Dei of Scripture scholar, Claus Westermann, as a "divinely conferred capacity for relationship," both vertically with God and horizontally with each other, as the one most conducive to framing the man-woman relationship as an image of divine communion. [9] Their communion, expressed by bodily difference, is also blessed with procreation through which they share in God's creative power. All this means that only in community do they mirror Him--not as individuals. Ouellet continues that together with New Testament revelation this "constitutes a solid scriptural base upon which to found the family analogy of the Trinity."[10] In the New Testament in St. Paul's Letter to the Ephesians man and woman in Genesis prefigure the Christ-Church union (Eph. 5:21-23); also Romans 5 is significant, which sees Christ as the new Adam; again in St. Matthew's gospel, Christ refers back to Genesis in re-establishing the indissolubility of marriage as it was in the beginning (Matt.19:12). This same text opens up the eschatological horizon of virginity for the kingdom. Here Ouellet refers to the relationships in the Holy Family, founded on virginal fruitfulness, which retain the man-woman complementarity.

Ouellet concludes: "Once the revelation of the intimate life of the Trinitarian 'We' is achieved, a new view on the original doctrine of the *imago Dei* becomes possible." This in turn provides a clearer understanding, starting with the Trinitarian mystery and God's covenant with man in Christ, of the creation of humanity as male and female. He notes how John Paul II made full use of this theological anthropology in his documents on women and the family and in his Wednesday Catecheses, his innovative reflection on man and woman imaging God even in their bodies.[11]

Besides the horizontal communion of love between man and woman, fecundity is an essential component of the family analogy of the Trinity. For John Paul II this is intrinsic to"the genealogy of the person" (LF 9) as well as in everything having to do with the child's growth. Yet it goes beyond that.

Ouellet speaks of a certain *common fecundity* between God and man. Eve's cry: "I have gotten a man with help of the Lord" (Gen. 4:1) reveals God's creative action in the one-flesh union. Here he cites von Balthazar that the gift of fertility "establishes an immediate relationship with God" because, in a sense, man can only be fruitful because of God, and yet God chooses to continue creation through the relationship between man and woman. Nevertheless the link of generation with death is an enigma, which is only resolved in Christ's suprasexual not asexual fecundity with the Church.[12] This means that: "In the light of Scripture and Tradition, it seems legitimate to affirm an authentic analogy between the Trinity and the Family."[13]

Further, through the sacrament of marriage and the Holy Spirit, the family becomes a "domestic church," linked sacramentally to the union of Christ and the Church of which it is a sign. While remaining a created reality, it is the sign of a greater mystery and participates in the fruitfulness of the Spirit even though it is surpassed by the higher spiritual fecundity of consecrated virginity.[14] With this new family analogy of the Trinity, the Holy Family, venerated as an "earthly Trinity," reveals its character as a credible model.

Angelo Cardinal Scola

Angelo Scola, former president of the John Paul II Institute for Studies on Marriage and Family at the Lateran University in Rome also attends to the Genesis texts with particular emphasis on what he calls the "asymmetrical difference" between man and woman and its likeness to Trinitarian relations. His interest is to elucidate John Paul's teaching on woman, especially in *Mulieris Dignitatem* (1988) and *Letter to Women* (1995). Noting that the pope began his pontificate with elaborating the anthropological and theological foundations of man and woman especially in his Wednesday Catecheses, but throughout in many other writings and speeches, Scola regards his teaching as marking "a considerable advance, both qualitatively and quantitatively."[15] He discovers two theses in the Pope's work above all: the likeness of the dual unity of man and woman to the communion in the Trinity and the fact that human sexuality is an integral part of the *imago Dei.* Referring to both the Priestly account of Genesis (1-2:3), which John Paul II calls the metaphysical, and the Yahwist account (Genesis 2:4-4:1), which expounds man's consciousness of his state in "the beginning," Scola uncovers four "ontological principles of dual unity."

Man exists always as either male or female. Each needs the other "I" for fulfillment. This both underscores man's contingent nature as well as his capacity for transcending himself. "He is not only an individual (identity) but also a person (relation/difference)."[16] Being in God's image means always existing in relation to another "I." Secondly, the relationship of male and female is one of both identity and difference. They are equal in their humanity while the difference, which in no way implies either inferiority or superiority, relates to their sexuality or gender. Thirdly, through this sexual difference there is a certain analogy to Trinitarian relations: "*Communio* as an essential dimension of man is part of his being in the image of God."[17] Lastly, Scola does not hesitate to define spousal love as the *analogatum princeps* of every kind of love determining man's relation with reality. Both virginity and marriage, the fundamental states of life, are spousal loves, expressed through the total gift of self as the ideal.

Scola also takes up the Christological aspect, which John Paul II draws from Vatican Council II: "The truth is that only in the mystery of the Incarnation does the mystery of man take on light" (GS 22). He argues that the hypostatic union of Christ's two natures remakes the dual unity of man and woman and becomes its new foundation.[18] The hypostatic union confirms that "difference without confusion and without separation is something positive, something that exalts, not destroys, unity."[19] He interprets the Incarnation as a spousal union. Furthermore it is only the Trinitarian relations, characterized by a unity of nature and a trinity of persons, that allows the Incarnation to be conceived from within the Trinitarian communion. Ultimately the dual unity of man, he concludes, therefore, is in the Trinity. He sees the Christ-Church pair, which flows from the Incarnation itself uniting God with humanity, as the original pair from which the man-woman pair is in a certain sense derived.

Focusing on the dignity of women, which was a major concern of John Paul II, Scola deepens his reflection on the nature of the dual unity. Too often in history this difference has been a cause of discrimination against women instead of being an enrichment for both. The foundation of their unity is their common humanity. The difference allows for the reciprocal gift of self. The pope warns against women imitating men to achieve equality and maintains that there is not just a distinction of roles but a more substantive difference. It constitutes an "otherness" which is both mystery and contingency. Scola goes so far as to say that without the revelation of the Trinitarian God, it is impossible to understand sexual difference in a positive light.

Scola then addresses the question of whether human sexuality is part of the *imago Dei*. Since man is created always as either male or female, ordered to procreation, the image is not just in his rational nature but in the totality of his body/soul unity. He draws attention to paragraph six in *Mulieris dignitatem,* where John Paul II includes the blessing of fertility in man and woman's creation in the image of God. Sexuality is, thereby, raised from mere animal sexuality to the level of the imago Dei. Scola calls this "an important innovation, which "cannot but have enormous consequences."[20] (Indeed the move is crucial for much of the thesis in this book) In John Paul II's earlier reflections on divorce in Matthew 19:4-6 in his Wednesday Catechesis, John Paul II refers the Pharisees to man and woman's creation "in the beginning," in the graced state of original innocence. The body in its masculinity and femininity constitutes a primordial sacrament which makes visible the invisible reality of the mystery of divine Trinitarian communion in which Man truly participates.[21] This was obscured in the Fall but not totally lost. With redemption by Christ, the sacramentality of the body was restored but it is now a task as well as the fruit of grace. The man/woman pair in the Letter to the Ephesians is also prophetic of the union of Christ and the Church in the "mystery hidden from all ages" (Eph. 3:9).[22] From all this Scola finds enough evidence for sexual difference to be integral not simply extrinsic to the *imago Dei* and that includes the one-flesh union between man and woman and procreation.

In Summary, we see that Ouellet follows a katalogical path from the Trinity to marriage and family as a communion of life and love, from Vatican Council II's by way of John Paul II and influenced by Hans Urs von Balthasar. He argues from Trinitarian relations to family relations. Scola can be said to start from below, from the dual unity of man and woman. Both find in the Incarnation the indispensable link to the Trinitarian relations. Both call procreation a share in God's creative power but Scola goes further in arguing for human sexuality to be integral to man and woman imaging God. Ouellet sees the Holy Family as a model for the human family but more in its virginal fruitfulness. As Ouellet says: "In their daily family life, Mary and Joseph were taken up into the divine human relationship that Jesus had with his heavenly Father.[23] This author argues that, as Jesus was both divine and human, the Holy Family, called an "earthly Trinity," is in some sense a model for both human and divine communion... We turn now to another theologian to show how the Holy Family is not the "ontological exception."[24]

The Holy Family not the Ontological Exception

Repeated reference has been made to "person" and the communion of persons both in the Trinity and in the creation of humankind. Unlike the "autonomous individual" of the Enlightenment, whose relations are either contractual or constructed, "person" contains the notion of relationality within substantial unity in the manner of the Trinitarian persons. The concept and term grew out of Christian reflection on the nature of the Trinity, primarily with the Incarnation of Christ.[25] Ratzinger in an article on the notion of person in theology shows how the term was coined from the Greek word *prosopon* meaning "mask" (or "face"), the mask actors wore when portraying a character in a drama.[26] The actor uses this device to introduce dialogue. The Greek Fathers noticed that not only do the prophets in the Old Testament engage in dialogue with God but within the Godhead itself dialogue takes place. For example, David says: "The Lord said to my Lord" (Ps. 110). Now these are not just roles but realities, "dialogical realities." "The 'role' truly exists; it is the *prosopon*, the face, the person of the Logos who truly speaks."[27] Ratzinger summarizes:

> The idea of person expresses in its origin the idea of dialogue and the idea of God as the dialogical being. It refers to God as the being that loves in the word and consists of the word as "I" and "you" and "we." In light of this knowledge of God, the true nature of humanity became clear in a new way.[28]

Christology came to the conclusion:

> Relation is not something added to the person, but *is* the person itself. In its nature, the person exists only as relation.[29]

This means that the divine person exists as the act of self-donation in knowledge and love.[30] The Son exists in total relativity to the Father, receiving everything from him.[31]

What interests us even more is what the article says about the hypostatic union. Without going into the misunderstandings arising from the Greek view of the human person, suffice it to say that Ratzinger sees the Tradition up to now as erroneously regarding Christ's union of his human and divine natures as "the simply unique ontological exception."[32] Christ is the new Adam as Scripture calls him. If so, then he reveals the fulfillment of what it means to be human. This raises the question of what it means to have two natures in one Person. Since being a person is pure relativity on the level of spirit, it transcends itself by going out beyond itself. "By being with the other it first becomes itself, it comes to itself."[33] The human spirit can transcend itself in this way, and it can be with the wholly other, God. The more it can be with the transcendent God, the more it can be itself. In the Logos this is realized radically, so that, in Christ, human nature reached its highest possibility. This is also the goal towards which all human nature tends but never fully reaches.

The last point Ratzinger makes is pivotal for seeing the Holy Family, which John Paul II calls the original domestic church, not as the ontological exception but rather as the true exemplar. *First* of all, in the Trinitarian relations, there is not simply "the pure 'I,' nor the pure 'you,' but on both sides the 'I' is integrated into the greater 'we.'"[34] What this means is that multiplicity has the same dignity as unity. Ratzinger charges that even in theology the dimension of the "we" was lost when Augustine's interior analogy of the Trinity was preferred. With this move the "I" and "you" of the dialogical relation eventually disappeared into a single transcendent being, negatively affecting the notion of the Trinity as a communion of Persons. As we shall see, the procreative or "we" dimension of the family eventually collapsed in Protestantism into the "I"- "You." With the Enlightenment it collapsed even further into the autonomous individual.[35]

Secondly, Christ is present in the family through the baptism of its members as the domestic church. Just as Christ was present in the Holy Family, making it the fulfillment of what it means to be family, so the more the members of the Christian family are conformed to Christ, the more it is family.

Starting with *Familiars consortio,* in the very last section, the pope firmly links the Holy Family to the ordinary Christian Family:

> Through God's mysterious design, it was in that family (the Holy Family) that the Son of God spent long years of a hidden life. It is therefore the prototype and example for all Christian families (FC, 86).

In *Redemptoris custos* he goes further. The apostolic exhortation on St. Joseph follows the two great documents on women, first on Mary, *Redemptoris Mater* (March 25, 1987) and then on all women, *Mulieris Dignitatem* (August, 15, 1988). In *Redemptoris custos,* he inserts a statement from a discourse of Pope Paul VI to the Equipes des Notre Dame (Teams of Our Lady): "The Savior began the work of salvation by this holy and virginal union, wherein is manifested his all-powerful will to *purify and sanctify the family* –that sanctuary of love and cradle of love" (RC 7). He then adds, "How much the family of today can learn from this!" In the accompanying footnote, he notes how similar praise of the Holy Family can be found in Leo XIII's apostolic letter, *Neminem fugit* (June 14, 1892) and the Motu Proprio *Bonum Sane* (July 25, 1920) of

Pope Benedict XV. He also finds warrant for this identification in the Second Vatican Council's *Lumen gentium* (RC 7) Indeed he places himself squarely in the Tradition by saying, "The Church deeply venerates this Family, and proposes it as the model of all families" (RC 21). He goes on to call the Holy Family "a true human family," even if through the Incarnation it "has its own special mystery" (RC 21).

This identification of the Holy Family with ordinary human families is even clearer in *Letter to Families.*

> The only begotten Son, of one substance with the Father, "God from God and light from light," entered into human history through the family: "For by his Incarnation the Son of God united himself in a certain way with every man...The divine mystery of the Incarnation of the Word thus has an intimate connection with the human family. Not only with one family, that of Nazareth but in some way with every family (LF 2).

Later in referring to Joseph's obedience on taking Mary found with Child into his home, the pope writes:

> And so, thanks to Joseph, the mystery of the Incarnation and, together with it, the mystery of the Holy Family, comes to be profoundly inscribed in the spousal love of husband and wife and, in an indirect way, in the genealogy of every human family. What St. Paul calls the great mystery found its most lofty expression in the Holy Family. Thus the family takes its place at the heart of the new covenant (LF 20). Finally in the last section the pope declares: "The Holy Family is the beginning of countless holy families" (LF 23). These citations leave no doubt that the ordinary human family can find its deepest meaning in the Holy Family even though continence is at its center.

One might ask how can this be? As a faithful son of the Church, from his earliest days as a university chaplain, Karol Wojtyla/ John Paul II sought to understand and present in a new way the Church's traditional teaching on marriage and the regulation of births. It was in response to his predecessor Pope Paul VI's encyclical, *Humanae vitae*, that he first developed his theological anthropology since he understood that without a true understanding of the dignity and personhood of woman it was not possible to live the truths of *Humanae vitae*. [36] Significantly, here is found the nucleus of his theology of the Holy Family in the discussion on continence for the kingdom. The Pope says that the history of the birth of Jesus certainly conforms to the revelation of the "continence for the kingdom of heaven" even though it was hidden from the disciples at the time. But what does the Holy Family have to do with the human family at the center of which is the one-flesh union of the spouses? Yet the following citation makes reference to "*the mystery* of the perfect communion of persons, of Man and Woman in the conjugal covenant."

> *The marriage of Mary with Joseph* (in which the Church honors Joseph as Mary's spouse and Mary as his spouse) *conceals within itself*, at the same time *the mystery* of the perfect communion of persons, of Man and Woman in the conjugal covenant and at the same time the mystery of this *singular "continence for the kingdom of heaven"*: a continence that served the most perfect *"fruitfulness of the Holy Spirit"* in the history of salvation. Indeed, it was in some way the absolute fullness of that spiritual fruitfulness, because precisely in the Nazarene conditions of Mary and Joseph's covenant in marriage and continence, the gift of the Incarnation of the Eternal Word was realized: the Son of God, consubstantial with the Father, was conceived and born as a Man from the Virgin Mary (MW 75:3).

The key here is the role of the Virgin Mary as icon of woman. The pope is well aware that woman has not historically been given her due as a person with full dignity in the communion of persons. Scola places special emphasis on John Paul II's 1988 encyclical on women, *Mulieris dignitatem*, for the fullest treatment of his theological anthropology of the meaning of being a man and a woman. It was in large part a response to the Synod of Bishops' call in 1987 to a greater understanding of the dignity and role of women in Church and society. Scola describes the pope's basic methodological premise:

Only by beginning from the proper foundations can one grasp the depth of the dignity and mission of women. In fact, only by going to the root of the personal being of man and woman, which implies identity and difference, is it possible to consider women as a being who is "other" and not just "another thing."[37]

So now we must turn to what it means to be a person in a communion of persons.

Part II: The Subjectivity of the Person: Foundation of a Communion of Persons

Original Solitude

It was Vatican Council II that turned Bishop Wojtyla's thoughts to theology, particularly theological anthropology, in response to Pope Paul VI's plea for biblical foundations for the Church's teaching on responsible parenthood in the 1968 encyclical, *Humanae vitae.* In response to this request John Paul II, now pope himself, issued in his weekly Wednesday homilies, a work already prepared, now known as The Theology of the Body, from September 5 1979 to November 28 1984. He was greatly assisted by the philosophical work he had already done on the person, and the communion of persons, especially in *Love and Responsibility, The Acting Person* and numerous essays and articles. Beginning with answer to the Pharisees on the indissolubility of marriage when Christ refers to the Genesis texts of creation, John Paul II lays out a complete theological anthropology. Pivotal is his analysis of what he calls "original solitude."

An Adequate Anthropology

Horizon	Original Solitude	Original Unity	Original Nakedness	Hermeneutics of the Gift
Beginning/norm	Image of God Person Double solitude Partner of the absolute Contingent being Incommunicable	Image of Trinity Communion of Persons Affirms original solitude	Original innocence Sharing in God's vision Interpersonal Communion	Creation ex nihilo Love source of creation Man and world a gift Person a "being-gift"
	Self-knowledge Self-consciousness Self-determination Openness to the "Other"—woman	Dual asymmetrical unity Sexuality constituent of person Conjugal union Union by conscious choice	Self-possession Self-mastery Lack of shame "Peace of interior gaze" Beatitude	Freedom of gift Awareness of gift Acceptance of the gift Mutual gift Mutual self-donation
	Openness to parenthood	Knowledge-generation link	No tension between sex and procreation	Child a gift
*Source: John Paul II's *Theology of the Body*	Rootedness in the body Body expresses the person	Union through the body	Spousal meaning of the body Harmony with creation	Body sing of gift Creation gift to man Man gift to creation
	Sacramentality of the body and creation	Marriage the primordial sacrament		

Adam was created first alone with all the attributes of a human in contrast with the animals. Man is rational and has free will. Although by the mere fact of being created, like the animals, he is in a contingent relationship with God, by the covenant of creation, he has been made God's partner in charge of the world. He is "partner of the Absolute." All this flows from his being made in the image of God. Even in his body, John Paul II declares he images God, since it is his body that allows him to engage in truly human acts. The pope makes it clear that Adam's solitude has two meanings, (1) alone as a person before God and (2) without a suitable partner. He is created not just as a self-enclosed individual but as a person intrinsically ordered to another like himself in the manner of the Trinitarian Persons. He is created for love, which is made manifest in the very orientation of his body to union. His body, John Paul II calls spousal from its ordering to a spousal relation of love. Eve is created by God himself, while Adam is in a deep sleep, as a double solitude, with spiritual faculties of intellect and will in every way equal to Adam in her humanity but with a different bodily manifestation. Like the communion of the Trinity the union between the man and the woman, affirms everything each is as a person. When Eve is brought to Adam for the first time, he cries out: "Here at last is bone of my bones and flesh of my flesh" (Gen. 2:23). The pope interprets this as first a sister relation before it is spousal:

> Before they become husband and wife (a little later Gen 4:1 speaks of it concretely), man and woman *come forth from the mystery of creation* first of all *as brother and sister in the same humanity.* The understanding of the spousal meaning of the body in its masculinity and femininity reveals the innermost point of their freedom, which is the freedom of the gift.
>
> It is from here that the communion of persons begins in which both encounter each other and give themselves reciprocally in the fullness of their subjectivity. In this way, both grow as persons-subjects, and grow reciprocally, one for the other, also through their bodies and through their "nakedness" free from shame. In this communion of persons, the whole depth of the original solitude of man (of the first and of all) is perfectly ensured and, at the same time, this solitude is

> permeated and enlarged in a marvelous way by the gift of the "other" (MW 18:5).

This "sister" relation corresponds to the "I-other" relation of the neighbor, which all are called to through their humanity and which ensures a true communion of persons. It also corresponds to the virginal state. As John Paul II says, it is rooted first of all in the covenant of creation, the partnership with God himself. It is noteworthy that there is not simply dependence on God as Creator but dependence on each other for fulfillment.

Subjectivity

What it means to be a human subject, which is the foundation of personhood in a communion of persons, was of central interest for John Paul II, as philosopher Karol Wojtyla before he became pope and helps to illuminate what he means by "original solitude." One might say that it was what attracted him to phenomenology. In 1976 he called the problem of subjectivity "of paramount philosophical importance today." Indeed the subjectivity of the person—particularly in relation to the human community—imposes itself today as one of the central ideological issues that lie at the very basis of human praxis, morality (and thus also of ethics), culture, civilization and politics. "[38] Subjectivity, he says, is a synonym for the irreducibility or incommunicability of the human person. "This human being is not just an individual of the species but a personal subject."[39]

Irreducibility and subjectivity are particularly expressed by acts of the will. No one can will for the person not even God. It is through these acts that he "creates" himself. Not only is the person directed to a certain value in what he is drawn to but he also in a way creates himself though his choice. He becomes either good or bad, for example, by his moral acts. As Wojtyla says, he governs himself and by good moral acts he comes to "possess" himself. The human suppositum that constitutes itself through its acts of self-determination, is called a self or an "I." Having experience of myself as a person, also gives me access, through consciousness, to others with the same personal structure of self- determination.[40] Later this analysis of the human person and his acts will assist John Paul II in interpreting *Gaudium et spes*, no. 24: "Man, who is the only creature on earth which God willed for itself, cannot fully find himself except through a sincere gift of self."

Philosophically Wojtyla used the term "participation" in a particular way to convey how the person can participate in the being of another without losing his or her subjectivity.[41] He finds the essence of participation to lie in the Gospel commandment to love your neighbor as yourself. Only if the other is affirmed as another human person like myself can true participation occur. This is known as an "I-Other" relation and is the foundation of participation. Knowledge of the other comes through *experiencing* him as another human like myself not simply by *cognition*. From this flows the more intimate "I-you" relation, which has a reflexive quality.

> Both the "I" and the "you" face each other in the fullness of self-determination, self- possession and self- consciousness. The "I" is enabled to have a more complete experience of itself by seeing itself in the light of another "I." It does not lead me out of my subjectivity so much as establish me more firmly in it. When the relationship is fully reciprocal it constitutes a communion of persons, *communio personarum*." [42]

Original Innocence and the Communion of Persons

In the "beginning" according to Genesis 2:25 Adam and Eve were "both naked and not ashamed." This phrase, John Paul II says, indicates a fullness of vision both of God and each other in their masculinity and femininity. They enjoy the *communio personarum* willed for them by their Creator. "They see and know each other, in fact, with the peace of the interior gaze" (MW 13:1). In this "beautifying" beginning, they could be a reciprocal gift to each other since:

> Communion of persons means living in a reciprocal "for," in a relationship of reciprocal gift. And this relationship is precisely the fulfillment of "man's" original solitude. (MW 14:2)

They had what the pope calls "the freedom of the gift." They were endowed with an innocence and inner purity that did not allow them to treat each other as mere objects. Such freedom resulted from perfect self-mastery and self-possession through which they could become a "sincere gift" to each other" (MW 15:2). It was the fruit of the grace of original innocence, a gift from the Creator, "who has willed (and continually wills) man, male and female, "for his own sake"(MW 17:3).

Revelation teaches us that Adam and Eve rejected the Creator's gift by listening to Satan's lies about God and his love. "They cast God out of their heart" (MW 26:4).[43] Adam and Eve's disobedience brought about alienation, first from God, who is the source of life-giving grace, then within themselves, since they now experience disorder in the soul-body union, and finally from each other since they can no longer accept one another as a "disinterested" gift. Instead they begin to use each other for their own selfish purposes. The person and the communion of persons was damaged at its root when Adam and Eve lost the gift of grace, the grace, through which they began to participate in divine Trinitarian communion. Along with banishment from Eden, however, was given the promise of a Redeemer (Gen. 3:15).

Mary's Fiat

From this it can be seen that a covenantal relationship with God, as Creator, is the foundation of the dignity of man and woman and the substratim of a communion of persons. When Adam and Eve preferred to listen to the lies of the serpent, their communion of persons was shattered. But Mary with her *fiat* began the work of restoration.

The divine plan of salvation in Christ, which includes everyone, "reserves a special place for the '*woman*' who is the Mother of him to whom the Father entrusted the work of salvation," says John Paul II (RM 7) "'Grace,' means a special gift," John Paul II reminds us in speaking of the Annunciation, "which according to the New Testament has its source precisely in the Trinitarian life of God himself, God who is love. (cf. 1 Jn. 4:8)" (RM 8). The pope will later stress that although becoming the mother of God was a pure grace of the Holy

To: John Martino

Thanks again so much.

May Sarasananden

Spirit, "through her response of faith Mary exercises her free will and fully shares with her personal and feminine 'I' in the event of the Incarnation." She acts as an "authentic subject" in the union with the second Person of the Blessed Trinity for God always respects the free will of the human "I" (MD 4).[44] In the apostolic letter, *Tertio millennio adveniente*, John Paul II says: "Never in human history did so much depend…upon the consent of one human creature" (TMA 2). It was in giving consent in faith that Mary and also Joseph most fully expressed their personhood, acknowledging obedience to God who reveals and, at the same time, exercising free will in authentic subjectivity.

Mary, Icon of What it Means to be Woman

As we saw, John Paul II continually looks back to the Council. [45] Certainly one of the reasons for his encyclical letter, *Mother of the Redeemer*, according to Josef Ratzinger, was to reconcile the two Mariologies that clashed at the Council, one seeking a separate document on Mary and the other integrating devotion to Mary into the Church. The former, whose piety was centered on Marian apparitions, favored the motto "*per Mariam ad Jesum,*" while the latter, immersed in the biblical and liturgical renewal, preferred "through Christ to the Father." In the final document, *Lumen Gentium,* Mary was inserted into ecclesiology. Ratzinger called the move correct but in the aftermath Mariology itself collapsed. [46] In 1974 Pope Paul VI issued *Marialis Cultus,* which was designed to restore the balance. Taking *Lumen Gentium* as his starting point, he examined the relationship between Mary and the liturgy and Mary as the model of the Church's living of the divine mysteries. He particularly highlights her faith and notes that she is both a teacher for the individual Christian and a model for the Church in the practice of divine worship (MC 16, 17, 21). He restores the balance between the two approaches by declaring that she is "the highest after Christ and the closest to us" (MC 27). John Paul II picks up the theme of the dual character of Mary as the one who "far surpasses all other creatures" (R M 10) and also walks the same pilgrimage of faith of all.[47]

In his encyclical letter, *Mother of the Redeemer*, he takes as his theme her pilgrimage of faith, which began at the Annunciation. "I wish to consider primarily that 'pilgrimage of faith' in which 'the Blessed Virgin advanced,' faithfully preserving her union with Christ" (RM 5). This pilgrimage of faith does not just concern Mary but the whole People of God. It is an "exceptional pilgrimage" since she is *"already the eschatological fulfillment of the Church:"* yet it is the path that all must walk in the Church (RM 6). Throughout the encyclical letter, Mary's role in the Church is emphasized including her spiritual motherhood of Christians but not her role in the family of Nazareth. That was left for the apostolic letter, *Mulieris dignitatem,* more than a year later on the occasion of the Marian year. While dwelling on Mary's exceptional role as Mother of God, *Theotokos,* John Paul II seizes on Christ's address of his mother as "Woman," to underline her likeness to all women, especially in her union with God: "The dignity of every human being and the vocation corresponding to that dignity find their definitive measure in union with God" (RM 5). It is significant that John Paul II takes the words of Elizabeth to Mary at the Visitation "Blessed is she who believed" as the overarching theme for his reflection on Mary in the encyclical letter, *Mother of the Redeemer* (RM 4). These words not only recall those of *Lumen gentium* but point also to Mary's dual role arising from her faith of becoming the Mother of God *and* of going before the People of God in their pilgrimage of faith. After comparing her faith to that of Abraham, the pope recounts key moments in her journey of faith from the prophecy of Simeon that "she will have to live her obedience of faith in suffering, at the side of her suffering savior" (RM 16); in her hidden life in Nazareth; and beside her Son on the cross. As his mother, she is in contact with the truth about her Son only in faith. "In the expression, 'Blessed is she who believed,' we can rightly find a 'key' which unlocks for us the innermost reality of Mary, whom the angel hailed as full of grace" (RM 19). The pope goes on to show how Christ looked upon faith in the Son of God as also the key to the pilgrimage of faith for all. The pope refers to the two passages in Luke, 11:28 and 8:20-21, where Jesus calls those who believe the word of God his mothers and his brothers (RM 20).

In his apostolic letter, *Redemptoris custos*, the pope compares the faith of Joseph to that of Mary at the Annunciation. Citing the Vatican II document on divine revelation, *Dei verbum* the pope says:

> The obedience of faith" must be given to God as he reveals himself. By this obedience of faith man freely commits himself entirely to God, making "the full submission of his intellect and will entirely to God who reveals," and willingly assenting to the revelation given by him." *This statement*, which touches the very essence of faith, *is perfectly applicable to Joseph of Nazareth* (RC 4).

By citing this Vatican II document, which refers to all Christians, this would seem to place St Joseph closer to imperfect Christians than to his immaculate spouse.[48] He continues:

> He was also the first to be placed by God on Mary's 'pilgrimage of faith." It is a path along which—especially at the time of Calvary and Pentecost—Mary will proceed in a perfect way" (RC 5).

Thus we see that John Paul II views the Holy Family as the preeminent model for the faith of all believers.

Mary's Chastity

The angel greeted Mary as "full of grace," (*kecharitomene*). Scripture scholar, Ignace de la Potterie, states that, in using the perfect passive participle, the angel's greeting to Mary at the Annunciation indicates that she had already been transformed by grace[49] in preparation for her becoming the mother of God, virginally, by the Holy Spirit. De la Potterie cites St. Bernard as interpreting the grace given as the "grace of her virginity." He also sees it as helping to establish the dogma of the Immaculate Conception. Mary, from the first moment of her conception, was preserved from original sin and all its consequences, especially concupiscence or disordered desire. Here we might turn to another author, Jean-Pierre Batut, professor of Dogmatic Theology in Paris, in his reflections on the chastity of Jesus.[50] Mary, he says, is the only one who fully understands the temptations of Jesus. Batut notes that Aquinas distinguishes between two types of temptation, those of the "flesh" and the "world" and those which have Satan as their author. The temptation facing Adam and Eve first and foremost attacked their faith in God and his promises.[51] When Christ was tempted after his sojourn in the desert, (Matt. 4:1-11) his very mode of existing as a Son, wholly oriented in loving obedience to the Father, was called into question by Satan: "If you are the Son of God. . . ." He concludes that in a certain sense, every sin in its roots is "a sin against chastity," because it turns man away from God and towards the "world." It denies his primary orientation towards a loving God, his creator and redeemer, before everything and everyone else.[52] In the Annunciation, Mary was faced with the temptation to doubt God's promises. With her *fiat* she surrendered her whole being to God and thereby, as the Fathers reiterated, undid the knot of Eve's disobedience. And as they also say: "She conceived this Son in her mind before she conceived him in her womb: precisely in faith" (RM 13).[53]

Mary as Theological Person

Finally, Marc Ouellet points out how the theologian, Hans Urs von Balthasar (who greatly influenced John Paul II) has specified a further concept of person when he is incorporated into Christ. He believes that, in spite of its philosophical diffusion, the term person needs to be referred to its origin to account for the irreplaceable dignity of the human person. So von Balthasar says: It is when God addresses a conscious subject, tells him who he is and what he means to the eternal God of truth and shows him the purpose of his existence ---that we can say of a conscious subject that he is a person."[54] In this way he makes a distinction between a "conscious person" and a "theological person," a "person in Christ." In Christ person and mission are identical. One can say that Mary became a theological person when the angel addressed her as "full of grace" (*kecharitomene),* in view of her becoming the mother of God. Such a concept also involves an intrinsic relation to the ecclesial community. The implications of this concept will be drawn out in subsequent chapters.

Summary

In this chapter, we have looked at the Trinitarian and Christological roots of the communion of persons and traced in brief the development of John Paul II's theology of the Holy Family as a model for all families. Following Josef Ratzinger's interpretation of the humanity of Christ in the hypostatic union, we have attempted to show that it is not an exception, as it has been viewed over the centuries. Just as by being united to his divine nature Christ's humanity reveals humanity in its perfection, so the Holy Family in having Christ as the center is the perfection of what it means to be family. Mary through the grace of the Immaculate Conception was endowed with a union with God beyond all other creatures in view of her becoming *Theotokos*, Mother of God. This exceptional union was expressed in the gift of "consecrated" virginity. John Paul II has shown in his theological exegesis of Genesis 2 how all, however, are created first in a virginal state as person-subjects, "original solitudes" before forming a communion of persons. In the Annunciation, Mary showed herself an "authentic subject, or feminine "I" by her *fiat* and marked out the path of faith, first for St. Joseph, and then for all of Christ's disciples in the Church.

In *Redemptoris Mater*, John Paul II brings out Mary's role as virgin, spouse *and* mother both in flesh and spirit. "She is a virgin who 'keeps whole and pure the fidelity she has pledged to her Spouse' and 'becomes herself a mother' for 'she brings forth to a new and immortal life child who are conceived of the Holy Spirit and born of God' (RM 6). [55] Forthcoming chapters will examine the "I- other," the "I- you" and the "we" relations as they are expressed in the communion of persons of the family, namely the spousal, paternal/maternal and filial dimensions.

CHAPTER 3

The Role of Joseph in Salvation

WHILE THE INAUGURATION OF THE Old Covenant depended on the faith of one man, Abraham, the inauguration of the new, as the Fathers of the Church often pointed out, depended on the assent of one woman, Mary.[1] Mary reversed the disobedience of Eve in listening to the serpent in the Garden of Eden. At the Annunciation Mary conceived by the Holy Spirit, Jesus, who was then born into an ordinary Israelite family. This chapter begins to unravel what this inconceivable irruption of divinity into human history means for the human family as a communion of persons. First of all, it is necessary to unpack the role of Joseph in salvation history in order to see the Holy Family as a defining model of a communion of persons for the Christian family in spite of obvious differences. Was he a true husband of Mary and father to Jesus? As a just or righteous man Joseph was completely imbued with the Old Testament ethos, expressed succinctly in being in right relationship with God.[2] Their ordinary life, lived according to this ethos,[3] nevertheless, concealed an extraordinary event, the virginal conception of Jesus by the power of the Holy Spirit.[4] Paradoxically it is both the continuity and discontinuity with the Old Testament, that allow the Holy Family to be par excellence the model for all families and to reveal the true depths of what it means for the family to be a communion of persons. This chapter traces Joseph's identity in the Gospel narratives, in the Fathers of the Church, in the Middle Ages to the 17th century to the final emergence of an understanding of his protective role in the Church in the 19th and 20th centuries.

Here it must be said that all revelation was completed by the death of the last apostle but not all aspects were immediately clear. It has taken long centuries to unpack the richness of Christ's life, death and resurrection. It is in that spirit that the salvation history of Joseph's role is being given. It is also important to note that there are two legitimate interpretations of Joseph. In the Eastern Orthodox Church, it is believed, following the Proto-evangelium of James, that Joseph was a widow with several children when he entered into a virginal marriage with Mary. However, in the Latin Church, which does not recognize the gospel of James as a canonical book, Joseph was a young man and took a vow of virginity when entering marriage with Mary. This is the path taken by the Western Church, particularly from the late Middle Ages. It is the one favored by the majority of the Fathers of the Church and the one that is followed in this book.

The Gospel Narratives

Right from the time of the evangelists there has been an ongoing search in the Church to understand and embrace the nature of Joseph's fatherhood. As all commentators point out, Gospel references to Joseph are few. In fact, he is mentioned in only three New Testament (NT) writings: Matthew, Luke and John.[5] Prominent in Matthew and Luke are the genealogies of Jesus, Matthew beginning with Abraham and descending through David (Mt 1:1-17) and Luke (3:23-38) starting with Joseph and working backward to Adam. The genealogies presented two problems to the early Christian exegetes: first, Joseph was assigned two fathers and secondly Jesus' ancestry was traced through Joseph, who was not the biological father. The levirate law of adoption was given to explain the first and the Jewish custom of tracing the ancestry through the head of the family to explain the second. In either case, as Francis Filas says, in Jewish law "an already existing fatherhood" was assumed.[6] To the question about Mary's ancestry, many Fathers cite the Jewish custom of marrying relatives. If they both went to Bethlehem for the census, they must have both been of the same tribe of David.[7] Both genealogies reference Jacob, whose son Joseph, sold into slavery in Egypt in order later to feed his brothers in time of famine, is often seen as an OT type for Jesus.[8]

Matthew, Fitzmeyer points out, ends his genealogy with: "Jacob, the father of Joseph, the husband of Mary of whom Jesus Christ was born," (1:16) thus attributing Joseph's fatherhood by implication to his marriage to Mary. The following Gospel passage further delineates the nature of Joseph's fatherhood. Joseph is advised in a dream by the angel to take Mary as his wife and to *name* Jesus. By Joseph naming him, Jesus will come to be called his son. Then by being warned also in a dream about Herod's designs on the child and fleeing to Egypt with Mary and Jesus, he is "depicted as the guardian of the family" as he is again in shepherding the family back to Israel, to Nazareth in Galilee.[9] Mary, herself, calls Joseph "father" when she asks the twelve-year old Jesus in the Temple, "Why have you treated us so? Behold your father and I have been looking for you anxiously" (Lk 2:48). Joseph is also present at the purification in the temple and hears the prophecies of Simeon and Anna (Lk 2:22 -40).

The Fathers of the Church

In spite of these gospel passages, "for the first millennium of Christianity," according to Joseph Leinhard, "St. Joseph was all but ignored in preaching, liturgical celebrations, martyrologies and theological writing."[10] Examples he gives are: no homilies by Church Fathers; no feast day until the seventh century and only in Egypt; and not until the 14th century a single treatise devoted to him. It was not just due to the paucity of reference in the canonical gospels (there also were several apochryphal gospels, the most important of which was the Protoevangelium of James, which contained such "facts" as the age of Joseph at marriage and his being a widow with children).[11]

There was a deeper theological reason. Filas presents the dilemma that faced the Fathers, who were mainly concerned with expounding the doctrine of Christ. Until she was declared *Theotokos*, Mother of God, at the Council of Ephesus (431), even devotion to and honoring of Mary remained muted until the main Christological doctrines had been formulated. As Filas says, "on the subject of the Holy Family, difficulties arose for them in every direction."[12] In what sense was Joseph both husband and father? How could it be a true marriage if it was not consummated by conjugal intercourse? Yet, if it was declared a true marriage, danger lay in denying the virgin birth. Against all attacks by heretics the Fathers had to find a way to affirm that it was a true marriage without compromising the divine origin of Jesus from Mary.

Filas begins his analysis of the Fathers' response to this dilemma with Origen in the third century. Reference had been made to the marriage in St. Ignatius of Antioch's Epistle to the Ephesians. He declared that one of the providential reasons for the marriage was to hide Mary's virgin birth from Satan.[13] For both Justin Martyr and Irenaeus in the second century, Joseph was only *thought* to be his father. Joseph had no part in the generation of Jesus. It was only in the third century with Origen that a serious investigation was made of the nature of Joseph's fatherhood, again in response to heresies. His solution is to refer to Joseph as legal and foster father.[14] Ephrem was more expansive. He called Joseph's fatherhood nobler than that of an adoptive father. Fatherhood belongs to him both by juridical descent and through his relationship to Mary. He also referred to him as adoptive father, and even more boldly as "father of God," indicating in some way a true fatherhood. Filas considers Ephrem's contribution a real advance in understanding Joseph, allowing in some sense his phrase "father of God" as "following the rules of '*communicatio idiomatum.*'"[15] Yet he acknowledges that it could be misconstrued. Ephrem is the first to use the simile of the palm tree, in which presence of the male palm is thought to make the female palm fruitful, an apt simile for Joseph's part in the Incarnation.[16]

The fifth century sees a diminishment of Joseph's role with Epiphanius who relies mostly on apochrypha and with Chrysostom, for whom the relation was an espousal and not a true marriage. Joseph was "like a father" and his paternal authority came not from the marriage but from the angel's pronouncement. Jerome, on the contrary, defended both Joseph's virginity and his rights of fatherhood through the marriage.[17] In addition, he denied claims of the apochrypha that Joseph was a widower with several children. Filas quotes him as saying, "Joseph was also virginal through Mary in order that from a virginal marriage a virginal child might be born.[18]

St. Augustine

It is Ambrose and Augustine who defended the marriage of Mary and Joseph as a true marriage, following Roman law by which consent not consummation established the marriage. The opposite view, according to Leinhard derived from a popular attitude.[19] Augustine sets out his views in detail in Sermon 51, using the terminology of Roman law on matrimonial consent and contract. It was not, however, the first time Augustine had taught the genuity of the marriage. In several of his treatises against heretics, he affirmed that "the heart of marriage is not carnal union, but the kind of union Christ has with his members."[20] In particular, in *On Marriage and Concupiscence* and *Against Julian*, he affirmed that all three goods of marriage, which he defined as fidelity, offspring and sacrament as indissolubility, were present in the marriage of Mary and Joseph.[21] It is not difficult to see how the goods of fidelity and sacrament are present in the marriage of Mary and Joseph. The leap that Augustine makes is to assert that the marriage was in Filas' words "*actually* fruitful. . . .Christ is the first of the three actual 'goods' of marriage, understanding 'good' as a property or blessing."[22] In some way the child, Jesus, drew his origin from the union not in a physical but a moral sense. Filas interprets Augustine's meaning as "*God gave the Child to this marriage*—namely to Joseph as well as to Mary; to Joseph united to Mary; and to Joseph because of, and through Mary."[23]

In Sermon 51, Augustine expanded on these ideas. He refers to St. Paul's Epistle to the Corinthians. "*It remains that these who have wives should be as though they had none*" (I Cor 7:29). He goes on:

> And we know many brothers and sisters bearing much fruit in grace, who by mutual consent withhold from each other in the name of Christ the desire of the flesh, but do not withhold from each other their mutual married love. The more the former is held in check, the stronger grows the latter. . . . So if the bond exists, if there is

> a marriage, if you can't say there isn't a marriage just because the act is not performed which can also be performed, but unlawfully, outside of marriage (and if only all couples could live like that, but many can't) then these people should not unjoin couples who so can live, and not deny that he is a husband or she is a wife, just because they don't come together in the flesh, but are tied together in their hearts.[24]

These and the succeeding paragraphs of Sermon 51 certainly indicate that, in Augustine's view, engaging in conjugal intercourse is done *either* solely to procreate children *or* out of lust, and he advises couples to refrain if they can. He compares the need to eat with the necessity to procreate the human species, saying "the wise and prudent and faithful person lowers himself to each out of duty, and doesn't dive in out of lust" or greed.[25] It is important to remember that Augustine's main concern in Sermon 51 is to establish the genuity of the celibate marriage of Mary and Joseph, on which Joseph's fatherhood rests. There is also a sense in which he sees Joseph's chastity contributing specifically to his role as father, referring to the genealogies of Jesus being traced through Joseph.

> Why? Because he's the father. Why is he the father? Because he is all the more definitely and solidly the father, the more chastely he is the father.[26]

Augustine's emphasis on Joseph's chastity may well have influenced his theology of marriage.

According to Joseph Atkinson:

> One will look in vain for a developed theology of the family in St. Augustine. For example in the whole Augustinian corpus the term *paterfamilias* (father of the family) occurs only 43 times.[27]

Yet Atkinson goes on to say that Augustine is the only Church Father to call the family directly a domestic church and he cites the letter, *De Bono Viduitatis.* This and another letter are addressed to the widow Julia, who is living with her daughter, a consecrated celibate. Augustine sees in Julia's family, which is living the Christian faith in prayer, celibacy and discipleship a domestic church (*domestic ecclesia*).[28] It is no accident that Augustine linked the celibate life with that of the family. Again we turn to Atkinson who notes that as a way of holiness, "*Christian* marriage and (what he called) 'conjugal chastity' were interchangeable."[29] There is a *gradus* or gradation between the chastity of the consecrated celibate and conjugal chastity. The man is called to the same purity as his wife. In fact, marriage, imbued by Christ and living conjugal chastity, is one of the three "ways of life" in the Church.[30]

Augustine's ideas on fatherhood are also arresting in his comparison of the ecclesial function of bishop with that of the father of the Christian family. Atkinson has drawn this out from *In Joannis Evangelium.* Like a good bishop, the father in the family is a teacher of the faith for all his family and in this way ministers to Christ, fulfilling in his own home an ecclesial office. "Through baptism, fatherhood has been assumed into the salvific process, and the manner in which a man exercises this role becomes part of the way in which he is working out his salvation."[31] Chrysostom also compared the father in the home to a Bishop. For him both the proper ordering of authority and the teaching of Scripture are paramount in the duties of a father. In this way there is a reciprocal relationship between the home and the Church although for Augustine it is *through* baptism and for Chrysostom it follows *from* baptism. Augustine and Chrysostom clearly prefer to draw out the comparison with a bishop rather than St. Joseph, which may well be due to reluctance to articulate more distinctly the nature of Joseph's fatherhood.

The Fathers of the Church, one can conclude, were inhibited from spelling out the full nature of Joseph's fatherhood by the initial imperative of establishing the dogma of the Incarnation of Christ as true God and true man. Yet there was a recognition and concern for the genuity of the marriage of Mary and Joseph, from which it was agreed Joseph's fatherhood flowed. Their holy marriage particularly influenced Augustine in his theology of marriage and conjugal chastity.

The Middle Ages to Seventeenth Century

Doctrinal Development

The 12th and 13th centuries saw a revival of Gnosticism, particularly the Albigensian or Catharist heresy, which abhorred the carnality of marriage and procreation. This set the stage for a dispute between Gratian, an Italian monk from Bologna, who published the *Decree* (a collection of Church laws) and the theologian Peter Lombard. Gratian held the use of the marriage bond (namely intercourse) to be virtually identical with marriage. Lombard, on the other hand, citing St. Augustine, especially Sermon 51 in his refutation, argued from the genuity of the marriage of Mary and Joseph that consent makes the marriage. As a theologian Lombard was highly influential with other theologians, so that his views prevailed in many medieval commentaries, including those of Albert the Great and Thomas Aquinas.[32] Nevertheless, consummation completed the marriage.[33]

Albert the Great and later Thomas Aquinas consider that Jesus fulfilled the *bonum prolis* dimension of marriage for Mary and Joseph, arguing from the nature of the marriage itself. According to Filas the word, *suscipio* (accept), which Albert used to explain how Joseph received the Child Jesus into the marriage, even though he did not generate Him, is highly significant. *Suscipio* was used in Roman times to indicate the father accepted the child into the family (otherwise the child might be abandoned). Albert takes the argument a step further than Augustine by saying: "Jesus belonged not simply to Mary, but rather to Mary as Joseph's virginal wife and therefore to Joseph's marriage and to Joseph himself."[34] Jesus was not just born but *conceived* in Joseph's marriage.[35]

Thomas Aquinas, whose texts are the foundation of modern theological discussion of Joseph's marriage and fatherhood, articulated two further conclusions.[36] Since the perfection of a thing consists in its form and "the form of matrimony consists in an inseparable union of souls by which husband and wife are pledged to each other with a bond of mutual affection that cannot be sundered," viz. the nuptial bond, the marriage was not deformed by the conditional assent to the "bond of the flesh," dependent as it was on the will of God. To distinguish from Jesus a child, born of adultery and adopted, Thomas says such a child is born *outside* the marriage and not according to God's will.[37] Mary and Joseph's marriage was specifically ordained for the birth and rearing of this Child by divine decree.[38] Furthermore, since both consented to virginity and a virginal marriage was necessary in God's plan, Joseph's consent was a key factor in preparing for the Incarnation.

William of Estius (+1613) developed and extended some of Augustine's principles. Notable was his assertion that "Christ's *procreation* itself belonged to the marriage." Since marriage is directed to procreation, "the wife's procreative powers belong to the husband as well."[39] According to the natural law, that children arise within the marriage, Jesus is brought forth by Mary to Joseph, her husband as the good of marriage. Therefore Joseph has a true fatherhood. Francisco Suarez (+1617) was significant not just in summarizing past doctrinal developments on Joseph's fatherhood, but in drawing out new insights. When Jesus on the cross shared his own sonship with the apostle John, Suarez argues he would not have given a title without meaning. Similarly, in the gospel of Luke, Joseph did not just share in the title of father of Christ but in the reality also, which included the capacity to be father in love, care and authority.[40] In a certain sense, Suarez maintains that Joseph, as husband of Mary, is the "lord of her body," so that he shares in the parenthood of Jesus. It was this "common ownership" of Jesus that ensured a true fatherhood of Joseph in the moral order.[41]

But Suarez' most significant development was to describe Joseph as partaking in the "order of the hypostatic union," because of his most intimate relationship both with Jesus and Mary.[42] Because of this privilege, Joseph's ministry, Suarez maintains, surpasses all but Mary's. Citing the Gospel of Thomas, he concludes, "The apostles are greatest by their ministry of the New Testament. Joseph's ministry, however, belonged neither to the New nor properly to the Old; but rather to the Author of each, and to the cornerstone uniting the two." The whole reason for the existence of Mary and Joseph was to be cooperators in the Incarnation. After Mary, Joseph's role was pre-eminent, so that together with Mary his place lies in the order of the hypostatic union "to the exclusion of all others."[43] Among other theologians, Bossuet (+1704) stands out as proposing that, since Mary's virginity belonged to Joseph by virtue of the virginal marriage, Jesus as the fruit belongs to Joseph as well. From this, he argues for some type of causative role in the Incarnation. "If, then, Joseph has so great a share in the saintly virginity of Mary, he also partakes of the fruit which she bears."[44]

The Rise of Devotion to St. Joseph

Bossuet is primarily known as a spiritual writer guiding souls through devotion to Jesus, Mary and Joseph. Indeed it was in the Middle Ages that devotion to the saint first took hold with a greater interest in his virtues. Devotion fed on previous theological interpretations, especially that of Augustine, and in turn influenced them. John Gerson (+1429), Chancellor of the University of Paris, authored eight works on St. Joseph, in which he developed the new idea that since Jesus was born in the land or property of Joseph as the spouse of Mary, it gave him a juridical right as father.[45] But Gerson was mainly interested in promoting a Feast of the Espousals of Joseph and Mary.[46] The writings of Gerson, along with those of Peter d'Ailly (+1420), greatly influenced the composition of Masses devoted to St. Joseph, which sprang up in the 15th century. Songs and prayers were imbued with Augustine's three goods of the marriage in which Joseph played a key role. The tributes to St. Joseph by Bernadine of Siena (+1444) were particularly incorporated into the liturgy. In preaching on the love of Joseph for Jesus, he intimated for the first time that Joseph in his fatherhood resembled the eternal Father in his relationship with Christ. The *Summa of the Gifts of St. Joseph* by Isidor de Isolani (+1530) reiterated this same likeness to God the Father.[47]

It was the Franciscans who took the lead in fostering devotion to St. Joseph.[48] Bernadine of Siena was one. Another was Cardinal Cisneros of Spain at the time of St. Theresa of Avila. According to Andrew Doze, "A Franciscan Pope, Sixtus IV, is the one who introduced St. Joseph into the breviary and set his first liturgical feast in the Church of March 19 by the Act of November 19, 1480."[49] With the establishment of Joseph's role in the marriage, devotion both to him and to the Holy Family could and did take place. The next chapter will detail the confluence of the rise in devotion to St. Joseph and the Holy Family, while the remaining portion of this chapter will outline increasing attention to Joseph in the papal documents of the Church.

Papal Documents

From the time of Sixtus IV, succeeding popes increased the solemnity of the Feast of St. Joseph from the 17th to the early 18th centuries.[50] But it was in the 19th century that the Church was both confident enough of the role of Joseph and received numerous petitions to elevate his role in worship. Pope Pius IX in *Inclytum Patriarcham* (July 7, 1871) stated:

> In these latter times in which a monstrous and most abominable war has been declared against the Church of Christ, the devotion of the faithful toward St. Joseph has grown and progressed to such an extent that from every direction innumerable and fervent petitions have reached Us. These were recently renewed during the Sacred Ecumenical Council [Vatican Council I] by groups of the faithful, and, what is more important, by many of our venerable brethren, the cardinals and bishops of the Holy Roman Church.

In response to these petitions, Pius IX had declared St. Joseph Patron of the Universal Church on December 8, 1870 and raised the level of his feast.[51] In *Inclytum Patriarcham,* he stipulated that he is to be invoked after the Blessed Virgin, and he added prayers to the breviary.

Pope Leo XIII, also citing a rise in atheism in society, turned to intercessory prayer to St. Joseph. Having declared October the month of Our Lady of the Rosary, he advocated invoking her "chaste spouse." It is of interest that both Pius IX (*Quemadmodum Deus*) and then Leo XIII in *Quamquam Pluries* (August 15, 1889) refer to Joseph's Old Testament namesake as prefiguring "the greatness of the future guardian of the Holy Family."[52] Just as the Patriarch Joseph presided over Pharaoh's household and by his actions saved the Kingdom of Egypt, so the second, "destined to be guardian of the Christian religion should be regarded as the protector and defender of the Church." He cites him as model not only of fathers in paternal solicitude, of spouses in love, peace and conjugal fidelity but also calls him the protector of virginity. Pope Leo XIII had written two foundational encyclicals, one, *Arcanum*, on marriage and another, *Rerum Novarum*, on the social situation, both under attack from the forces of the industrial revolution.

The threats accelerated in the 20th century, especially with the outbreak of the Communist revolution in Russia in 1917. Pope Benedict XV once again turned to Joseph, calling for celebration of the 50th anniversary of Pius IX's declaration of St. Joseph as Patron of the Universal Church in 1870.[53] The pope speaks of an increase of devotion to St. Joseph in the horrors of World War I but acknowledges a much greater plague has arisen in atheistic communism with its materialism and class warfare. In addition the family, weakened by the separation of spouses during the war, is undergoing a consequent corruption of morals. Pius XI "speaks of Joseph as the 'tender and vigilant head' of the Holy Family, and the guardian of the divine child."[54] In this encyclical Pius declared St Joseph patron against atheistic communism. "This patronage is part of Joseph's patronage of the Universal Church, which, with regard to the mystical body of Christ, is the logical extension of the Saint's fatherhood of our Lord."[55] Here once more we see the connection between devotion to St. Joseph and renewal of the family through meditation on the Holy Family, which will be considered in detail later.

As the power of communism increased, Pius XI issued an encyclical on the Feast of St. Joseph, 1937 on its evils. At the end he appealed to St. Joseph:

> To hasten the advent of that "peace of Christ in the kingdom of Christ" [48] so ardently desired by all, We place the vast campaign of the Church against world Communism under the standard of St. Joseph, her mighty Protector. He belongs to the working-class, and he bore the burdens of poverty for himself and the Holy Family, whose tender and vigilant head he was. To him was entrusted the Divine Child when Herod loosed his assassins against Him.[56]

The next great champion of St. Joseph in the Church is Pope John XXIII. On the Feast of St. Joseph, 1961, he gave what is called "the longest papal document, (an apostolic letter) ever written on St. Joseph." Its primary purpose was to declare the saint Patron of Vatican Council II.[57] He appealed to St. Joseph as "Protector *Universalis Ecclesiae*." On December 25, the pope convoked Vatican Council II to meet sometime in 1962.[58] Once again, he drew attention to the entrustment of the Council to St. Joseph. At the close of the Council, Paul VI again invoked St. Joseph, who, together with John the Baptist, was a patron of the Council.[59] St. Joseph was not mentioned in the documents of the Council itself. However, Filas argues for the fittingness of devotion to St. Joseph in the inclusion of devotion to Mary in *Lumen gentium*, Chapter Seven.[60] What he finds even more significant is John XXIII's order to include St. Joseph's name in the Canon of the Mass on November 13, 1962.[61] Fifty years later on May 1, 2013, the Congregation for Divine Worship and the Discipline of the Sacraments issued the decree *Paternas vices* by the authority of Pope Francis that the name of St. Joseph, spouse of the Virgin be inserted together with Mary (cum beato Joseph, *eius Sponso*) into Eucharistic Prayers II, III, and IV. This was initiated by Pope Benedict XVI and confirmed by Pope Francis.[62]

The papal document that has not yet been mentioned is John Paul II's Apostolic Exhortation, *Redemptoris Custos*: (Guardian of the Redeemer) On the Person and Mission of Saint Joseph in the Life of Christ and the Church, issued August 15, 1989, on the century of Pope Leo XIII's *Quamquam Pluries*. Of all the papal documents, it is most clearly imbued with reverence for the Holy Family as a communion of persons.

Emergence of Joseph's Role in Salvation History

In this chapter we have seen how it was necessary for Joseph's role in the Holy family to be virtually ignored in the early centuries of the Church so that it could be worked out how Christ could be true God and true man in the Incarnation. Yet Scripture had to be taken into account, which spoke of Joseph as father of Jesus, tracing his ancestry through him and described as such by Mary. The Fathers variously called him putative, foster or adoptive father. Attention was focused on the genuity of the marriage, which was determined to be the source of Joseph's fatherhood and essential in God's plan for the Incarnation to take place in a family. It was not until the Middle Ages that attention was given to the person of Joseph and his attributes as father of Jesus. Devotion, both personal and liturgical, arose at the same time. Chief among Joseph's attributes was his role as guardian of the Holy Family. In the 19th century, Joseph was recognized as Patron of the Church.

In the 17th century Francis de Sales in a letter to St. Jane de Chantal, spoke of "the splendors of this Husband of the Queen of the whole world, named Father of Jesus and his first worshipper next to his divine Spouse."[63] While these three titles "perfectly interlock" (first husband, then father and worshipper of Christ), Andrew Doze comments that "the Church is far from having integrated [this fact] into her thought and practice."[64] It has had to wait until the late 20th and 21st centuries for Joseph as spouse to be officially recognized. Nevertheless, it is noteworthy, particularly in the later Middle Ages how frequently *relations* between the members of the Holy Family are cited to validate Joseph's true fatherhood. In other words, the *communion* of the Holy Family was paramount.

St. Joseph's Role in a Communion of Persons

John Paul II first gave an apostolic exhortation on St. Joseph, *Redemptoris custos* Guardian of the redeemer) in 1989, two years after his encyclical letter on Mary, *Redemptoris mater* (Mother of the Redeemer). He reflects on Joseph within the context of the whole Christian mystery of the Incarnation.

> This is precisely the mystery in which Joseph of Nazareth "shared" like no other human being except Mary, the mother of the Incarnate word. He shared it with her: he was involved in the same salvific event; he was the guardian of the same love, through the power of which the eternal Father "destined us to be his sons through Jesus Christ." (RC 1)

As Chorpenning brings out, the pope's approach firstly is conciliar, christological and ecclesial.[65] He highlights the Second Vatican Council's teaching of the pilgrimage of faith in *Lumen gentium*.[66] For example, Joseph was united in a special way to Mary by his faith, which paralleled hers (RC 4). By embarking on this "pilgrimage of faith," Joseph became *"a unique guardian of the mystery* 'hidden for ages in God'. . . .*Together with Mary, Joseph is the first guardian of this divine mystery"* (RC 5). Secondly, his vision is *personalist, trinitarian* and *relational*, making full use of the theological anthropology of *Gaudium et spes*.[67] Right at the beginning of *Redemptoris custos*, in just two paragraphs the pope refers to Mary's motherhood, her spousal relation to Joseph and his fatherhood (RC 2, 3).

It is primarily the anthropology of the Holy Family as a communion of persons that this work seeks to draw out. Other aspects will be brought in as they relate to the underlying theme.

After referring to Joseph's sacrifice (his "gift of self") in accepting virginity for Mary's sake, the pope writes:

> This *bond of charity was the core of the Holy Family's life,* first in the poverty of Bethlehem, then in their exile in Egypt, and later in the house of Nazareth. The Church deeply venerates this Family, and proposes it as the model of all families. Inserted directly in the mystery of the Incarnation, the Family of Nazareth has its own special mystery. . . . Together with human nature, *all that is human, and especially the family*—as the first dimension of man's existence in the world—*is also taken up* in Christ (RC 21).

Two other quotations are a fitting close to this chapter on Joseph's role in salvation history. Both are from *Redemptoris custos* and will serve as a prelude to more detailed explorations of the Holy Family as a communion of persons that follow.

> Whereas Adam and Eve were the source of evil which was unleashed on the world, Joseph and Mary are the summit from which holiness spreads all over the earth. (RC 7)

and

> "The family has *the mission to guard, reveal, and communicate love*, and this is a living reflection of and a real sharing in God's love for humanity and the love of Christ the Lord for the Church his bride" (FC 17). This being the case, it is in the Holy Family, the original "church in miniature (*Ecclesia domestica*)" that every Christian family must be reflected. "Through God's mysterious design, it was in that family that the Son of God spent long years of a hidden life. It is therefore the prototype and example for all Christian families" (FC 85) (RC 7).

The next chapter will show how Joseph's role in salvation, now recognized as both spouse and father, are essential for a full theology of the Holy Family as a communion of persons.

CHAPTER 4

Joseph and the Holy Family

In the last chapter, we saw the emergence of Joseph's role in salvation both as husband of Mary and father of Jesus, as well as his role as protector of the Church. Parallel with this development came an appreciation of the Holy Family, on the one hand, as an "earthly Trinity" and, on the other, as a model for Christian families. How this came about is the burden of this chapter. Only with the emergence of Joseph's role in salvation could the Holy Family be seen as a communion of persons and a true family. This chapter takes the liberty of condensing a thousand years of salvation history in order to show the trends that have affected the family since the Middle Ages with special emphasis on the emergence of Joseph and a theology of the Holy Family. The lens through which the historical perspective will be examined is through the understanding of the Holy Family as a communion of persons. This means that who they are in their identity as person, spouse and mother, father or child will be examined primarily to see how the integrity of each identity contributes to a true communion. [1]

Beginning with the Gnostic heresy of the Albigensians, the chapter moves from the Church's response of a more incarnational theology of the family to its own partial rejection of such an anthropology, which contributed to the dualism of modernity and subsequent fracturing of the family in the 20th century by contraception, abortion and reproductive technologies. The Church's contemporary response, epitomized by St. John Paul II, in R*edemptoris custos*, invokes the "personalist, Trinitarian and relational approach" of Vatican Council II. Without these developments the Holy Family could not be viewed as a credible model for the family as a communion of persons.

Methodology

So far in tracing the development of Josephology in the Church much reliance has been placed on Francis Filas for good reason. He has exhaustively studied the understanding of Joseph's role in the Fathers of the Church, in the rise of devotion in the Middle Ages and in increasing papal pronouncements on his place in the Church by modern popes. This chapter will also depend heavily on another theological expert, Joseph Chorpenning, since he has both made a particular study of the development of devotion to the Holy Family and its relationship to Josephology, culminating in St. John Paul II's encyclical, *Redemptoris custos*.[2] He has also brought together other theologians, who contribute to its illumination.[3] But contrary to the last chapter, in which the main sources brought forward were from inside the Church, in this chapter sources both inside and outside the Church, the latter neutral or even hostile, will be consulted to give a fuller picture of the acceptance or non-acceptance of the Holy Family as a model for families.

For example, secular cultural historian Albrecht Koschorke in *The Holy Family and Its Legacy*, engaging with images (which are, in fact, a major source of the theology of the Holy Family) and heavily influenced by Freudian ideas, portrays the history of the Holy Family as a struggle for power between society and the Church. He writes:

> Joseph's importance rises and falls, depending on the extent to which the position of the man at any given time fits the overall plan of social order. The figure of Jesus' marginalized foster father demonstrated that the authority of the natural father had to be weakened to allow a different, supernatural power—one that transcended the biological frame of reference both spiritually and politically—to prevail. It was only after that operation had been completed that Joseph could take on a new task; supporting and passing on the transcendentalized authority through his humble human means. At that point, however, Josephean piety could also be used once again by the retreating church to *oppose* the state's secular claim of universal jurisdiction.[4]

Far from denying the power of the Holy Family as a symbol, Korschorke, in fact, ascribes to it great power. Surveying in his book its impact on Western culture, he ends with these words: "A series of coincidences has, in retrospect, made it possible to recount the past two thousand years as the after history of the Holy Family."[5]

Two things have been pointed out by Joseph Chorpenning: (1) "Joseph must be seen as an active, full-fledged participant in the Holy Family before it is possible to consider Jesus, Mary and Joseph as forming an integral and credible family unit."[6] And (2) a major development occurred, when attention was "focused more on the communion of life they shared, rather than on each of them as individuals." One of the salient facts that Chorpenning's ongoing research has brought to light is the strong link between St. Joseph and the Holy Family in the New World. While he traces the origin of the term "Holy Family" to St. Bernardine of Siena (1380-1444), he points out that it did not take hold for several centuries because "until the seventeenth and eighteenth centuries the word 'family' in Western Europe was understood to mean 'extended family' (or all those living under the authority of the *paterfamilias*) rather than 'nuclear family' as it does today."[7] Instead, the Holy Family was viewed apart from the human family and more akin to the heavenly Trinity as an "earthly Trinity."[8]

Now we will look briefly at three phases in the development of the Holy Family as a communion of persons (although that term was not used until the 20th century): The early to high Middle Ages, from the 11th to the 15th centuries, the Protestant Reformation and the Enlightenment, from the 16th to the 19th, with particular reference to America, and finally the 20th century development of a theology of the Holy Family by St. John Paul II. Each phase could be said to be responding to a threat to the Church either through erroneous theological views or aberrant behavior within the clergy or families.

The Middle Ages

In the 11th and 12th centuries the Church faced a heresy that attacked the core of the spousal mystery as it was lived in the Church, the family and society with far-reaching implications. As was noted earlier the Albigensian heresy, a revival of the Gnostic heresy, which threatened early Christianity, particularly attacked the procreative dimension of marriage. [9] Since the Cathars believed that matter is evil they regarded procreation which enfleshes new souls to be evil also. [10] One of the ways to counteract the dualism of the Cathars was to encourage women's spirituality centered on their nurturing bodies.[11] The Dominican order had been founded to convert the Cathars. A weapon in their arsenal was the prayer, Ave Maria. As Noonan says, "The central tenet was indirectly denied by the prayer . . . blessed is the fruit of your womb."[12]

This emphasis extended to nursing the child at the breast. In *Holy Feast and Holy Fast: the Religious Significance of Food to Medieval Women,* Carol Walker Bynum has detailed the images of both the nursing Christ and the nursing Virgin that were common to both men and women, although men tended to identify more with being nourished than nourishing. As Bynum says, "Both men and women. . drank from the breast of Christ, in vision and image."[13] For example, Bernard of Clairvaux, commenting on the Song of Songs: "Not only are they (his breasts) better than wine, but smelling sweet of the best ointments too, for not merely do you refresh those present with the milk of inward sweetness, you also spray the pleasing perfume of good repute over the absent ones."[14] When the bride receives the "kiss of his mouth," says Bernard, "So great is the potency of that holy kiss, that no sooner has the bride received it than she conceives and her breasts grow rounded with the fruitfulness of conception, bearing witness, as it were, with this milky abundance."[15] In late Medieval art the lactating Virgin was often associated with the Eucharist, so that there are images side by side of the Virgin offering her breast while Christ exposes the wound in his side."[16] This aspect of the life of the Holy Family, which portrays the communion between Jesus and Mary, will be treated in more detail later.[17]

The Feudal Family

According to Georges Duby, a prominent social historian particularly of France, social conditions at the time set the stage for a romantic type of love to take root among the nobility. Through the custom of primogeniture, marriage was limited to the eldest son alone so that the inheritance, especially of land, was not divided. All the younger sons remained bachelors at the court. They were permitted to take mistresses, usually of a lower class but not to marry. In order to tame their wild ways, the game of love, in which "bachelors" (*iuvenes*) sought to woo the lady of the House, was encouraged. The troubadours, wandering minstrels of romantic tales, initiated the practice of what came to be called courtly love.[18] Thus, a new concept of romantic love which emerged in the Middle Ages in relations between the sexes, though deficient had some positive contribution to make to the love between man and woman, and the Church eventually sought to incorporate it into marriage.

The Artisan Family

While primogeniture made its mark on the families of the nobility, another family model arose with the emergence of the new commercial class in the cities.[19] The families of craftsmen, shopkeepers, and petty merchants all lived under one roof. The wife was usually the business partner, continuing her craft in marriage so that from the beginning she made a more equal contribution to the family. In this way, the communion of persons was affirmed because they shared work together. Ties were not so much with the extended family as with professional and craft guilds. Artisan mothers also nursed their own infants. While this ensured a propitious start for the child, it was the custom in a few years for these same children "to be pushed out of the nest into an often harsh apprenticeship."[20] On widowhood, the working class mother usually remarried, introducing an often indifferent step father, while the widow of the nobility preferred not to remarry and risk losing her children, who were surrounded by a loving extended family.[21]

Monastic Friendship

At the same time particularly among monks the theme of spiritual friendship was explored. For Cistercians, especially, friendship played an important role in monastic life. Bernard of Clairvaux, for example, espoused a positive view of human affection and its place in the path to union with God, based on experience.[22] First in the ascent to divine union comes carnal love. It is not opposed to God but precedes it. The order of nature is reversed when the sinfulness of cupidity comes in and love of self is preferred to love of God. He concludes that to be free from this natural necessity would mean being without bodies. The goal of Cistercian spirituality is to rectify the will through mortification so that nature can become a reliable guide. This allowed room for human affection.[23] One can easily see how it would fit the marriage of Mary and Joseph.

Etienne Gilson is emphatic that Cistercian love is radically different from the secular form of romantic love described by Duby. Both claimed their "disinterested" love had its origin in Cicero's *De Amicitia* (Treatise on Friendship). In courtly love the reward remains always out of reach, which is, in fact, a defect of love, since by its nature love ought to be reciprocal. To transpose that, for example, to divine love, means loving God without His loving in return, an impossibility, because God has loved us first. It is a love says Bernard, "both disinterested and rewarded."[24] While restraint and/or sublimation of carnal desire played a role in both types of love, the one, courtly love, because it subscribed to only a limited good, is defective. Nevertheless, it did raise love between the sexes beyond the purely physical plane.[25]

Miracle Plays

Another development in the Middle Ages brought the Holy Family closer to the ordinary life of the human family from its exalted role as an "earthly Trinity" – the medieval mystery play. Scott R. Pilarxz, S.J. has made a study of these plays particularly those of York, England, of which a full cycle of 48 plays survive. Originally presented by Churchmen on church premises in Latin (along with miracle and morality plays), the mystery play dramatized salvation history from Adam and Eve to episodes in Christ's life from the Annunciation to the Crucifixion. In the 13th century, lay craft guilds took over and the strictly religious nature declined.[26] Pilarz describes how the plays humanize the biblical characters. For example, Joseph and Mary become a poor Yorkshire couple, and to inject some humor, Joseph refuses to ask directions on the way to Egypt. As Pilarz says, "While some scenes in the life of the Holy Family are certainly played for laughs, others model a pattern for marital sanctity that is surprisingly progressive," so that "while watching their friends and neighbors play Jesus, Mary and Joseph, they would have had good reason for wanting to become what they beheld, holy families.[27] At the time the laity, excluded from daily communion, were struggling to carve out for themselves a spiritual role, giving dignity to the ordinary events of their lives. The 14th century was called the golden age of the laity, in contrast to the 13th and 15th.

The Theological Contribution

Angelo Scola has shown how Thomas Aquinas, by incorporating the philosophical analysis of Aristotle, deepened the profoundly Christian and incarnational understanding of love and affection that was developing in all these ways.[28] He shows how in Questions 22 and 26 of the *Summa Theologica* especially,[29] Thomas affirms the goodness of the passions, while noting the effect of original sin in turning them away from their original orientation to the Creator. Of particular interest is Scola's commentary on affection as a *Passio* in Question 26. In defining it as "the subject's ability to react, through the appetite, to the provocation of a desirable object," he takes a step further in affirming that affection is a particular type of *passio* called *amor.* [30] For Thomas, the structure of undergoing a passion occurs on three levels. On the first level the human simply undergoes something without reacting to it. On the second level the subject reacts in a manner proper to the appetite. On the third level there is an actual modification of the body and the more intense that is, the more we know, according to Thomas, that a passion is present. Affection belongs to the second level. As linking both the sensible and spiritual appetites, affection as a passion has an "inexorable tendency" both downwards and upwards. When it is ordered to the higher spiritual cognitive level, affection is purified. It is integrated into love at the level of the will.[31] As we shall see, these experiential and philosophical reflections on love and affection bore fruit in a deeper understanding of the love between Joseph and Mary and in marriage.

Development of Theology of Marriage

Duby has pointed out how marriage in the Middle Ages was both supported and undermined by the competing interests of feudal society and the Church. The household and the married couple were the central cell of lay feudal society; a public marriage ceremony was the sole means of legitimation; both condemned abduction and adultery; and finally procreation was the purpose of marriage. The goals in conflict concerned "youths" (*iuvenes*) denied a legitimate marriage, who continued adventuring and the continuation of consanguineous marriages often between close cousins.[32] Society and the Church having so much in common allowed for some of the greatest developments in the theology of marriage to take place, epitomized later by Thomas Aquinas and Bonaventure.[33] A major task of the Church was to affirm both the dignity of women and of marriage by moderating the role of the family in arranged marriages, in which the woman could become a virtual pawn in the goal of protecting property and inheritance. Arranged marriages were not *per se* opposed by authorities but the free consent of the couple had to be assured.[34]

The marriage of Mary and Joseph contributed greatly to the resolution of the continuing debate in the Middle Ages on whether consent or sexual intercourse established the marriage.[35] From the time of St. Augustine, Christian couples could live "spiritual marriage" on the pattern of Mary and Joseph, which, as we saw in the last chapter, was considered a true marriage.[36] Hugh of St. Victor, for example, affirmed with St. Augustine that when a couple consents to marriage, they agree to surrender their entire self to the other in a primarily human partnership. The generation of children according to Genesis 2:24 rests on a previous commitment made by each to the other. This opposed the long-dominant social tradition that marriage had to be consummated to be complete.[37] The latter view was bolstered by theologians, who considered conjugal intercourse a fitting symbol of Christ's union with his body, the Church. As we saw in the last chapter, consent as forming the marriage prevailed but its indissolubility is confirmed further with consummation.[38] In the Holy Family, while there was no consummation through sexual intercourse, the birth of Jesus fulfilled the procreative dimension.

Marriage as image of the union of Christ and his Church, has its roots in Scripture (Eph. 5: 31-33) and is the foundation of liturgy before it is the subject of theology (*lex orandi, lex credendi*).[39] While a plethora of authors and historians attribute negative attitudes toward conjugal as opposed to celibate spousal love in the Middle Ages, new research is discovering a more positive paradigm.[40] F. Stan Parmisiano has made a study of late medieval marriage liturgies in England. The nuptials are celebrated with the solemn Mass of the Trinity. Not only is the pallium (sacred mantle) placed over the couple during the ceremony, while the priest blesses them, but the bride and groom are blessed with a Trinitarian blessing at the end when the marriage chamber and bed are also blessed.[41] The marriage homily emphasizes the equal and complementary role of both the man and the woman, often pointing out that while Adam was formed from the dust of the ground, Eve's origin was higher, being born from his flesh. The preacher counsels the couple: "As you shall be one in body, flesh, and in blood, likewise be steadfast and perfect with unity in love in your souls without discontinuance" in the image of the Trinity.[42] In the 13th century certain preachers characterized marriage as a religious order in the manner of traditional religious orders, even suggesting that since marriage was instituted by God, it surpasses them. One Dominican preacher pointed out that it "was instituted in the state of innocence. . . was the only order saved by the flood; it is the order in which the blessed virgin was a member. . . ." His praise also included the conjugal act. [43] Consequently, it has its own kind of holiness, arising specifically from its sacramental nature as imaging the union of Christ and the Church. But this positive view was not sustained.

Imbalance of the Three Goods of Marriage

It is significant that in placing the greatest emphasis on the sacrament as the spousal union imaging Christ's union with the Church, Parmisiano finds in his review of the liturgies that the other goods of marriage—fidelity and procreation—were mentioned only in passing. He comments that contemporary theologians, especially Thomas Aquinas, forthrightly taught procreation as the chief end of marriage (although from another perspective, he regarded the sacrament as the highest good). [44] In spite of the canonical emphasis on procreation, an imbalance did develop, and it is to that imbalance we must now turn, since it helps to explain why a theology of the family lagged behind a theology of marriage as Angelo Scola has charged, and highlights the importance of the Holy Family in restoring the balance of the family as a communion of persons in the image of the Trinity. It is noteworthy that the authors of *Christian Marriage: A Historical Survey* in the chapters on the early and High Middle Ages devote only two pages to the Holy Family. Olsen comments: "Though fascination with the Holy Family was mostly a late medieval and early modern development, from Carolingian times it played a modest role in developing theological understanding of the family."[45] He goes on to say that the typical iconographic representation was of Madonna and Child, and the message was more likely that of the Incarnation than of childhood and the family, with the emphasis on holy mothers.[46] This is undoubtedly true, but the fleshly union of mother and child is a key component of a communion of persons in the family.[47] Tradition teaches that Jesus's birth was miraculous but Mary nursed her own Son as was the Jewish custom (see Luke 11:27-28). As we saw earlier, in a response to the Albigensian heresy which despised the body, the Church encouraged particularly women's spirituality linked to the nursing Madonna.[48]

Duby has noted how ecclesiastical and secular views on marriage shared important features but also diverged, in regard to endogamous, arranged marriages, concubinage and divorce. Duby also pointed out the significant role of the lady of the house as a lure for the *iuvenes* in the game of love, another way in which the woman was objectified. Whatever the cause, it became the custom, particularly in France, for the Church to make a cultural exception from nursing for the women of nobility attending court.[49] So we can see two contradictory views of nursing in the Middle Ages, one as a religious symbol associated with the Virgin Mary in the Holy Family and another secular custom of women of the nobility eschewing nursing in favor of wet nurses.[50] Prudence Allen in her discussion of women mystics and analogical thinking and Margaret Miles have pointed out that as a religious symbol the Nursing Madonna elevated women as mothers. In fact, Miles comments, "Women seem to have enjoyed more respect in societies in which the breast was regarded as a powerful symbol of nourishment and loving care than in those societies in which it was viewed as an erotic and/or medical object."[51] Miles goes further:

> Looking beneath the rich surface of Christianity's symbolic resources, we notice a . . . profound loss, namely the incremental disappearance of human bodies as symbols of religious subjectivity. The Christian doctrine of Creation, Incarnation, and Resurrection each pointedly and emphatically identify bodies as both locations of, and symbols for, Christian truth. . . The loss of the female breast as site and symbol of religious meaning was a significant moment in a gradual shift within Christianity, from the affirmation of bodies—both male and female—as essentially engaged in religious commitment, to the female body as object and spectacle.[52]

In spite of the development of this imbalance between the three goods of marriage, it can be seen in summary, how the Middle Ages set the stage for an understanding of the Holy Family as a communion of love between Jesus, Mary and Joseph. Although defective, courtly love, by its exaltation of a woman's beauty and virtue, enhanced the appeal of chastity in man-woman relations, as did the monastic exploration of spiritual friendship. The artisan family, on the other hand, promoted a greater equality between the spouses. While the abandonment of breastfeeding by the nobility did not value the true needs of the child, the childhood apprenticeships of the artisan family disrupted the communion at a later stage. The Church's emphasis on consent as essential to marriage greatly strengthened personal subjectivity, especially of the woman, although other trends in feudalism, including the use of wet nurses undercut her subjectivity and role as mother. The emphasis on the sacrament of marriage as an image of Christ and the Church raised spousal relations to a new level but the constant suspicion of the goodness of sex, in spite of the life-affirming anthropology of theologians such as Aquinas, prevented its full contribution to the communion of persons. At the same time, the marriages, especially of the nobility and later members of every social class in the cities, emphasized the one-flesh union of the spouses at the expense of the fleshly union of mother and child. Although theologians, such as Thomas Aquinas, stipulated that a mother has a moral duty to nurse her child, the Church, especially in France but in Italy as well, tended to favor the husband's need for conjugal intercourse over the mother's moral duty. As Miles relates, there was a loss of religious symbolism, which one might venture to say, affected the image of the Church as well as the Holy Family as a model for families.[53] This is developed in more detail later.

St Joseph and the Counter Reformation

Two major changes occurred in the 15th century with regard to the roles of both Mary and Joseph. Donna Spivey Ellington has made a study of sermons in the transition that occurred from the 15th to the 16th centuries. She found a sharp contrast between Mary's role as Mother of God, co-sufferer with Christ at Calvary and heavenly intercessor in late medieval sermons compared with those in the 16th and 17th centuries. "Historians are beginning to understand," she writes "that Mary's bodily nature was the cornerstone of the entire late medieval edifice of the Virgin's cult."[54] Although her popularity flourished and even increased in the 14th and 15th centuries, "a crisis or revolution of religious sentiment" begins to take place in the 15th.[55] The changes in the spirituality of the body that began to take place Ellington, herself, puts down to the invention of printing and the decline of oral transmission which required bodily presence.[56] Regardless of the cause, Ellington documents a very different Mary that surfaced with the Counter Reformation.[57] Her humble obedience was stressed in the 16th and 17 centuries as the perfect role model for Christians. Whereas her contemplative role, secluded from public life, belonged to both eras, the new more passive virgin contrasted vividly with the active co-operator in the Incarnation of medieval piety.[58]

Since the Holy Family is a communion of persons, with the diminution of Mary's role one might expect Joseph's to be augmented. Mention was made in the last chapter of the promotion of Joseph in devotion in the 15th century by Jean Gerson and Pierre d'Ailly. Joseph was transformed from an old man to a young and vigorous protector of Mary, an image and role that the Counter Reformation adopted.[59] Two doctors of the Church, St. Teresa of Avila and St. Francis de Sales, as well as Jean Jacques Olier, founder of the Sulpicians, were greatly responsible for the new devotion to St. Joseph, which was inseparably united to devotion to the Holy Family. It was bound up especially with reform of the priesthood and religious orders.

St. Teresa's devotion to the Holy Family as a whole and to its individual members was both personal and an integral part of the reform of Carmel. Losing her mother at the age of twelve, Teresa turned to the Blessed Mother. Later, when she attributed a cure to St. Joseph's intercession, she took him as "this Father and Lord of mine."[60] Subsequently, he became for her a powerful intercessor and protector of all her journeys to found monasteries, with the first called after him. Teresa thought of her convents as another Nazareth or Bethlehem and placed statues or paintings of Joseph and Mary in key places, such as over the entrance or the altar. As Christopher Wilson writes:

> Each convent attains paradisal status because, according to Teresa's writings, it is the dwelling place of Jesus, watched over by Mary and Joseph. As the abode of the Holy Family, like the house of Nazareth, it is a restoration of heaven on earth.[61]

At the invitation of a carpenter's guild in Rome and requested by the Master of the Sacred Palace of St. Peter's, Jerónimo Gracián, spiritual director of St. Teresa of Avila, published a compilation of the "excellencies" of St. Joseph.[62] According to Chorpenning, "The Summary is a watershed in the historical development of the veneration of St. Joseph;" not only as a compendium of previous literature but because it was the "most widely circulated work on St. Joseph in Spain and Europe."[63] Sources of the summary were Scripture, the Fathers, Doctors of the Church, medieval ecclesiastical and mystical writers, John Gerson, and Isidore of Isolani's *Summary of the Gifts of St. Joseph.*"[64] The spirituality of the Summary was the primacy of love. St. Joseph was the recipient of the most sublime divine love. He reciprocated this love by his faithful loving service to Jesus and Mary as guardian and husband so that he is a model of paternal and conjugal love in the real world. Gracian reflects on his intimacy with both Jesus and Mary. No husband was loved by a wife as much as Joseph by Mary, since they both shared a "mutual experience of divine love," through the presence of Christ in their midst.[65] Tradition even held that love was the cause of Joseph's death. Gracian goes on to present Joseph as an exemplar of the beatitudes, lists his virtues, especially chastity and purity of heart, his fifty privileges and his tribulations. He is upheld as the model of the union of the active and contemplative life. Chorpenning comments that Gracian's work "had a decisive impact on universal devotion to St. Joseph." It was also pivotal in iconography.[66]

Francis de Sales and the French School

The 16th and 17th centuries brought a more interior spirituality epitomized by St. Francis de Sales and the French School, Cardinal Berulle, St. John Eudes, Jean Jacques Olier and the Carmelite superior, Madeleine du Bois de Fontans. For an account of St. Francis de Sales and his theology of the Holy Family we can do no better than turn to Joseph F. Chorpenning, a contemporary theologian, himself a Salesian, who, in making a particular study of the Holy family, has broken new ground. In his view: "While Francis's theology of St, Joseph has been studied by scholars, his equally rich and well developed theology of the Holy Family, which is a natural outgrowth of his theology of Joseph has not received comparable attention."[67] According to St. Francis, the purpose of Joseph's marriage to Mary was to provide a human family for the Son of God. Salesian spirituality of the union of hearts was modeled on the union of hearts of Jesus, Mary and Joseph. Quoting Francis's words, the Holy Family represents to us, "the mystery of the most holy and adorable Trinity . . . .it was a trinity on earth, representing in some sort the most holy Trinity—a trinity worthy to be honored and greatly esteemed."[68] Francis emphasized the gentleness and mildness of relations in the Holy Family, the significance of little things and hiddenness as a model for all families. He firmly believed that holiness is not reserved to a spiritual elite but meant for all.[69]

In opposition to Jansenism, the French School developed a theology of the heart, centered on the love of Jesus and Mary while at the same time remaining Trinitarian and Christocentric.[70] Particularly notable is St. John Eudes, who fostered devotion to the Sacred Heart of Jesus and Most Holy Heart of Mary.[71] John Saward forthrightly states that the French School of spirituality gave the Church devotion to the Holy Family. Cardinal Berulle studied

Christ in all his "states" and "mysteries," regarding all his human actions as revelatory. He particularly emphasized Christ's three births, as Son of God, his birth within Mary and from Mary especially favoring devotion to Jesus in the womb of Mary.[72] Joseph, on the other hand, is in the place of God the Father and his obscurity is part of a pattern in the life of Christ. Christ hides his divine identity in the bosom of his earthly father, in the womb of his mother, in his childhood in exile and in Nazareth, in the ignominy of his death, and after his resurrection in the Eucharist.[73] Saward concludes that at the time of Berulle's death in 1620 there was an "explosion" of devotion to the Holy Family in both the New and the Old worlds.[74]

THE NEW WORLD

The French School, through its missionary orientation transported devotion to the Holy Family to New France, (Canada).[75] In 1624, St. Joseph was named "patron of the new country and protector of the growing church."[76] The new land was marked in more ways than one with the stamp of the Holy Family. As part of a special missionary vocation it was revealed to Blessed Marie of the Incarnation in 1635 that she was to build a house where Jesus, Mary and Joseph would be honored. Then a layman, in conjunction with Fr. Jean Jacques Olier, established the Notre Dame Society (consisting of 27 men and eight women), which was eventually responsible for the founding of Montreal. In 1642 it met and "consecrated the Island of Montreal to the Holy Family of Our Lord, Jesus, Mary and Joseph, under the special protection of the Blessed Virgin."[77] Roland Gauthier concludes: "It is quite evident that, in the spirituality of the first pioneers of Canada, a special place was reserved for the three members of the House of Nazareth."[78]

The Jesuits were also active in promoting devotion to the Holy Family. The Jesuit, Louis Lallemant, asked to be sent to the foreign missions, especially Canada for three years.[79] Although he did not go himself, he formed other missionaries, many of whom were martyred.[80] In 1662, a Jesuit from Italy, together with a devout laywoman, established a Confraternity of the Holy Family, which was approved by the Bishop Laval of Quebec in 1664, who, himself, composed rules for the confraternity.[81] Being devoted to the

Holy Family, Bishop Laval placed the Seminary under its patronage as well as dedicating several parishes in his diocese to the Holy Family. Some noted paintings of the Holy Family, two as an earthly Trinity, reflect this devotion in 17th century Canada. Elsewhere in the Americas such as in Spanish colonial art, St. Teresa of Avila is often depicted with St. Joseph and the Holy family, reflecting her great influence in spreading this devotion.[82]

With the Counter-Reformation, in summary, Joseph came into his own as vigorous protector of the Holy Family, guardian and chaste husband of Mary. He became the model for paternal love, substituting for God the Father in the Holy Family. As for Mary, her humble obedience was stressed. Their conjugal life together was blessed with great intimacy and imbued with gentleness and mildness. Joseph became the model for the union of the active and contemplative life. While the Holy Family "came out of the shadows" as it were, nevertheless, devotion to the "earthly Trinity" was aimed primarily at priestly and religious life. However, Francis de Sales sought to bridge the gap between consecrated and lay spirituality, which made the Holy Family more accessible as a model for the ordinary interior life of families.

The Protestant Interpretation of the Holy Family

What about Protestant Europe? Was all trace of Holy Family iconography and devotion erased, along with the sacramentality of marriage and the abolition of celibacy? In one sense a loss ensued, in another sense there was gain. Let us look at the question under the following headings: marriage ceased to be a sacrament but became a covenant with the word of the Scripture superseding sacrament; marital sex was lauded but the person remained a sinner; monasticism, celibacy and asceticism were rejected while marriage was raised to a holy estate; the pastor's wife was given a holy role as wife and mother but convents, which encouraged women's education, prophetic and leadership roles were dismantled; the equal companionship of husband and wife was advocated but public roles for women discouraged; emphasis on companionship facilitated contraception; and with the abolition of devotion to Mary and the saints, the body became less and less important.

Marriage as Covenant

It is generally agreed that the Reformers ceased to regard marriage as a sacrament, preferring simply to call it a covenant. Although marriage was not considered one of the seven sacraments until the Middle Ages, from the time of the Fathers, the theology of marriage was centered on the union of Christ and the Church in Ephesians 5:25-33, with its sacramentality emphasized. The Reformers, on the other hand, considered that God had instituted marriage at creation and they chose covenant phraseology to indicate its likeness to God's covenant with the Israelite people.[83] (John Paul II was later to make full use of the covenant analogy for marriage in his Catechesis on Human Love, authorized by Vatican Council II's Gaudium et spes, no. 48. As Polish he was likely to take his inspiration also from Eastern Orthodox Marriage liturgy.)[84] Not regarding marriage as a sacrament removed it from ecclesiastical jurisdiction. Since some regulation was necessary marriage came under the jurisdiction of the State.[85] Luther adopted the idea of the two kingdoms; indissolubility, for example, was required in the spiritual kingdom of the "justified" but not in the worldly kingdom. While he did not regard indissolubility as an inherent characteristic of marriage, it was imposed by secular authorities for the common good. Marriage was part of God's plan to redeem society but it was not sacred.

Marriage as Holy Estate

A positive aspect of the Protestant Reformation was the new attention to marriage as a holy estate, since a cardinal tenet was the priesthood of all believers. This was especially true of the pastor's family. Because of the concubinage of priests, the pastor's wife sought to elevate the role and she became an icon of the new order. Such wives were "expected to model 'wifely' obedience and Christian charity and serve their husbands and church in silence and modesty."[86]

The husband was head of the household, not according to natural law but according to the order of Redemption, but his headship was "precedence with mutuality." [87] This mutuality is regarded by some as a new development, but, as we saw earlier, the artisan family already exhibited mutuality. This was further emphasized by the view that procreation, while a blessing, took second place to mutuality.[88] In Luther's doctrine of the total sinfulness of the believer before God, sex was tainted but through justification by faith alone, the believer could regard sexual love in marriage as a good to be enjoyed in marriage, since "sexual love gives meaning to all other experiences.[89]

Rejection of Celibacy, Monastic Asceticism and Images

The asceticism of monastic life and celibacy was roundly rejected, leaving no other path than marriage, which was especially detrimental for women. In the 16th century when most production was still centered on the home, the role of wife and mother was not as confining as it became with industrialization in the 19th century. Stjerna points out how convents had provided education and a prophetic role for women. Spiritual discipline was now centered on the home but any public role was denied women. While reading the Word of God became primary in church and home, a major loss occurred in devotion to holy images, which celebrated the bodily aspect of the Faith. Eamon Duffy details how this was imposed for the most part unwillingly on the lay faithful in Elizabethan (Protestant) England.[90]In Calvinist Switzerland, Lee Palmer Wandel sees the destruction of images in churches as the way "evangelical iconoclasts participated, through their own "language" of acts, in "Reformation."[91] Wandel continues: "At stake for the iconoclasts, in Reformation was "presence": How was God to be present in the world? For the iconoclasts, that presence centered not upon the question of two natures that theologians had discussed since the beginning of Christianity. For them, the theological question of 'presence' centered upon relations, between God and human beings and between one human being and another."[92] In other words, they favored a communion of persons in which the body was only incidental.[93] The mediation of Mary, the saints, the sacraments (except for Baptism and a limited concept of the Eucharist) and reason as a way to truth were rejected as were monasticism and asceticism as a path to virtue.[94] The whole of man's nature was considered depraved by the Fall; along with this went a belief in the predestination of the elect, whose corollary was the futility of works to attain salvation. Such a rejection of human nature, combined with an affirmation of the goodness of creation and of pleasure in marital intercourse produced an ambiguity in Protestant treatment of sexuality, which can be seen most clearly in the American context.[95]

Protestantism in America

The Puritans who settled New England had a vested interest in increasing the population. "Theological principles supported the emphasis on procreation including the biblical injunction to 'be fruitful and multiply' and the view that childbearing was women's 'calling.'"[96] Although breastfeeding was used to space pregnancies (during which time the husband usually abstained) the emphasis was on increasing family size. At the same time affectionate relations between husband and wife with pleasure in intercourse was expected.[97] The higher fertility levels gradually declined in the 19th century.[98] As Americans reduced their fertility with the availability of contraceptives, they adopted a romantic attitude towards marriage so that it became "more important as a union based on love and affection."[99]

Several factors accentuated the emphasis on romantic sexual satisfaction, which Peter Gardella chronicles in *Innocent Ecstasy,*[100] among them popular Freudianism, which implied that sexual repression is harmful. On the religious front the Great Awakening with visionaries such as Amy Simple McPherson and Phoebe Palmer and the Methodist doctrine of Christian perfectionism with its stress on the primacy of love also contributed. Surprisingly Gardella sees Bernadette and the youthful appearance of the Virgin at Lourdes as enhancing the infatuation with innocent female ecstasy. Margaret Sanger capitalized on this attitude in her contraceptive crusade.[101] Yet the ambivalence towards the Virgin and the asceticism of celibacy remains among Protestants[102]

Thus we see the Protestant Reformation, despite some regarding the body as totally corrupted by original sin, contributes to affirming the goodness of marital sexuality. However, it combines such affirmation with a suspicion of asceticism, so essential to self-mastery and the eschatological dimension where there is no marriage. The role of the child as central to the communion of persons declines with the increasing use of contraceptives, obviating breastfeeding as a means of spacing. The rejection of the sacraments, particularly marriage as a sacrament, weakens the transcendental dimension, diminishes the grace available during difficult times and opens the way to divorce, which fractures the communion. Rejection of the saints such as Joseph and especially Mary does not allow for the veneration of the Holy Family or even its existence. Yet when Protestant families make study of the Word of God intrinsic to their family life, which puts Christ at its heart they give rise to many a devout Christian family

The Enlightenment and the Family

René Descartes

A graver threat to both a transcendental and incarnational perspective, but in a way prepared by ambivalence toward the bodily aspect of Christianity, began in the 17th century. It is generally agreed that the philosophical and mathematical reflections of French philosopher, René Descartes (1596-1650), with his defining aphorism *cogito ergo sum* (I think, therefore I am), ushered in modernity with its abiding emphasis on the scientific method as the primary path to knowledge. Jacques Martain, in a thorough review of Descartes' method calls it "the sin of *angelism*. . . .What he saw in man's thought was the *Independence of Things*."[103] Maritain describes angelic cognition as intuitive in mode, innate in origin and independent of things as to its nature. Descartes posits ideas directly from God not from objects. No longer are the body and senses necessary for cognition. Instead, the body and matter become a mere *res extensa* or instrument. He has dispensed with discursive reasoning, so that thought has become an operation of the will and not the intellect, even if deduction follows from this initial judgment.[104] Deduction takes the form of combining intuitions, with mathematics given a privileged place in the process. Maritain calls this "lust for pure spirituality"[105] and charges that "it rates the mathematics of phenomena above theology, science above wisdom." [106]

Maritain does not explore what predicated this revolutionary philosophical move by Descartes. Biographers see a turning point on the night of November 10, 1619 when he experienced three dramatic dreams. Karl Stern has analyzed these dreams from a psychiatric perspective, primarily to see their significance for the Cartesian dualism that permeates modernity.[107] Descartes, himself, woke up from his dreams with a vague sense of foreboding "that the *scientia mirabilis* implies a dreadful devaluation of *poetic knowledge*," combined with a massive depletion of faith.[108] Descartes, himself, retained a belief in God and in poetry but his system created, or was in tune with, a *climate* that eventually permeated the whole of society. Stern explains the distinction as follows:

> Poetic knowledge is acquired by union *with* and attachment *to* the object; Scientific knowledge is acquired by distance and detachment *from* the object. The poetic relation to nature is one of embeddedness, the scientific one is that of confrontation. Scientific knowledge is associated with disassembling and breaking up. The poet knows the object by an act of fusion which cannot be reduced to anything more basic; the scientist knows the object by an act of piercing which can be broken into steps.[109]

Stern then looks at the circumstances of Descartes' life. His mother died in childbirth when he was a year old. He had a life-long devotion to his wet nurse, who seems to have been a domestic servant, and he even fathered a child by her. Losing the bodily presence of his mother was instrumental in his doubt of any carnal presence. "The certainty of the flesh which is the foundation of all certainty *had* to be conjured away—because it was here where the terror and pain of abandonment lurked."[110] The scientific method gave him the illusion of manageability. The organism gave way to organization. Stern describes this as the *masculinization of thought.* The maternal dimension of Wisdom is rejected.[111]

In *The Third Revolution: A Study of Science and Religion*, Karl Stern elaborates further. He calls the "searching reason of science…a masculine, aggressive principle."[112] This is not to devalue, in turn, the contributions of the scientific method to the great technological advances that have been made in Western society. It is to question its predominance to the exclusion of all other modes of knowledge, especially knowledge from faith. Faith flourishes, above all, in relationship. This has been brought out well in John Paul II's encyclical letter, *Fides et Ratio* (On Faith and Reason). There he points out the close link between reason and faith. Human beings are intrinsically relational. More truths are believed not from personal verification, but on the credibility of others. Such knowledge can seem less sure, but it can often be richer, because it involves a personal relationship of deep entrustment to another.[113] Such truth is not primarily empirical or philosophical. What is sought is the "truth of the person." He sums up, "Human perfection, then, consists not simply in acquiring an abstract knowledge of truth but in a dynamic relation with others. It is in this faithful self-giving that a person finds a fullness of certainty and security" (FR no. 32).

In his Catechesis on the theology of the body, the pope finds special significance in the biblical use of the term "know" for conjugal intercourse because it raises the act from the biological to the personal. He sees two aspects in the biblical use of the word "know," both intentionality and the reality of the union in one flesh. Both the husband and wife know each other reciprocally and by doing so discover who they are in their own specific masculine or feminine "I" (MW no. 20:5). It stands to reason, then, that whatever diminishes the ability to be in relation will diminish the capacity to know truth in all its fullness. The earliest and foundational relationship is that between mother and child. As Stern says, "In order to have faith, we have to be childlike."[114] To be childlike in our dependence on God, secure maternal and later paternal figures, are normally a requisite. Neither can be dispensed with.

Rousseau and the French Revolution

Jean Jacques Rousseau (1712-1778), born some sixty years after Descartes' death, a leading figure of the Enlightenment, and central influence on the French Revolution, experienced a similar loss of his mother in infancy. He was raised by his wet nurse and an aunt.

He also married a woman of the servant class, like his wet nurse, with whom he fathered five children.[115] There the likeness ends. Descartes conjured away the body with his radical *cogito, ergo sum*. Rousseau, on the contrary, embraced the senses. They are opposite sides of the same coin, a split between body and soul. Says Maritain, "He turns our hunger for God towards the sacred mysteries of sensation, towards the infinite of matter."[116] Rousseau also had a "conversion" or life-changing experience, on considering the question of whether the arts or the sciences had done more to corrupt morals.[117] Rousseau answered both, arguing that civilization does not make men happier. Rousseau espoused the theory of man's natural goodness in the state of nature, the primitive state being one of total freedom. This differs from the Thomist teleological view of nature as ordered to fulfillment through virtue. In order to live in society, man must submit to a fictional general will, "*born*" says Maritain in interpretation of Rousseau, "*of the sacrifice each has made of himself and all his rights on the altar of the city.*"[118] Yet he continues to obey only himself. The ideal is the solitary free man in a state of nature.[119] When he moves into society, only by ruling himself can he remain free. [120] There is a conflict between a moral idea of freedom and freedom not to be subjected to any man.

There is also conflict between what is required of men and women. While Rousseau grants the diversity of the sexes, he is ambivalent about their unity. "In everything not connected with sex, woman is man."[121] What they have in common belongs to them as species, while their difference is tied to sex. From a Christian perspective, one can agree with much that Rousseau writes about the differences between men and women. In this sense as in others, Maritain says, "He perceived great Christian truths which his age had forgotten, and his strength lay in recalling them; but he perverted them."[122] One of those he recalls is the importance of the mother nursing her own child. "When mothers deign to nurse their own children, then there will be a reform in morals; natural feeling will revive in every heart; there will be no lack of citizens for the state."[123] The mother nursing her own child was to be a major way of taming the man in the state of nature for society.

The French Revolution and Women

Both the French Revolution and the Enlightenment proved problematic to the role of women in the communion of persons of the family. Feminist scholar, Rebecca Kukla, has delved deeply into the significance Rousseau placed in the body of the nursing mother. First she cites Rousseau, himself, on the "depravity" of wet nursing and contrasts it with the benefits from maternal nursing to society. The nursing mother played a major role in creating "second nature." A paradox lies at the heart of Rousseau's politics. "First nature," instead of being the ground of culture, is opposed to it. How to tame it to cooperate in society? The "natural" nurture of maternal breast-feeding forms a "second nature," which induces love of country so that civic acts become free acts. "The natures instilled at the maternal breast," says Kukla, "get their *normative* status as *proper* natures only when they succeed in *perfecting* first nature in accord with the contingent needs of the state."[124] She goes on to show how Rousseau brought about a revolution in maternal practices by linking breast-feeding to the establishment of the Republic. The nursing or bare-breasted mother became a symbol of the State. Whereas before the Revolution scarcely five percent of Parisian mothers nursed their own infants, only twenty years later that figure had jumped to more than 50 percent.[125] But these high numbers did not last.

While Rousseau laid emphasis on sexual difference and maternal bodies, the legacy of Descartes was invoked for the primacy of reason and a dualistic separation of mind and body. The key to the Bastille, according to philosopher Prudence Allen, "can be seen as analogous to the discovery that *reason* could free an individual from constraints of custom, tradition and despotism."[126] This gave rise to a group of philosophers called "Cartesian feminists" or "Reason's Disciples." Well before the French Revolution they argued for the equality of nature and rights for women. The storming of the Bastille, which began the revolution, was led by women, yet in the French bill of rights the right to vote and hold office was limited to men only. Women reacted to this loss of dignity. So we can see that a greater and greater disruption of family relations occurred which motivated popes on the part of the Church to promote the Holy Family as a model for families.

The egalitarian and anti-patriarchal spirit of the Revolution entered the home according to secular historian Rudolf Binion. He sees it as responsible for the dramatic decline in fertility of the family and its eventual breakdown in both Europe, beginning in France, and the United States. In fact, he argues that "the spirit of the age that rejected ancestral patriarchal authority in the political sphere also rejected it in the domestic sphere by the same token."[127] Binion cites Daniel Scott Smith, "American women who espoused the liberal, egalitarian values of the Revolution, only to find themselves excluded from public life despite those very values, reacted by taking control of their family life, and in particular of their own bodies, inasmuch as they refused to accept unrestrained childbearing against their will.[128]

The Contraceptive Revolution and the Structures of Sin

Rudolf Binion's interest centers on "group processes in history." He describes group process as "the psychohistorian's term for actions in concert that run their course independently of individual volition."[129] As illustration, he has taken the changes in reproductive life and the family in the 19th and 20th centuries. From a theological perspective, one might call these group processes "structures of sin" when they are informed by a faulty theology and/or anthropology. In the opening of a chapter called "The Guilty Family" Binion writes:

> Group process rides roughshod over whatever individual sentiments or scruples would bar its way. In the late-nineteenth-century Europe the adaptive imperative of fertility retrenchment left a trail of moral casualties behind it as it overrode Europe's inveterate resistance to birth control in marriage.[130]

He determined that a "creative response" surfaced in the literature of the time, "thereby easing the moral transition from 'natural fertility' to 'planned parenthood.'" There follows an exhaustive and enlightening survey of what he calls "antifamilial literature," beginning with Ibsen's *The Wild Duck* (1884). The characters in the novels rail against the way marriage restricts the freedom of the individual, confines women to the role of wife and mother in an unequal partnership, exacerbates the battle of the sexes, may do violence to children, driving them to suicide or parricide and leads to the death of love. Binion calls this antifamilial literature unprecedented and in seeking the cause, lays it squarely at contraception, which became endemic in Europe at the end of the 19th century. "The generalized adoption of contraceptive sex within marriage marked a daring and dizzying reversal of Europeans' basic attitudes toward their bodies and souls alike, a collective transgression of an age-old, Christianized taboo that had carried over intact even into post-Christian mind-sets."[131] He concludes: "Once the natural family was on the line so too was the family all in all."[132]

The Enlightenment in accentuating the autonomy of the individual ended by isolating both men and women from each other. Contraception made this a fait-accompli in marriage. Once the unitive and procreative dimensions of marriage were severed by contraception, all technological manipulation of human reproduction became possible in the 20th century, and the communion of persons has suffered severe damage as a result.

The 20th Century

John Paul II and Redemptoris custos

It is against this backdrop of fragmentation of the nuptial mystery that John Paul II offers his innovative insights on the Holy Family as a communion of persons and model for families. We have seen two parallel developments in this brief history of the Holy Family and the human family as a communion of persons. While the Holy Family gained prominence as a *bona fide* family, since it was the consent of Mary and Joseph that made the marriage and Jesus was its "fruit," the theology of the human family suffered an imbalance, especially with regard to fecundity, as Angelo Scola charges. The fecundity does not just refer to physical fecundity, although that is at stake with the adoption of contraception and abortion as a means to secure women's intellectual and spiritual fecundity, but to the fecundity of the communion of persons itself, the harmony between the members as persons made in the image of God, and their communion as persons, spouse, mother, father and child. It was John Paul II's special genius that he divined the profound meaning of the Holy Family for human families. To quote Joseph Chorpenning: "No pontiff has offered as extensive, developed, and incisive a theological reflection on the 'special mystery' of the Holy family of Jesus, Mary and Joseph as has Pope John Paul II."[133] He goes on to say, "The pope consistently exalts the Holy Family as the nascent Church and the original domestic Church."[134] Chorpenning speaks of John Paul II's *well developed* (italics added) theology of the 'special mystery' of the Holy Family of Nazareth."[135]

CHAPTER 5

The Spousal Relation

IN AN EARLIER CHAPTER WE saw how new theological reflection on the family locates its origin in the Trinitarian communion of love among Father, Son and Holy Spirit. What is key is the loving interaction between the divine persons of total self-gift. The Christian family as "domestic church" is called to be an icon of this divine communion of Persons. The second part of the chapter outlined the essential element of what it means to be a person. Made in God's image, the human person's first relationship is with God as Creator. John Paul II has coined the term, "original solitude" from the Genesis text to highlight this aloneness before God, which is prior to any relationship of Adam with the woman. Adam was created as a bodily person with intellect and will in a unique relation with God. Eve, too, was created as a personal subject in direct relation with God. This is expressed in a preeminent way by a life of virginity. John Paul II emphasizes Mary's authentic subjectivity in giving her consent in faith to the angel, becoming a mother, while remaining a virgin. The chapter ends with John Paul II's reflection on the meaning of masculine-feminine difference in the conjugal relation and the true headship of the husband as expressed by St. Paul in Ephesians 5:21-33.

The Ontological Exception?

Since motherhood in the created order comes about through conjugal intercourse, which separates marriage from every other type of relationship, it would seem that in this fundamental way, the Holy Family could not be a model for families. This chapter takes up this question beginning with the theological concept of *Eros* in the thought of John Paul II and Pope Benedict XVI and its relation to the mutual gift of self in the spousal relation. Particular attention will be paid to the body as intrinsic to man and woman imaging God in their communion. Next to be considered will be the teaching of Thomas Aquinas, based on Aristotle's teleology and endorsed by the Church, on the natural inclinations and their contribution to conjugal love, especially as interpreted by Servais Pinckaers. This will lead to a better understanding of the reciprocal gift of virginity in the marriage of Mary and Joseph and how it relates to the reciprocal gift in marriage of the one-flesh union of all baptized couples.

Eros *in the Spousal Relation*

John Paul II in his Wednesday Catechesis on the theology of the body first mentions *eros* at the end of his reflections on the creation accounts of Genesis (1-4:1) referring to what he calls "the *biblical cycle of knowledge-generation.*" He takes particular notice of the biblical term of "knowledge" for their conjugal union and asks whether Adam's exclamation on first seeing Eve, "This at last is bone of my bones and flesh of my flesh" (Gen. 2:23) is not the equivalent of the Greek *eros?* He takes up the concept of *eros* in greater detail in his discussion of Mt 5: 27-28 on committing adultery in the heart. In an extensive footnote, he distinguishes Plato's understanding of *Eros* as a love that is neither purely human nor purely divine. Although it is never free from the desire to possess, it differs from purely sensual love in always reaching for the sublime.[1] In the text, while acknowledging that in Plato *eros* means the inner attraction to the good, the true and the beautiful, he asks, "whether *eros* connotes the same meaning that is present in the biblical narrative (above all in Gen 2:23 -25), which doubtless attests to the reciprocal attraction and the perennial call of the human person—through masculinity and femininity—to that 'unity of flesh,' which at the same time should realize the union-communion of persons" (MW 47:2). Therefore it is important to understand what the Sermon on the Mount means. Only if *eros* is understood to be more than the sensual attraction of concupiscence and to draw the person to the true, the good and the beautiful, can it then be applied to Christ's words which bring a new order of values (*ethos*). John Paul II concludes that "it is necessary continually to discover the spousal meaning of the body and the true dignity of the gift in what is 'erotic'" (MW 48:1). This accords neither with the Manichaean nor the Freudian suspicion of the goodness of sexual desire. But it is a task that man and woman need to take up or their attraction will remain at the level of concupiscence and they will not experience what is authentically 'erotic' in its fullness made possible by Redemption.[2]

The third place where the pope introduces the concept of *eros* is in his exegesis of the Song of Songs. He notes immediately that although spousal love is part of the great analogy between God and his people, the Song of Songs is simply, first of all, before all else, a song of love between the bride and the bridegroom (MW 108: 1, 3). In interpreting it as such, the pope draws extensively on contemporary historical textual criticism, at the same time not excluding the possibility of analogical interpretations. Atkinson has given a masterful account of Israel's conception of marriage, citing Schillebeeckx's designation of marriage as "first and foremost a secular reality."[3] The transcendence of the Israelite God precluded any type of sacred marriage or sex among divine beings or between gods and humans.[4] "The methodological linkage between the earthly and divine realms was ...completely severed."[5] Atkinson goes on to say that "sexuality resides in man, but like everything else in creation, it receives its constituent nature from Yahweh, who has determined its purpose and meaning."[6] John Paul II says the Song of Songs must be read within the context of the "reality of the primordial sacrament" in the "beginning" (MW 108: 3) to which Christ refers the Pharisees in their question on divorce (Mt 19: 3-7). In other words, it pertains to before the Fall. John Paul II sees in the poem "all the richness of the language of human love" (MW 108: 4-5). He finds in the address of the bridegroom as "my sister, my bride" an eloquent testimony to the original peace of "disinterested tenderness," the "peace of the body" expressed in the sister relation as the first meaning of "bone of my bones, flesh of my flesh" (MW 110:2). It is the first experience of the masculine and feminine "I" in their common humanity belonging to the same Father, which is the foundation of a communion of persons in the one-flesh union as we saw in the last chapter.

John Paul II does not shy away from the sensual aspects of the lovers' dialogue but sees it as rooted in the concept of sister and brother.

> If "being a person" means both "being a subject" but also "being in relation," the term "sister" seems to express in the simplest way *the subjectivity of the feminine "I"* in its personal relation, that is, *in its openness* toward others, toward the neighbor the particular addressee of this openness becomes *the man understood as "brother."* The "sister" in some sense helps the man to define and conceive himself, she becomes, I would say, a challenge in this direction (MW 109:4).

The pope goes on to distinguish between the term "sister" and "friend," although the latter is always necessary in marriage. The term "sister" applies particularly to the language of the body so that their relation is not determined by *libido* alone. *Eros* itself leads them beyond themselves. "*In reaching each other*, in experiencing closeness to each other, *they ceaselessly tend toward something*; they yield to the call that goes beyond" (MW 112:1).

Both John Paul II and Benedict XVI refer to the Old Testament in their discussion of *eros.* A true Christian understanding cannot be gleaned outside its roots in the Old Testament.[7] Although marriage and sexuality are a secular reality, biblical scholar, Gordon Wenham, says "the whole of man's life must be lived out in the presence of God."[8] The Israelites are a people set apart by God. The book of Leviticus details what is known as the Holiness Code (Lev 17-26), laws that mandate the separateness of the Jewish people. As Atkinson says, it is not so much separation *from* surrounding nations as separation *to* God.[9] At least two-thirds of the Book of Leviticus detail what is known as the Holiness code (Lev. 17-26) laws directly related to behavior that affects the family, first separating it from the immorality of its pagan neighbors. Within the Israelite community itself there were other separations such as the taboo on approaching a woman during her menstrual period.[10] Finally there were severe punishments for violating the code, including the death penalty for adultery, incest, homosexuality and bestiality. The prophets in comparing idolatry to adultery, which John Paul II elaborates on in his Wednesday Catechesis on the language of the body, confirm the close link between God's covenant with his People and the manner of living the conjugal relation (MW 103-107).

In his encyclical letter, *Deus Caritas Est,* Pope Benedict XVI takes up the unity of love in creation and salvation. Because it involves both body and soul and gives a glimpse of a promise of happiness, among all loves, the love between man and woman stands out. The pope distinguishes between the three terms for love used in the Greek New Testament, *eros, philia (*friendship), and *agape.* The latter is a "new and distinctive form of Christian love" (DCE 3). Although the Old Testament opposed the expression of *eros* in the fertility cults, it did recognize its relation to ecstasy towards the divine, but it needed purification. At Jewish weddings, songs celebrated and exalted conjugal love. The two words for love used in the Old Testament are *dodim* (pl) meaning indeterminate, insecure and searching, and *ahaba,* which the Greek Septuagint translates as *agape,* meaning a real discovery of the other and seeking the good of the beloved. Such love becomes exclusive and forever. "Love is indeed 'ecstasy,' not in the sense of a moment of intoxication, but rather as a journey and ongoing exodus out of the closed inward-looking self towards its liberation through self-giving, and thus towards authentic self-discovery and, indeed, the discovery of God" (DCE 6). Christ shows the way by his own total self-giving love on the cross. By his sacrifice, he "portrays the essence of love and of human life itself" (DCE 6).

Eros and Agape

Pope Benedict then asks if there is any contact between the two types of love since they are often regarded as opposite, one, *eros,* ascending and the other, *agape,* descending, known in Christian philosophy as *amor concupiscientiae* and *amor benevolentiae.* He answers that they can never be fully separated. In fact, if *agape* does not enter into *eros* it ends up being impoverished. But Man cannot live on oblative love alone. *Eros* is somehow rooted in man's very nature and drives him toward marriage, in which it is fulfilled and, one might say, surpassed by *agape.* In God himself the two are intrinsically united. "God is both Logos (philosophical reason) and *Eros* (passionate love). "*Eros* is thus supremely ennobled, yet at the same time, it is so purified as to become one with *agape* (DCE 10)."[11]

This is how John Paul II explains the two types of love in his Wednesday Catechesis. He reflects on two Old Testament passages, the Song of Songs, which celebrates *eros* and the Book of Tobit where *ethos* is central. While the body has an indispensable role to play in marital love, the pope finds limits even in such a physical panegyric as the Song of Songs. As he says, "*Love* shows itself *as greater than what the 'body' is able to express*" (MW 112:5) and notes that although the Song of Songs as a canticle of human love is outside the great analogy of God's love for his people, it, nevertheless, belongs to the core of biblical teaching in its affirmation of the goodness of sexual love between a man and a woman (MW 108 1: fn 95,97). In fact the pope links it, as has already been noted, to what he calls the "primordial sacrament" which pertains to original innocence "in the beginning" (MW 108: 3). While it is caught up in the 'reciprocal fascination' of the 'language of the body,' it seems unaware of the conflict between good and evil, which is at the heart of Tobit and Sarah's struggle as a result of the first sin.

The Song of Songs is a celebration of *eros*, while *ethos* is at the center of Tobit and Sarah's love. As John Paul II says: "Truth and the strength of love show themselves in the ability to place oneself between the forces of good and evil that fight in man and around him" (MW 115:2). The language of love is expressed in choice and acts as well as in "the mystery of life and death." In this aspect, especially, it has the power to become the language of liturgy. But for this it must be reread in the context of the "integral truth of man." The prayer of Tobit and Sarah on their wedding night harkens back to the creation of man and woman in Genesis. They unite "not out of lust," nor simply from their emotions, but from a consciousness of "the depth and weight of existence itself." (MW 116:2). In expressing this truth in their bodies, they image God's eternal covenant of love with man.

Anticipated Signs of the Gift and the Natural Inclinations

This brings us to the place of the body and the sexual drive in the mutual self-gift of marriage. In *Love and Responsibility*, in a discussion of the sex drive,

Wojtyla/John Paul II says: "The drive is something more fundamental than the very psycho-physiological properties of woman and man, even though it neither manifests itself nor acts without them."[12] While in the animal world only the sex instinct is operative, in the world of persons, the sex drive has a natural tendency to turn into love of the other for his own sake. "The drive is subordinated to the person, and the person can use it at his discretion."[13] Not only is this the case in an individual encounter between man and woman, but in all social relations the drive manifests itself as a "common, universal human property" in the coexistence of persons of different sex.[14] It arises out of man's contingency and needs to be complemented by the other sex. Later on in *Veritatis splendor* John Paul II refers to the anticipatory signs of the gift in the body. "The person, by the light of reason and the support of virtue, discovers the anticipatory signs, the expression and the promise of the gift of self, in conformity with the wise plan of the Creator" (VS no. 48). The meaning of the body is always the dignity of the human person who must always be affirmed for his own sake.

The Pope's teaching on the sexual drive in *Love and Responsibility* is in conformity with Aquinas on the natural inclinations, although he has greatly enriched it with the concept of the spousal meaning of the body in his Wednesday Catechesis on the theology of the body and its fulfillment in the communion of persons. Servais Pinckaers, drawing on Thomas Aquinas, has recovered in a masterly way the liberating Christian understanding of the natural inclinations and their place in the moral life.[15] The modern tendency, influenced by nominalism, is to think of nature and freedom as contrary.[16] In this view, everything depends on the will to control the natural drives which are "blind and coercive." For St. Thomas, who followed Aristotle and many of the Greek and Latin Fathers of the Church in accepting nature as the foundation of morality, the natural inclinations in man orient him to truth and goodness. While they are determining in animals, in man the natural drives are moderated by reason. Pinckaers points out that the natural inclination to truth at the origin of the intellectual life is not a blind tendency since darkness cannot engender light. The intellect is, in fact, illuminated by the dazzling splendor of divine light. So the attraction to the good in natural inclinations is not blind but "is the deepest source of that spontaneity that shapes our willing…this inclination should be described as higher than morality and supremely free, even a sharing in the freedom, goodness and spontaneity of God."[17] He goes on to say:

> We must therefore regain at any cost the sense of this spiritual "naturalness" inherent in our earliest inclinations. Our entire conception of morality depends on this question.[18]

For St Thomas

> The inclinations, like the natural law, were God's most precious work in the human person, a direct unique participation in his wisdom, goodness and freedom and the emanation of the eternal law.[19]

In this view freedom and nature are not opposed. Under the ethics of obligation, in a former theological tradition, an external law is super-imposed on the natural inclinations. On the contrary, the inclination to the good is the first principle of practical reason. The good is what all men desire. It is closely linked to the desire for happiness. In the core of every person there is the desire for the good and the true even though through original sin the person may be deceived as to what is in reality the good. The true good is determined by man's last end, which is God. With a morality of the good combined with a morality of man's last end, which is a sharing in divine goodness and freedom, Aquinas affirmed a freedom for excellence. This differs radically from an ethics of obligation, in which the agent giving the law is seen to determine the good, unrelated to man's natural desire. Pinckaers adds, however, that two kinds of love must be distinguished, the love of concupiscence and desire and the love of friendship. In the love of concupiscence, I love something such as wine for a reason other than for itself alone but in the love of friendship, I love someone for his own sake. This is the good properly so called. The love of concupiscence is ordered, if not subordinated, to the love of friendship.

The love of concupiscence, or ordered sexual desire, is a natural inclination operative in the sexual union for the generation and rearing of offspring. It is one of the five basic inclinations. These are shared with the animals but realized differently in man due to his spiritual nature. Peter Lombard had proposed a theory of "excuses" to justify marriage due to a confusion of sexual desire, as a natural inclination, with lust. With his teaching on the natural inclinations, St. Thomas provided a new point of view. Pinckaers summarizes:

> Sexuality had originated in a primordial inclination of human nature. As such it was the work of the Creator, according to the Genesis account of the creation of man and woman. Therefore whatever might be the deficiencies caused in the individual person by sin and concupiscence, the seat of unbridled desires, sexuality was recognized as something basically good and a source of moral excellence.[20]

When subject to the interior mastery of reason and grace, the natural inclinations can be the foundation of the virtue of chastity. In marriage when imbued with charity, they can contribute to the work of salvation in a positive way. Above all there is a need to establish a close link between chastity and love.

Chastity and the Reciprocal Gift of Self

This was precisely the task Wojtyla/John Paul II set himself in his book, *Love and Responsibility*. A complete chapter is devoted to "The Person and Chastity," following "the Person and Love." In the latter he emphasizes the incommunicable mystery of the human person, whom it is never permissible simply to use, but must always be received for his own sake. He also analyzes the difference between sensuality and sentimentality. The male is drawn more to the sensual values in the woman, while she is drawn to his masculinity. In a certain sense sensuality, which focuses on the sexual values of the body, is more "objective," while sentimentality, which encompasses the whole person, is more subjective. Sentimental susceptibility is the source of affection and appears to be free of concupiscence while sensuality is full of concupiscence. The desire in affection is for nearness to the beloved person. Both are the raw material of love but they need to be distinguished by the intellect and integrated at the level of the will.

It is only in the interpersonal communion of love in the spousal relation that the integration takes place, whether the person surrenders himself to God or another human being in an inalienable way. Here the pope notes a paradox in the sexual relation; while the man seeks to possess the body of the woman, she has the experience of being possessed. This is overcome by the man simultaneously giving himself in return for the woman's gift of herself in a mutual act of self-surrender.[21] The woman can only fully surrender if she is convinced she is valued first as a person and the man recognizes the greatness of the gift. There is also a paradox in the relation of freedom to love as self-giving. Both spouses limit their freedom on account of the other person, since love consists in a commitment of freedom. Only the truth of the person as incommunicable and loved for his own sake makes the limitation of freedom something joyful and positive.[22]

> Love engages freedom and fills it with what the will clings to by nature: it fills freedom with the good. The will tends to the good, and freedom belongs to the will, and therefore freedom is for love, for through love man most fully participates in the good.[23]

A struggle usually takes place between sensual desire, focused on enjoyment, and the will, that seeks the absolute good of the beloved— happiness. While the sexual drive wants to use the other, love wants to give. Friendship between spouses, which affirms the other "I," must always be paramount. This brings the pope to the virtue of chastity in the spousal relation.

Chastity in the Spousal Relation

Chastity can only be understood in the context of love. "To be chaste," says John Paul II, "means to have a 'transparent' relation to the person of the other sex—chastity is the same as the 'transparency' of interiority, without which love is not itself, for it is not itself as long as the wish to 'use' is not subordinated to the readiness to 'love' in every situation."[24] It is not so much a "no" to sexual values as a "yes" to the value of the person; "the value of the 'body and sex' must be embedded and confirmed in the value of the person."[25] Chastity is thus not a negative value but it docs require humility. "The human body should be 'humble' toward the greatness that is the person: this is the true and definitive greatness of man."[26] Above all, the body must be "humble" toward the true happiness of man both in the human spousal relation and in his union with God and not try to impose its imperious demands. Here the pope adverts to the analogy of marriage in the Old and New Testaments for God's relation with mankind, first with the chosen people and then with the Church, to affirm its greatness.

Chastity is part of the cardinal virtue of temperance, which moderates desire according to reason. Wojtyla/John Paul II gives it the name of self-mastery, which aims at the perfection of the person and realizes love in the world of persons, especially in the spousal relation between man and woman. This means finding the proper "measure" of sensuality and affection in a love relation. Chastity, in conjugal love, does not consist in blindly smothering these impulses but in harnessing them towards the objective value of the person. Affection is helpful here in *feeling* the value of the person. In this way, affection becomes an ally in self-mastery and the virtue of chastity. [27]

The pope devotes several paragraphs at the end of the chapter to tenderness, which is particularly salient in the conjugal love of Mary and Joseph, in which there was no sexual intercourse but a supreme abundance of affectivity and friendship, as the Fathers of the Church and subsequent theologians have stated.[28] Tenderness, he says, "possesses a very specific meaning and performs a specific function in human life, especially in the interaction between a man and a woman—the sublimation of their reciprocal relation is to a large extent based on tenderness."[29] Tenderness is a kind of co-feeling for the various creatures we come in contact with, intuiting their interior states. It comes, in a way, from man's connection and union with all of nature especially with other human beings. It is above all "a sensitiveness to the other's lived experiences and states of the other person's soul." [30] Furthermore there is a possibility and a need to communicate this to him. The closeness proceeds from affectivity. It is expressed physically by holding hands, embracing or by certain forms of kissing. It is important to mark a boundary between such gestures of affection and sensuality so that it expresses benevolence, not sensual desire, which only comes with self-mastery. The pope asks if there cannot be a right to tenderness, especially on the part of the weak and vulnerable. It is a critical factor in love especially in the spousal relation. A woman particularly needs it in the challenging events of pregnancy, childbirth and all that accompanies them. It is through the sacrifice and self-denial of continence that such tenderness can flourish.[31]

Tenderness is a theme favored by Pope Francis from the encyclical at the beginning of his papacy, *Evangelii gaudium,* to many subsequent speeches and homilies. For example, he writes: "Whenever we look to Mary, we come to believe once again in the revolutionary nature of love and tenderness (EG 288). He then cites this passage on his apostolic journey to Cuba in September, 2015. He follows it with the words: "We are asked to live the revolution of tenderness as Mary, our Mother of Charity did." [32]

The Spousal Relation of Mary and Joseph

Cognizant of the virtues involved in such tenderness it is possible to discuss the spousal relation of Mary and Joseph and to understand Mary's gift of virginity, and, as a corollary, Joseph's. In the context of the resurrection of the body, John Paul II introduces continence for the kingdom of heaven when he comments on the words of Christ (Mk 12:25) that there is no marriage nor giving in marriage in heaven as well as Matthew 19:11-12. In the resurrected state "man, male and female, finds at one and the same time the fullness of personal giving and of the intersubjective communion of persons, thanks to his whole psychosomatic being in the eternal union with God" (MW, 73, 1). This state, without the beatific vision, is anticipated by those given the exceptional gift of consecrated virginity by the Holy Spirit in this life. Both vocations of marriage and of celibacy for the kingdom are spousal relations expressed in the body. Celibacy for the kingdom points to the eschaton where there is no giving or receiving in earthly marriage but perfect union with God and perfect "inter-subjectivity" between man and woman. In fact, the spousal meaning of the body is the foundation of this call to continence in a total self-giving to Christ. In the marriage of Mary and Joseph, both spousal meanings are expressed.[33]

The dogma of the Immaculate Conception affirms that Mary was totally free from original sin, and, as the Catechism of the Catholic Church states, "by a special grace of God, committed no sin of any kind during her whole earthly life" (CCC 411). This means that with perfect harmony of body and soul her love was totally pure. What about Joseph? As we saw, the Tradition was conflicted about Joseph being subject to original sin. In the Middle Ages in art, he was depicted as an old man, possibly widowed, in whom the fires of concupiscence had been extinguished.[34] While the Church has made no definitive statement about Joseph, some arguing for his sanctification in the womb like John the Baptist, it is clear that only Mary was immaculately conceived.[35] Basil Cole, a Dominican, has written and reflected on St. Joseph and the Holy Family. As a disciple of St. Thomas Aquinas, he is well versed in the work of the Angelic Doctor. Although Aquinas did not endorse Mary's Immaculate Conception,[36] he gave cogent arguments for her sanctification in the womb. Basil Cole has taken those arguments and applied them to Joseph.[37] In the *Summa Theologiae,* III, 27 1 and 6, Aquinas answers the question of whether Mary did not experience the first movements of sin, resulting from the effects of original sin. Applying them to Joseph, Cole would say that at some point in his mother's womb he was given an abundance of grace from sanctification in the womb, like St. John the Baptist. This was fitting for one who was to be the human supernatural father of the Incarnate Son. He was also kept by divine providence from inordinate movements of sensuality. According to tradition, when Christ was born, his presence ensured complete freedom from sinful inclinations (analogously, we shall see later how the Eucharist acts as a purifier for sinful human beings). Cole concludes:

> These explicit thoughts on Mary in the text of Aquinas, and implicit ones that I have brought out and applied to Joseph, enable the theologian to see how important the marriage of Mary and Joseph really was. These ideas give a glimpse into how they were able to maintain virginity while, at the same time, be the best of friends.[38]

Next, Cole turns to John Paul II's apostolic exhortation, *Redemptoris custos,* in order to bring out Joseph's gift of self as a husband and father. He quotes the following passage concerning Joseph taking Mary into his home (Mt. 1: 24):

> Are we not to suppose that his *love as a man was also given a new birth by the Holy Spirit*? Are we not to think that the love of God which has been poured into the human heart through the Holy Spirit (cf Rm 5:5) molds every human love to perfection? This love of God also molds – in a completely unique way – the love of husband and wife, deepening within it everything of human worth and beauty, everything that bespeaks an exclusive gift of self, a covenant between persons, and an authentic communion according to the model of the blessed Trinity (RC 19).

As Cole says, grace does not destroy nature but elevates it. John Paul II continues in *Redemptoris custos:*

> The deep spiritual closeness arising from marital union and the interpersonal contact between man and woman have their definitive origin in the Spirit, the giver of life (cf. Jn.6:63). *Joseph, in obedience to the Spirit found in the Spirit the source of love*, the conjugal love that he experienced as a man. And this love proved to be greater than this "just man" could ever have expected within the limits of his human heart (RC 19).

What follows about the nature of celibate love is, in no way, meant to denigrate the conjugal act but to show the priority of love of the person to any form of sexual pleasure.[39] Cole comments that renouncing conjugal acts to preserve Mary's virginity, far from eviscerating conjugal feelings for his wife, purified them.[40] Cole turns to the spiritual friendship of the saints to show how virginal or chaste love, which affirms love "for the sake of the other rather than for personal usefulness or pleasure" [41] actually increases tenderness, friendship and caring. He cites another Dominican, Paul Conner, in his book, *Celibate Love,*[42] which reveals from their letters that theses saints were not only channels of grace for each other but deeply cared about each other and felt sorrow when separated. Because their friendship was rooted in God, it enabled them to increase in holiness. Rightly ordered conjugal love enables the spouses, too, to increase in holiness and friendship. While the spiritual friendships of the saints are similar in shared intimacy and affection, they are not the same as the marriage of Joseph and Mary which was marked by the exclusivity characteristic of conjugal love.

Cole finds especially relevant to the holy marriage of Jesus and Mary, the experience of Bartolomeo de Dominici in the presence of St. Catherine, a beautiful young woman. Although having deep feelings of attachment, his sexual feelings were quieted. Cole concludes: "since Mary was immaculately conceived and St. Joseph was probably consecrated in the womb, without the conjugal act, they possessed the greatest possible intimacy that two friends could have on earth."[43] The self-mastery, implicit in the virtue of chastity, is required in both celibate and conjugal love. In a later chapter, Cormac Burke shows how, since the Middle Ages, there has been an unfortunate denigration of the conjugal act as implicitly lustful. As we saw above, this has been corrected by both St. John Paul II and Pope Benedict XVI.

Here, what Livio Melina has to say on the analogy of love is pertinent. All human love is a *response*, originating from divine love. From this it follows that there is "a fundamental analogy between the original love and a love that is originated springs forth."[44] The specific form of analogy, which accords with the fundamental structure of love as a relation between the good and the beloved, is known as the *analogia caritatis.* Only through consciousness of this original divine gift is it possible to live all our loves in God. It is God's presence in the beloved that "becomes the moving force in the life of man."[45] Not only is God present in the love between Mary and Joseph as lover and beloved, but Christ, himself, is present as both the source, reason and fruit of their union.

The Prophetic Role of Joseph

While marriage harkens back to creation, virginity for the sake of the kingdom points forward to the resurrected state. Tradition holds that Mary was predisposed to the virginal state as the fruit of her immaculate conception.

Joseph, however, was steeped in creation's blessing of fertility in the Old Testament going back to Genesis 1:28. What prepared him to accept without question the announcement of the angel that Mary's pregnancy was of the Holy Spirit and to take her into his home (Mt. 1:20 - 24)? Giorgio Buccellati gives several reasons:

> The first is what I call the Old Testament "catechumenate," i.e., the deep spiritual attitude that the Old Testament had made possible in even the simplest of people, as Mary and Joseph culturally were. In this light, the Annunciation is not an hallucination along the lines of a visit from outer space but rather an understandable epiphany of a reality already known, however dimly, and one that could be meaningfully conceptualized.[46]

All the prophecies of the Old Testament prepared for this event. Matthew gives the appellation "just" to Joseph (Greek *dikaios)*, which has a specific connotation in the Old Testament. For the Greeks, the word denoted primarily a social virtue of not transgressing the rights of others, mainly a juridical view. The biblical view has to do above all with man's relations with God and his walk with him.[47] Buccellatti, along with contemporary biblical exegete Ignace de la Potterie, refuses to take the view that Joseph was motivated by a legalistic attitude in putting Mary away. Buccellatti contends Joseph was motivated by reverential fear of what had taken place within her. Just as Peter exclaimed to the Lord after the miracle of the fish, "Depart from me for I am a sinful man," likewise, Joseph did not feel worthy of "the Mystery," and so proposed to separate himself from Mary.[48] It was his immersion in the prophecies that gave him a dim awareness of what it might mean. John Paul II does not explicitly endorse this view, but he uses the word "astonishing" to describe Joseph's view of Mary's motherhood, thus opening a way for such an interpretation. He seems to be aware of it also in his reference to "the mystery of Mary's motherhood" when he comments on the passage (RC 3).[49]

Buccellati proposes that Joseph's commitment to virginity was not due to a previous vow, but rather in response to the Annunciation.[50] It was this confrontation of both Mary and Joseph with the Incarnation that became the defining feature of Christian virginity and characterized its novelty. Although at times, an unhealthy emphasis on the idea that sex and even the spousal relationship are impure, combined with a focus on "a release from the outward fetters of married life" has undermined consecrated virginity's true meaning, (See Cormac Burke in Chapter 9) it has not obscured the extraordinary vitality of the Catholic tradition of the virginal life. Following the example of Mary and Joseph, "The secret of the truly miraculous tradition of Christian virginity begins and ends with the contemplation of the Incarnation seen as a Trinitarian explosion."[51] Buccellati calls it a prophetic proclamation. In this sense Joseph's faith in living with the mystery is like that of Abraham. Without any manifestation of its extraordinary nature, he was witness to it in "a glass darkly."[52]

It is above all the faith of Mary and Joseph, both challenged and permeated by the presence of Christ, that makes the Holy Family a model par excellence for all Christian families. Just as Mary, committed to virginity according to the Tradition from an early age, surrendered her limited human perspective to God's will that she enter a marriage with Joseph, so the "just man" Joseph, heir to the generous fruitfulness of the covenant of creation, submitted to a virginal marriage with Mary for the sake of the Incarnation of Christ. This was not to be without suffering. Even Mary asked "Why?" when they discovered Jesus in the temple after three days of searching (Lk. 2: 48). Whether called to virginity for the kingdom or to sacramental marriage, it is the task of every Christian to live out this vocation to life in Christ in total trust, modeled on Mary and Joseph in the Holy Family.[53] Such submission to God's will may mean ten children or none, an abundance of conjugal intercourse or possibly none if physical disability or some canonical defect such as a previous marriage, that has not been annulled, intervenes. Yet such a marriage, in spite of or even because of the purification of great suffering, when centered on union with Christ and mutual self-gift, can be imbued with physical tenderness and deep intimacy and friendship. As John Paul II says:

> The Holy Family is the beginning of countless other holy families. The Council recalled that holiness is the vocation of all the baptized. In our age, as in the past, there is no lack of witnesses to the gospel

of the family, even if they are not well known or have not been proclaimed saints by the Church (LF 23).

Josephite Marriages

Living marriage without conjugal intercourse because of a sacramental or physical impediment differs from a couple choosing what was traditionally called a Josephite marriage. While the Church has always acknowledged the right of Christian couples to make this choice, it has not been encouraged. For example, the parents of St. Therese of Lisieux were advised to consummate their marriage. For the Church Fathers, says, Dyan Elliott, the only type of such spiritual marriage that was endorsed was moving from normal conjugal relations to celibacy.[54] Elliott points to several competing interests in the practice: the desire of married couples to elevate the spirituality of their marriage, a certain suspicion of the goodness of conjugal intercourse, that has persisted to modern times;[55] and the desire of clergy and religious to make a clear demarcation between the two states.[56] She also draws attention to woman's desire for greater equality. As John Paul II points out in *Love and Responsibility*, in conjugal intercourse the man has the sense of possessing while the woman experiences being possessed[57] and "parenthood . . . is realized much more fully in the woman" (MD 18). Elliott notes that women "generally were the ones who agitated for spiritual marriage. [58] She concludes that the "move to chastity [in the sense of celibacy] had an empowering effect on the woman."[59] It was not until the development of marriage as a communion of persons within the context of the encyclical, *Humanae vitae*, and John Paul II's theology of the body that the proper place for chastity in marriage could come to the fore and give full value to the equality and diversity of roles of men and women. (This is dealt more fully in later chapters.)

Subject to One Another Out of Reverence for Christ (Eph. 5:21)

In his *Letter to Families* John Paul II proclaims that "St Paul's magnificent synthesis concerning the great mystery [of God in Christ and the Church in

Ephesians 5:32] appears as the compendium or *summa,* in some sense, of the teaching about God and man which was brought to fulfillment by Christ" (LF 19). This text is key in the Pope's eyes for understanding the asymmetrical difference of masculinity and femininity in the family and society and it is based on the union of Christ and the Church, which in turn has its origin in the Trinity (MW 87 no. 3). The idea of body is central both to the metaphorical meaning of the Body of Christ, which is the Church, and the concrete meaning of the human body. Going back to Genesis and referring to the analogy of God's spousal love for his People in the union of Christ and his Church, John Paul II seeks to discover what the text says about the sacramentality of marriage particularly in terms of the theology of the body. Here we are not so much concerned with the sacrament of marriage as with the instructions on how to live family life as a communion of persons and how the Holy Family conformed their life to these instructions. As the pope says in describing "the *two main guiding lines* of the whole Letter to the Ephesians: the first is the mystery of Christ, which is realized in the Church as an expression of the divine plan for man's salvation; the second is the Christian vocation as the model of life for baptized persons and particular communities, corresponding to the mystery of Christ or to the divine plan for the salvation of man" (MW 88 no. 3). These instructions apply not just to the spouses but to children as well. In this chapter, the emphasis will be only on the spousal relation, especially the admonition, "Be subject to one another in the fear of Christ" (Eph. 5: 21).

Commenting on this scripture passage, the pope notes that there is both a vertical and horizontal dimension of the spouses with Christ and each other. Their reciprocal communion must be imbued with a reverent fear (transcendent awe) of Christ, a sense of holiness. It is within this context of mutual submission to Christ, that the wife is called to be subject to her husband (Eph. 5: 22). It is by no means a one-sided submission. "Christ is the source and at the same time the model of that submission" (MW 89 no. 4). Although the pope does not in the text refer to the Trinitarian relations, it is helpful to look at the meaning of the word St Paul uses, *hypotassomai* and how it is used scripturally with reference to the Trinity. It does, indeed, mean submission but depending on its context its meaning can range from active subordination to voluntary submission. In the Hellenic world in the active voice it means "to place under" or "subordinate." However, in the Septuagint it means to acknowledge someone's power, for example to surrender to God. In the New Testament it is confined to Luke, St. Paul, James and 1 Peter. Most statements in the active voice are Christological with special reference to Ps. 8:6 "Thou has put all things under his feet" (cf. 1 Cor. 15:28; Heb. 2; Eph. 1:22). In these instances its use suggests that the phrase is considered part of the early Christian confession.[60] St. Paul uses it for important theological statements. For example, in 1 Cor. 15-28 the Son subjects all things to himself, then subjects himself to the Father. It is important to keep this Trinitarian dimension in mind.[61]

When it is used as an exhortation it denotes a sacred order as a child submitting to his parent's discipline. In the Letter to the Hebrews (12:9), the comparison is made between submitting to the discipline of an earthly father and God the Father, in some way linking the two. The same middle voice is used in Luke 2:51 of Jesus submitting himself to Mary and Joseph. [62] It is in this sense of voluntary submission that it is used in Ephesians 5:21 and is first used of both husband and wife submitting to Christ. When the sentence continues without the repetition of the verb, it goes into an ecclesial statement about the wife's submission to the husband as the body of the Church submits to Christ as the head. The husband is called to love his wife with the love of agape just as Christ loves the Church and gave himself up for her.

John Paul II has an extensive reflection on the passage in his Wednesday Catechesis. The analogy goes in two directions; on the one hand, the spousal love of marriage illuminates the mystery and on the other, it is in turn illuminated by the mystery. "Marriage corresponds to the vocation of Christians only when it mirrors the love that Christ the Bridegroom gives to the Church, his Bride, and the Church (in likeness to the wife who is 'subject,' and thus completely given) seeks to give back to Christ in return" (MW 90: 2). There follows an analysis of the meaning of Christ as head. "As head, he is the savior of his body and, at the same time, as Savior, he is the head. As head and savior of the Church, he is also Bridegroom of his Bride." (MW 90:5) The union of head and body is organic in nature, which St. Paul applies also to the union of the spouses, especially with the reference to the one-flesh union of Genesis.

The pope considers Ephesians 5:22-23 as decisive for the analogy: "Wives be subject to your husbands as you are to the Lord." (The Lord here is interpreted as Christ whose total self-gift on the cross is the model for husbands.) In no way does the analogy imply any loss of "personhood" on the part of the wife. Both in the cases of the unity of Christ and the Church and the spouses, they remain distinct persons-subjects. The analogy describes the different way the man and woman are called to love one another:

> *The husband* is above all *the one who loves* and the wife, by contrast, is *the one who is loved.* One might even venture the idea that the wife's submission to the husband, understood in the context of the whole of Ephesians 5: 22-23, means above all the experiencing of love (MW 2:6).[63]

How then does this analogy apply to the marriage of Mary and Joseph? John Paul II talks about a moral unity in which the love that unites them does so spiritually so that the "I" of the one who loves becomes the "you" and vice versa. As we have seen, the love between Mary and Joseph was above all a disinterested love, in which Joseph even surrendered his conjugal rights to Mary out of reverence for Christ. Mary, in spite of the privilege of being Theotokos, at all times gave the "headship" to Joseph. It was Joseph who was instructed by the angel to take her into his home and, at another time early in the marriage, to flee to Egypt. Yet Mary showed herself a person-subject through her response to Gabriel at the Annunciation, no matter what might be Joseph's response. In the communion of persons, the relationship with God in original solitude, always precedes and grounds the love of the spouses.

The pope takes up again the analogy of Ephesians 5 in *Mulieris Dignitatem,* stressing once again that as established by the Creator in the "beginning," marriage has the ethos of a communion of persons, corresponding to the truth of their being as man and woman. "In this love," he says, "there is a fundamental affirmation of the woman as a person" (MD 24). The newness of the gospel is to affirm the mutuality of the subjection "out of reverence for Christ." While the analogy places the husband as the initiator of love with regard to his wife, in relation to Christ's divinity, he is on the side of Church. All men and women are recipients of God's love in Christ first. All are called to be the "bride" of the Redeemer. "In this way 'being the bride,' and thus the 'feminine' element, becomes a symbol of all that is 'human,' according to the words of Paul: There is neither male nor female; for you are all one in Christ Jesus" (Gal. 3:28) (MD 25). (This feminine element of all being on the side of the Church in relation to Christ has been forgotten, but this in no way denigrates from man's role of initiation in the man-women relation.) All this recalls the words of Vatican Council II, *Lumen Gentium*, from which John Paul II takes his theme for *Redemptoris Mater, Mother of the Redeemer,* "Blessed is she who believed." Just as Abraham initiated the covenant of the Old Testament through his faith, so it is the faith of the woman, Mary, who initiates the New Covenant. Mary's faith preceded that of Joseph and all the redeemed to come (RM 26).

CHAPTER 6

Paternity and Maternity

The "We" Dimensions of the Communion of Persons

The last chapter looked at the Holy Family as a communion of persons specifically in the "I-Thou" dimension. Although not engaging in conjugal intercourse, Mary and Joseph enjoyed a profound interpersonal communion. This interpersonal communion did not exist for its own sake but for their mission to "serve the person and mission of Jesus" (RC 8). In this sublime task, Mary and Joseph discovered the "we" dimension of communion as father and mother, sharing in the care and upbringing of their Son. Karol Wojtyla/John Paul II has described the "I-Thou" relationship as "particularly compatible with the person as subject." In the same way, the "We" denotes more than one subject working towards a common good. A prime example is the family, when the couple take on a task together. Although they do not cease to be an "I" and "Thou," they discover in themselves a new dimension. Wojtyla says that "the confirmation of the subject 'I' in the community 'We' agrees profoundly with the nature of this subject."[1] In no way is there any distortion or diminution of personal subjectivity of each unless there is some defect in the "I-Thou" relationship. John Paul translates this into theological language in his Wednesday Catechesis on the theology of the body. In his analysis of the Genesis texts of creation, he passes from original solitude, the person, to original unity, the first communion of persons, to the cycle of knowledge-generation through which Adam and Eve become father and mother.

> Procreation brings it about "that the man and the woman (his wife) *know each other reciprocally in the 'third' originated by both.* For this reason, this 'knowledge' becomes in some way a revelation of the new man, in whom both, the man and the woman, again recognize each other, their humanity, their living image" (MW 21:4).

He goes on to say:

> The woman stands before the man as mother, subject of the new human life that is conceived and develops in her into the world. In this way what also reveals itself is the mystery of the man's masculinity, that is, the generative and "paternal" meaning of the body (MW 21: 2).

Once again we must ask in what way the Holy Family can be a model for families as a communion of persons, when there is no generation in the one-flesh union.

This chapter begins by expanding on John Paul II's idea that the genealogy of the person and, therefore, of the family has its origin in the Trinity especially through the writings of Angelo Schola and Marc Ouellet. Then fatherhood, motherhood and shared parenthood will be considered through four perspectives critical for a communion of persons: (1) the meaning of each, (2) the transition to the new state, (3) the virtues of fatherhood and motherhood (4) the place of prayer and liturgical celebrations and (5) Work. A section on shared parenthood will also be given. Reference to the Holy Family as model will be considered in each segment.

Genealogy of the Person and Fecundity

In *Letter to Families*, John Paul II, citing Ephesians 3: 14-15, explains how human fatherhood and motherhood transcend mere biology. As made in the image of God, man is called to an eternal destiny in the Trinity.[2] "The genealogy of the person is thus united with the eternity of God and only then with fatherhood and motherhood, which are realized in time" (LF 9). From these and various Scripture passages, both Angelo Cardinal Scola and Marc

Cardinal Ouellet, locate a theology of fecundity itself as well as its origin in God, the Creator of human nature. In discussing the nuptial mystery and fruitfulness Scola, who defines the nuptial mystery as consisting of sexual difference, love and procreation, places the full meaning of spousal love in the communion of the Trinity.

> *Communio personarum* exists in its perfection in the Three in One, because the Father gives himself completely to the Son without keeping anything of his divine essence for himself. The Father generates the Son. The Son himself gives back the same, perennial divine essence. This exchange between the two is so perfect as to be *fruitful* in a pure state: it gives rise to another Person, the Holy Spirit.[3]

While there is no sexuality in God, Scola posits suprasexual fecundity in the unity in distinction in the Trinity that finds its echo in the human *communio personarum*. "In its truth, human love is this communion between two persons of different sexes which is open to a third person." If this is the case, Scola asks if it is possible to identify the specific kind of fruitfulness proper to each. Generation is the prerogative of the Father and the Son is begotten not made.[4] It is through the power of the Holy Spirit, the fruit of the perfect love between Father and Son, that Christ is conceived virginally in Mary. In the dual unity of the human couple, the third is not simply a member of the human species but a personal subject, made in the image of God. The conjugal act is thus a procreative act. While a certain likeness exists between human and animal sexuality and reproduction (which responds solely to instinct) the love and fruitfulness that should always inform the conjugal act raises it to a communion of persons by the total gift of self and thus to a certain analogy of the Trinitarian communion of persons. [5]

Ouellet also takes as his starting point, based on *Redemptoris custos,* that motherhood and fatherhood find their source in the Trinity. In no way can they be fully explained from below but must pass through creation in Jesus and the Christ-Church union. In developing a "'theology' of matrimonial and family sanctity,"[6] Ouellet proposes that holiness in the communion of persons embraces both the bond *and* fecundity. He avers:

> If the baptismal grace of sonship introduces the Christian into the intratrinitarian relation of the Son and the Father, matrimonial grace confers upon the couple a new participation between the divine Persons. . . . With the Son comes the Spirit of Love who assumes authentic conjugal love into God's love, to make it a privileged expression of the Father's fecundity within the covenant between Christ the Bridegroom and the Church his Bride.[7]

He echoes Scola in saying that since Trinitarian life is communion in fecundity, analogously the "third" which is first generated is the unity of the couple. The "third" in the faith-filled couple is also grace given by the Holy Spirit, which gives "a new unity that is not only human, but Trinitarian."[8] From this perspective, although there is no direct continuity, it is possible to see how earthly fathers and mothers are linked to their heavenly father. They receive not only the gift of a child created in God's image but spiritual fruitfulness through the gift of the Paschal Mystery. Ouellet goes on to say that in loving obedience to Christ, "they must therefore place their love for God above every other love, including even that of their own parents, spouse and children."[9]

The Holy Spirit is the one who seals the human "we" in the family in image of the eternal "We" of the Trinity and brings about a new communion of love. This love, animated by the Holy Spirit, Ouellet likens to electrical energy circulating in the reciprocal life of the couple. Ouellet posits three stages of marital love: (1) the passage from "being in love" to loving the person; (2) conjugal charity modeled on the sacrifice of cross; and (3) the gift of children when love becomes paternal and maternal. He quotes *Familiaris consortio* that the family's "mission is to guard, reveal and communicate love" (FC 17).

Ouellet concludes:

> In the daily relationship of love in the family, the interlacing Trinitarian relations of fatherhood, sonship and fruitful unity, which constitute Trinitarian holiness shine forth. The Incarnate Word, shaped by the Holy Spirit through the hands of Mary and Joseph, brought forth this

> mystery in our midst and made possible the sacramental encounter between the Trinity in heaven and that on earth, the family, icon of the Most High.[10]

It is now time to consider human fatherhood and motherhood in its various dimensions as a communion of persons in the image of the Trinity.

Fatherhood

The Meaning of Fatherhood

The apostolic exhortation, *Redemptoris custos*, is the closest that John Paul II came to writing anything specific on human fatherhood yet it is clear from his own family life, his witness and scattered references in his other documents that understanding the true nature of fatherhood was of immense importance to him. Aware of feminist excoriation of "patriarchy" he is careful to distinguish between the mystery of divine fatherhood and human fatherhood. In *Letter to Families* he refers to the universe in its immensity and the world of all living beings as "inscribed in God's fatherhood" (LF 6:1). In reflecting on God's covenant with his chosen people and the text of Ephesians 5: 25-27 with its analogy of spousal love, he says: *"The first dimension of love and election*, as a mystery hidden from ages in God *is a fatherly dimension and not a 'conjugal' one" (MW 95:5).* This means that the mystery of adoption as sons in Christ is first linked to the very fatherhood of God. The analogy of spousal love only appears when God reveals himself as Redeemer and it is this spousal analogy that links human marriage to the union of Christ and the Church. The pope is always careful to confine the family image of the Trinity to communion and not to the gendered persons per se. Christ as redeemer is one with the Father, as he says in John 14: 8-12 to Philip. Ultimately the relationship of human fatherhood to divine is a mystery.

In *Letter to Families*, the pope is even more specific about the limits of the analogy between human and divine fatherhood. "Although man is created in God's image, God does not cease to be for him the one 'who dwells in unapproachable light' (1 Tm. 6:16): He is the 'Different One,' by essence the 'totally Other'"(LF 8). He refers to the "masculine" and "feminine" qualities that are ascribed to God; his love sometimes presented as the love of a bridegroom, father and sometimes as the care of the mother. What, therefore, does human fatherhood look like in the perspective of the mystery of the fatherhood of God? One might say that the fatherhood of Joseph is the essential link between the majestic fatherhood of God and human fatherhood. Here Joseph's humility, chastity, deep affection for, guidance and protection of Jesus and Mary have particular relevance.

In reflecting on original sin, the pope says, "man turns his back on God-Love, on the Father" (MW 26:4). As a result what "comes from the Father" is cut off from man's heart and he is left a prey to what "comes from the world" (MW 26:4). In the second Scripture passage on Matthew 5:27-28 the pope notes how casting the Father out of the heart is particularly linked to concupiscence or disordered desire especially between man and woman. It is at the core of "original shame." Although both man and woman are adversely affected, the man is more at risk of treating the woman as an object of sexual desire so that the transition to fatherhood may be a special challenge.

Transition to Fatherhood

As bishop of Cracow and later as archbishop, Karol Wojtyla gave retreats to young people.[11] During one of these retreats he addressed both the men and the women separately. His talk to male students is particularly enlightening in view of his later reflections both in his Wednesday Catechesis on adultery and the encyclical, *Veritatis splendor.* Wojtyla selects the passage from St. Matthew's gospel of Jesus's encounter with the rich young man (Matt. 19: 16-22).[12] After Jesus invites him to follow Him if he wishes to be perfect, not simply to obey the commandments, the young man turns away sad. Wojtyla chooses to interpret the passage from "a human perspective."[13] He sees a certain arrogance in the young man's approach as if claiming he is already living a virtuous life. When Jesus challenges him to give up his possessions, his unwillingness to give of himself becomes apparent. Wojtyla calls these two male characteristics typical: arrogance and a lack of willingness to give. A third is the spirit of conquest. Including himself in the male sex, Wojtyla comments:

> We are quite ready to take, or conquer, in terms of enjoyment, profit, gain and success—and even in the moral order. Then comes the question of giving...The element which is so characteristic under other forms in the spiritual portrait of women is barely perceptible in men.[14]

The bishop's analysis does not end there. He finds a tendency in men to view religious devotion as primarily for women, to lack a deep interior life and to try to make God's truth fit his convenience, in effect being tempted to "place myself 'above' Christ."[15] He continues that nowhere is this truer than in the area of sexual morality, where Christ places demands on men.[16] Since his desire is stronger, he urges the woman on and then expects her to "pay" for both. But he is forgetting that God as Creator and Father has shared his creative power with him and he is ignoring the fact that the life is created within the woman. He is in danger of exploiting her unless he uses his interior strength to mature into the role of father.

Wojtyla fleshed out these themes in his play, *Radiation of Fatherhood*, especially focusing on the struggle of the protagonist, Adam, to mature into fatherhood. The subtitle of the play is "A Mystery," which, the introduction explains, recalls the medieval mystery plays. Adam is in some sense Everyman. As the genre, "theater of the word," the action is subordinate to the interior states of the three protagonists, Adam, Monica, the child, and the Mother who is not given a name. In a dialogue with God the Father, Adam cries out, "You could have left me in the sphere of fertility...without placing me in the depths of a fatherhood to which I am unequal."[17] He prefers God to leave him in loneliness, although he is ambivalent, realizing that he has not been made "closed."

> You want me to love. You aim at me through a child, through a tiny daughter or son—and my resistance weakens.[18]

Adam comes to understand that God does not want him to become a father unless he first becomes a child, the reason his Son came into the world, for he comes to understand that "Fathers return through their children; the father always through the soil of a child's soul."[19]

At this point the Woman, the Mother, speaks. She exclaims how motherhood is an expression of fatherhood. Motherhood can never be truly separated from fatherhood.[20] "It must always go back to the father to take from him all that it expresses. In this consists the radiation of fatherhood."[21] It is the child who restores the father as bridegroom. Here we have the circumincession of the communion of persons in the family. In his essay on the play, Polish theologian, Rev. Prof. Josef Tischner sees "creative interaction" as the key to the drama. We become who we are through our interaction with others.[22]" In Trinitarian circumincession,

> The Son comes from the Father, and the Holy Spirit comes from the Father and the Son. Every Person of the Trinity is Himself thanks to another Person. The God of Christianity is not an Absolute Solitude but an Absolute Interaction.[23]

We see this played out in the scenes between Adam and Monica. Monica is wrestling with memories of an absent father who died before the play begins. She grows to love Adam as another father. He, in turn, struggles to be the father Monica seeks. Suddenly a snake rustles in the nearby grass. His instinct to protect the child takes over and the realization that in some way he gave life to Monica matures him into fatherhood. He understands that fatherhood involves a choice. "Love," Adam says, "is always a choice and always born by choice."[24] He concludes: "Giving birth this way through perpetual choice, we give birth to love."[25]

Turning now to the Holy Family, Joseph had a difficult passage into fatherhood of the Christ Child. First, the Child was not from his own seed. Until he was enlightened by the angel he had a painful decision to make. Once assured of his role in God's plan, he took Mary immediately into his home. Shortly afterwards he departed with his pregnant wife to Bethlehem to fulfill the Roman census. Since in Bethlehem there was no room at the inn, he suffered the indignity of Jesus being born in a stable. To escape from Herod the new father shepherded the Holy Family to Egypt, returning to Nazareth only when Herod died.

The Virtues of Fatherhood

Let us look at the virtues of fatherhood through St. Joseph. The pope refers to Joseph's sacrifice of virginity as "a husband's 'gift of self'" (RC 20). In Joseph's life John Paul II sees his "total gift of self" made possible, both by his commitment to the interior life and the presence of Jesus and Mary. He speaks of the silence of Joseph in the Gospels as *"a silence that reveals in a special way the inner portrait* of the man" (RC 25). It is "only in the light of his profound interior life" that his self-sacrifice is understandable (RC 26). The pope cites the same discourse of Pope Paul VI. "It was from this interior life that 'very singular commands and consolations came, bringing him also the logic and strength that belong to simple and clear souls, and giving him the power of making great decisions—such as the decision to put his liberty immediately at the disposition of divine designs, to make over to them also his legitimate human calling, his conjugal happiness, to accept the conditions, the responsibility and the burden of a family, but, through an incomparable and virginal love, to renounce the natural conjugal love that is the foundation and nourishment of the family'" (RC 26). (The conjugal act, which may or may not lead to fruitful procreation is the prime way for the man to express in his body his total gift of self to his wife. While all other gestures of affection were available to Joseph, this expression was uniquely denied). [26] The pope adds, "St. Joseph was called by God to serve the person and mission of Jesus directly *through the exercise of his fatherhood;"* and "Joseph showed Jesus 'by a special gift from heaven, all the natural love, all the affectionate solicitude that a father's heart can know'" (RC 8)

As we saw in the third chapter it took centuries to unpack the nature of Joseph's role in salvation as husband and father and only then could there be a theology of the Holy Family. It is noteworthy that his role in salvation was only decided through the "interaction" of his marriage with Mary. Throughout the long centuries of reflection on his role in salvation history, reference was made to the virtues he exercised as husband and father. These can be subsumed under the headings of faith, second only to that of Mary, purity of heart and chastity, love and conjugal fidelity, the role of protector, humility, industriousness and uniting the contemplative and active life. (The 17th century French School of Spirituality especially valued humility.[27]) As guardian of the mystery of the Holy Family from the 19th century onwards, St. Joseph was given an ecclesial role as protector of the Church.[28] In *Redemptoris custos* John Paul II particularly stresses his role as protector or guardian linked to his role as father.[29] Not only did he claim his fatherhood by naming the Child and having him circumcised, but he fulfilled a father's protecting role in the flight into Egypt to escape Herod.

While John Paul II lists all of these in his apostolic exhortation, *Redemptoris custos*, he goes further and integrates them into a vision of the Holy Family as a communion of persons. Above all, he sees Joseph as a model for what it means to mature into fatherhood. Citing the encyclical, *Familiaris consortio:* "the family has the mission to guard, reveal and communicate love," the pope exclaims: "How much the family of today can learn from this!" (RC, 7). He finds a passage from a March 19, 1966 discourse of Paul VI as "concretely" expressing St. Joseph's fatherhood "in his having used the legal authority which was his over the Holy Family in order to make a total gift of self, of his life and work; in having turned his human vocation to domestic life into a superhuman oblation of self, an oblation of his heart and all his abilities into love placed at the service of the Messiah growing up in his house" (RC 8). He stresses above all his role as guardian of the hidden or private life of Jesus.[30] "God placed him at the head of his family, as a faithful and prudent servant, so that with fatherly care he might watch over his only begotten son" (RC 8).

Above all John Paul II stresses the primacy of St. Joseph's interior life. No word of Joseph, only his actions are recorded by the evangelists. We have already spoken of Joseph's silence. St Joseph combined both the active and contemplative life. He was able to combine both *love of truth* –that pure contemplative love of divine the truth which radiated from the humanity of Christ—and *the demands of love*—that equally pure and selfless love required for his vocation to safeguard and develop the humanity of Jesus, which was inseparably linked to his divinity" (RC 27).

Liturgy and Worship

Pope John Paul II is very much aware of Joseph's rootedness in the Old Covenant: "*This just man,* who bore within himself the entire heritage of the Old Covenant, was also *brought into the 'beginning' of the New and Eternal Covenant of Jesus Christ.*" Christ, by subjecting Himself to the lineage of Joseph, was heir to all the rituals and promises of the Old Covenant and of this particular family of which Joseph was the head. He called on all in the Church to "*learn from him how to be servants of the 'economy of salvation.'*"(RC 32). In the Old Covenant, the man is the founder of the family. The family points both to the past and the future so that the family is not merely the father's house but the house of the fathers. "It is the continuity that makes the father's house and family."[31] This can be seen in the genealogies of Jesus in Luke and Mathew, where both the continuity and discontinuity are laid out. Through his adoptive father, Jesus' human ancestry is traced back to Abraham (Matthew) and Adam (Luke). In *Redemptoris custos,* the pope cites the liturgy for the Feast of St. Joseph, "God placed him [Joseph] at the head of the family, as a faithful and prudent servant, so that with fatherly care he might watch over his only begotten son" (RC 8). His fatherly authority was exercised with love coming from the Father "from whom every family in heaven and earth is named" (Eph.3: 15). Once again John Paul II refers to the fulfillment of the Old Testament in the life of the Holy Family. This is particularly true of Joseph naming Jesus, thus declaring his own legal fatherhood and performing the ceremony of circumcision, the first religious obligation of the father. As the pope says:

> As with all the other rites, circumcision is "fulfilled" in Jesus. God's covenant with Abraham, of which circumcision was the sign (cf. Gen 17:13), reaches its full effect and perfect realization in Jesus, who is the "yes" of all the ancient promises (cf.2 Cor 1:20).

Now it is baptism, not circumcision, prefigured by the baptism of John (Mt 3:11) that initiates the child into the New Covenant, as heir to all the promises of the Old Covenant as well.

The celebration of Sunday, which harks back to but replaces the Jewish Sabbath, which was observed both in the home and in the Temple, John Paul

II observes is of particular significance for family life. As part of the "important task of 'raising' Jesus, that is, feeding, clothing and educating him in the Law and in a trade with the duties of a father" (RC 16), the Sabbath observance was primarily Joseph's responsibility as it is for every Christian father to keep Sunday holy.[32]

> Remember the Sabbath day to keep it holy. Six days you shall labor and do all your work; but the seventh day is a Sabbath to the Lord your God . . . . for in six days the Lord made heaven and earth, the sea, and all that is in them and rested the seventh day and hallowed it (Ex. 20:8-11).[33]

and

> Observe the Sabbath Day to keep it holy, as the Lord your God commanded you. Six days you shall labor and do all your work; but the seventh day is a Sabbath to the Lord your God . . . .You shall remember that you were a servant in the land of Egypt, and the Lord your God brought you out thence with a mighty hand and an outstretched arm; therefore the Lord your God commanded you to keep the Sabbath day (Deut. 5: 12-15).

These two scriptural readings provide two different reasons for observance of the Sabbath, creation (Exodus) and redemption from slavery (Deuteronomy). According to contemporary Jews, "Every Shabbat, when we lift the *Kiddush* cup for blessing, we remember the One who created the universe and blessed our people with freedom."[34] The Sabbath is intrinsically bound up with both action and refraining from action since the Jewish religion is one that is based more on action, *mitzvah,* than creed.[35] This action includes the *mitzvah* of joy, of sanctification and of rest on the Sabbath. It also encompasses a variety of physical acts in preparation such as cleaning, cooking and decorating the table; almsgiving; lighting the Sabbath candles, reciting the *Kiddush* or blessing over the wine, delighting in the Sabbath meal. While the observance of

Sabbath distinguishes the Jewish people as a covenant people, it is primarily a family event. For example the lighting of candles in the synagogue is no substitute for the lighting of candles (*headlakat hanerot*) in the home, which marks the beginning of the Sabbath. Two candles are customarily lit, "corresponding to the words, *Zachor* ("Remember') and *Shamor* ("Observe") in the two versions of the Decalogue."[36] The candles are a symbol of holiness.

With Christ's resurrection on the 8th day of the week, Sunday as the day of the "new creation replaced the Jewish Sabbath. In the apostolic letter, *Dies Domini* John Paul II called it "the day which recalls in grateful adoration the world's first day and looks forward in active hope to "the last day," when Christ will come in glory (cf. *Acts* 1:1-11; *Th* 4:13-17) and all things will be made new" (DD 1). The Sabbath, according to the first pages of the bible, was instituted when God rested on the seventh day after creating the world. The Old Testament also links the Sabbath to the liberation of the Jews from Egypt so that there is both a distinction and close connection between the orders of creation and salvation. The pope points out that both covenants are set within the bridal relation of God with his People; in other words not within cultic stipulations but within the ethical context of how to live the moral life in Deuteronomy. "Israel and then the Church declare that they consider it not just a matter of community religious discipline but a defining and indelible expression of our relationship with God" (DD 13).

The very heart of Sunday is the obligation to take part in the Eucharistic Assembly; the *dies Domini* is also the "*dies Ecclesiae"* since not only the resurrection but the Church was born at Pentecost on a Sunday (DD 35). It is also the *dies homini;* just as the Jews were expected to celebrate the Sabbath with the mitzvah of joy so Christian families are called in the same way. There is no necessary conflict between Christian joy and true human joys. The pope notes the importance of a day of rest both for worship and for rest from labor in civil society. "Rest is something "sacred," because it is man's way of withdrawing from the sometimes excessively demanding cycle of earthly tasks in order to renew his awareness that everything is the work of God" (DD 64). Activities chosen should always enhance the spiritual life of the family, its solidarity and dignity.

Man's Work

As was noted in earlier chapters on St. Joseph and the Holy Family, his work as a carpenter was singled out. For example, "The Excellencies of St. Joseph" by Jerónimo Gracián, St. Theresa of Avila's spiritual director, was initiated by a carpenter's guild in Rome. Joseph's role as manual worker particularly came to the fore with the advent of the industrial revolution in the 19th century. Leo XIII especially commends him as model for all "the poor and those who live by the labor of their hands."[37] Benedict XV at the outbreak of communism warns: "Those who make their living by their labor are especially at risk from the contagion of socialism." Therefore St. Joseph is proposed as a *model.* The Son of God wished to be called the son of a carpenter (*fabri filius*) and graced Joseph with outstanding virtues, which was fitting for the spouse of the Blessed Virgin and "putative" father of Jesus Christ. "So let the poor not trust in the promises of seditious men, if they are wise, but in the example and patronage of the blessed Joseph and in the maternal care of the Church." [38]

Later Pius XI exclaimed:

> In a life of faithful performance of everyday duties, he left an example for all those who must gain their bread by the toil of their hands. He won for himself the title of "The Just," serving thus as a living model of that Christian justice which should reign in social life.[39]

Work, St John Paul II stressed even more is "the daily expression of love in the life of the Holy Family" (RC 22). "If the Family of Nazareth is an example and model for human families, in the order of salvation, so too, by analogy, is Jesus' work at the side of Joseph the Carpenter" (RC 22). In this way human labor, especially manual labor, was redeemed. Work that transforms nature and man himself is a human good reaching back to God's command to Adam and Eve at creation, which with Original Sin had become arduous and dehumanizing. With redemption in Christ, the pope sees it as belonging to the sanctification of daily life and showing that great deeds are not necessary to become a true follower of Christ. The pope notes that the Gospel gives work, especially manual labor, a prominent place. Work itself was taken up in the mystery of the Incarnation by the Son of God sharing in the work of Joseph for so many years (RC 22).

In *Laborem exercens* John Paul II's encyclical letter on human work, he refers twice to Christ's work in the family of Nazareth, pointing out the importance of the subjective dimension over the objective. It is not so much what work is done but man as subject. His dignity must always be safeguarded. Just as through his work, Joseph supported the Holy Family, "work constitutes a foundation for the formation of *family life*, which is a natural right and something man is called to . . . In fact the family is simultaneously a *community made possible by work* and the first *school of work,* within the home, for every person" (LE 10). Here one might note the different work that belonged to Joseph as father in the education of Jesus.

Motherhood

The Meaning of Motherhood

Now let us turn to Mary's motherhood. In the encyclical letter, *Redemptoris Mater*, John Paul II was intent on highlighting Mary's ecclesial role. It was a year later that he placed in dialogue her physical maternity with that of women in the apostolic letter, *Mulieris Dignitatem.* Released at the end of the Marian year, it was in response to the request of the Synod of Bishops for a greater understanding of the anthropological and theological bases of the dignity of being a man and a woman in order to address contemporary problems in Church and society first and foremost related to women. In the first part the pope highlights Mary's role as *Theotokos*, mother of God, pointing out that in the sending of the Son "a woman is at the center of this salfivic event" (MD 3). Mary is truly God's mother "because motherhood concerns the whole person, not just the body nor even just human nature" (MD 4). The grace that was given to her to fulfill her role as mother he says "signifies the fullness of perfection of 'what is characteristic of woman,' of 'what is feminine'" (MD 5). Motherhood, belongs intrinsically to the personal dignity of woman. Even before motherhood, the union with God, which was uniquely Mary's as *Theotokos,* determines in some way the dignity of all human beings.

In *Mulieris Dignitatem* the pope refers to the 'beginning.' All men and women derive their dignity from the common 'beginning' with the creation of Adam and Eve. "Man is a person, man and woman equally so" (MD 6). This is stressed again and again. "Both man and woman are human beings to an equal degree, both are created in God's image" (MD 6). Therefore any relation between them must affirm them both as persons. But man exists always as a "unity of the two" since "being a person in the image and likeness of God . . . also involves existing in relationship, in relation to the other "I". . . "To be human," he says, "means to be called to interpersonal communion" (MD 7). That is an "indispensable point of departure." Woman has been entrusted to man both as sister in humanity and as spouse. She must always be treated as a gift not an object of use.

Having defined the two essential aspects of woman's dignity and vocation, union with God (as virgin) and motherhood, present in a complete way in Mary, John Paul II recalls the biblical anthropology, beginning with Genesis that he developed in his Wednesday Catechesis. The equal dignity of man and woman in the "beginning" is put at risk by the sin of Adam and Eve. Their disobedience to God obscures their creation in His image and likeness. When they cease to treat each other as a gift, wanted for their own sake, their *communio personarum* is fractured and distorted. This is especially disadvantageous for the woman. The biblical phrase, "Your desire shall be for your husband and he shall rule over you (Gn. 3:16)" points to the disturbance in the communion of persons, "since domination takes the place of 'being a sincere gift' and therefore living 'for' the other (MD 10). In *Mulieris Dignitatem* the pope holds up Mary as the new Eve, who, by her obedience to God, reverses Eve's disobedience to God.

> In Mary, Eve discovers the nature of the true dignity of woman, of feminine humanity. This discovery must reach the heart of every woman and shape her vocation in life (MD 11).

In Mary the two vocations of women, motherhood and virginity are united. John Paul II addresses physical motherhood first. There are three specific points he wishes to make: (1) "motherhood implies a special openness to the new person (MD 18); (2) motherhood is linked to the concept of gift and (3) both the man and the woman share parenthood. In this section only the first two will be considered.

Openness to the New Person and Mary's Motherhood

The pope speaks of motherhood having "a special communion with the mystery of life as it develops in the woman's womb" (MD 18). He draws attention to the confirmation of this observation in scientific analysis but warns against remaining at the biophysiological level, since it is linked to the concepts of person and gift. Ratzinger notes how contemporary culture trivializes sex and the body. While it seems to bring man and woman freedom, treating biology as a mere thing affects the deepest being especially of women because woman is "the true keeper of the seal of creation."[40] Since marriage and family are the "sacrament of creation" in John Paul II's language, how can the Holy Family and Mary, specifically, speak to the couple when there was no one-flesh union of conjugal intercourse and the Tradition of the Church holds that Christ's birth took place with her virginity in-tact?[41]

We have already seen how from the time of the Fathers, special significance was given to Christ dwelling in Mary's womb, and the 17th century French School embraced a spirituality of both the womb and the heart. What was unique to the Middle Ages was a veneration of the nursing Madonna. In nursing the child, a woman expresses a profound openness to the new person. (See chapter 4 and next chapter.)

Motherhood as Self-Gift

In *Redemptoris mater* John Paul II relates how Mary understood her motherhood as total self-gift to Christ in God's plan of salvation. We have already seen how from the Fathers of the Church through the Middle Ages and beyond, Mary's self-gift of conceiving Christ in her womb was celebrated.[42] It was uniquely in the Middle Ages that her self-gift of nursing her Son was praised and held up as a model for mothers' own bodily self-gift. Caroline Walker Bynum, who has studied women's medieval religious practice extensively, speaks of "the new religious significance of the body acquired in the period, 1200-1500."[43] Medieval thinkers both emphasized the soul body unity and associated the body with woman. They also associated the body with God, more than the early Church Fathers. "The body of Christ was sometimes depicted as female in medieval devotional texts—partly, of course, because *Ecclesia,* Christ's body, was a female personification, partly because the tender nurturing aspect of God's care for souls was regularly described as motherly."[44] In art, there were images of Mary as priest offering the flesh of God in the Eucharist. Hildegard of Bingen repeatedly supported the denial of the priesthood to women because they were "the body of Christ not merely his representatives."[45] This flowed from the fact that Christ's body came entirely from his mother and the Holy Spirit who is called the quasi-soul of the Church by Venerable Pius XII. Also, woman's body was associated with breast milk as the first essential food of the human being. Bynum calls the cult of the Virgin's milk, "one of the most extensive in late medieval Europe. . . The allegorical figure *Ecclesia* was also frequently shown as a nursing mother."[46]

Dominican Basil Cole calls a child's birth "an interpersonal event welcoming the newborn in the way of love."[47] He notes how a mother normally welcomes the child at birth through offering her breast and lists the many advantages, physical, psychological and spiritual that ensue. Mary, as a Jewish mother, was no exception. Cole comments that Mary's fulfillment of this role brought her many graces because her vocation was to foster maternal-infant communication and communion." [48] He goes on to say:

> Motherhood, like birth, is difficult, but with the help of natural inclinations, learned skills and God's grace, a woman can give herself to her infant's needs. The gift of nursing is a maternal sign of the donative meaning of the body (phrase of John Paul II) in the communion of persons.[49]

In a study of Mary and Jesus' maternal-infant bond, William D. Virtue concludes:

> Jesus and Mary as the exemplar couplet express the beauty and truth of the maternal-infant bond which is symbolically referred to in the two key sacraments of birth – Baptism – and of nourishment—Eucharist. Mary nursing Jesus is the moral exemplar of the first formation in a loving bond.

and

> In the moral theology of motherhood, the primary principle is that of embodied self-giving. . . . Through this motherhood "according to the Spirit," the child is opened up to the mode of existence which is charity, i.e., mutual giving and receiving in love – the mode of 'gift' – which is the life of God in the Triune Communion of Persons.[50]

It must never be forgotten that, important as the natural inclinations are in fostering communion on the human level, priority must always be given to communion with Christ, as Jesus responds in Luke 11:27-28. This is a consoling thought for those women, who, for various reasons, may be unable to nurse their children directly or are not given the gift of husband and children. In a profound sense, the self-gift of the spousal and maternal relation is a true analogy of spiritual openness and fruitfulness whether in the married or single state.

Transition to Motherhood

John Paul II notes the link between the woman's motherhood and the paschal mystery. The Gospel refers to the pangs of birth, but when a child is born the mother experiences joy (Jn. 16: 21-23). Mary, according to the Tradition experienced no pain in childbirth, such pain being a fruit of original sin, but she experienced the perplexity of Joseph on revealing her pregnancy. Thus many mothers may experience consternation at news of an unexpected pregnancy. John Paul II emphasizes the shared parenthood of man and woman as the fruit of their communion in love. "Experiences teaches," he says, "that human love, which naturally tends towards motherhood and fatherhood, is sometimes affected by a profound crisis and is thus seriously threatened" (LF 7).[51]

The Virtues of Motherhood

We have already referred to Mary's faith as her outstanding characteristic. Both Mary and Joseph were called to exercise faith to a pre-eminent degree. As we saw earlier *Karol Wojtyla* (John Paul II) refers to faith or the spiritual life being a particular characteristic of women.[52] In *Mulieris dignitatem* he highlights woman's call above all to love and be loved, which flows from her spousal role. "In God's eternal plan, woman is the one in whom the order of love in the created world of persons first takes root (MD 29). This section on *Mulieris dignitatem* is the most complete on the nature and dignity of woman.

> The bridegroom is the one who loves. The bride is loved. It is she who receives love in order to love in return. . . . The dignity of woman is measured by the order of love, which is essentially the order of justice and charity (MD 29).

In the call of the husband to love his wife in the Letter to the Ephesians, there must be a "fundamental affirmation of the woman as person" (MD 24). Woman has been entrusted to man as a task but she is also responsible for herself. In other words she must guard her own personhood. Both man and woman are called to interpersonal communion. Each strives for self-realization in order to become a gift to the other but a special prophetism belongs to the woman in her femininity since in the universal priesthood, both men and women are on the side of the Bride in relation to Christ as Bridegroom. In being equal to man as the image and likeness of God, woman is "equally capable of receiving the outpouring of divine truth and love in the Holy Spirit;" (MD 16) nevertheless the woman must not take on masculine characteristics in order to offset the domination that comes from original sin. As the pope says in "Letter to Women" too many women are still more valued "for their physical appearance than their skill, their professionalism, their intellectual abilities, their deep sensitivity; in a word, the very dignity of their being."[53]

As we saw, in motherhood the woman has a special openness to the new person, the child. The pope describes Mary's service in the home at Nazareth as an "authentic 'reign.'" She was first and foremost the "handmaid of the Lord" (Lk 1:38).

> Through obedience to the word of God she accepted the lofty yet not easy vocation as wife and mother in the family of Nazareth. Putting herself at God's service, she also put herself at the service of others."[54]

Serving others according to God's will is the true meaning of authority. As he said in his Apostolic Letter, *Ordinationio Sacerdotalis* on Holy Thursday 1994, "the ministerial priesthood, according to Christ's plan 'is an expression not of domination but of service' (No. 7)."[55]

Liturgy and Prayer

John Paul II does not spell out the particular role of the mother in fostering prayer in the family. Perhaps he thought it obvious from her close relation with the child. Certainly God's will cannot be discovered without prayer. The first real section on prayer in the family occurs in *Letter to Families*, although in *Mulieris dignitatem* he has said, "If man is the image and likeness of God by his very nature as a person, then his greatness and dignity are achieved in the covenant with God, in union with him" (MD 9). Its place in *Letter to Families* right at the beginning is significant. Prayer, the pope says must become a major part of the Year of the Family in the Church, "Prayer by the family, prayer for the family and prayer with the family.

> It is significant that precisely in and through prayer man comes to discover in a very simple but profound way his own unique subjectivity. In the human "I" the person more easily perceives what it means to be a person. This is also true of the family (LF 4).

The pope's concern here is to strengthen the subjectivity of each person in the family. In other words prayer is the foundation of the communion of persons in the family. . . It is also essential to the family as "domestic church, which he highlights in the document.[56]

Prayer does not directly enter into the section on the educational task of the parents, but one could say it is assumed from this early section. The more the family is rooted in prayer, the more it can fulfill its role in fostering a civilization of love. The pope calls the educator "a person who 'begets' in a spiritual sense" (LF 16) and this occurs in a major way from the very fact that the mother carries the child in her womb, which, in its turn, has an effect on the mother. It is clear from the Gospels, that Mary shared with Joseph in the rituals and pilgrimages to Jerusalem incumbent on the Israelite family.

Woman's Work

The place of a woman, especially a mother, in the public sphere arouses perhaps the most controversy today. While Joseph epitomizes the ordinary work the man does to put bread on the table, Mary is above all a mother. The pope has much to say about the particulate toil of women in the care and nurturing of children, without down-playing their public role. In the papal *Letter to Women* issued on July 10, 1995, John Paul II addresses the issue head-on. He begins by citing his word of thanks in *Mulieris dignitatem* "for the 'mystery of woman' and for every woman—for all that constitutes the eternal measure of her feminine dignity, for the 'great works of God,' which through human history have been accomplished in and through her" (No. 31). He then thanks women as mothers, wives, daughters and sisters, praising especially women's sensitivity, intuitiveness, generosity and fidelity. He thanks women who work for "an indispensable contribution to the growth of a culture which unites reason and feeling, to a model of life ever open to a sense of 'mystery,' to the establishment of economic and political structures ever more worthy of humanity."

Next he acknowledges the many abuses throughout history, even in the Church, that have prevented women from exercising their gifts on behalf of humanity. Such detriment of their dignity is in contradiction to the teaching of Jesus Christ in the Gospel. While deploring discrimination in the work place, he notes particularly discrimination against those who have chosen to be wives and mothers. He returns to his Catechesis on the Book of Genesis to affirm woman's equal dignity with man, the call of both to procreation and dominion over the earth but in different capacities. He especially praises women's work of education. Above all he holds up Mary as "the highest expression of the 'feminine genius.'" Through obedience to the word of God she accepted the lofty yet not easy vocation as wife and mother in the family of Nazareth. Putting herself at God's service, she also put herself at the service of others: a service of love. Precisely through this service Mary was able to experience in her life a mysterious, but authentic 'reign.' It is not by chance that she is invoked as 'queen of heaven and earth' (LW 10).

Mary and the Church as Feminine

Mary's motherhood from the Fathers of the Church into the Middle Ages was not seen apart from the motherhood of the Church. As Hugo Rahner states, "Mary, the mother of Jesus, in virtue of the ineffable dignity of being the mother of God made Man, became the essential symbol of the Church our Mother."[57] Again, "His own body He fashioned from Mary and the Church He fashioned from the wound in his side, when the spear pierced his breast and there flowed out for us the twin redeeming mysteries of the water and the blood."[58] Two other Scripture passages are cited for this identification, Jesus giving the "woman," his mother, to the care of St. John at the crucifixion and the descent of the Holy Spirit at Pentecost.[59] Mary is also identified as "Daughter of Zion;" she is the true Ark of the Covenant. Just as Yahweh dwelled "in the womb" of Israel, Jesus dwells in Mary's womb. "Everything said about the *Ecclesia* in the Bible is true of her, and vice versa: the Church learns concretely what she is and what she is meant to be by looking at Mary."[60]

With the identification with Zion, Mary unites the Old Testament with the New. Such a "typological identification" Josef Cardinal Ratzinger calls a spiritual reality that is rooted in the faith of the Fathers.

It was a favorite theme of the Fathers that, through her obedience of faith, Mary is the second Eve and like the Church is both Virgin and mother. Unlike the Church, she gave birth to Christ physically while Christians only give birth to Christ through the Spirit. Without losing her place in the communion of saints she is Christ's helpmate.[61] Above all, Mary has the mission of motherhood of the members of Christ. [62] Ratzinger points how out John Paul II "shows that Mary's maternity is not simply a uniquely occurring biological event; he shows rather, that she was and, therefore, also remains a mother with her whole person."[63]

Hugo Rahner throughout his seminal work, *Our Lady and the Church* emphasizes that in the Middle Ages, Mary was still identified with the Church. But it was in the early part of the Middle Ages that concepts of Mary and the Church began to be separated. Instead, "a tender human cult of Our Lady sprang up quite distinct from a merely legal view of the Church."[64] Rahner's volume was part of the recovery in the 20th century of the identification of the Church with Mary. Ratzinger concurs, saying, "It is, I believe, no coincidence, given our Western masculine mentality, that we have increasingly separated Christ from his Mother, without grasping that Mary's motherhood might have some significance for theology and faith."[65] The Church is more than a "structure and action: the Church contains the living mystery of maternity and of that bridal love that makes maternity possible."[66]

At the end of *Letter to Women*, this is what the pope wants to emphasize. Mary's femininity speaks of a true diversity of roles. In the sacramental economy there is "a kind of inherent 'prophecy' (cf. MD 29) a highly significant 'iconic character,' which finds its full realization in Mary and which aptly expresses the very essence of the church as a community consecrated with the integrity of a 'virgin' heart to become the bride of Christ and the 'mother' of all believers" (LW 11). Saints Catherine of Siena and Theresa of Avila, doctors of the Church, serve as examples of the genius of women. By emphasizing in *Redemptoris mater* Mary's pilgrimage of faith, John Paul is showing the path for all women to fulfill their vocation in the private or public sphere according to God's will for them.

Shared Parenthood

Although the mother's relation with the infant takes precedence in the early stage of life, John Paul II is at pains to emphasize the joint nature of parenthood. He writes:

> There can be no doubt that the *state of parenthood* in the man as father and in the woman as mother objectively produces *a new dimension, a new qualification, in their personal and social life.* The objective dimension, however, should be accompanied by subjective awareness and experience—in every single instance, in each conception and birth. Otherwise the *communio personarum is disrupted.* [67]

He reiterates that the man's fatherhood always occurs through the woman's motherhood and vice versa and it is through the *communio personarum*, which comprises an anthropology of gift, that the woman, especially, is confirmed in her motherhood. In his encyclical on women, the pope is emphatic not only that parenthood is shared, but that the woman has the more demanding part.

> It is the woman who "pays" directly for this shared generation, which literally absorbs the energies of her body and soul. It is therefore necessary that the man be fully aware that in their shared parenthood he owes a special debt to the woman (MD 18).

It is the task of the parents to make "a mature gift of humanity" to the child.[68] This they do first and foremost by who they are as persons and then by various educational activities. It is truly a gift of their whole being. Acknowledging different cultural milieus, the pope notes there are fundamental structures in the family that belong to it as a communion of persons. He turns to

Scripture for these principles. The parents wield authority over their children, which must always be exercised in an interpersonal atmosphere of love. Later in *Letter to Families,* John Paul II will admonish parents in reference to the fourth commandment of the Decalogue: "You parents, the divine precept seems to say, should act in such a way that your life will merit the honor (and the love) of your children!" (LF #15) While the Father's presence is beneficial to their children's formation, the pope cites *Gaudium et Spes*: "The care of the mother at home, which is needed especially by the younger children, should be ensured."[69]

The gospels tell us very little of the daily life of the Holy Family. Since Mary and Joseph were seen as an ordinary Israelite family, biblical scholars have extrapolated from what was expected of parents in such a family. The extended family was the norm both vertically and horizontally, whether living under the same roof or close by.[70] Matthew makes reference to Jesus's mother and brothers coming to see him (Mt. 8: 19-20). As noted earlier the Israelite family was *patrilineal* so that the ancestry of Jesus was traced through St. Joseph. It was also *patrilocal* (Joseph took Mary into his home) and *patriarchal*, the family was in the father's charge. The father's responsibilities rather than his privileges were stressed. These can be divided into those duties concerning fidelity to worship of Yahweh and instruction in the Scriptures; providing for and protecting the family; maintaining family well-being; and representing the family to the outside world. In addition, the father had special responsibilities toward first-born sons, which, the Gospels record, were fulfilled by St. Joseph together with Mary, i.e. naming Jesus, consecration in the temple and circumcision. As a "just" man, imbued with the righteousness of the Old Covenant, he fulfilled all these to a preeminent degree. The book of Proverbs presents a wife and mother of "initiative, creativity and energy." While she is subordinate, she is in no way subservient. The practice of family purity precludes treating the woman simply as a sexual object and was ordered to procreation as the fulfillment of marriage.[71] From both Mary and Joseph, Jesus would have learned the signs and prophecies recorded in the Old Testament of his heavenly Father's plan of salvation. As St. Luke records, when Jesus at the age of twelve "was found in the temple, sitting among the teachers and asking them questions. . . all who heard him were amazed at his understanding and his answers" (Lk. 2:46-47).

Familiaris consortio quotes Vatican Council II: "They (parents) have a most solemn obligation to educate their children" (FC 36). From the sacrament of marriage they are empowered for their vocation, which St Thomas compares to priestly ministry. Not only are they called to introduce their children into the mystery of salvation through attendance at the liturgy but they must educate them in prayer and evangelization. John Paul II sees two key principles in the rearing of children, (1) each person is called to live in truth and love and (2) all find fulfillment by a sincere gift of self. Since this is true both for the educator and the one being educated, the mutual communion of persons plays a vital role. Even before birth, the child is shaped in the womb by the mother and in turn influences her. The father's part is to recognize her motherhood as a gift and be attentive. Ultimately, the process of education by the parents and others leads to self-education. The child must in a certain way distance himself from his parents to find his own path. The true meaning of human education is to become a child of God and is "part of God's own pedagogy" (LF 16). Jesus revealed this dramatically in the three days he stayed behind in the temple at the age of twelve.

It is instructive to see how the pope views the solution to these challenges of maternity and paternity as belonging to its structure as a communion of persons. A brief survey bears this out. It begins with God's creation of man and woman in the likeness of Trinitarian communion. The family through fatherhood and motherhood "are a community of persons united in love *(communio personarum)*"(LF 6). "Only persons are capable of living in 'communion'" (LF 7). "Their unity . . . opens them to a new life, towards a new person" (LF 8). "The new human person is called to live as a person" (LF 9). "Marriage is a unique communion of persons, and it is on the basis of this communion that the family is called to be a community of persons" (LF 10). The common good is "the good of the person, of every member of the family community" (LF 11). "Education is thus a unique process for which the mutual communion of persons has immense importance" (LF 16).

> The family is a community of persons and the smallest social unit. As such it is an institution fundamental to the life of every society (LF 17).

When at the end of the Letter John Paul II describes "fairest love," it is in the context of the communion of persons in the Holy Family, the interaction of both Mary and Joseph in the upbringing of Jesus. Thanks to Joseph, both the mystery of the Incarnation and the mystery of the Holy Family came to be "profoundly inscribed in the spousal love of husband and wife" (LF 20). Just as Adam reveals himself to Eve, newly married couples reveal themselves to each other and become a new community in Christ with sacramental marriage. Mary was revealed to Joseph as 'sister and bride.' While Mary was the first to enter the great mystery of the Incarnation she introduced Joseph to it. Together they underwent the dangers surrounding Jesus' birth in Bethlehem and the vicissitudes of the hidden life of Nazareth. Just as the Holy Spirit made possible "fairest love" in the hearts of Jesus and Mary, so he does for each family. He ends the letter with a prayer: "May the Holy Family, icon and model of every human family, help each individual to walk in the spirit of Nazareth" (LF 23).

CHAPTER 7

Childhood Divine and Human

In the beginning was the Word and the Word was with God and the Word was God (Jn 1:1).

And the Word became flesh and dwelt among us, full of grace and truth; we have beheld his glory, glory as of the only Son from the Father (Jn 1:14).

THE WORD BECAME FLESH IN the womb of the Virgin. The Creator of the universe was born as a helpless infant, entrusted to the care of Mary and Joseph. The Incarnation of the second Person of the Blessed Trinity, the union of the divine and human natures, is the key to our salvation as it was succinctly expressed by the early Church Father, Tertullian, "*caro salutis est cardo.*"[1] It was with Mary's *fiat* at the Annunciation that "a decisive change took place in the relationship between God and material creation."[2] This change began in the Holy Family at Nazareth and our era has made a particular contribution to its meaning for marriage and family. As John Paul II said at the beginning of his pontificate:

> *This family is at the same time a human Family. . . .Holiness imprints on this Family, in which the* Son of God came into the world, a unique, exceptional, supernatural character. And at the same time all that we can say of every human family, its nature, its duties, its difficulties, can also be said of this sacred family.[3]

The last two chapters have considered the spousal "I-Thou" and paternal and maternal "We" relationships in the family and in the Holy Family from the point of view of the two persons who form the original bond of love. The fruit of their love is the child, in the case of the Holy Family, Christ, the Son of God. For a true communion of persons to flourish, each person in the family must be given full value and this is especially true of the child since the mission of the family is to "guard, reveal and communicate love" (FC 17). As noted earlier Angelo Cardinal Scola holds that for two millennia in the Western world, marriage and family were lived as an organic unity encompassing sexuality (the person, masculinity and femininity) love (marriage) and fruitfulness (family) but with the advent of contraception that synthesis was broken. The well-being of the mother-child communion, hence of the child, became a casualty of the increasing emphasis on the marital relationship, accompanied by contraception, medicalized birth and bottle feeding at the end of the 19th century. In the Catholic world, however, the icon of Madonna and Child kept the core significance of the child and childhood, even if its importance was not fully understood for the communion of persons in martial relationships.

This chapter will look at the meaning of childhood in the Holy Family and by analogy in all families.

An Apostolate of Childhood

John Paul II did not write an encyclical or apostolic letter on childhood per se, but his concern for the child is evident in his major documents related: to the family, *Familiaris consortio* and *Letter to Families;* to life, *Evangelium vitae;* and to men and women, especially as mothers and fathers, in *Mater redemptoris, Mulieris dignitatem* and *Redemptoris custos.* In an early Angelus address, he spoke of the significance of childhood:

> Christ attached enormous importance to the child. He made the latter almost the spokesman of the cause proclaimed by him and for which he gave his life. He made the child a representative, the simplest one, of this cause, almost a prophet of this.[4]

The pope emphasized that the child is a witness to the innocence lost by Adam and Eve. God the Father by calling us to his house, helps us to regain (not without much effort) that innocence so that the child becomes a source of hope. John Paul II even spoke of "the apostolate of Jesus" as "a certain apostolate of childhood."[5] In commenting on Matthew's gospel (18: 2-4), when Jesus drew a child to himself and presented him as the model for entry into the kingdom of heaven, the pope gave a symbolic significance to the state of childhood in itself.[6]

Hans Urs von Balthasar and Childhood

The 20th century theologian, who has done the most to uncover the significance of childhood as a state, drawing on Jesus' childhood and his words in the Gospels, is Hans Urs von Balthasar.[7] He notes that with Christianity came a change in attitude towards the child. The Greek word used for both child and slave is *pais* since the child was considered inferior like the slave. Specific Gospel events lie at the foundation of this new Gospel of childhood. Jesus calls a child to himself and says that unless you become like children you will not enter the kingdom of heaven (Mt. 18:1-3; cf. Mk 10:15). In John 3:10 he responds to a teacher of the Law about the necessity to be born again to enter the kingdom of heaven. In yet another passage he states that whoever receives one of these little ones in his name, receives Jesus himself (Mt. 18:5). "A child, therefore," says von Balthasar, "is not merely a distant analogy for the Son of God. . . [in welcoming any child] that person is welcoming the archetypical Child who has his abode in the Father's bosom."[8] He considers that Jesus' Sonship of the Father and our adopted sonship inter-penetrate each other. Christ's identity itself is "inseparable from his being a child in the bosom of the Father."[9] At the same time our rebirth in the spirit is inseparable from the mystery of Christ.

Nature of Human Childhood

What is it about the human child that reveals the nature of Jesus' childhood and vice versa? John Paul II speaks of the child being a witness to lost innocence. Von Balthasar describes this as the child living in a sphere of wholeness: "That zone or dimension in which the child lives . . . reveals itself as a sphere of original wholeness or health, and it may even be said to contain an element of holiness, since at first the child cannot yet distinguish between parental and divine love."[10]With the age of reason, the child must make a conscious choice of either good or evil at some point in his early life.[11] The original intuition of goodness, truth and beauty is clouded over. Adult morality often sets itself apart from the original intuition, seeing the good as a law to be obeyed in an abstract and juridical way. While Jesus sees this as an almost inevitable path of human development, he calls his followers to a maturity that embraces the original childlike trust in "Abba, Father!"

The mother-child relation has a critical part to play in development. Von Balthasar sees a double "arch identity" in the child dwelling in the mother's womb and then being born into visible reality. Although a profound unity exists between mother and child in the womb, the child is always a separate entity, comprising the seed of both mother and father from their one-flesh union of love. Furthermore, the child is a gift and not a possession since his spirit is infused by God, who has his own designs for him. The unity does not cease with birth, for the child at the mother's breast is like an extension of the child in her womb. As the child awakens to the love of the mother, her smile arouses in him a reciprocating smile so that the unity continues even if they are not physically joined. Von Balthasar comments: "The love between a 'Thou' and an 'I' inaugurates the reality of a world which is deeper than simple being because of its absolute boundlessness and plenitude," because love is both human and divine.[12] He calls this the original intuition of the unity of goodness, truth and being as a gift from God. If the unity between the parents or one parent and child is fractured or disturbed, it can cause deep wounds which may never fully heal psychologically. The helplessness of the child means it has a sacred right to care, but only the care given freely out of love suffices for proper development. When such care is given it is the nature of the child to respond with trust and later obedience.

Jesus' Childhood and Becoming God's Children

Jesus' childhood was unique as both divine and human. Because he had a "primal trust" in the Father through the Holy Spirit of love between them, it could never be clouded with mistrust. As the Father's love was always present, so Jesus remained a "child" even as an adult. He must reciprocate his Father's love with obedience. Von Balthasar says this does not negate the mother-child relation. On the contrary one might say that Mary's nursing of Jesus formed his foundation as man, with a parallel trust in being human.[13] More and more, psychology is uncovering the essential contribution of the mother-child relation for good or ill to the adult and adult relations such as marriage because the mother-child bond is a primary relationship which informs every other relationship.[14] Since both Mary and Jesus were sinless, Jesus did not suffer any wound in this relation, unlike the majority of human beings. More will be said later of the significance of these relations in the life of the child.

The apocryphal gospels in the early centuries and other narratives through the ages have attempted to fill in the silent years at Nazareth. "The human childhood of Jesus," says von Balthasar "is draped with closely woven veils; the attempt to lift them –through psychology for example—will always miss the mark."[15] Before turning to Von Balthasar's treatment of Jesus' identity and consciousness of his divine mission, it might be worthwhile to speculate on why the Gospels lift the veil when they do, with specific reference to the human family. This occurs in the first years of Jesus' life from his conception to the flight into Egypt; when Jesus was twelve years old; and at the beginning of his public ministry with the marriage feast of Cana. Might it not be because these transitional events are the ones that can be the most difficult for families? The conception of both Jesus and John the Baptist challenged particularly the fathers-to-be, Joseph and Zechariah. For both Elizabeth and Mary the pregnancy was unexpected, one occurring before a marriage is normally consummated and one at the waning end of fertility. Jesus was born in poverty in spite of being a king yet his birth was the occasion of great joy. The Holy Family suffered exile in solidarity with many families throughout the ages. For three days the Christ child was missing, causing his parents great anguish. On finding him in the temple, "his mother said to him, 'Son, why have you treated us so? Behold your father and I have been looking for you anxiously'" (Lk. 2: 48). At the marriage feast of Cana, Mary, herself, now totally trusting in her Son and his Father's plan for him, initiates his public life and his departure from her side (Jn 2:1-11).

Von Balthasar takes as his starting point Luke's words following the narration of the prophecies of Simeon and Anna and the return to Nazareth, "And the child grew and became strong, filled with wisdom; and the favor of God was upon him." (Lk 2:40) Like every human child, Jesus must have grown in stages. After cautious speculations on Jesus' burgeoning consciousness of his identity, the Swiss theologian avers that the first thirty years also give him an increasing understanding of his mission. Mary and Joseph through their instruction in Scripture, recitation of the psalms and attendance at the annual Jewish festivals, formed him as a son of Israel, which von Balthasar calls a certain divine Sonship. Jesus' own experiences of his deepening relation with his Father, combined with the prophecy of Simeon and the Old Testament promise of a messiah, who would be a light to the nations, must also have initiated him into his mission.

Human childhood, according to von Balthasar, presents a certain likeness to Jesus' filiation with the Father. Our own adoption as sons is not simply juridical but we are born again into Christ's Body, the Church, through Baptism and the Eucharist. As such we must become like him in childlikeness. Von Balthasar concludes his reflection:

> To be a child of the Father, then, holds primacy over the whole drama of salvation, since it is what leads the Son of God from his human childhood through his public ministry and rejection by man all the way to his high priestly office on the Cross. That same reality of being the Father's Child is what takes the Church, born herself as a child from the wound in Christ's side, up into the consenting realization of the priestly ministry of the Cross which is continually renewed in the Church's daily life and Eucharist.[16]

But human childhood also presents differences, since human childhood bears both the characteristics of the permanent childlikeness that ought to persist into maturity, and the immaturity and weakness that separate it from adulthood. Von Balthasar refers to at least three types of immaturity spoken of in the New Testament: (1) being untutored, (2) being untutored and therefore easy to lead astray and (3) being weak in faith. Jesus praises the wisdom of the simple, who grasp his message when it is concealed from the learned and clever (Mt 11:25 and Lk 10:21). He castigates those who would lead the simple astray (Mk 9:42) but St. Paul also compares new Christians to the child still needing milk (1:Pet. 2:2) because he has not grown into a mature faith. Above all, for Jesus, being childlike, which does not depend on age, means loving confidence in the Father and unquestioning obedience. He posits a strong link between his eternal relation to the Father and natural childhood. It is such childlikeness that belongs to those who would enter the Kingdom of God, expressed especially in trusting the Father to provide every need, including those of the body. This emphasis on the *Logos* as child von Balthasar calls unique to Christianity

In a reflection on what he calls the "logic of childlessness in modernity," David L. Schindler draws from the 1983 Lenten retreat preached by Joseph Cardinal Ratzinger on Jesus' address to his Father as "Abba."[17] Schindler asks how childlikeness can be a perfection in an adult. He classifies modernity as interested in "being" as only useful for man's construction, so that adult constructive power is given precedence over allowing something simply to "be" as given. The child and childlikeness witness to such givenness. "Birth and being born," he says, "reveal the logic of being given, of being from another and Jesus in his Sonship reveals just this logic of coming from another." For Ratzinger, the beatitude, "Blessed are the poor" applies particularly to the child, who possesses nothing yet is rich in who he is as a gift given by God. "Indeed Ratzinger says that anyone among us who is not able to sustain this sense of richness as given by God loses 'that childlikeness without which we cannot enter the kingdom of God.'"[18]

Human and Divine Trust

This trust in the Father, who is the source of both motherhood and fatherhood (LF 6), Von Balthazar sees particularly in the mutual smiles of mother and child. They bring about an "archetypical identity," since the mother's adoring gaze is a particular revelation for the child of who he is as a person regardless of his attributes. The child responds to this revelation with an answering smile. "Here is where the miracle occurs that one day the child will recognize in its mother's face her protective love and will reciprocate this love with a first smile."[19] Such affirmation, the Swiss theologian considers necessary for the child to awaken to his true dignity and uniqueness.[20] However, he asks whether this affirmation of the mother or any human being can secure the consciousness of the child in its uniqueness, for it can be withdrawn. Ultimately no human being can reveal to another who he is in himself. "The most emphatic affirmation can only tell him who he is *for the one who values him* or loves him."[21] Such knowledge of who he really is can only come from the "absolute Subject, God." Von Balthasar says this happened, when at the baptism in the Jordan, Jesus was given his eternal "definition" by the Father, as "my beloved Son" (Mt. 3:17).

As we saw earlier, Von Balthasar sees a difference between simply being a person and being a theological person when a person's mission is revealed to him. Jesus' primal experience of trust was in the Father. Yet he also had a primal experience "of being at home in the mother's bosom." [22] He asks how this dual experience can be accounted for? Since the deepest experience is of the Father's love slumbering in the Son's soul, the awakening by his mother's love radiates within him "the personal Face of his Father, personally turned towards him."[23] The sense of being a gift is mediated by both the mother and father and is so important that if a child misses what is proper to him as a human being, Ratzinger says, he "has missed him or herself." Man's original sin was to bypass childhood in favor of a false autonomy. As John Paul II says in the Wednesday Catechesis, "man turns his back on God-Love, on the 'Father.' He casts suspicion on creation as a gift" (JP II, MW 26:4).

In the ordinary child a distinction between divine and human parental love comes about quite late; in Jesus there must have been consciousness of his Father's love, at least implicitly, from conception. It is this consciousness of being the child of the Father that perdures into adulthood. For the human infant, the mother's love plays a much greater role for good or ill, either affirming the child's identity or fragmenting it, affirming what psychologist Erik Erickson calls basic trust in the goodness of reality or generating suspicion and doubt but the father's unique love is also important. We shall look at this in greater detail later in this chapter.

The Obedience of Nazareth

"And he went down with them and came to Nazareth, and was obedient to them; and his mother kept all these things in her heart. And Jesus increased in wisdom and stature, and in favor with God and man" (Lk 2:51-52). With these words, Luke completes the infancy narratives. Apart from the three days in the Temple at the age of twelve unbeknownst to his parents, Jesus' first 30 years were spent in loving obedience to his mother and father in Nazareth. John Paul II in commenting on these words, which describe the obedience of a son to his parents, noted how "this obedience of Jesus at Nazareth to Mary and Joseph occupies nearly all the years he lived on this earth, and is, therefore the longest period of that complete and uninterrupted obedience he rendered to the heavenly Father."[24] As a result, the mystery of our redemption belongs in a significant way to the Holy Family. The pope also sees in these words the educative aspect of the family.

> This submission, obedience, readiness to accept the mature examples of the human conduct of the family, is necessary on the part of children and of the young generation. Jesus, too, was "obedient" in this way.[25]

This places great responsibility on parents to model mature behavior. They must always keep in mind also that the child has been entrusted to them by God and they do not bring him up for themselves alone as Jesus taught Mary and Joseph when they found him in the Temple at the age of twelve.[26] This counterpoint between obedience to human authority and to God is brought out decisively by St. Ignatius of Loyola in the *Spiritual Exercises* in relation to the specific vocation God designs for each of us, religious and lay alike.[27] It presupposes obedience, especially, to the fourth commandment of the Decalogue to honor one's father and mother and at the same time, placing God's call paramount.[28]

Honor Thy Father and Mother

In *Letter to Families* John Paul II devotes a complete section to the Fourth Commandment of the Decalogue. He calls the family, its solidarity or interior unity, the real subject matter of the commandment. The word "honor" he finds particularly appropriate, because it expresses what the family is, namely a community of subjects; in other words, a communion of persons who should treat each other with honor.

> The family is a community of particularly intense interpersonal relationships between spouses, between parents and children, between generations. It is a community which must be safeguarded in a special way (LF no. 15).

The pope notes that the commandment is placed immediately after the three commandments that enjoin worship and love of God before all else. Because the parents have given life to the children and introduced them into a particular family line, nation and culture, they act in a way as God's representatives. They deserve honor which is "a certain analogy here with the worship owed to God" (LF no. 15).

John Paul II next asks if the fourth commandment is one-sided, demanding nothing of the parents. On the contrary, honor comprises both love and the allied virtue of justice. The pope links it to his philosophical concept of neighbor, asking "who is more of a neighbor than one's own family members, parents and children?" (LF no. 15). Since honor is primarily an attitude of unselfishness, it calls for the "sincere gift of self" that is at the heart of a communion of persons. So parents must deserve the respect and even love of their children, and if this does not happen, honor is still owed for having received existence from them, a debt which can never be fully repaid. Above all, it is in the family that the child learns how to be human, how to be a son or daughter of one's society and of the world. Can we say that Jesus learned from Mary and Joseph how to be human amidst the vicissitudes of daily life in Nazareth? The Holy Family was, indeed, imbued with an attitude of unselfishness, of sincere self-gift and mutual honor.

It has been pointed out that although Jesus declared that he did not come to abolish the Law and the Prophets, some of his sayings seem to contradict the commandments, none more so than the fourth commandment (Mk 7:9-11).[29] Reference can be made to Luke 11: 27-28 where Jesus exalted anyone who kept the Word of God over the mother who nurtured him or to Matthew 12: 46-50 when he called those doing his Father's will his mother and his brothers. In Luke 14: 27-28 his words seem harsher, declaring that no one, who preferred his mother or brothers before him, was worthy to be his disciple; or in Matthew 10: 34-36, where he announces that he had come to bring division even in the sanctuary of the home. John Paul II in *Letter to Families* notes that the commandment was given to fragile human beings as a "task" to be accomplished with the help of grace. We know that few mothers and fathers exercise their role faultlessly so that there is both need of the fourth commandment and the recognition that beyond human paternity there is the divine Fatherhood of God.[30]

When Jesus' urges that no one should call anyone on earth his father since only God is Father (Mt 23:8-9), this does not negate the human father but points to the same Father all have, which makes them brothers. The Father of Jesus Christ as creator, and together with the Son and Holy Spirit, redeemer and sanctifier, is more *real* than any human father because He is reality itself. Whatever is symbolic in human fatherhood or motherhood finds its ultimate source in the paternity of God. In this way, Christ, with these gospel sayings, "gives us the means to *discover* what in either of them is truly *symbolic;* he corrects for what is missing in life and whatever remedies psychologists and psychiatrists might try to apply to it."[31] Jesus, himself, perfectly witnessed the honor given both to Mary and Joseph as well as to his heavenly Father in the Holy Family of Nazareth.

The Analogy of Human Fatherhood in the Life of the Child

In commenting on the biblical portrait of God as Father, Scripture scholar, John W. Miller asserts that "Israel's faith in *God* as a dynamically caring father created an environment that gave birth to new modes of human fathering."[32] This became the context for Christian fathering. The significance of Abraham's near sacrifice of Isaac lies in Judaic rejection of infant sacrifice, which was prevalent in surrounding pagan cultures. The God of Israel was revealed as a caring Father, "a major force for good in the life of the world."[33] He was not only powerful and assertive, not countenancing any worship of an alien God, but he was the cause of creation and in his goodness liberated his people from slavery. By contrast, Mesopotamian myths portrayed a weak father, saved from destruction at the hands of his wife by a powerful and courageous son, who ruled in his place.

One of the chief ways in which the concept of God as a caring father was translated into human fathering was through the various father-friendly rituals. The redemption of the first born in the Temple recalled the substitute of a ram for Isaac in the land of Moriah (Gen 22:2). The father formally takes responsibility for the child. Procreativity and circumcision as a mark of the covenant are closely linked. During the ceremony those present respond: "As he has been entered into the covenant, so may he be introduced to the study of the Torah, to the marriage canopy and to good deeds."[34] Miller points out that while circumcision and redemption of the first born took place only once in the life of the child, Passover, commemorating God's deliverance of His People from slavery, was celebrated annually, and was presided over by the father in the home. "Through it fathers in Israel, as in no other culture we know of, appropriated to themselves an identity as redemptive caretakers, with an ongoing and permanent stake in the life of their families."[35]

Besides the witness given by St Joseph in the Holy Family, Miller proposes three ways in which Jesus fostered fatherhood. Firstly, he opposed the divorce allowed by the Mosaic law; indissoluble marriage is the foundation of the family. Secondly, he stressed the importance of children and modeled, as we have seen, the child's relation with the Father through the affectionate term "Abba." Thirdly, he himself modeled the Father.[36] So while Jesus' disciples replaced his biological family as an adult, the pre-eminence of the Father and his mercy, through numerous parables such as that of the Prodigal Son, took central place in his preaching and his actions. This translated into an emphasis on spiritual fatherhood, especially in the West with the rise of the monastic movement and the celibacy of the priesthood.

Raising and educating children in the home also involves spiritual fatherhood. As noted before, according to John Paul II, "the educator is a person who begets in a spiritual sense" (LF 16). All education must be given in love, with the love between the parents being the primary teacher. "Kindness, constancy, goodness, service, disinterestedness and self-sacrifice are the most precious fruits of love" (FC 36). In both *Familiaris consortio* and *Letter to Families* the pope devotes whole sections to the education of children. Since that has been dealt with in a previous chapter, here the "unique and irreplaceable importance," in John Paul II's words, of the father is stressed.

> As experience teaches, the absence of a father causes psychological and moral imbalance and notable difficulties in family relationships, as does, in contrary circumstances, the oppressive presence of a father, especially where there still prevails the phenomena of "machismo," or a wrong superiority of male prerogatives which humiliates women and inhibits the development of healthy family relationships (FC 25).

Distinguished psychologist Paul Vitz has made a study of leading atheists in Western society and their experience of either absent or abusive fathers. Vitz states that "in the Judeo-Christian view, God can be understood as a perfect attachment figure: an all-knowing, all-powerful, all-loving personal being available throughout life to provide safety in times of distress."[37] He reports that a new theory of atheism as the defective father hypothesis has been developed as an extension of the attachment insecurity hypothesis in childhood.[38]

Joseph, Shadow of the Father

Joseph has been called "adoptive father" just as we are called "adoptive children of the Father." A chapter in a book on adoption in Australia is entitled, "The Shadowy Fathers."[39] The term "shadowy" is coined to indicate the continuing presence of the birth father in the life story of his child. This is the negative side of the term "shadowy father," illuminating both the presence and absence of the birth father. French author, Andrew Doze, calls St. Joseph, "Shadow of the Father" illuminating the presence of God the Father in the fatherhood of the saint. He links him to the pillar of the cloud that hovered over the Israelites as they escaped from Egypt and which went before them in the desert for forty years. This exodus was foretold by the patriarch Joseph, with whom Mary's spouse is often compared and whose bones were taken to the Promised Land (Ex 13:19). Doze writes: "Joseph is the one in whom the father conceals himself to welcome this child and, in turn, to hide it, to surround it with love, to protect it, to help it to increase in every way."[40] After the episode in the temple, where Jesus' divine Fatherhood is made manifest, the Son disappears into this "shadow" for eighteen years. Doze concludes that "this profound and lasting formation would have lasting effects on the life of Jesus as well as on the life of the Church of all ages."[41] Like the cloud, St. Joseph performed a protective role, which is uniquely that of a father and reveals the caring, nurturing role of God the Father.

The Mother-Child Relation

Fathering, according to Miller, "is a predominately cultural achievement, due to the fact that it is so much less nature-determined than is mothering."[42] While this is, no doubt, true since the child is conceived, gestated and breast-fed by the mother, modernity is more and more determining motherhood and childcare through technology and distance rather than through nature and presence. The womb is no longer the inviolable home of the growing infant. Apart from abortion, which is now widely and legally available, with reproductive technologies, the child can be conceived in a Petri dish and gestated in the womb of a woman who is not the biological mother.[43]

How is the Holy Family and above all, Mary, who conceived by the power of the Holy Spirit, the model for all children in whatever manner they were conceived, born and nurtured? When Mary gives her *fiat* to the angel for Christ to be conceived by the Holy Spirit, she shows the priority of God's loving action in the creation all human beings—whether conceived in conjugal embrace or through reproductive technologies. God chose a properly constituted Israelite family for his Son with two loving parents united in the bond of marriage, indicating the ideal setting for human flourishing. Yet he knew that, as a result of original sin, many, perhaps the majority of families, would not achieve the ideal. It was to save the human race wounded by sin that he sent his Son into the world. Through his Church he provided the healing presence of Christ and gave us his own mother to make up for the deficiencies of human mothering both through her example and care, and our devotion.

The Significance of Gestation and the Nursing Mother

Although there was no conjugal intercourse in the Holy Family, Mary engaged in a profound fleshly union with Jesus in nurturing him in her womb and at the breast. Could this not be a profound affirmation of the goodness of the body and its role in human love, whether in birth, gestation, breastfeeding or conjugal union? Theologian Fr. John Saward in his book, *Redeemer in the Womb* writes: "In the stable at Bethlehem, Mary can at last hold in her arms and feed at her breast, see with her own eyes, the Child-God who for nine months has been hidden in the hermitage of her womb."[44]

> Apart from the saving novelty of its saving manner, the conception of Christ is in all respects like ours. For us, then, as for him, it is the moment from which we are fully and completely human, endowed with rational soul as well as body."[45]

Saward focuses on the nine months Jesus spent in Mary's womb tracing its treatment in theology, liturgy, poetry and iconography from the Fathers of the Church through the Middle Ages and the Age of the Baroque to our own times. Apart from the Middle Ages, as we have seen, there has not been much reflection on Mary nursing Jesus, which is physically an extension of life in the womb.

The teaching of the Church, founded on the philosophy of Thomas Aquinas is clear. Nursing is a natural duty of motherhood and, therefore, in most cases, an obligation. Fr. William Virtue, who has researched the Church's teaching in this area, cites a Bishop Kelly Ross of Ireland as making one of the few ecclesiastical pronouncements in the 20th century on the traditional moral teaching on breast-feeding. Citing another source in 1907 he comments:

> The obligation of maternal nursing is of the constant and received *moral teaching* of the Church, as based on natural law as well as the revealed law of the Decalogue in the *fourth commandment* on *parental duties.* For centuries this duty was taught, and was in the moral manuals up to relatively recent times.[46]

Pope Benedict XIV (1675-1758), who headed the Church from 1740-1758, gave a comprehensive statement of traditional teaching on the moral obligation of maternal nursing. He drew on the commentaries on Genesis of Cornelius A. Lapide, S.J. and other Salmaticenses' summaries of the doctrine, as well as on Saints Gregory the Great, Clement, Basil, Ambrose and John Chrysostom.[47] The mother, indeed, is free of grave sin if she does not nurse, provided she has reasonable cause and provides a substitute, but he continues to affirm the duty of a mother to nurse her own children. Fr. Virtue goes on to argue that there has been a regression in Church teaching in this area.[48] Secular science has led the efforts to re-instate breastfeeding in western industrialized countries with mixed success and, at the same time, promoted its continued use in non-western countries.[49] In an address on breast-feeding, science and society organized by the Pontifical Academy of Sciences and the Royal Society of Great Britain in 1995, St. John Paul II commented:

> The very individual and private act of a mother feeding her infant can lead us to a deep and far-ranging critical rethinking of certain social

> and economic presuppositions, the negative and moral consequences of which are becoming more and more difficult to ignore. Certainly, a radical re-examination of many aspects of prevailing patterns of socio-economic patterns of work, economic competitiveness and lack of attention to the needs of the family is urgently necessary.[50]

Since the pope had already written his major encyclicals and apostolic exhortations on women, the family, the laity and work, he did not incorporate these insights into any major document.

Reference has already been made to the article by Niles Newton on the interrelationships between sexual responsiveness, birth and breastfeeding. Here it is pertinent to revisit it in more detail. Newton points out that the male has only one reproductive relationship with females, coitus, while the woman has three reproductive acts, two of which, birth and breastfeeding, are related to the child. Newton writes:

> The survival of the human race, long before the concept of "duty" evolved, depended on the satisfactions gained from the two voluntary acts of reproduction—coitus and breastfeeding (Newton & Newton, 1967. These had to be sufficiently pleasurable to ensure their frequent occurrence. Thus it is not surprising to find the following marked psychophysiologic reactions between lactation and coitus."[51]

Newton goes on to list them, from uterine contractions, including orgasm, to skin changes, and emotions similar to those aroused by sexual contact. Feelings of well-being are engendered by both. They are also similar in neurohormonal reflexes; sensitivity to environmental disturbances; and the triggering of care-taking behavior through the release of hormones, especially oxytocin and prolactin.[52] The physiologic acts, themselves, cannot ensure care-taking behavior but satisfying mating relationships traditionally have induced the man to protect and defend the mother of his child, and the woman to make a home for him and be psychologically committed. In a similar way, the ecstatic reactions of natural childbirth and nursing encourage maternal behavior.

Sheila Kippley, who, with her husband, John, has been a pioneer in promoting the Church's teaching in *Humanae vitae* and also breastfeeding, sees eleven "simple points of comparison between breastfeeding and the marriage act."[53] On the physical side, both are necessary for life, contribute to the health of the family, and, therefore, of society, and both involve physical pleasure. The two orders of nature and the personal order are intertwined. On the psychological dimension, both are freely chosen acts between two persons; the woman makes a gift of her body to her husband and her child; love comes about through physical intimacy and emotional bonding; and both acts involve a mutual gift of self, which unites them in love. In Scripture, the love of the spouses is an icon of God's love for his people (Eph 5: 21-33) and the mother nursing her child also reveals God's love (Isa 66:12-13). In the Middle Ages, as we saw, charity was depicted as a nursing mother and an analogy was made between the nursing Madonna and Christ feeding his people from the wound in his side. Finally, Kippley sees both acts as illustrative of the theology of the body.[54]

From John Paul II to Pope Benedict XVI, there has been a greater appreciation than in previous centuries of passion in betrothed union both spiritual and physical.[55] Pleasure accompanies both. Could one not regard the physical, nurturing relationship in gestation, birth and breastfeeding of Jesus and Mary as a perfect fleshly union, dissimilar in the freedom from original and all other sin of the mother and in the holiness of the Child but similar in self-donation of body and soul. Even though there was no one-flesh union between Mary and Joseph, their total self-gift was expressed virginally which shows the priority of the eschatological state. Yet the fleshly union between Mary and Jesus affirms the goodness of the body and its ordination to love.

The Family as a Communion of Persons and Nursing

How, then, does maternal nursing contribute to the family as a communion of persons? Some authors refer to the "enfacement" phenomenon. Margaret Miles, citing Jessica Benjamin, writes: "Within a few weeks after birth, the infant has learned that he can expect to be fed when he is hungry, so that 'hunger may be less pressing than his interest in his mother's face.'"[56] According to Benjamin the infant needs to see the mother as a separate being, not simply as an object to satisfy his hunger or he will extend that into other interpersonal relationships, which then spreads out into culture. There needs to be mutual recognition and acknowledgement. She has coined the term "intersubjectivity" to describe this mutuality. Miles goes further: "Rather, the gaze of mutual recognition between mother and child is based on a fundamental *intercorporeality*, an erotic recognition of the other's body."[57]

Obviously the relationship between mother and child at the infancy stage is primary. It is advisable for the mother to "fall in love" with her baby. This is similar to, but distinct from, romantic "falling in love" leading to marriage. The experience is well expressed by Mayra Bloom, a breastfeeding mother. "What you cannot anticipate…is that you will fall in love with your child."[58] Then she refers to the "romantic isolation" that sets in when mother and baby are totally absorbed in one another. Citing Herbert Ratner, M.D., Rev. William D. Virtue speaks of the co-naturality of the mother with the child. For example, both have a smooth soft skin; the infant can only hear high tones like the mother's soprano voice; the infant needs to be cradled in the woman's soft arms; without peripheral vision, the eyes of the nursing infant focus on the mother's face.[59] There is a danger of the father feeling left out of this dyad. New research shows that father-infant attachment does take place and have coined the phrase "engrossment" for this phenomenon.[60] This left-out feeling can refer to the spousal relation as well. The father's role of presence and support, as well as the new mother not neglecting the spousal role, can restore the communion of persons in the family.

Giving the child to a wet nurse for a minimum of two years and sometimes for longer, often in the distant home of the care-giver, served to rupture the communion of persons in the family with unforeseen consequences. One of these consequences has been a negative effect on the moral life because, as John Paul II emphasizes in his encyclical, *Veritatis Splendor*, at the heart of morality is a loving interpersonal relationship, formed first in the closeness of mother and child.[61] The subsequent loss of the child-spacing effect of breastfeeding has already been noted, leading to hyper fertility, which in time fueled the demand for contraception. With the mass production of condoms in the 19th century, the technological separation of the procreative and unitive dimensions of sexuality began in earnest. The effects on culture already have been considered in chapter four.[62]

Significance of Dogmas of the Immaculate Conception and Assumption

As we saw in Chapter Four, both Protestantism and the Enlightenment espoused an ambiguous if not contradictory relation to the body and woman which resulted in a distortion of the communion of persons. Protestantism, on the one hand, elevated the companionship of the couple in marriage to one of greater mutuality; on the other, it denied the woman a public role and eventually, by embracing divorce and contraception, put marriage and motherhood in jeopardy. With the rejection of Mary as *theotokos*, the sacraments and the Church, the feminine role in salvation was obscured. The Enlightenment went further in fracturing the communion of persons. Although it ostensibly promoted the freedom and subjectivity of the individual, it damaged its innate relational identity by rejection of God and endorsement of contractual relations even in marriage. The significance of the body making visible what is invisible, which will be brought our further in the next chapter, became problematic.

Certainly the declaration of the dogma of the Immaculate Conception came significantly on December 8, 1854 when attacks on the body had accelerated through the spread of contraception. When rubber was vulcanized in 1843, it enabled the mass production of the condom. Historian, Rudolf Binion, as we saw in Chapter Three, has chronicled the negative effect on the family expressed in the fiction of the time:

> What gave rise to this mainstream fictional repudiation of the family throughout Europe that began around 1879? The first place to look for an answer is the family itself, to see if something there did not change radically in those same years. And something there did change radically. For those were the years when conjugal birth control first spread.

The dogma of the Assumption, by which it was confirmed that Mary's totally sinless body was assumed into heaven, was also promulgated at a significant time, in 1950, just a decade before the mass use of hormonal contraception, which fueled the sexual revolution of the 1960s and less than 25 years before Roe vs. Wade, which enshrined abortion as a right in the U.S. Constitution. What the bodily Assumption of Mary into heaven teaches, among other lessons, it seems to me, is the goodness of the fleshy unions of birth, gestation, maternal nursing and conjugal union when rightly ordered. They are designed to nourish the union of all three persons in the family, a communion that is gravely disturbed by contraception, abortion and reproductive technologies, all of which attack the child. Both Mary and St. Joseph are witnesses to the priority of union with Christ and spiritual fruit in marriage. Nevertheless, as this book has sought to show, the fleshly unions of both the marital and nursing couple are good in themselves and ordered to communion. It is not insignificant that St. Joseph was called to the sacrifice of physical union, which is generally hardest for the male.[63] Mary, on the other hand enjoyed a profound physical union with Jesus through breastfeeding, which is the union that women are most likely to reject or cut short.

From this it can be seen on the one hand how pivotal the child (an adopted child or spiritual fruit for those unable to conceive) is to the communion of persons in the family and on the other how a true communion of persons, which gives full value to the unity of body and soul, ensures the physical and spiritual flourishing of the child. In all this, the Holy Family is an exemplary model.

CHAPTER 8

Presence, Divine and Human in the Family

THE PRECEDING THREE CHAPTERS HAVE focused on the nature of the family as a communion of persons modeled on the Trinity and the Christ-Church union. They have tried to show in what ways the Holy Family, although centered on a divine Person and characterized by the virginity of Joseph and Mary, can be a true model for human families. To accomplish this, the different dimensions of being a communion of persons have been presented, from what it means to be a person, to the spousal union, paternity and maternity and childhood. This chapter initially has two, purposes, (1) to show that Christ, as the Son of the Father in the Blessed Trinity, is also at the center of Christian families through the baptism of each member and (2) to begin to unpack the significance of Christ's presence in the family as a communion of persons in the manner of the Trinity and Christ-Church union. Special attention is given to the role of bodily presence for communion. This chapter, therefore, begins by considering the family as the "domestic church" through the perspectives of John Paul II, Scripture scholar Joseph Atkinson and Marc, Cardinal Ouellet. Ouellet is particularly concerned to rectify the lack of attention to fruitfulness as an essential element in a communion of persons, a lack, which he finds remedied, in the Church's teaching on responsible parenthood. After reviewing how Christ's presence in the sacraments transforms the Christian family into the "domestic church," the chapter moves to consideration of the meaning of bodily presence, both divine and human for the communion of persons. The initial guide for this section is José Granados, followed by consideration of the role of presence to fertility as gift and its signs in the body, which is at the heart of the OT practice of family purity and of the contemporary methodology of responsible parenthood.

The Presence of Christ in the Domestic Church

John Paul II

In *Redemptoris custos,* citing *Familiaris consortio,* John Paul II writes:

> The family has *the mission to guard, reveal and communicate love,* and this is a living reflection of and a real sharing in God's love for humanity and the love of Christ the Lord for the Church, his bride. That being the case, it is in the Holy Family, the original "Church in miniature *(Ecclesia domestica),*" that every Christian family must be reflected (RC 7: 19).

In *Letter to Families* John Paul II makes at least five references to the family as "domestic church," linking it especially to the "civilization of love." Right at the beginning he comments that Vatican Council, his perennial inspiration, applied the term to the family and he hoped it "will always remain in people's minds" in spite of changed conditions in the family (LF 3). He mentions it again in discussing the two civilizations, the anti-civilization of use and the "civilization of love" for it is in the family that the person becomes a sincere gift to another (LF 13, 14, 15); and he links it to *Gaudium et Spes* no. 22: "Christ . . .fully discloses man to himself and unfolds his noble calling" (LF 13). Again noting that in the "civilization of love" fatherhood and motherhood are critical dimensions, especially in the education of the child, the pope highlights their irreplaceable role of "religious education, which enables the family to grow as "domestic church" (LF 16). Finally he joins the meaning to the "great mystery" of Christ and the Church. In some way Christ's Incarnation is "recapitulate[d] in the event of baptism." He caps this by saying:

> The family itself is the great mystery of God. As the domestic church, it is the bride of Christ. The universal church, and every particular church in her, is most immediately revealed as the bride of Christ in the domestic church and in its experience of love: conjugal love, paternal and maternal love, fraternal love, the love of a community of persons and of generations (LF 19).

JOSEPH ATKINSON

Scripture scholar, Joseph Atkinson, in his study of the biblical foundations of the domestic Church, explains that the Hebrew concept of corporate personality carried over into the New Testament and is crucial in understanding the effects of baptism in the family.[1] Referring to St. Paul in 1 Cor.7:12-16 on the marriage of a pagan to a Christian, he shows how everyone in the family is affected by the baptism of one. *"The family is, therefore, a privileged place where Christ in one member affects the many;"*[2] and "Through Baptism, the family becomes a sphere of eschatological activity."[3] He goes on to say that "the early Church Fathers were particularly sensitive to this transforming effect of baptism on the whole family, its new identity in Christ, and its role in the order of salvation."[4] The most important texts of the Fathers are to be found in St. Augustine and St. Chrysostom. Atkinson finds in St. Augustine, especially, a warrant for the family as domestic Church. He was, for example, the only Church Father to use the term directly. St. Augustine fostered the concept of the holiness of marriage, which includes conjugal union. Marriage, redeemed by Christ, he infers is a vocation. Although Augustine does not use the term "vocation," he employs many equivalent terms, such as *professio, officium, vita, genus.* Atkinson concludes that as a result of baptism: "Christian marriage was clearly one of the 'ways of life' which was *situated* in the Body of Christ and participated in the activity of the Holy Spirit." [5]

Marc Cardinal Ouellet

While Atkinson comes to the "domestic Church" from the point of view of Scripture and corporate personality, Ouellet reflects on the Trinity-family relations from the perspective of the family's participation in the mystery of the Church. Like Atkinson, he notes that Vatican Council II re-introduced the term, domestic Church, into the contemporary theology of the family. Both Paul VI and John Paul II elaborated on its meaning. Ouellet states:

> The search for a Trinitarian anthropology of the family passes through the theme of the domestic Church which concretizes, as it were, a new dimension of the relationship between the Trinity and the family, namely the dimension of grace or, in patristic terms, the dimension of the divine likeness in view of which the image was created. . . We must now enter into that "sanctuary of life" the family, to discover the "Presence" which gives to each person and to the communion of persons a sacred and inviolable character.[6]

As noted earlier, the Holy Family has been traditionally called an "earthly Trinity" from the presence of the second Person of the Blessed Trinity. In a similar way, it is the presence of Christ in the baptized members of the family that constitutes it as a "domestic Church," called to love in the image of the Trinity.

Through an in-depth analysis of *Familiaris consortio*, Ouellet discovers three categories in the text related to the domestic Church: (1) an actualization of ecclesial communion by the Word, the sacraments and by its unity; (2) its evangelizing mission; and (3) as a domestic sanctuary of prayer and worship. These are an actualization in the family of the principal characteristics of the Church, communion, mission and worship. The family is not just an image of the Church but a true "ecclesial reality." This can be deduced from

Ephesians 5:21-33. The Christian couple participate in the love of Christ for his Church. As Eastern theologian, P. Evdokimov writes:

> By virtue of the sacrament of matrimony, *every couple marries Christ.* Therefore, in loving each other, the spouses love Christ.[7]

The Holy Spirit, the third Person of the Trinity, is the seal of their covenantal union.

Ouellet then turns to the theological foundations of the ecclesiality of the family. He draws particularly on von Balthasar, who, as we saw earlier, placed the primacy of Christ at the core of theological anthropology. [8] Like John Paul II he holds that the person's subjectivity is only formed in communion. It is constituted by the interpersonal relations of the I-Thou-We. Human freedom is not autonomous but intersubjective and realized in a giving and receiving of love. The reason for this is because infinite freedom is a freedom of communion, "which engenders the other in order to be one with him in love."[9] In Christ, therefore, finite freedom can be provided a space of giving and receiving where it can be fulfilled in love. Christ is the original model of what it means to become a person in the event of the hypostatic union. In the same way, the persons in the family find their identity and mission in Christ. The person and community [of the Church which is the Mystical Body of Christ], interpenetrate. Since the interpersonal relations between the spouses are elevated by grace to the dignity of a sacramental sign of Christ's love for his Church, the Christian family can be said to participate in the mystery. Those "who are in communion by virtue of their mission constitute the very identity of the Church."[10] It is by virtue of communion that the Church is an *ecclesia de Trinitate* and the family an *ecclesia domestica.*

Interface of the Divine and Human

Fr. William Virtue, in his doctoral dissertation at the Angelicum in Rome, *Mother and Infant: The Moral Theology of Embodied Self-Giving in Motherhood in Light of the Exemplar Couplet, Mary and Jesus Christ,* seeks an understanding of the Incarnation, especially in the relation of Jesus and Mary in the

Holy Family. [11] He proposes a three-fold interface between the divine and human, grace and nature, in conception, birth, and breastfeeding in the Holy Family. Because of his divine nature God is not subject to the laws of nature in creation. The Incarnation introduced (or re-introduced, John Paul II might say, since Adam and Eve were clothed with grace in the Garden of Eden (MW 19:2) the principle of grace "that not only perfects the promise of nature but goes beyond to elevate nature to glory by participation in the divine life of God."[12] In the Incarnation, Virtue sees a dialectic of both presence and absence.[13]

While Mary provides Jesus' human nature in the conception, the human paternal contribution is absent. Here the supernatural predominates over nature. Although Jesus is gestated for nine months in Mary's womb, the birth is in some way miraculous in being free of pain and preserving her virginity (CCC 499). Again the divine predominates but the birth takes place within the natural order. Mary's nursing of Jesus, on the other hand, is wholly within the order of nature. Yet nursing, as we saw, is the apt foundation of a loving bond between mother and child. Since moral action flows from a loving interpersonal relation, it is also at the heart of morality. Virtue concludes: "In the exemplar couplet of Jesus and Mary all human conception, birth, nursing and bonding is taken up into the new order of grace...Jesus and Mary, in their loving bond, perfectly realize our covenant with God who is a communion of persons."[14]

Since, we have argued, the Holy Family is not the "ontological exception," the same presence and absence, same and other, is also characteristic of the human family as a communion of persons. The sacrament of marriage, as the foundation of the family, is first of all a created reality, which in the OT is gradually revealed as an analogy of God's spousal love for his People and in the NT of the union of Christ and his Church, especially in the Eucharist. (Eph. 5:21-33) In a very real sense, the divine predominates in the conjugal act, so that it is fenced around with more prohibitions both exterior and interior.[15] Procreation takes place in this act. Each child's soul is created directly by God who is love. It is, therefore, wrong to usurp God's authority over life and how it is achieved especially as he has designed the most loving way for a child to be conceived. With regard to childbirth, Virtue points out the acts of sexual intercourse and birth have similar physical manifestations. "Both involve the same canal and both have an ecstatic abandon. Both acts are about giving life."[16] Yet the divine still predominates; to destroy life in the womb or at birth is evil and an offense against God. With regard to nursing, which is wholly of the natural order, not to breastfeed is less grave, but the Church, as we saw, has always considered it a mother's moral duty to nurse her own child for the benefits of nutrition and bonding.[17]

Interpenetration of Divine and Human Love

This, being so, the family's essence and identity is ultimately defined by love, both human and divine. Ouellet traces the beginning of such a view of family relations to the encyclical, *Casti Connubii* (Pius XI, 1930). Vatican II further emphasized communion and the identity with Christ especially in *Gaudium et spes* nos. 22 and 24, which John Paul II made the foundation of his theological anthropology. The three traditional goals of marriage, offspring, fidelity and sacrament, received a new emphasis. Procreation as a distinct end was folded into "fruitful conjugal love."[18] The Catechism of the Catholic Church defines two ends of marriage, "the good of the spouses (*bonum conjugum*) and the procreation and education of children" (CCC 2249). (More will be said on the *bonum coniugum* later).

Ouellet then sees three focal points with regard to love as: (1) total self-giving, (2) openness to life, and (3) the sacrament of Christ's love for the Church. If the family does, indeed, find its model in the Holy Family, then Mary and Joseph witness to these three categories and are a credible icon of Christian family life. It is noteworthy that this new emphasis on love is first found in an encyclical whose main purpose was to reiterate the Church's two thousand year old commitment to the precept of God forbidding contraception, in the face of contemporary endorsement of contraception as the path to greater love in marriage.[19] The teaching from God, of course, was upheld by Pope Paul VI in the 1968 encyclical, *Humanae vitae*. While that document appealed more to reason,[20]a less well-known document, spoke eloquently of the love of the couple.[21]

It was to provide a more theological account of this teaching that John Paul II, even before he became pope, turned to Scripture to illuminate the doctrine, resulting in the ground-breaking Wednesday Catechesis on the theology of the body (MW 133: 4).

Ouellet begins by quoting *Humanae vitae* no.9. "Conjugal love comprises a totality involving all aspects of the person—the call of the body and instinct, the force of emotion and affectivity, the aspiration of the spirit and the will; it aims at a profoundly personal unity, one which, beyond the union in one flesh, leads spouses to become one heart and one soul: it demands indissolubility and fidelity in a definitive reciprocal gift; and it opens into fruitfulness."[22] Love is essentially a gift. By its nature, when the couple give themselves to each other, they also give the possibility of a third, the child, who is a living reflection of their love and gives them a new identity as mother and father. Contraception not only prevents the conception of a child but falsifies the language of total self-gift in conjugal union, so that it cannot image the union of Christ and the Church or divine Trinitarian communion. This is not the case with periodic abstinence because, unless motivated by selfishness, the couple do not sin against the fecundity of love. Each person is received in his or her totality as the natural periods of infertility of the woman are respected. Thus they engage in authentic conjugal intercourse. Such a method accepts the partner as gift received from the hand of a loving God. This is discussed more fully later.

Love as Fruitful

Since God is the author of life, when a couple close themselves to the generation of new life through contraception, they objectively exclude God from their marriage, no matter what their subjective desires may be. In doing so, they also exclude spiritual fecundity, which is the fruit and most important gift of marriage. It is the love between the Father and Son in the Trinity that generates the third, the Holy Spirit. As Ouellet says: "Human love is the reality which most explicitly bears the mark of the Trinitarian character of love."[23] In conjugal union, the couple transcend themselves, becoming fruitful in the bond of love itself before the child. In other words, thc spiritual fecundity of the bond, precedes the physical fruitfulness of the child. Such transcendence, according to von Balthasar, shows that the body belongs to the Spirit. He cites 1 Cor. 6: 19-20 where St. Paul calls the body the temple of the Holy Spirit.[24] It would follow from this that the love between Joseph and Mary was the first fruit of their marriage bond, which preceded the conception of Jesus. In this way, St. Joseph's love for Mary could be said to be a "cause" of the Incarnation, as John Paul II says:

> In the words of the "annunciation" by night, Joseph not only heard the divine truth concerning his wife's indescribable vocation; he *also heard the truth about his own vocation.* This "just" man, who, in the spirit of the noblest traditions of the Chosen People, loved the Virgin of Nazareth and was bound to her by a husband's love, was once again called by God to this love (RC no. 19).

He goes on to suppose that, with Jesus' conception by the Holy Spirit, Joseph's love as a man was also given new depth. And he asks:

> Are we not to think that the love of God which has been poured forth into the human heart through the Holy Spirit (cf. Rm 5:5) molds every human love to perfection? This love of God also molds—in a unique way—the love of husband and wife, deepening within it everything of human worth and beauty, everything that bespeaks an exclusive gift of self, a covenant between persons, and an authentic communion according to the model of the Blessed Trinity (RC no. 19).

Christ's total self-gift on the cross was the price for our bodies to belong to the Spirit. In the Eucharist, Christ joins us both physically and spiritually to himself. "That is why Christ's total self-gift," says Ouellet, "has become the model *par excellence* of the fruitful self-gift of the spouses; and this self-gift has become the sacrament of the union between Christ and the Church."[25]

Through the sacrament of marriage Christian spouses not only imitate but participate in Christ's gift of himself, combining their fruitfulness with his. Simply stated, Ouellet says, "The sacramental mission of the family is to mediate Christ's love for the Church, that is, the Trinitarian love for the world."[26] When their communion is not marred by sin, the spousal and familial relationships participate in the very relationships of the Holy Trinity. In this way the family is both a *saved* community, receiving Christ's love, and a *saving* community. For this, prayer and regular participation in the Eucharist are necessary. Nourished in this way, the family will increase in respect for the dignity of the human person, especially the woman, and rediscover the sacredness of human love, sacred because imbued with and witnessing to the love of Christ for the Church. Ouellet concludes:

> The covenant between the Trinity and the family in Christ, thus signifies a wondrous exchange of human and divine love in which spouses give their nuptial love to Christ and in exchange Christ gives them the very Love of God under the nuptial modality of the Gift of the Spirit. Such an exchange entails the demands of fidelity and fecundity.[27]

The Bonum Conjugum

To return now to the *bonum coniugum.* In 1983 with publication of the revision of the 1917 code of canon law, a new terminology entered the Church's treatment of the ends of marriage, the *bonum conuigum,* translated the "good of the spouses."[28] It then entered the new Catechism of the Catholic Church.[29] Little has been written on what actually defines this good, but former rotal judge of the Roman Curia, Cormac Burke, traces its origin to the new personalist understanding of marriage, in which love between the spouses was promoted sometimes even over the more traditional view of procreation as the end of marriage. He traces the official recognition of such a personalist understanding of marriage to the 1930 encyclical, *Casti Connubii,* which affirmed the Church's teaching against contraception. *Humanae vitae,* in its turn, spoke of the inseparable connection between the unitive and procreative dimensions of human sexuality. The Commission tasked with revising the Code of Canon Law rejected an individualist interpretation of the *bonum coniugum* as simply personal love, security and satisfaction but gave it a more objective sense. Burke calls the inseparability of the two ends, the *bonum coniugum* and procreation as the key. He cites the first pages of Genesis as the warrant for both, with the former coming from the Yahwist account of man's creation. He concludes: "The 'good of the spouses' regards not primarily their passing happiness but their maturing in the love that brings one to eternal happiness."[30] Both indissolubility and the care of children help to mature them as a couple. "Conjugality and procreativity taken together draw man out of his original solitude, which limits him as a person and is an enemy of his self-realization, of his *bonum*."[31]

Burke addresses both the new way of understanding consent as central to a true interpretation of the *bonum coniugum* and the personalist value of openness to life. He points out that Christian personalism is not self-centered individualism but ordered to self-gift, so that matrimonial consent is a pledge to both give oneself to and accept the other without reserve. Furthermore, since our true good is God himself, marriage is directed to the perfection of love and sanctification of the spouses. "Marriage is a genuine *vocation*, a personal call from God to a way of life aimed at achieving sanctity."[32] He goes on to develop a personalist argument for procreation and he cites John Paul II as saying that by destroying the power to give life, the spouses also destroy the power to give love. What makes the conjugal act unique in contrast to friendship is the power to give life. To give one's seed is much more tangible than words. The person says, "With you alone, I am prepared to create new life." When the life orientation of the conjugal the act is deliberately excluded physically or chemically, its essential power to signify union is destroyed. Here Burke echoes John Paul II's categorization of contraception as a lie and not love because it says, "I prefer a sterile you, not all of you."[33] Acceptance of the other without reserve is nullified. This emphasizes the centrality of the body as presence in conjugal love. As John Paul II says the body is spousal.

The Body: Touchstone of Presence

Christ began the work of salvation through his bodily presence in the womb of Mary, at the heart of the Holy Family. The work is continued through the sacraments of his Body, the Church, especially Baptism and the Eucharist. It is the burden of this section that, since the human being is a unity of body and soul, P/presence, both divine and human, is inextricably linked to the body, love and communion.[34] The section will begin with reflections by José Granados, who has made a study of the meaning of the body in theology, on a recovery of the language of the body by Vatican Council II, specifically in *Gaudium et spes,* (nos. 47-52), on treating of the family and its relationship to the human body, and the presence of Christ in the Church including the domestic Church. It will continue with John Paul II's encyclical letter, *Ecclesia de Eucharistia* with its frequent reference to divine presence. It will conclude with an excursus on "the face" in Scripture and the Apostolic Letter, *Novo millennio ineunte.* Moving to the human family, it will show how essential is the fullness of presence to a true communion of persons, drawing together the theology of communion laid out in the preceding three chapters as well as showing how presence to fertility as gift enhances the communion of persons.

An overarching purpose of Vatican Council II, according to José Granados, following John Paul II, was to bridge the gap between the objectivity and subjectivity of faith, in order to speak to modernity, which, since Descartes, had set human consciousness as the criterion of the freedom of an autonomous, self-enclosed individual. Only if human consciousness is founded on God's foundational love is the way open to relationship.[35] *Communio* was recognized as the key to Vatican Council II's response, especially in its teaching on marriage and family, where love, the body, person and communion are intertwined. *Gaudium et spes,* which took up the topic of marriage and family, was faced with the question of whether making love central, would blur the line between the objective and subjective aspects. Adopting the language of covenant rather than contract was a crucial move that allowed the language of love, responsibility, person and freedom to address the concerns of modernity. However, this raised two problems, first, how to integrate the personalist approach with nature, including fecundity and second, the relation of the family to society. Christian faith has always recognized the priority of the love of God, who is the author of marriage. As to the body and nature, an analysis of the bodily character of love was necessary. As Granados says: "It is through the body that man perceives an original language, a language he has not created but is nonetheless anterior to him, and that allows him to love."[36] The body is by nature open to the transcendent. Even though a full theology of the body was not developed until after the Council, the section on marriage and family in *Gaudium et spes* does give a glimpse of it.

Divine Presence

Granados draws particular attention to no. 48, which speaks of the human love of the spouses caught up in divine love as it is enriched by the sacrament of marriage and modeled on Christ's own union with the Church. By placing within the context of love the relation between Christ and human persons, the text makes it clear that relationship is what defines both Christian revelation and human nature. This context emphasizes the importance of the body, which is not closed but opens up through personal love to another. Granados goes on to say: "The relational nature of the body, which the sacrament of marriage makes explicit, plays a crucial role in the explanation of the way Christ is united to us."[37]In fact, he considers it a significant contribution of the Council "to present God in interpersonal terms, as a God who is love."[38] Also as a God who is available to us through bodily touch. The love God has for us takes on bodily form in the sacraments. It is here, says Granados, that the link between the body and love is critical for the question of God. God reveals himself, not just through the sacraments, but through words and deeds in history (cf. DV, 2). "This is precisely what the connection between the body and love tells us: in the experience of love the body is no longer seen as a limit to our autonomy, but as a place of encounter with others, as the beginning of a path toward ever new horizons, and thus as the perfect place for God [as Trinitarian communion] to appear in the world."[39] The connection of love with the body, which takes place concretely in the family, is critical for understanding God, so that how marriage and family are lived has a direct bearing on preaching the Gospel. The Church's mission today is to present a true understanding of love. This puts the family "at the center of the Church's presence in the world, inasmuch as it is in the family that love, true love, sustains its meaning."[40] And that love is connected to bodily presence both in the Church and in the family.

God's presence is especially associated with a physical space, from the Ark of the Covenant to the Temple. The Temple, as God's holy abode, must be kept from any type of pollution. The Jewish people themselves were called to be a holy nation and that entailed avoiding certain types of impurity. Two-thirds of the Purity codes of Leviticus, which are designed not so much to separate them *from* surrounding peoples but *to* God, concern the family. For physical and moral pollution affected not only the individual but the very tabernacle where God dwells among his people. As biblical scholar Gordon Wenham says, God's enduring presence, not simply in worship but in the ordinary circumstance of family life, is the defining feature of the book of Leviticus. Obeying the Torah, along with rituals such as sacrifice, preserved God's presence and holiness, especially in the Temple. A certain ambiguity surrounded the human body in relation to the Temple. Immoral acts such as adultery always required purification before entering the Temple. But certain bodily processes relating to sexual intercourse and childbirth, not impure in themselves but from their association with life and death, also required cleansing rituals, since everything associated with death must be kept from the dwelling of the immortal God. This changed with Christ's triumph over death in his resurrection.[41]

The new People of God is the Church. Here we turn again to Granados, who considers how the Church is present in the world. The family is crucial for understanding Vatican II's ecclesiology. According to *Lumen gentium*, two related terms define the Church, sacrament and *communio*. As a sacrament, the Church is a visible sign and instrument of salvation based on the Incarnation. "The consideration of the Church both as sacrament and as *communio*," says Granados, "points to the need to analyze the concept of the Body of Christ."[42] St. Paul's analogy, is not only that of the body/head relationship, in which the body is presented as an organism with all parts cooperating and animated by the Spirit, but "body" means for him also wife, thus including the nuptial dimension crucial to the Apostle. "The *una caro* of Adam and Eve points to the union of Christ and the Church, and this connection between the beginning and fulfillment constitutes a *magnum sacramentum*, a great sacrament, as St. Paul said."[43] It is from this bodily *communio* that all the other relations of mother, father, brother and sister, which are intrinsic to the *communio* in the family, take their origin. As Granados concludes:

> The Church's Temple, the only one she truly needs for her liturgy, is the temple of the body. Christianity does not depend on any concrete area of worship—not Jerusalem, not Rome—but it needs an area that is very real and concrete: the temple of the body. Marriage and family constitute the environment in which the body is honored as Temple and appears as such in the world.[44]

The Eucharistic Presence

The Body, par excellence, in the Church is the body and blood of Christ.

At the beginning of the encyclical, *Ecclesia de Eucharistia* John Paul II writes:

> The Church draws her life from the Eucharist. This truth does not simply express a daily experience of faith, but recapitulates *the heart of the mystery of the Church.* In a variety of ways she joyfully experiences the constant fulfillment of the promise: "Lo, I am with you always, to the close of the age" (Mt 28:20), but in the Holy Eucharist, through the changing of the bread and wine into the body and blood of the Lord, she rejoices in this presence with unique intensity (EE no. 1).

Throughout the Letter, the pope emphasizes presence along with the theme of the Eucharist as sacrifice and banquet (EE, 61). He refers to Christ's "saving presence"(EE, 9); "this central event of salvation becomes really present" and "This sacrifice is so decisive for the salvation of the human race that Jesus Christ offered it and returned to the Father only *after he had left us a means of sharing in it* as if we had been present there" (EE, 11). Christ's sacrifice in the Mass, John Paul II says "involves a most special presence," and he refers to the words of Paul VI: It "is called 'real' not as a way of excluding all other types of presence as if they were 'not real,' but because it is a presence in the fullest sense: a substantial presence whereby Christ, the God-Man, is wholly and entirely present" (EE, 15).[45] In the same way, it "absolutely requires the presence of an ordained priest" (EE, 29). He "alone is qualified to offer the Eucharist *in persona Christi.*" (EE, 32).

In the final chapter, John Paul II links the Eucharist to Mary and the Incarnation. "In a certain sense, Mary lived her *Eucharistic faith* even before the institution of the Eucharist, by the very fact that *she offered her virginal womb for the Incarnation of God's word"* (EE, 55). He sees a close analogy between Mary's *fiat* at the Annunciation and the faith of the Christian, who believes that in the Eucharist Christ is present in his full humanity and divinity. At each Eucharist, Mary is present as she was present at the Cross as the Mother of the Church and as our Mother (EE 57). "Gazing upon Mary, we come to know the transforming power present in the Eucharist" (EE 62). He links the beginning of the encyclical letter on the "Eucharistic face of Christ"(EE, 7) to the end where he recommends Mary as the guide in contemplating Christ's face.

The Face and Presence

The Israelites had strict laws against making any representation of God as a form of idolatry. Yet repeated references, especially in the psalms, are made to "seeking God's face." This exception of the "face of God," proposes Jewish-born physician and philosopher, Herbert Ratner, is linked especially to the face-to-face attachment of the nursing infant.[46] Ratner sees a powerful image in the one-flesh union of the nursing couplet of mother and child.[47] (In a succeeding paragraph, it is noted that the human is the only creature that has conjugal intercourse face to face which underscores the importance of the face in interpersonal communion.) The *humanus* is different from all other creatures in the way it communicates through the face. The newborn has an innate attraction to the mother's face.[48] The breastfeeding infant, (the norm in Israelite culture) with no peripheral vision for two months, is ideally positioned to fasten his eyes on the mother's face initiating a union of trust and love. Ratner points out how often the psalms petition to see God's face, which he traces directly to this experience, citing for a start: Ps, 67:1, "Make his face smile on us;" 31:14-16 "let your face smile on your servant;" 42: 1-2 "when shall I go to see the face of God?;" and 27:7-9, "Yahweh, I do seek your face; do not hide your face from me."[49]

Giorgio Buccellati, a scholar of Ancient Near Eastern Studies, has distinguished the absolute originality of biblical anthropology from surrounding polytheistic cultures. He has traced the concept of "person" and "Trinity" even in the Old Testament, which he calls the Catechumenate of the New.[50] He sees reference to the face as linked to understanding God as a person and ultimately the communion of persons in the Trinity. The Fathers of the Church made use of the Greek word for face, *prosopon* to illuminate the Trinity as a communion of persons. Representation of Christ and the saints changed with the Incarnation of Christ, as St. John of Damascus demonstrated in defending the use of images to foster devotion,[51] but the over-riding importance of the face as encounter both with God and others remains, especially in worship and in the family.[52]

Contemplating Christ's face is a major focus of John Paul II's Apostolic Letter, *Novo Millennio Ineunte*, issued at the beginning of the new millennium, and of his Apostolic Letter, *Rosarium Virginias Mariae.*[53] Issued January 6, 2001, *Novo Millennio Ineunte*, reflected on the jubilee year 2000. Section II was devoted to the contemplation of Christ's face. It noted first the historical dimension of the Word made flesh, (NMI, no. 18). Yet "regardless of how much his body was seen or touched, only faith could fully enter the mystery of that face" (NMI no. 19). Entering the mystery of the two natures in one Person is a gift of God and can only take place through the gift of grace. John Paul II then links the contemplation of Christ's face to the fulfillment of the desire expressed in the psalms to see God's face. By becoming man, Christ also revealed "the true face of man," (NMI, no. 23) and his destiny to participate in divine Trinitarian life. But "in order to bring man back to the Father's face, Jesus not only had to take on the face of man, but he had to burden himself with the 'face' of sin" (NMI, no. 27) and die in extreme agony. Yet the Church always passes from Christ's bleeding face to the face of the Risen one. John Paul II recommends prayer, especially the Rosary as the path to contemplation of Christ's face.[54]

Prayer and Presence

Our reflections on what it means to be a communion of persons began with the foundational understanding of the person as created in the image of God. First and foremost man and woman each have a relationship with God as Creator. Developing that relationship through Faith and being present to God is essential both for each member of the family and the family itself. As John Paul II says at the beginning of *Letter to Families*:

> It is significant that precisely in and through prayer man comes to discover in a very simple yet profound way his own unique subjectivity: in prayer, the human "I" more easily perceives what it means to be a person. This is also true of the family, which is not only the basic cell of society, but also possesses a particular subjectivity of its own (LF 4).

Mary's faith, nourished by the whole Israelite tradition of worship of God, preceded the Incarnation of Christ in her womb. It was likewise the faith of Joseph, the "righteous man" of the Old Testament, that together with Mary's, sustained the Holy Family through the long years and vicissitudes of the hidden life.

Presence to one another centered on prayer is also key in the spousal relation. As John Paul II says:

> The sacramental union of the two spouses, sealed in the covenant which they enter into before God, endures and grows stronger as the generations pass. It must become a union of prayer . . . Prayer needs to become a regular habit in the daily life of the family (LF 10).

Human Presence in the Family

What does this tell us about the significance of presence and the face-to-face encounter in the Church and in the family? First of all, presence and face-to-face encounter are required of all the sacraments in an "I-Thou" relationship. Presence is also required in the liturgy of the Church, especially the sacrifice of the Mass where the "We" dimension of the Body of Christ comes to the fore. The nature of the bodily presence on the part of individual members may vary in intensity but Jesus Christ is the same, yesterday, today and forever. Transposing this to the family, we can say that bodily presence and personal encounter are or should be defining characteristics. And this is especially the case in the fleshly unions of family life, beginning with conjugal intercourse, through gestation in the womb and breastfeeding. The human person is the only creature who engages in both sexual congress and nursing at the breast face-to-face. Both are profound interpersonal encounters and the foundation of *communio,* as are the daily interactions in the family of conversations, discussions and expressions of affection. All are enhanced by bodily presence.[55]

It is clear from John Paul II's "theology of the body" and the whole biblical tradition that sexual intercourse has a different meaning in and outside marriage because the body has a language of which it is not the author. Within marriage it speaks the language of total mutual self-gift. It is for this reason that it is the context for the conception of a new human person. One might also say that giving the breast by the nursing mother speaks a similar language to her child, although the inference is not as clear since alternative modes of feeding by a wet-nurse or by the bottle might be necessary for the survival of the child, whose mother is unable to nurse. Yet, in the past, it was almost universally recognized that the child imbibed the character of the wet nurse with the milk, so that great care was often taken to ensure the virtuous background of the wet nurse. In any event, this brought about a split in the child's experience between the actual mother and the substitute mother, with effects the science of psychology has only recently uncovered.[56] This is not to say that the bodily relation of conjugal intercourse or the mother nursing her own child necessarily brings about the interpersonal encounter. One might say that bodily presence facilitates the encounter but does not ensure it. Husbands find out quickly that conjugal delight in the bedroom depends in large measure on what happens in the rest of the couple's life together. With regard to the mother constrained to bottle feed her child, her simple bodily presence greatly facilitates the encounter, as does the supportive presence of the father.

Such presence sets the pattern for the later stages of the life of the child and the family. The more we learn about the family life of the People of Israel, it is manifest that not only was their conjugal life ordered to the primacy of interpersonal encounter, not simply sexual satisfaction, through the practice of family purity, but the mother was expected to breastfeed her own child. The education of the child, shared by both mother and father took place in the home. Their family life was enriched by religious rituals such as the Passover Feast as well as regular pilgrimages to the temple in Jerusalem for holy days. In the case of the Holy Family, Jesus was apprenticed to Joseph as a carpenter. In today's society that may not be possible, but without both divine and human presence, there can be no true culture of the family or the home. This is brought about in all the everyday interaction of family life, which make it a true communion of persons, of which the Holy Family, an "earthly Trinity," is the model. What this means is that whatever activities both spouses engage in outside the home, they should strive for them always to enhance not detract from the communion of persons in the home.

Signs of Fertility in the Body and Communion

A major way spouses can enhance the communion of persons in the family and be present to each other is through the practice of responsible parenthood, as expressed in the methodology of natural family planning, which is a way of both achieving and avoiding pregnancy by monitoring the signs of fertility and abstaining if the goal is family spacing or limiting. We might ask if such attention to the signs of fertility in the body and abstinence is new. On the contrary, it was central to the practice of Family Purity in the OT, which has already been mentioned several times.

Family Purity

A contemporary Jewish author, Norman Lamm has given an account of Family Purity, which has been called a "profoundly *spiritual, religious* institution."[57] Both the husband and wife are expected to come to the wedding in a state of chastity and free of any negative views of the goodness of sex in marriage, which is both for procreation and loving communion. The institution (religious practice) of "Family Purity" protects both. As we saw, a Jewish husband may not approach his wife during menses and seven days afterwards. During this time they are expected to show respect and affection towards each other but to avoid physical caresses. At the end of the period the wife immerses herself in the *mikvah* or bath, after which relations may be resumed.[58] This ascetic dimension has implications for the Christian practice of responsible parenthood.

When the temple, in which God's presence dwelt, was destroyed, there was no longer the same rationale for purity laws. Yet, to preserve the Jewish identity in the Diaspora, Rabbinic sages and scholars "created fences around the Torah." One of these was the practice of Nidah, which was expanded to include seven days of "whitening." In rabbinic times, "the Mitzvah of *Tamarat hamishpacha (Laws of Family Purity)* is considered so vital that rabbis enjoin Jewish communities to erect a *mikvah* even before the synagogue is built. Because of its contribution to Jewish life, this mitzvah has enormous consequences for Jewish couples and Jewish continuity," says Rahel R.Wasserfall.[59] Norman Lamm particularly wants to encourage the discipline of "Family Purity" in Jewish family life.[60] Lamm sees the practice of "family purity," with its period of abstinence as "crucial in protecting the marriage bond," arguing that unrestricted sexual access creates boredom.[61] Not only is periodic abstinence a way of civilizing sex since the partner does not become a sexual object, but sexual congress always remains fresh. It is significant that Lamm argues that such abstinence from sex in marriage needs to have a religious sanction: otherwise the separation "will no longer be elevating or ennobling."[62]

Modern Family Planning and the Communion of Persons

Elsewhere, this author has given a brief account of the same scientific discoveries that lie behind both the major contraceptive and natural methods of family planning.[63] What is significant for our purposes is to show how the communion of persons is enhanced by the natural methods when used rightly. This can be readily seen under the headings chosen by John Paul II, "original solitude" or person, original unity or "I-Thou" and the "We" dimension of community. First and foremost, the woman is affirmed as a person endowed with the gift of fertility when her husband shares with her the decision either to have a child or to abstain. Fertility itself has its origin in God. As John Paul II says, "Every Act of begetting has its primordial model in the fatherhood of God . . . The genealogy of the person is inscribed in the very biology of generation." In the case of Mary, for example, the angel Gabriel sought her acceptance first before she was overshadowed by the Holy Spirit. The pope cites St. Augustine and other Fathers of the Church: "she conceived this Son in her mind before she conceived him in her womb" (RM 13); and "With her *fiat* Mary becomes the authentic subject of that union with God . . . All of God's action in human history respects the free will of the human "I." And such was the case of the annunciation of Nazareth" (MD 4). In the case of the human couple, monitoring the signs of fertility tells them when pregnancy is most likely to result in order either to achieve or avoid pregnancy so that they can make a joint decision.

Although the decision was Mary's in direct relation with God, it necessarily involved Joseph, since she was betrothed to him. In other words, it is part of the "I-Thou" dimension or original unity. In awe of what was conceived in Mary, Joseph, once the angel had assured him that her conception was from God, abstained from any relations with her. Through the practice of Family Purity, periodic abstention was not foreign to him, but he was given the grace of complete abstinence as a sign of the new dispensation of a total gift of self to Christ as well as to confirm Jesus' divine origin. His virginity also pointed to the *eschaton*. For the human couple periodic abstinence is a sign not only of respect for the personhood of the spouse and of any future child, but, when it is according to God's will, strengthens self-possession for self-gift and calls down grace. The "We" dimension comes into being with the conception and birth of the child. Charting the signs of the body gives the couple almost immediate knowledge of the pregnancy so that the husband often uses the expression "we are pregnant." [64]

Cycle Awareness: A New Form of Communication

In the early days of introducing modern hormonal methods of family planning, much research centered on factors that contributed to a) their use and b) their effective use in avoiding pregnancy. The author has detailed many of the studies in her previous work, so that here mainly the conclusions will be given.[65] First, all the studies from many different countries showed that a minimum of husband-wife communication is necessary for a couple to adopt a method of family planning. The researchers distinguished between *verbal* communication on family planning, *agreement* between the spouses and *empathy* "defined as a correct perception of the spouse's attitudes and opinions."[66] It was found that a high degree of empathy did not necessarily translate into avoiding pregnancy. These couples found joy in welcoming a new child. This was a consistent finding across the studies. It was also found that if the husband is the more "dominant" partner, the couple were more likely to use a "natural" method, and those that require joint cooperation. The majority of NFP couples (who are a declining minority in most countries)[67] report that in spite of difficulties with abstinence, the method enhances their interpersonal communication since they need to discuss at a minimum where they are in the cycle and decisions on sex and pregnancy.

Dr. Thomasina Borkman, now emeritus professor of sociology, George Mason University, and this author, from their own study of NFP couples, hypothesized that the body provides another unique form of communication, which they call "cycle awareness."[68] Such information on the fertility cycle gives a form of communication that the couple do not usually have access to. It especially gives information about the way the cycle can affect a woman's moods so that she and her husband can adjust their responses. Both husbands and wives find it gives a new quality to their relationship, with a certain reverence for the way the body is made, so that it is, in truth, spousal.[69] The gift of fertility is recognized as mutual. [70]

Presence Through Ecological Breastfeeding

John Kippley, founder of the Couple to Couple League and now of NFP International, considers that there are two kinds of natural family planning, ecological breastfeeding and periodic abstinence.[71] During ecological breastfeeding, which provides a period of amenorrhea from one year to three, with careful monitoring of the signs of returning fertility there is no need for the husband to abstain.[72] At the same time, the wife and mother is present to the child in a unique way.

The practice of the mother nursing her child increases the well-being and communion of all in the family. First of all the husband does not need to abstain from conjugal intercourse as long as the amenorrhea from ecological breastfeeding lasts. Only then is he called to abstain through NFP if more spacing is called for. Nursing provides many physical benefits to both mother and child from immunity to disease to better brain function in the child. The most important benefit is the bonding between mother and child, which nursing uniquely provides. If, however, the mother, for various reasons, is unable to breastfeed her child, she can still be present to her child in many other ways.

NFP and the Language of the Body

John Paul II writes: "Woman's constitution differs from that of the man; in fact we know that it is different even in the deepest bio-physiological determinants" (MW 21:3). This difference, especially with regard to the gift of fertility, has not always been viewed favorably. [73] Routinely in studies of the effectiveness of different methods of family planning an unexpected pregnancy is termed a" failure" or "unwanted." NFP researchers, on the contrary use the term "surprise" pregnancy, since a child is always a gift even if circumstances might be difficult. . Indeed, language has a powerful effect on the way couples are present to their bodies and fertility, as John Paul II clearly saw when he coined the phrase "the spousal meaning of the body."

Summary

This chapter has looked at the centrality of Christ, in the baptized family, which, according to the early Church fathers and Vatican Council II, transforms it into the "domestic church." John Paul II links it further to the "civilization of love." Not only is Christ's presence in the family pivotal but human bodily presence of each member to the other is essential for communion. This extends to the most intimate aspects of the body, which husband and wife share in the practice of NFP. The next chapter is devoted to a fuller understanding of the Church's teaching on responsible parenthood in *Humanae vitae,* and shows how the Holy Family can be a true model in its commitment to God's will for love in the family.

CHAPTER 9

Humanae Vitae, the Communion of Persons and the Holy Family

Introduction

In the last chapter it was seen how central is the body to divine and human communion. Not only did Christ take on a human body in the Incarnation but he has left us his glorified body in the Eucharist. The body, itself, is sacramental, making visible what is invisible. In original innocence the body is

> Understood as a *sign that* efficaciously *transmits in the visible world the invisible mystery hidden in God from eternity.* And this is the mystery of Truth and Love, in which man really participates. . . It has been created to transfer into the visible reality of the world the mystery hidden from eternity in God, and thus be a sign of it (MW 19:4).

The imaging of God occurs through masculinity and femininity. The way couples live the language of the body in marriage has, therefore, profound implications for revealing divine truths. The Church's perennial teaching on the inseparability of the unitive and procreative dimension of marriage is designed not only to safeguard these truths but to ensure human happiness and fulfillment, albeit a challenge for post-lapsarian humans.

This chapter focuses specifically on how living the truths of *Humanae vitae* helps to heal and restore the communion of persons in the family with a fresh understanding of marital chastity. Previous chapters have sought to show that John Paul II's anthropology of person, gift and communion especially, based on *Gaudium et spes* (nos. 22 and 24), is key to living marriage as it was designed in creation and redemption. It has corrected some deficiencies in the way marriage has been understood since the Middle Ages. A particular deficiency, to be addressed by Cormac Burke in this chapter, concerns the *remedium concupiscentiae*, which was used to justify marriage as a license for lustful intercourse. This license led to a ready acceptance of contraception as a response, which, while claiming to restore marital intimacy, in fact harms it. More grievously it undermines the very truths of revelation concerning man and woman and their call to communion in the image of the Trinity. *Humanae vitae,* on the contrary, opens the way to a fuller understanding of the Church's teaching on responsible parenthood and the family as a communion of persons. As this chapter shows, the Church has been in the forefront of promoting scientific research on natural methods, which make use of the naturally occurring fertile and infertile phases of the woman's cycle, as a morally licit way of achieving or avoiding pregnancy for serious reasons. Chastity is not only central to this method but it accords with the Holy Family as the model for all families called to image the Christ-Church union and to participate in divine Trinitarian communion.

This chapter shows how the new framework of marriage as a communion of persons in the image of Trinitarian communion both removes the suspicion of the goodness of conjugal love and affirms the full meaning of conjugal chastity as not simply purification of the conjugal act, but, above all, of conformity to God's designs of life and love in marriage and the whole of life. Cormac Burke begins by challenging the interpretation of the *remedium concupiscentiae* as a license for lust in marriage. The contribution of two NFP pioneers, one who remained faithful and one, who ultimately took the path of dissent, along with a brief discussion of the role of science, highlight the foundational character of what John Paul II calls "the prophetic truth of that historic document." Married couples can now see the chastity of the Holy Family not so much as an exception but intrinsic to living marriage in accord with God's designs, however many children they are blessed with.

Marriage as *Remedium Concupiscentiae*

Cormac Burke, a civil lawyer, doctor of canon law and a judge of the Roman Rota, is forthright in castigating the Church's misuse through the centuries of the meaning of marriage as *remedium concupiscentiae* or remedy for concupiscence.

> The term, *Remedium Concipiscentiae*, presented up to 1983 as a "secondary" end of marriage, has been seriously misapplied over the centuries. In practice it has been taken to imply that marriage gives a lawful outlet to sexual concupiscence (or lust) and hence married couples can yield to it, since it is now legitimized.[1]

It was held that lust was automatically purified by marriage. Provided the procreative end was respected, couples could give free reign to concupiscence, but that was not the view of Augustine and Aquinas. Burke charges that the "legitimizing of concupiscence has for centuries impeded the development of a positive and dynamic notion of marital chastity."[2] He refers to the work of John Paul II's theology of the body in showing the good of sexual desire and marriage not as "a second class Christian way, but seeing it for what God wished it to be: a full vocation to holiness precisely to be attained in and through the married state."[3] Burke notes that in Vatican Council II and subsequent documents there is no direct or indirect reference to the *remedium concupiscentiae.* (It was virtually replaced by the *bonum conjugum* as a good of marriage.) In spite of its long use from the time of St. Paul,[4] he charges that it lacks "theological and anthropological structure" and its misinterpretation meant that the Church failed "to develop a theological and ascetical consideration of marriage as a way of sanctification."[5] Love does, indeed, need purification, but the answer is not to legitimize lust at the expense of a positive role for sexual intercourse in marriage.

This attitude persisted until the mid-Twentieth century. Then the Magisterium began to offer "startlingly new perspectives," which Burke later refers to as "a step forward of extraordinary significance in magisterial teaching"[6] Burke cites a passage from the pope's theology of the body. "As much as concupiscence darkens the horizon of the inward vision and deprives the heart of the clarity of desires and aspirations, so much does 'life according to the Spirit" (that is the grace of the sacrament of marriage) permit man and woman to find again the liberty of the gift, united to the awareness of the spousal meaning of the body in its masculinity and femininity."(MW 101: 5) The fulfillment of sexual desire when it is subordinated to conjugal love is a good and the way the couple express marital chastity. Concupiscence, even in marriage, on the contrary, wants to use the other person. In conjugal acts respecting the person, Burke cites *Humanae vitae* and *Gaudium et spes*, the latter referencing married love as "eminently human" (GS 49 and HV 9).[7] The human nature of the act does not just lie in being open to procreation. It "also lies in its being an act of intimate self-donation to, and union with one's spouse: a reconfirmation in the body of one's singular choice of him or her, a reconfirmation that is expressed not only in the giving and receiving of pleasure but even more essentially in the care, respect, tenderness, and reverence accompanying the physical act."[8] Both anti-procreative and anti-unitive attitudes and actions vitiate the act.

The remedy for concupiscence is not giving into lust but purification by chastity. Only self-mastery through chastity gives true freedom to love, the freedom brought by Christ. Sexual intercourse, itself, is not the only bodily expression of love in marriage. The other physical expressions of affection in marriage also play an important part. None of this is easy for "fallen" man. Burke cites John Paul II on marriage being a "difficult love."[9] Continence seems to and does cause tensions in marriage, but, says the pope, enduring such tensions is the only way truly to free man for a deeper spousal love and to prepare him for eternal love.

Loving in a Human Manner (Modo Humano)

Humans respond to love and are not just prey to instinct like animals. French theologian, Jean Guitton, author of *L'Amour Humaine,* contrasts animal and human sexuality.[10] Animals, he points out, respond to automatic compulsive drives to fulfill the biological function of reproduction and preservation of the species. Man, however, is not so compelled but can choose not to exercise his reproductive function for the sake of a higher purpose and still live well. Guitton further contrasts animal need, which is finite, with human need, which has infinity added to it from man's rational nature, so that need transforms into desire, even passionate desire. A further difference pertains to the interchangeability of animal sexual partners versus the personal nature of human sexuality. A man loves a particular woman. If he simply seeks out any woman to satisfy his sexual need as in prostitution, he debases his sexuality not just to the animal level but to a lower level, since the goal of animal sexuality is a new member of the species.

St. Paul VI emphasized the *human* nature of spousal love, when expounding his encyclical on responsible or conscious parenthood in *Humanae vitae*, 1968. "Married love is before everything else a love distinctly *human*, that is, of the senses and the spirit." [11] It is also a matter of a "*full* love, a special form of personal friendship in which husband and wife generously share with each other." He continues: "Whoever truly loves a spouse, loves not so much because of what is received, but because of who the other is, and loves willingly so that the other may be enriched by the gift of one's self" (HV 9). Spousal love is, in addition, steadfast, exclusive and fertile. "It is not exhausted by the communion between husband and wife but is destined to continue raising up new lives" (HV 9). Section 10 is crucial in articulating the Church's teaching. Mindful of developments in modern society, which he has laid out at the beginning of the encyclical, namely, rapid increase in population, economic challenges, the new position of women, and the value placed on love in marriage, the pope advises cultivating awareness of the biological processes that bring about life. These, together with "inborn impulses and emotions," must be subjected to reason and will in order to bring about self-mastery for self-gift. Couples are encouraged, after examining the physical, economic and psychological conditions, to decide both prudently and generously to raise a large family or for serious reasons to avoid conception "for a definite or indefinite period of time"(HV 10).

However, the means to do this must be moral. Pope Paul VI speaks of the "unbreakable connection between the meaning of unity and the meaning of procreation,"(HV 12) and reiterates that if one partner imposes their will on the other it is not "a true act of love"(HV 13). While contraception was promoted by Margaret Sanger as a way to foster sexual intimacy in marriage, critics have pointed out that, in fact, the personal nature of married love is *ipso facto* debased. Contraception by its nature makes the partners a means to an end, rather than individuals joined in a unique and irreplaceable relation.[12]

Science and *Humanae Vitae*

Based on sound scientific research, Natural Family Planning (NFP) is a method, that has been developed to implement the Church's teaching on the moral way to space or avoid pregnancy if there are serious reasons to do so. It must always be understood within the overarching concept of "responsible parenthood" and, one might say marital chastity. It has been said that the couple using contraception need reasons to have a child while those committed to responsible parenthood need reasons *not* to have a child. Debates on the licit use of hormonal contraception and even of natural family planning have raged in the last forty plus years, especially among theologians. This is not the place to rehash them. It is pertinent, however, to give briefly some papal and Vatican pronouncements on the licit use and promotion of NFP. Opposite is a table with papal encyclicals from 1930-1981.

Papal Encyclicals and Documents on Marriage and Responsible Parenthood

	Marriage	Offspring	Fidelity	Sacrament	Nature
Casti Connubii (Dec. 31, 1930)	• Divine Institution • Divine Laws govern • Souls linked more than bodies	• Primary end is procreation/education of children • Sexual intercourse belongs only in marriage • Periodic continence acceptable	• No lustful looks at others • Obedience of wife • Practice of continence in early years aids fidelity • Contraception against fidelity	• Indissoluble by nature • Source of grace • Prototype of Christ's union with Church • Grace enough for difficulties	• Power over our own body only according to nature • Nature part of Divine Plan
Gaudium et spes (1965), Nos. 47-52	• Is human and involves whole person • Is perfected in the marital act	• Duty of education, especially religious education • Conjugal love ordained to children • Parents make decision, but not arbitrarily • Children supreme gift of marriage	• Mutual gift of two persons • Called to total fidelity • Irrevocable covenant • Conjugal chastity essential	• God author of sacrament • Must obey Church	• Nature ordered to bearing and rearing children • No contradiction between divine laws and love and life
Humanae Vitae (July 25, 1968)	• Fully human • Involves integral vision of man's natural/supernatural end	• Duty to transmit life • Deliberate and generous decision to raise large family, but for grave reasons, may limit or avoid completely • Hierarchy of values – God/family/society; union of unitive and procreative	• Total, faithful and exclusive • Contraception causes loss of respect for woman	• Strengthened by grace, couples witness to God's holy law	• Knowledge and respect for biological processes • Natural law expression of God's will • Couples ministers to design of Creator

		• Periodic continence acceptable • Openness to life			• Abortion, contraception, sterilization against nature
***Familiaris Consortio* (Dec. 15, 1981)**	• Sexuality not purely biological, but total • Natural love perfected by supernatural • Love is vocation of all in marriage or celibacy	• Transmission of life fundamental to marriage • Fecundity also implies passing on culture • Even weak/suffering human life is God's gift	• Equal dignity of women, but maternal role above public • Chastity essential	• Church recognizes difficulties of families and population problems • Recourse to sacraments in difficulties • Sexuality is redeemed by Jesus	• No contradiction between Divine Law and marital love • Choice of natural relations involves dialogue and reciprocal respect • Contraception and periodic continence irreconcilable concepts

John Paul II took every opportunity to foster scientific development of the natural methods. Shortly after his election in 1979 he addressed two groups of international researchers, encouraging the men of science, doctors and specialists present "to provide practical help to couples to live this responsible parenthood."[13] Again, in 1981, in an address to the First Congress for the Family of America and Europe, he referred to "the most urgent need today "to develop methods in collaboration with the design of the Creator, who "has provided the human organism with structures and functions to assist couples in arriving at responsible parenthood."[14] In greeting participants at an NFP course sponsored by the Centre for Studies and Research on the Natural Regulation of Fertility of the Catholic University of the Sacred Heart he insisted that the natural methods are not a 'licit' variation of contraception. "In practicing natural methods, science must always be joined to self-control, since, in using them, virtue—that perfection belonging specifically to the person—is necessarily a factor."[15] He goes on to say: "This intrinsic connection between science and moral virtue constitutes the specific and morally qualifying element for recourse to the natural methods."[16] In 1992, while noting that "the methods which the Church finds morally acceptable are today receiving the support of ever new scientific confirmation," the pope asserts that thanks to "the generous contribution of scientists and married couples, one can speak of a turning point in the defense and promotion of the dignity of conjugal life."[17] More than a decade later it is, unfortunately, hard to see this turning point since the separation of the unitive and procreative dimensions of sexuality through technological means proceeds apace with the fragmentation of the family continuing to accelerate and the statistics on NFP use stagnating at approximately 2% of couples of child-bearing age.[18]

In spite of this or rather because of it, the Church continues to call for implementation of *Humanae vitae*, even when, as John Paul II advises, "one is often laughed at, accused of lack of understanding, and of severity and of other things besides."[19] But "the *real* difficulty is that the *heart* of man and woman is prey to concupiscence: and concupiscence urges freedom not to consent to the authentic demands of married love." In 1990 the pope spoke forcefully about the difficulties.

> In truth, only *within the framework of responsibility for love and life* can the underlying reasons for prohibiting "actions which have the aim of and are used as a means for making procreation impossible" (*Humanae vitae* 14) be understood. Only within the context of values such as these can spouses find the inspiration to overcome, with the help of God's grace, the difficulties which they inevitably face when, under unfavorable social conditions and in an environment marked by readily available hedonism, they seek to follow a path which conforms to the Lord's will.[20]

Furthermore, it is only within the context of these values that the "difference both anthropological and moral, between contraception and recourse to the rhythm of the cycle (FC 32)" can be grasped. The following tables, "Philosophical and Psychosocial Differences" and "Dissemination of Natural Family Planning" highlight some of the differences

Philosophical and Psychosocial Differences

Natural Family Planning	Contraception
Balances procreative and unitive dimensions	Emphasizes unitive at expense of procreative
God is ultimate giver of life	Man has total control of his life
Man cooperates with God in sexuality	Man manipulates his sexuality
Heterosexuality is the norm	Homo-, bi- and heterosexuality equally valid
Emphasis on virtue; pleasure a bi-product	Emphasis on sexual pleasure
Emphasis on childbirth/breastfeeding	Emphasis on coitus
Emphasis on relationship, especially husband/wife and children	Emphasis on autonomous individual
Men and women can be chaste	Sexual urges are overwhelming
Enhances communication	Diminishes communication
Enhances equality	Creates inequality
Promotes unconditional love	Promotes limited love
Enhances self-differentiation/unity	Increases fusion/separation
Can both achieve and avoid pregnancy	Only avoids pregnancy

Dissemination

Natural Family Planning	Contraception
Endorsed by health profession	Endorsed by health profession
Fully educational approach	Given by prescription with minimum education
Neglected by governments, population agencies and health professions	Promoted by governments, population agencies and health professions
Promoted by Church and NFP users, some feminists and ecologists	Counseled by educational and health professionals
Linked to pregnancy counseling	Linked to abortion counseling
Taught in context of marriage and family	Taught in context of varied sexual lifestyles
Linked to chastity education	Linked to contraceptive and STI education
Varied cost in initial teaching phase; minimum cost later	Initial cost varies, but ongoing cost for devices and pathological effects
Miniscule public and private funds spent on NFP dissemination	Billions of dollars spent on promotion of contraceptives

Medical Science

Most people are unaware that the same discoveries of the hormonal phases of the menstrual cycle are at the base of the development of the contraceptive pill and of periodic abstinence (natural family planning) but applied to a different purpose, in one case to suppress fertility, in the other to monitor and work with the naturally occurring phases of fertility and infertility.[21] As has already been pointed out, John Paul II notes that the difference in the constitution of the man and the woman is evident at even the deepest bio-physiological level (MW 21:3). Medical science reveals this difference, correcting some false notions of generation that prevailed in the past that did not affirm the woman in her full subjectivity.[22] Elsewhere I have shown that the Church's insistence on the inseparability of the procreative and unitive dimensions of conjugal intercourse led directly to the development of natural family planning with concomitant research on the properties of cervical mucus, which allow the couple to identify the fertile period in advance.[23]

In his Wednesday Catechesis, John Paul II coins a phrase, "rereading the language of, the body in truth." This is a crucial phrase in his whole argument, since it links his biblical reflections on the spousal meaning of the body with *Humanae vitae.*[24] Only if the spouses reread the language of the body in truth do they image the union of Christ and the Church and divine Trinitarian communion. The Church has always held that there can be no conflict between faith and reason, represented in our day by scientific knowledge. In his encyclical, *Fides et ratio* the pope reiterates this teaching:

> Faith and reason are like two wings on which the human spirit rises to contemplation of truth; and God has placed in the human heart a desire to know the truth –in a word, to know himself—so that, by knowing and loving God, men and women may also come to the fullness of truth about themselves (cf. Ex.33:18; Ps. 27:8-9; 63:2-3; Jn. 14:8; 1 Jn. 3:2)[25]

He goes on to say, "The more human beings know reality and the world, the more they know themselves in their uniqueness, with the question of the meaning of things and of their existence becoming ever more pressing" (FR 1). Significantly this is illustrated, as noted earlier, in the medical textbooks on the human reproductive system, which employ a "language of the body" that, unfortunately, conforms more to its fallen rather than its redeemed state. This language conveys a meaning, which has been criticized as hostile, especially to women.[26] Sperm are called "foreigners in a hostile body" which "assault" the egg.[27] Is it any wonder that contraceptives, which block the sperm, become a preferred medical solution. These textbooks are in marked contrast to NFP instruction manuals, as noted earlier, where words like "gift," "union," "harmony" predominate. Both set of textbooks and instruction manuals affirm the vital importance of rereading the language of the body in truth. Since the body "expresses the person," a false reading can affect every level of the couple's relationship.

Hanna Klaus, ObGyn., when asked for her medical evaluation of contraception responded:

> While the culture, especially in the West, has enthusiastically embraced the separation of sex and procreation by technological means, the body has its own truth which asserts itself directly via psychophysical distress resulting from the use of steroid contraceptive hormones or male or female sterilization and by behaviors resulting from the notional removal of the procreative capacity from sexual intercourse. Despite denial of significant side-effects from contraceptive hormones by those who promote their use, the weight of complaints on social media by thousands of women can no longer be denied. Manufacturers have tried to decrease side effects by changing formulations and lowering doses, but the fact remains that the steroids alter moods and wellbeing of a significant number of users, as well as causing well documented serious medical side effects such as blood clots leading to strokes, heart attacks and death from pulmonary embolism. While advocates claim that contraceptive use has helped many young women to delay childbearing while completing their education and starting careers, this benefit has only accrued to those with long term goals, but has had

> almost no economic impact on the poor. All socioeconomic groups have experienced profound changes in a decrease in marriage and an increase in single parenthood and divorce. Men and women do not need to commit themselves fully to a relationship that excludes their ability to go beyond themselves by total self-gift.[28]

Psychological Implications

Current statistics on the breakdown of marriage and family life, which has greatly accelerated since the introduction of the hormonal contraceptive pill in the 1960s, witness to the effect of contraception on the couple's relationship. Since this is not a psychological but a theological work, suffice it to say that this author has written extensively before of the effect of practicing responsible parenthood on the relationship of well-disposed couples.[29] The argument could be made that these accounts are biased in favor of the Church's teaching and cannot be applied to the ordinary couple. To counter such a charge, a review of *Love One Another: Psychological Aspects of Natural Family Planning* by John Marshall, who came out in favor of the Church changing its teaching on contraception, is printed in the appendix.[30] When he wrote the book, John Marshall was Emeritus Professor of Neurology, University of London with an impressive array of medical credentials. The second chapter details the scientific development of NFP. He is fair in his assessment of the effectiveness of the method in preventing pregnancy. The crux of his concern is the role of abstinence in using the method to avoid pregnancy. He questions the term "user failure" particularly for NFP. He asks:

> A breach of the rules may indicate that the method (in this case abstinence from sexual intercourse) was too demanding for that particular couple. Is this event to be attributed to the method, as being too demanding, or to the users, as not trying hard enough or to both?[31]

Faced with this situation, he eventually opted for contraceptive use. As an original member of the Papal Birth Control Commission, which was established by Pope John XXIII in 1963 and later expanded under Pope Paul VI, he voted with the majority to change the teaching of the Church to allow contraception. But his conversion to the majority view was gradual.

Humanae Vitae and the Language of Love

John Marshall, MD

Marshall approaches marriage from the point of view of love, noting that it is not the traditional path but accords with couples' experience. He defines love as the desire to possess the other, to give in a spirit of sacrifice and create community. He is insistent that the creative aspect of love covers more than the biological so it should not be limited to procreation. In searching for a word that encompasses these three aspects of married love, he says: "Coitus is the most profound commitment one human being can make to another."[32] It is a total act, physical, psychological and spiritual like the union of Christ and the Church. It is also exclusive and faithful. Since it is consent that makes the marriage, love is necessary but that does not mean equating love with emotion. To arrive at his understanding of coitus, Marshall interprets Pope Pius XII's allocation to Italian midwives in 1951 as formally stating that married couples have a duty to procreate. In his own words:

> The point about the allocation of Pius XII was that no longer was it possible to see marriage as a quasi-religious state in which sexual activity was in some way a concession. The Pope firmly declared that marriage was a vocation established for the service of new life. Procreation was no longer a biological necessity which provided the justification for sexual activity; it was a manifestation of the love and service specific to the married state.[33]

In the Introduction, he discusses his use of terms. Since, he notes, "sexual intercourse" refers to all relations between the sexes, he has chosen "coitus" for genital sex which involves the whole person, reserving "copulation" for sex between animals. He restricts "procreation" to the union of the sperm and the ovum and prefers the term "creation, creative" because it is not limited to the child but refers to the "whole interplay between two persons" leading to their fulfillment and development together with their children.[34]

John Kippley

"Coitus" is still very much a biological term, in spite of the broad meaning Marshall seeks to give it. John Kippley chooses a more Scriptural term, "covenant." He, too, begins with an analysis of the word "love" looking at it specifically in the area of sex. He asks two questions: (1) "In the interpersonal order of creation, is there meant to be an intrinsic link between sexuality and love?" and (2) "Within marriage, are sexual relations necessarily expressive of authentic married love?"[35] In the marriage ceremony, man and woman enter a covenant with each other, a sacramental and spiritual bond, recognizing God as the Author. The covenant has a structure independent of the couple, who must, however, give their free consent. They promise both to help each other and let their love produce life. The sex union expresses in a physical way their marriage covenant.

> The sex union now is morally good, because it is the renewal of the marriage covenant; it has become more than physical; it has become sacramental, an outward expression of the interpersonal and God-made covenant of marriage. The criteria for evaluating sexual activity is not just physical; it is not just psychological and intentional; it is sacramental which means that the criteria is truly human.[36]

The argument against contraception is that it becomes the refusal to accept the possible results of the marital act and so it does not renew the marriage covenant. It excludes trust and faith in God and his designs and purposes. Kippley draws his covenant theory from Scripture, in which sexual relations are viewed as an analogy for God's covenant with his people as well as the New Testament analogy of Eucharistic communion. He notes that it accords also with natural law.

John Paul II

How do these two languages compare with that of John Paul II in his Wednesday Catechesis on the theology of the body? In the final homily, no. 133, he explains how the final section on *Humanae vitae* is not artificially added to the previous sections, each of which draws on a particular Scriptural quotation, but is closely connected to it, "because *it is from this topic that the questions spring* that run in some way through the whole of our reflections" (MW 133:4). For the pope, marriage as a sacramental sign is paramount. Referring back to Genesis 1-2 he says in an earlier homily:

> The structure of the sacramental sign remains, in fact, in its essence the same as "in the beginning." What determines it is *in some sense "the language of the body,"* inasmuch as the man and the woman, who are to become one flesh by marriage, express in this sign the reciprocal gift of masculinity and femininity as the foundation of the conjugal union of the persons (MW 103:4).

The "spousal meaning of the body," drawn from the covenant analogy of God's relation with his people, "gift," "reciprocal donation" and marriage as a communion of persons in the manner of the Trinity, are all central to John Paul II's analysis of marriage and the conjugal act. Before becoming pope he had already developed a coherent philosophy of conjugal relations, which also accords with Scripture. The pope goes one step further and shows how it also corresponds to the deepest experience of the human person.[37] This experiential aspect is important since it appears to be a major reason John Marshall and the Birth Control Commission, set up by Pope John XXIII in 1963 to study the licitness of the Pill came out in favor of contraception. It might be said that Marshall's language of love centered on "coitus" was more in keeping with some of the new theologies of sexuality embraced by dissident theologians, such as Charles Curran.[38]

The Birth Control Commission: Crisis of Faith

Since Marshal was one of the original members of the Birth Control Commission, it is worth tracing his passage from faithful Catholic to dissenter on *Humanae vitae.* Above all it is important to acknowledge the pressures faced by himself and other members of the Commission, not to mention the ordinary person in the pew, from both inside and outside the Church, such as the United Nations and World Health Organization, the population control movement, the media, and powerful, prelates--pressures that still exist.[39] In his book, Marshall also records ignorance on the part of doctors faced with patients knowledgeable on NFP as well as medical opposition to use of the method.

One woman wrote:

> I think, particularly at the present time, one's psychological reactions to the method are bound to be influenced by external pressures. I know my own fear of pregnancy is as much a fear of medical disapproval as of anything else. I feel constantly on the defensive about our use of the method. I feel we are being watched for signs of tension, maladjustment and even insanity, and this in itself produces tension and unease.[40]

Marshall, himself, does not speak of any such response to his own involvement from the medical profession, but it could not have been easy. His own account of the Birth Control Commission is printed in the appendix with permission of *The Tablet.* It is ironic that he was persuaded ultimately not by a scientific argument but by an outdated theological argument. He concludes with the insight that dissent from *Humanae vitae* differs from previous disagreement with Church teaching. Formerly if someone disagreed they might argue:

> "I know the Church says this is wrong, but what else can I do in the circumstances? The Lord will understand." Now, however, the judgment of many was: "The teaching reaffirmed in *Humanae vitae* is wrong. I cannot accept it as the word of God."[41]

This effectively shuts out God's merciful love, especially through the Sacrament of Reconciliation, and makes growth in the couple's relationship problematic.[42] As Marshall and the Commission theologians understood, it was, indeed, an attack on the very foundations of the Church as well as on the authority of the pope.[43] John Paul II made the nature of this attack the theme of his ground-breaking encyclical on moral theology, *Veritatis splendor.*

> "It is no longer a matter of limited and occasional dissent, but an overall and systematic calling into question of traditional moral doctrine on the basis of certain anthropological and ethical presuppositions." At the root of these presuppositions is the more or less obvious influence of currents of thought which end by detaching human freedom from its essential and constituent relationship to truth (VS 4).

Humanae vitae brought these "currents of thought" to a head, which were essentially opposed to chastity as a fundamental good of the person.

The Full Significance of Marital Chastity as the Foundation of the Person and Communion of Persons

Chastity and Humanae Vitae

The attack launched against Pope Paul VI's encyclical in 1968 was nothing new in the history of either Judaism or Christianity. The purpose of the hormonal contraceptive pill, (later followed by the legalization of abortion) was to free sexual enjoyment from its procreative end. As such it ushered in a cult of sexual pleasure in the name of certain goods, deemed necessary for modern society, especially population control, women's liberation from the burden of pregnancy to enable them to participate in public life, and creation of the "wanted" child.[44] The great attraction of modern contraception is not achievement of these goods per se but "surrender to the sexual drive," in the words of author, Patrick Riley. Modern technological means brought about what had been institutionalized by sacred prostitution and child sacrifice in the Canaanite religious cult, which the Israelites found when they first entered the promised land and which the prophets continually inveighed against throughout Israel's history. "As a religion of sexual abandon and child sacrifice, it struck two lethal blows at the family, one at its root, and the other at its fruit."[45] Riley comments that it was "not only an assault on the worship that forged the nation of Israel but, as an assault on chastity, was an assault on the family."[46] The great analogy, of course, in Israelite worship, was faithful marriage as an image of God's spousal covenant with his people and worship of alien gods was likened to adultery.[47] The fact that the Israelites continually surrendered to the sexual drive and idolatrous worship illustrates the challenge of marital chastity that is the foundation of family life, especially in a Christian context.[48]

John Paul II, in his analysis of Christ's words on the Sermon of the Mount in his Wednesday Catechesis on the theology of the body, traces the history of the Israelite people's understanding of the Mosaic commandment, "Thou shalt not commit adultery." From a mere transgression of the Law, in which the wife was regarded simply as property, the Chosen people were brought, especially by the Prophets, to an analogy of adultery with idolatry. On the positive side, "God-Yahweh makes the covenant with Israel (without any merit on its part); for Israel he becomes a Bridegroom and Husband who is most affectionate, attentive and generous towards his Bride" (MW 37:3). The Bridegroom's love is an act of "sheer mercy." The pope goes on: "Adultery is sin because it is *the breaking of the personal covenant between the man and woman*" (ME 37:4). Although the Wisdom Tradition focused more on the heart, in the Sermon on the Mount, Christ introduces a new ethos. It does not negate the lawful desire of a man for his wife, but acknowledges that through the disorder of concupiscence arising from original sin, man has a tendency to look with lust even on his own spouse, which disrupts the communion of persons. The pope calls these words demanding but in no way do they condemn the body. "The Christian ethos is characterized by *a transformation of the human person's conscience and attitude*, both the man's and the woman's, *such as to express and realize the value of the body and of sex* according to the Creator's original plan, placed as they are at the service of the 'communion of persons,' which is the deepest substratum of ethics and culture" (MW 45:3).

If chastity, however, is not linked to love it is meaningless. Emile Mersch, a Jesuit, writing before World War II, states that "it is respect for our human nature, through charity towards man that Christianity sets up such limitless requirements." He goes on to say that Christian doctrine is "not in the first place a declaration of war, but a formula of union."[49] He acknowledges that to rid ourselves of sin will be a struggle. Mortification is essential to the Christian, which involves not so much a flight from sin but positive action. For "Christianity in its entirety is before all else positive and love of the good."[50] Although the exigencies of purity are hard and all must struggle against weakness, including psychological deficiencies, habits and temperament, the "foundation of chastity is not terror but love."[51] Sexual love is ordered to union and implies a reciprocal donation of self for life.

Paul M. Quay, another Jesuit, who has reflected deeply on human sexuality, comments that if we want to know the fullness of human good, we must look to Jesus and Mary because our nature is fallen and theirs is not. He makes three important statements on chastity.

- We can get a right picture of human sexuality—or anything else in our nature—only insofar as it is contained in Christ.[52]
- It follows, since integral human nature is understandable only in Christ, that integral human sexuality is a mystery of faith.[53]
- Any truly human sexual behavior is essentially an element, aspect, or component of Christian chastity.[54]

Quay, like St. John Paul II, compares the abuse of sex to lies, as its natural symbolism. In adultery, the body speaks the language of total commitment, while one or both partners are already committed to another in marriage. Coercive intercourse, intercourse only for selfish pleasure or without true concern for the other's needs, belies the language of love expressed by the body. In fornication the body expresses a permanent love that the couple treat as transient. For the same reasons, masturbation and homosexual activity cannot express true love. It is chastity that ensures the true symbolism of human sexuality, both in and outside marriage.

Quay has much to say on the symbolism of premarital chastity, taking as his text the biblical verse of the Song of Songs: "A garden enclosed is my sister, my bride; a garden enclosed, a fountain sealed" (4:12). He concludes, "The symbolic meaning of a man's virginity, then, is a dominion over the subhuman world for the good of his prospective family, that images God's dominion over the entire universe for the good of his family, the whole people of God."[55] He asks what is the meaning of man's physical powers coming to maturity before he, himself, is ready for marriage? The young man is called upon to master his sexual desires so that in marriage he procreates in response to love not lust. "If a husband is not capable of perfect self-control, he is incapable of giving himself perfectly to his wife."[56]

John Paul II, himself, addresses chastity from a phenomenological perspective in *Love and Responsibility.* His approach is above all personalist. The person, especially in the sexual relation, is both a subject and an object, but he is not a "something," nor simply an individual member of the species. He has an inner life from his rational nature, which enables him to communicate with God and others. He also has the power of self-determination, which makes him the arbiter of his own decisions. No one else can will for him, unless he permits it. Because he has intelligence and freedom, it is never legitimate to treat him simply as an object or a mere means to an end, for example, sexual satisfaction. Love demands the couple subordinate sexual enjoyment to the good of the person. A basic, although not the only, reason for chastity is the potential for creating a new human person. When a person respects this potential, he or she grows in the power of self-determination and self-possession by exercising the virtue of chastity. Such self-mastery enables the person to become a gift, so that conjugal relations then become mutual self-gift. Pleasure is not absent from their union. On the contrary, it becomes all the greater when subordinated to love.[57]

The Wounded Heart

Love, being a property of the person, does not depend on sexual intercourse for its expression. Unfortunately, according to Ashley Montagu, author of *Touching, the Human Significance of Skin*: "The frenetic preoccupation with sex that characterizes Western culture is in many cases not the expression of a sexual interest at all, but rather a search for the satisfaction of the need for contact."[58] His researches led him to conclude:

> Tactile stimulation appears to be a fundamentally necessary experience for healthy behavioral development of the individual. Failure to receive tactile stimulation in infancy results in a critical failure to establish contact relations with others.[59]

Personal identity must be grounded in bodily feeling. [60] Jean Vanier, founder of the l'Arche for the mentally disabled, confirms these findings. He writes about a boy, who was abandoned by his mother and did not receive the warmth and bodily affection he needed. He was obsessed with the desire to touch and caress women.

> His need to touch and be touched was not primarily a genital need. It was not in the literal sense a sexual urge; it was a cry of his deprived body longing to be loved and appreciated by a woman-mother.[61]

Vanier continues:

> The links which unite genital sexuality and this call to be loved, held and caressed are so profound that they lead a person to a state of confusion and fear. The cry for relationship gets mixed up with sexual desire.[62]

Since this is a theological, not a psychological treatise, specific psychological deficiencies are outside its scope to treat in detail. They are not, however, outside the scope of the sacraments to heal through grace and the support of a loving community, which Vanier explains in his chapter on "Community: Place of Sexual Integration."[63]

The Nature of Christ's Chastity

Reference was made earlier to Jean-Pierre Batut on the meaning of Christ's chastity. Drawing on Aquinas' reflection on the temptations, (*Summa Theologiae* III, q. 41) that Christ underwent, Batut asks what the relationship might be between Christ's temptations and his chastity. He notes that Aquinas makes a distinction between the temptations that have the flesh and the world as their object and those which have the devil as their direct author. Because, as a result of the Fall, all are born with a tendency to concupiscence, which even Baptism does not remove, all are subject to temptations of the flesh and the world. This is not the case with Christ or with Mary, who was conceived without original sin. So what was the nature of Christ's temptation? Batut defines Christ's innocence, the innocence that Adam and Eve possessed in the Garden of Eden, as complete orientation to God in all thought and action. The original sin was when man began to distrust God and his love. The first act then is a "*disfigurement of God,*" turning him into "an avaricious, self-serving master."[64]

In the creation account Satan begins by misrepresenting God and his word to Eve. Sin begins to exist as soon as Eve accepts this misrepresentation. As Batut says:

> The commandment of life appears arbitrary (Gn 3:3), and even wicked (Gn 3:4); and, because the true reality has been lost from sight, *that which does not exist begins to exist* (Gn 3:6). For the desirable character of what we substitute for God is but a construction of our minds. It is God alone who is desirable, and it is for this reason that the rest is good and quite truly belongs to us when we receive it from him.[65]

Chastity, then, is a "refusal to grasp" (in contrast to Eve grasping the forbidden fruit) and it relates first and foremost to God. Batut calls every sin in its essence, a sin against chastity—in its effects but also in its roots.[66] The sin of our first parents did not first concern the desirable object but God and his promises. For this reason it is the *only* temptation that can be ascribed to Christ. In the temptations in the desert, Satan questions Christ's Sonship. Again on the Cross, his Sonship is challenged (Mt. 27:40, 42-43). Batut concludes that our faith in Christ the Redeemer rests on his never being prey to the temptations of the flesh and the world that follow from the refusal of Sonship.

Marital Chastity

How does this meaning of chastity as refusal of Sonship relate to marital chastity? We have already discussed the role of chastity in fostering self-mastery for self-gift, by which the couple struggle to overcome the temptations of the flesh and the world. With redemption in Christ these temptations can be overcome and man can live his calling as a son in the Son. They can be a true witness of Christ's self-giving love for his bride the Church and an icon of divine Trinitarian communion. Here Batut cites St. Paul:

> You did not receive the spirit of slavery to fall back into fear; you received the *Spirit of sonship* by which we cry out: Abba! Father! The Spirit in person joins himself to our spirit in order to attest that we are children of God. If children, then heirs; heirs of God, and co-heirs with Christ, because we suffer with him in order that we may be glorified with him" (Rm. 8:15-16).[67]

Contraception, as has been shown, not only precludes total mutual self-gift in marriage but the couple cease to be a true icon of divine Trinitarian love in which the Father pours himself out to the Son and the Son is total receptivity, with the Holy Spirit, Person and gift, the bond of their love. Nevertheless, the man and woman, who use contraception, still engage in the sexual act. However, once contraception has been declared a good in separating the unitive and procreative dimensions of conjugal intercourse, there is, in reality, no limit to what might be declared a good, including *in vitro* fertilization and the so-called marriage of gay persons.[68] One must ask if our contemporary technological culture is not now seeking to obliterate the call to be a son in the Son and obscuring man's creation to image God both as Person and Communion of Persons?

Christ's chastity, in this understanding, consisted of adhering to his Father's will even in the greatest suffering and at the point of seeming abandonment. It was not *his* fecundity he chose but that of the Father.[69] As sons in the Son, we are called to do the same. The Church's teaching in *Humanae vitae* and *Donum vitae* spell out the limits of human mastery over the power to give life and express love. Marital chastity, understood as first and foremost our filiation to the Father, means that it extends beyond not distorting the sexual relation by contraception and destroying life through abortion to respecting the conjugal act by rejecting artificial insemination and *in vit*ro fertilization. In other words, it means accepting life according to God's laws, which are inscribed in our nature, not creating our own reality through technological means.

Accepting a child, conceived in the normal way, through adoption respects God's laws on life and love. It is an expression of his mercy to the child, to the mother who cannot care for the child and to the family, suffering from infertility, who adopts him. Moreover, the adopted child is an icon of our own adoption by the Father as sons in the Son. Indeed, St. Joseph's fatherhood of the Christ Child has been compared to that of an adoptive father. Adoption is a generous response to infertility, but it is not the only response. Spiritual fruitfulness can be expressed by service to others so that the suffering of infertility can be transformed into a new kind of fruitfulness.

The Holy Family as Model of Chastity

The chastity of Mary and Joseph has traditionally been seen as a barrier to their being a true model for families. However, their chastity as the obedience of faith in radical adherence to God's plan for their marriage provides a supreme model for married couples. The contrast between Eve and Mary as the second Eve is a favorite theme of the Fathers of the Church. Eve, before coming together with Adam, listened to the Serpent and, choosing to disbelieve God's promises, disobeyed him by eating of the tree of good and evil. Mary believed in God's promises and conceived the Son of the Most High in her womb.[70] John Paul II chose the theme of Mary's obedience in faith for his encyclical, *Redemptoris mater.* He also praised St. Joseph's faith in *Redemptoris Custos.* Once he had been reassured in a dream of the nature of Mary's conception, he did not hesitate to take her into his home. For both Mary and Joseph, what was asked of them was not expected, yet they both embraced God's plan for them completely. In doing so, John Paul II asks if Joseph did not find an even greater love as husband/father.

In the same way, the pope calls married couples to be "interpreters of God's plan" for their marriage and family, following Vatican Council II:

> Through this sense of responsibility for love and for life, God, the Creator invites the spouses not to be passive operators but rather "co-operators or almost interpreters" of his plan (*Gaudium et spes* no. 50). In fact they are called out of respect for the objective moral order established by God, to an obligatory *discernment of the indications of God's will concerning their family.*[71]

John Paul II's description of what is required of couples practicing periodic continence could well refer to the marriage of Mary and Joseph. "It *requires a profound understanding of the person and love.* In truth, that requires mutual listening and dialogue by spouses, attention and sensitivity to the other spouse and constant self-control: all of these are qualities which express real love for the person of the spouse for what he or she is, and not for what one wishes the other to be."[72]

CHAPTER 10

The Universal Call to Holiness

Introduction

LIVING THE TRUTHS OF *HUMANAE vitae* John Paul II calls "demanding" because it calls for marital chastity. Is it an ideal or is it a path all are called to in imitation of Christ? This, in turn, raises the question of whether the Holy Family, which, traditionally, has been viewed as containing both virginity and marriage provides the model for the universal call to holiness put forward by *Lumen gentium* of Vatican Council II. This chapter considers the meaning of the call, specifically through deification, its revival through a new understanding of unity in the mystical body of Christ and John Paul II's appropriation of *Lumen gentium* in his call to holiness in communion.

The universal call to holiness, while acknowledging the hierarchy of the state of life of virginity versus marriage, also bridges the gap between them. It raises the relevance to the lay state, especially marriage, of the evangelical counsels, of poverty, chastity and obedience. Do they belong in marriage and if so, how are they understood and practiced? Our guides for a brief consideration of the topic will be St. John Paul II, pre-Vatican Council II theologian Emile Mersch, and David Crawford, who draws freely on the thought of Hans Urs von Balthasar. Finally, since sinful man cannot live the call to holiness without suffering, reflections from St. John Paul II's encyclical, *Salfivici dolores,* with special reference to the Holy Family, will round out the chapter.

Vatican Council II

The Holy Family is not only the model for the family as "domestic Church" (RC 7) but encompasses within itself both states of the Christian life, virginity and marriage. According to Vatican Council II

> As St. Ambrose taught, the Mother of God is a type of the Church in the order of faith, charity and perfect union with Christ. For in the mystery of the Church, which is itself called mother and virgin, the Blessed Virgin stands out in eminent and singular fashion as exemplar both of virgin and mother (LG 63).

Her motherhood took place within her marriage to Joseph.[1] As St. John Paul II says

> And thanks also to Joseph, the mystery of the Incarnation and, together with it, the mystery of the Holy Family, comes to be profoundly inscribed in the spousal love of husband and wife and, in an indirect way in the genealogy of every family. What St. Paul will call the great mystery found its most lofty expression in the Holy Family. Thus the family truly takes its place at the very heart of the new covenant (LF 20).

He goes on to explain: "It [the family] is a treasure which grows out of the rich tradition of the old covenant, is completed in the new and finds its fullest symbolic expression in the Holy Family in which the divine Bridegroom brings about the redemption of all families" (LF 23). Just as the Israelite family was called to be holy, so the Christian family is called to an even greater holiness, a teaching that had been obscured during the centuries until recovered by Vatican Council II and taken up particularly by John Paul II in his documents on the family and in his reflections on the Holy Family. "Whereas Adam and Eve were the source of evil which was unleashed on the world, Joseph and Mary are the summit from which holiness spreads all over the earth" (RC 7).

Vatican Council II, while maintaining the division and hierarchy of the ordained and consecrated orders, nevertheless put new emphasis on the way the faithful share in the one priesthood of Christ. For they "exercise that priesthood too by the reception of the sacraments, prayer and thanksgiving, the witness of a holy life and active charity" (LG 10). The Council unequivocally states that all Christians, whether consecrated or lay, have received a universal call to holiness. In Section 11, the document states that all the faithful "are called by the Lord to that perfection of sanctity by which the Father himself is perfect." Again in section 39, "All in the Church, whether they belong to the hierarchy or are cared for by it, are called to holiness," and "All Christians in any state or walk of life are called to the fullness of Christian life and to the perfection of love, and by this holiness a more human manner of life is fostered also in earthly society" (LG 39). Specifically, "in virtue of the sacrament of Matrimony by which they signify and share (cf. Eph. 5:32) the mystery of the unity and faithful love between Christ and the Church, Christian married couples help one another to attain holiness in their married life and in, the rearing of their children." (LG 11)

Deification

The warrant for the universal call to holiness is what is known as the "formula of exchange" as expressed in the words of Pope Benedict XVI: "This exchange consists of God taking our human existence on himself in order to bestow his divine existence on us, of his choosing our nothingness in order to give his plenitude."[2] The Incarnation, passion, death and resurrection of Jesus Christ enable us to become adopted sons of the Father. This is not a new teaching in the Church, but was obscured over the centuries, although it is central to the Gospels, the epistles and the Church Fathers.[3] The latter state that the primary means of appropriating this "exchange" are baptism and the Eucharist. In baptism, the Holy Spirit comes to dwell in the soul. With the erasure of original sin—although not its effects—the Christian grows more and more into the likeness of Christ by participating in the Eucharist and the other sacraments. In Baptism and the Eucharist, there is a real participation in the sufferings, death and resurrection of Christ; the Eucharist is a "real incorporation into Christ." The *goal* of deification—of the "admirable exchange"—is to be conformed to Christ and transformed into his image. While deification is a gift from above, which man cannot merit, nevertheless he is called to respond with his freedom. "Through prayer and a life of asceticism, communion with the Triune God is deepened and our likeness to Christ grows."[4]

The Mystical Body of Christ

With the rise of Scholaticism, Jansenism and the separation of various theological disciplines, particularly of morality from the ascetical and mystical life, sadly, deification ceased to take central place.[5] It was the recovery of the Church as the mystical body of Christ that led to a rediscovery of holiness in all its members.[6] Jesuit Theologian, Emile Mersch shows how Vatican Council I led the way in restoring the true nature of the relation between Christ and the Church, which culminated in *Lumen gentium* in Vatican Council II. For Emile Mersch, the outstanding mark of the Church is its unity in Christ, from which flows the holiness of all its members.

> The "mystery" is before all else a prodigy of unity. God has raised to a supernatural perfection the natural unity that exists between men. Henceforth they are one, but one in Christ, one with a unity so sublime that they are as little able to attain it by their unaided efforts as they are to comprehend it by their unaided reason.[7]

He goes on to say that we are made holy, just and pure before God, solely because of Christ and in him as the second Person of the Blessed Trinity. Mersch sees the Mystical Body of the Church prefigured in the Old Testament. The Chosen People comprise a unity in whom God dwells and through whom he shines his holiness. The Hebrews are one whole, one spouse, one person whom God loves passionately. Mersch here outlines implicitly the idea of corporate personality, discussed earlier. When Christ is compared to Adam, it is not as an isolated individual, but as the prototype of humanity, who are all regenerated in Him. Citing the Epistle to the Ephesians, he calls Christ the supernatural unity of all creation and God's plans in it.[8]

St. John Paul II

The Call to Holiness in Communion

John Paul II devoted his first encyclical to "The Redeemer of Man, Jesus Christ, [who] is the center of the universe and of history." Although the pope does not use the term "deification," the whole encyclical centers on the transformation of man in Jesus Christ through the Church, his body. The Vatican Council II document, *Gaudium et spes*, in his words, "a stupendous text," particularly section 22, inspired him. "Christ, the new Adam, in the very revelation of the mystery of the Father and of his love, *fully reveals man to himself* and brings to light his most high calling." Man must draw near to Christ. "He must, so to speak, enter into him with all his own self, he must 'appropriate and assimilate the whole of the reality of the Incarnation and Redemption in order to find himself.'"[9] Through Christ, man becomes fully aware of his own dignity, the "dignity of both the grace of divine adoption and the inner truth of humanity" (RH 11). This is accomplished through the sacraments of the Church, particularly the Eucharist. He calls it "the center and summit of the whole of sacramental life, through which each Christian receives the saving power of redemption, beginning with Baptism, in which we are buried into the death of Christ, in order to become sharers in his resurrection" (RH 20). Christ's death on the cross has made us "children of God," "adopted sons" and "a kingdom of priests" (RH 20).

Later that same year, in preparation for the 1980 Synod on the Family, John Paul II initiated the four-year series of Wednesday homilies on Scripture texts related to marriage, later published as *Man and Woman He Created Them: A Theology of the Body* (MW). It is in this Catechesis that he spells out what the "universal call to holiness" means. He first addresses the topic of holiness in the homily of January 30, 1980. "If creation is a gift given to man . . . then *its fullness* and deepest dimension is *determined by grace,* that is by participation in the inner life of God himself, in his holiness," which is love (MW 16:3). This homily on man's original innocence and holiness comes directly after a reflection on the spousal meaning of the body. The body in its masculine and feminine dimensions, its sexuality, reveals the essence of man and woman's existence as a gift, to be lived as mutual gift. It thereby witnesses to Love as the source of the gift and their rootedness in love. Because the man and woman in original innocence are free from any constraint of the body and sex, having the "freedom of the gift," they are able to receive each other as God intended. In the act of receiving one another, they affirm each other, first as persons, and this reciprocity creates the communion of persons. In other words, their relationship is not determined by sexual desire but by their existence as person-subjects capable of becoming a complete gift in the one-flesh union of marriage. It is the grace of original innocence that both *"manifests and constitutes the perfect ethos of the gift"* (MW, 18:5).

In his answer to the Pharisees' question on divorce (Mt. 19:8) Christ appeals to the graced beginning of man in original innocence. In the "beginning" man was called to holiness. In his theology of original innocence, John Paul II spells out in more detail this holiness and its link to the creation of man and woman as gift ordered to a relationship of mutual self-giving. He links it especially to the Genesis text 2:25 "they were naked and not ashamed." Immunity from shame implies that they possessed the perfect "freedom of the gift," so that:

> *Together with man, holiness has entered the visible world,* the world created for him. The sacrament of the world, and the sacrament of man in the world, comes from the divine source of holiness, and is instituted, at the same time, for holiness. Original innocence, connected with the experience of the spousal meaning of the body, is holiness itself, which permits man to express himself deeply with his own body, precisely through the "sincere gift" of self. Consciousness of the gift conditions in this case, the "sacrament of the body": in his body as man or woman, man senses himself as a subject of holiness (MW 19: 5).

Transforming Nature of Redemption

John Paul II draws attention particularly to texts of St. Paul to show the transforming nature of Redemption after man and woman have sinned and lost the grace and holiness of original innocence.. Among these passages he cites 1 Thessalonians 3-5: "For this is the will of God, your sanctification: that you abstain from unchastity; that each of you know himself in holiness and honor, not in the passion of lust . . . For God has not called us in uncleanness, but in holiness." Holiness is linked to purity, a virtue, which brings about self-mastery through human effort responding to the gift of grace. Through this self-mastery, the person gradually acquires the "freedom of the gift." It is a "capacity" rooted in the will and at the same time a gift of the Holy Spirit. The body's dignity now rests not just in being united to man's spiritual faculties but from its Redemption in Christ. "*The redemption of the body* brings with it the establishment in Christ and for Christ of a new *measure of holiness of the body*" (MW 56:4). The body is indwelt by the Holy Spirit and has become the temple of the Holy Spirit (1 Cor. 6:19) so that sins against the body are sins against the Holy Spirit.

After a discussion on the resurrected state, when there will be no marriage or giving in marriage, but the body will receive a new state of spiritualization, John Paul II turns to Christ's words on continence (eunuchs) for the kingdom of God. The passage in Matthew immediately follows the conversation with the Pharisees on divorce. It is in this context that John Paul II talks about the virginal marriage of Mary and Joseph. He had already called continence for the kingdom of heaven a "charismatic sign" of the resurrected state pointing to the eschatological "virginity" that pertains there. He says of this state: "the absolute and eternal spousal meaning of the glorified body will be revealed in union with God himself, by seeing him face-to-face," glorified moreover through the union of a perfect intersubjectivity that will unite all the "sharers in the other world," men and women in the communion of saints" (MW 75:1). By his own virgin birth in a virginal marriage, Christ elevates virginity beyond the Old Testament's preference for marriage. Yet it was not a repudiation of marriage. Rather:

> *The marriage of Mary and Joseph . . . conceals within itself,* at the same time *the mystery* of the perfect communion of persons, of Man and Woman in the conjugal covenant and at the same time the mystery of this *singular "continence for the kingdom of heaven"*: a continence that served the most perfect "*fruitfulness of the Holy Spirit"* in the history of salvation (MW 75:3).

Traditionally, consecrated virginity has been the path to holiness in the Church especially since the fourth century. In his treatment of celibacy "for the Kingdom," John Paul II does not negate this teaching but gives it a greater nuance. Celibacy for the kingdom is grounded in the same spousal meaning of the body as marriage but the spouse is the Divine Bridegroom. It is "a gift-of-self understood as a *renunciation* but realized above all *out of love*" (MW 80:1). He refers to the Old Testament understanding of holiness as first having an ontological character before a moral one. To be holy meant to be set apart for God, belonging only to Him. This is true of the consecrated virgin, who ought also to be distinguished by moral purity. In the first letter to the Corinthians, St. Paul refers to the "*transitoriness of the world* and of human life in it" (MW 84: 6). For this reason alone, the virginal state is better as it liberates the person from immersion in worldly affairs. It also points to man's destiny to the "future life." However, it is not continence by itself that leads to the state of perfection. "*The perfection of Christian life is measured*, rather, *by the measure of love*" (MW 78:3). Although a life based on the evangelical counsels of poverty, chastity and obedience help the person to reach a fuller love, a person living outside an institutionalized religious state, can reach perfection flowing from love "*through faithfulness to the spirit of the counsels.*" (MW 78: 3) Redemption of the body makes both paths to holiness possible. The hypostatic union, which took place in the Holy Family, witnesses to the superabundant fruitfulness of consecrated virginity, while, at the same time, taking place within the covenant of marriage of Mary and Joseph --a perfect communion of persons (MW 75:3).[10]

Practical Implications

In his apostolic letter, *Novo millennio ineunte*, ushering in the third millennium, John Paul II stressed that it is imperative to uncover the full pastoral significance of *Lumen gentium's* "universal call to holiness." He notes that the Council Fathers speak of the universal call to holiness, not just to embellish the Church superficially but to make it "an intrinsic and essential aspect of their teaching on the Church."[11] As a result, in his words, "the rediscovery of the Church as 'mystery,' or as a people 'gathered together by the unity of the Father, the Son and the Holy Spirit,' is bound to bring with it a rediscovery of the Church's 'holiness,' understood in the basic sense of belonging to him who is in essence, the 'thrice Holy'" *(cc. Is 6:3).* As the bride of Christ, who gave himself up for her, the Church is holy so that an objective gift of holiness is given to all the baptized. He goes on to say "the gift in turn becomes a task, which must shape the whole of Christian life" (NMI 30). Furthermore, "the time has come to re-propose wholeheartedly to everyone this *high standard of ordinary Christian living*: the whole life of the Christian community and of Christian families must lead in this direction" (NMI 31). This means adhering to the "radical nature of the Sermon on the Mount," and eschewing a "life of mediocrity" (NMI 30).

It also means married couples adhering to magisterial teaching on life and love. It is noteworthy that *Humanae vitae* was *the* reason John Paul II wrote his ground-breaking theology of the body (MW 133:4). As he said, "In some sense, one can even say that all the reflections dealing with the "Redemption of the Body and the Sacramentality of Marriage *seem* to constitute *an extensive commentary* on the doctrine contained precisely in *Humanae Vitae* (MW 133:2). From his earliest day as pastor and Bishop, the future pope John Paul II saw the New Testament appeal "'Be perfect...,' a call to self-perfection through love" as addressed to everyone. "By calling to perfection, the Gospel, at the same time, presents the truth about grace for us to believe. The action of grace places man in the orbit of God" (LR 243).

Therefore, to be trained in holiness, Christians must learn the art of prayer. St John Paul II does not shy away from recommending to Christian communities the great mystics and teachers of prayer such as St. Teresa of Avila and St. John of the Cross. Christians must enter into an intense dialogue of love with God which opens the heart to love of others. The goal of mystical prayer is to be totally possessed by the divine Beloved in spousal union. Liturgical prayer and the sacraments, especially Reconciliation and the Eucharist, are the efficacious means for purifying the soul and transmitting grace so as to bring about transformation in Christ. The pope says:

> It is prayer, which roots us in truth. It constantly reminds us of the primacy of Christ and, in union with him, the primacy of the interior life and of holiness (NMI 38).[12]

Pastoral Implications for Morality

Emile Mersch had already considered some of the pastoral implications for morality. In his view, God's holiness, justice and purity that "flow into" the members of the Mystical Body, produce vital effects on Christian ethics. "It establishes a new, purer, supernatural code of morality; it calls for a Christian holiness, for a Christian chastity and above all, for a Christian charity."[13] Mersch calls the Trinitarian dogma of unity in love "the great principle for the morality of Christians inasmuch as they are united to Christ."[14] Such a morality does not de-nature man. On the contrary, Mersch argues, men are called to become like God through their humanity. While Christ's death separated body and soul, it did not separate his humanity and divinity so that nothing in our nature is despised. This means, among other effects, that all man's affections must be respected. For those belonging to Christ's body there is no individual holiness. A Christian always acts as a member among members, which implies both attachment to Christ and to all other members through charity. Both Christian asceticism and sanctity, although they belong to the individual as part, are inconceivable outside the whole of the Mystical Body.

The Evangelical Counsels

If one and the same holiness flows in all, the question arises as to whether the evangelical counsels of poverty, chastity and obedience have a more universal application than simply to the consecrated state? In what way could the laity, especially the married, be called to live the "spirit of the counsels?" Since the counsels are so intimately linked to holiness, reference will be made to authors who have considered the question in depth.

Emile Mersch

Mersch begins to answer this by first looking at obedience. He finds obedience indispensable. Just as charity, the overriding virtue, causes us to love as a member of the Church, obedience directs our will so that it subordinates itself to the other parts of Christ's body, but always in a spirit of charity. He distinguishes first obedience that is owed to God who is the source of all authority; it comprises obedience to conscience and to the natural law, which he calls "sacred and obligatory before all others."[15] The obedience of children in the family and citizens in society also call for yielding one's will to another. Redemption brings a new way of acting in dependence on Christ. Grace makes possible this new way of life, which demands at the minimum obedience to the Ten Commandments. The way of perfection of the consecrated demands more. It involves emptying oneself to be filled with the divine will. Here Mersch clearly makes a distinction between the ordinary way and the way of perfection.

His most innovative reflections center on love, marriage and chastity. They flow from his theology of the Mystical Body. With redemption, conjugal love ceases to be just human and becomes a "thing of grace."[16]It has been greatly ennobled and transfigured by Christian charity. Mersch sees it as an "urgent duty" for Christian married couples to realize the full splendor of their state. "They must be shown how their state has its place, its very own place, in the Church of God, among the martyrs and confessors, the virgins and the pontiffs."[17] He calls on religious, while valuing their own commitment to total chastity, to love and honor marriage as another state of life. There needs to be a new understanding of purity and its relation to human love. Mersch is above all intent on rescuing conjugal love from any denigration. Even if man has degraded it with concupiscence, love itself comes from God, who is especially present in the creation of a new human being. "To sin against it, is to sin against God, where he is most present in the natural order."[18] Mersch goes so far as to say that "to change into a sensualist egoism the movement of the giving of self . . . is to pillage one's soul."[19]

Mersch argues from the perspective of the perpetuation of the human species, which takes place in the union of the man and woman. Their love "has its reason for being, its energies, and thence its requirements, not from the individual, but from the species."[20]As such they are the passive instruments of a force that is greater than themselves. God, who is the Author of our nature and raised it to a new dignity by the Incarnation, requires us to strictly adhere to his designs. The theologian does not mince his words. "To take as a toy the august function which alone assures its (humanity's) existence, is to sin grievously against the first principle of all society and against the essential subordination of the individual to the species."[21] Beyond the life-giving dimension, the conjugal act is intimately tied to love. In its intensity it has the power to move the man and woman "to a splendid life of devotion and forgetfulness."[22] For this reason the virtue of purity is the more necessary. Unlike other virtues, where the will is in more direct control of bodily acts, the virtue of purity in this act is incarnated in the corporeal activity itself. For those intent on right action, it is only possible "with great struggle [to] make brightness penetrate the depths."[23] The theologian expresses here a profound realism, going so far as to say "a man must labor and bleed in order to purify and to spiritualize slowly those shadowy regions where the past of our species has allowed too many evil roots to sink in."[24]

Mersch sees the sixth commandment as requiring above all mutual respect in marriage. The union that follows from the act of love must be exclusive, faithful and permanent. Because it plays such a large place in human, hence, in Christian life, it is fitting that it is a sacrament of the Church. Surrounded by dangers, and especially as the source of future members of the Church, it is in need of a consecration, so that marriage, which realizes the unity of humanity, is given a higher kind of perfection in Jesus Christ. Mersch calls the sacrament the "very essence of marriage" as a union of love; it participates in the union between Christ and the Church, between humanity and the Word. He sees the crucifix hovering over marriage, noting that it does not have all its perfection without sacramental consecration. Having given such a eulogy of marriage, Mersch is at the same time committed to the teaching expounded by the Council of Trent that consecrated virginity is a higher state of life.[25]

David Crawford

David Crawford links his discussion on the public vows of the consecrated religious more explicitly to the marriage vow. He follows in the footsteps of Hans Urs von Balthasar, who, in turn builds on the theology of Aquinas on the meaning of a vow. For Aquinas, the vow is a "promise made to God"[26] and, as such, is an act of religion. Because it belongs to "divine worship"[27] and is like a sacrifice to God, a work performed in fulfillment of a vow is more meritorious than without. It is clear that Aquinas sees the vow as something sacred, pertaining to God in its nature and fulfillment. Aquinas explains why a vow is necessary:

> [R]eligious perfection requires that a man give his whole life to God. But man cannot actually give his whole life to God, because that life taken as a whole is not simultaneous but successive. Hence man cannot give his whole life to God otherwise than by the obligation of a vow.[28]

God finds the vow highly acceptable because a person renders to him his liberty, which, Aquinas says, "is dearer to him than aught else."[29]

According to von Balthasar, when Aquinas frames the vow primarily in the context of religious life, he does not bring out its full relationship to the very nature of love. He goes beyond Aquinas in asserting that "*every true love has the inner form of a vow:* It binds itself to the beloved—and does so out of motives and in the spirit of love."[30] For Aquinas, the evangelical counsels, in as much as they are the means to the perfection of charity, are an instrumental cause of charity and not charity itself. Like virtues, they are useful tools in directing life to our ultimate end, love of God. In this understanding they are usually associated with the consecrated state but charity itself is the call of every Christian. Yet Aquinas also sees them as a form of personal identification with Christ's self-immolation.[31] When considered as such, they cease being merely instrumental and constitute "the actual giving away of self in love."[32]Under this light, the counsels can be viewed as the very form of self-gift, which paves the way for regarding vows as *central* to all Christian identity arising from the Gospel.

Indeed, Crawford proceeds to draw out the implications of von Balthasar's analysis for all true love that seeks to give itself away in total self-gift. Although the paradigmatic state is consecrated virginity, the implications include marriage, friendship and parental love. He declares:

> Only an irrevocable vow is capable of taking up the whole of a person, including his future, in such an act of open-ended self-commitment. We might say, then, that explicit vows are the "objective" actualization of love itself, because they do not simply lead to but in fact *constitute* love's giving away of self. Love, in other words, is manifested outwardly and becomes a human action in the form of an explicit vow.[33]

In this view, vowed love is not simply one form of love but the inner form of love itself, because it has an interior ordination to vows. Its deepest meaning and inner structure are "directed toward communion, which is finally only realized in explicit vows."[34] Crawford further states that a "presupposition of our discussion of vows is that love finds its culmination in self-gift and vows are the means by which human creatures, who are situated in a world of time and movement, can take up and give themselves away."[35]

Crawford makes this even plainer in his book, *Marriage and the Sequela Christi*. Marriage, he says, is the ecclesial "framework for the training of desire."[36] Purity of heart, which enables self-gift through the virtues and gifts of the Holy Spirit is fundamentally agapic and Christo-formic. Married couples, like the consecrated celibate, are called to struggle to overcome the effects of concupiscence. This exercises the person's freedom at the deepest level. The struggle does not destroy *Eros,* which can only find fulfillment in a horizon beyond itself. Like virginity, marriage is a nuptial or spousal response, activating the human vocation to love. Belonging to the created order, marriage has also been raised to an ecclesial reality by Christ. *Both* virginity and marriage are contained in the nuptials of Christ and the Church. Given the above, he concludes that "the counsels become the archtypical moral response to which marriage is called, and in which it shares as an ecclesial and sacramental reality."[37] However, it must always be remembered that the public vows of consecrated virginity in their radicality point to the resurrected state where there is no marriage or giving in marriage.[38]

John Paul II

As we have seen, Vatican Council II, especially through *Gaudium et spes,* brought new attention to the human person imaging God, not simply in his spiritual faculties of intellect and will but even more in communion with others.[39] In addressing both marriage and consecrated celibacy, John Paul II made this Trinitarian anthropology his primary framework. In his apostolic exhortation on consecrated life, *Vita consecrata*, he sees a Trinitarian dimension in the evangelical counsels.

> The deepest meaning of the evangelical counsels is revealed when they are viewed in relation to the Holy Trinity, the source of holiness. They are in fact an expression of the love of the Son for the Father in the unity of the Holy Spirit. By practicing the evangelical counsels, the consecrated person lives with particular intensity the Trinitarian and Christological dimension which marks the whole of Christian life.[40]

Chastity manifests the "undivided heart," that links the divine Persons in infinite love; poverty expresses the total gift of self each is to the other and obedience shows the trust that is both "filial" and "liberating" at the heart of the harmony of the Trinity.[41]

Man and woman truly find themselves through this total self-gift either to God or to a human spouse in sacramental marriage. The vows taken by consecrated religious and of sacramental marriage share in common a total, permanent and exclusive self-gift to another. Through baptism all are called to love Christ before all others, but through public vows to the evangelical counsels, consecrated religious give a living witness to an all-embracing commitment to Christ. Once final vows have been professed the commitment is unconditional and permanent.[42] In John Paul II's words to consecrated religious:

> *The profound essence of your consecrated life* consists . . . in a permanent gift to God that translates itself into an *espoused and total gift of self to the Lord.* Your gift of self is an *unconditional response to a declaration of love*, a response which is nourished by faith and prayer, after the example of the Virgin Mary, the perfect model of union with Christ the Redeemer.[43]

The permanence and spousal nature are also made evident in the ceremony of religious profession of consecrated virgins. For example, the bishop in giving the candidate the ring says, "*Receive the ring that marks you as a bride of Christ.* Keep unstained your *fidelity to your bridegroom*, that you may be admitted to the wedding of everlasting joy."[44] John Paul II refers to the specific "consecration" of the vocation of married couples spoken of by Vatican Council II. He sees both states not only complementing each other but also learning from and supporting each other.[45] While they are mutually exclusive they are harmoniously combined in Mary and Joseph, who, with Christ, are the model for both states. While these authors are moving toward a greater unity of the states of consecrated celibacy and marriage, it is a unity in difference in the universal call to holiness. Both are expressions of the unity of Christ and the Church.

In *Letter to Families*, John Paul II, in reference to Ephesians 5: 21-33 declares: "St. Paul's magnificent synthesis concerning the great mystery appears as the compendium or *summa*, in some sense, of the teaching about God and man which was brought to fulfillment in Christ." The pope echoes Mersch:

> The great mystery, which is the Church and humanity in Christ, does not exist apart from the great mystery expressed in the 'one-flesh (cp. Gn. 2:24 and Eph. 5:31-32), that is the reality of marriage and family.

> The family is the great mystery of God. As the domestic Church it is the bride of Christ. The universal Church and every particular Church in her, is most immediately revealed as the bride of Christ in the domestic Church and in its experience of love: conjugal love, paternal and maternal love, fraternal love, the love of a community of persons and of generations (LF 19).

The Universal Call to Holiness and Suffering

All these family relations and with them the community of the family, the first communion of persons, are put at risk by the separation of procreation from the conjugal act. Aided by new reproductive technologies, the separation results in daily more and greater fracturing of family relations. Pope Paul VI was well aware of the danger, and spelled them out in his prophetic 1968 encyclical, *Humanae vitae.* Not only are marriage and family put at risk in their human dimension, but they cannot image the total self-giving union of Christ and the Church, let alone divine Trinitarian communion, which St. John Paul II so eloquently expounds in his Wednesday Catechesis and many subsequent Church documents. Fortunately for humanity, God does not depend on weak and wayward humanity to reveal either his designs for mankind to participate in divine Trinitarian communion or his faithful and merciful love, but he does call for a free human response. This means living a life of virtue, integrity and holiness, which inevitably brings suffering to post-lapsarian man, who is subject to the threefold concupiscence of the flesh, of the eyes and the pride of life, which are not of the Father but of the "world" (See 1 John 15-17).

Indeed, the asceticism of marital chastity is required of couples using NFP when they have good reasons to avoid a pregnancy for a limited or even indefinite period (HV 10). Such restraint can undoubtedly cause suffering, but, as study after study shows the benefits for the majority of couples in increased intimacy, love and respect, outweigh the difficulties.[46] It is pertinent, then, to look at the place of suffering in the Christian life, especially since the suffering of the Cross is at the heart of the good news. Central to Christianity is the paradox of the cross of Christ, as St. Paul says: "The word of the cross is folly to those who are perishing, but to us who are being saved it is the power of God...For Jews demand signs and Greeks seek wisdom, but we preach Christ crucified, a stumbling block to Jews and folly to Gentiles, but to those who are called, both Jews and Greeks, Christ the power of God and the wisdom of God. For the foolishness of God is wiser than men, and the weakness of God is stronger than men" (1 Cor. 1:18, 22-25).

Salvifici Dolores, *The Gospel of Suffering*

Why, when Christianity proclaims the goodness of God and of the world he has created, is there suffering? John Paul II notes that man has always asked this question, especially since suffering in the world, particularly of the innocent, often causes man to deny God's existence. The answer is that *love* is the fullest answer to the meaning of suffering. Love was expressed in the cross of Jesus Christ, God's only Son, who was given to man to liberate him from evil, which is the meaning of salvation. The problem of suffering must be seen in the perspective of the love of the Father who gave his only Son out of love "to protect man against this definitive evil and against *definitive suffering*" (SD 14). Christ conquers sin by his death and death by his resurrection. "As a result of Christ's salvific work, man exists on earth *with the hope* of eternal life and holiness" (SD 15).

This does not eliminate temporal suffering but throws a new light on all suffering both physical and moral, the light of salvation. And that is the good news of the Gospel. By taking suffering on himself, from fatigue to misunderstanding, from persecution to the pangs of death, Christ drew near to all who suffer. At the same time he spent his public life healing all manner of disease and sickness. Suffering now is linked to love, "to that love which creates good, drawing it out by means of suffering, just as the supreme good of the redemption of the world was drawn from the cross of Christ, and from that cross constantly takes its beginning" (SD 18). Furthermore, every man now, by joining his suffering to Christ, can share in the mystery of redemption. To share in the sufferings of Christ is also to share in the glory of the resurrection.

John Paul II cites St. Paul, "But far be it from me to *glory* except in the *cross* of our Lord Jesus Christ, by which the world has been crucified to me and I to the world" (Gal. 6:14). To share in the sufferings of Christ is to become worthy of his kingdom. Here the pope speaks both of "maturity" and "spiritual maturity" brought about by suffering, referring to "this *spiritual tempering* of man in the midst of trials and tribulations" (SD 23). Suffering is a school of virtue, especially the virtue of endurance. Bringing about both hope and joy, it reveals the creative character of suffering. There is another way that suffering releases love; by relieving it in another. And here the example given is the parable of the "Good Samaritan."

While Christ, Himself, is the supreme model of the relationship between suffering and love, the one closest to him, Mary, whose heart Simeon prophesied would be pierced by a sword, is rightfully called Our Lady of Sorrows. The pope makes particular reference at the end of the encyclical to the sufferings Jesus's mother endured at Bethlehem, Nazareth and at the foot of the Cross.

The Holy Family and Suffering

Although Mary was sinless and Joseph was sanctified by the presence of Christ, the Holy Family was by no means free from suffering. At the end of the next chapter, in discussing the role of mercy in the Christian, indeed, human life, it is proposed by John Paul II that Mary received the greatest mercy in being conceived without sin; she also underwent the greatest suffering. Suffering accompanied her and the Holy Family from the moment of the conception of Jesus in her womb. The gospels of Matthew and Luke recount the suffering surrounding Mary's pregnancy, from the dilemma facing Joseph (Mt. 1: 18-19) to birth in a stable because there was no room at the inn (Lk 2: 7). This was followed by the slaughter of the innocents by Herod, the flight into Egypt and another uprooting with the return to Nazareth (Matt. 2: 7-18). Luke tells of the loss of the child Jesus for three days and the anxiety of his parents: "Son, why have you treated us so? Behold, your father and I have been looking for you anxiously" (Lk 2:48). These are the sufferings and vicissitudes that can happen to any family and call for endurance, patience and trust in God and each other.

There were additional sufferings, which especially affected Joseph, but also Mary. Joseph, in his appellation of "righteous," was heir to all the blessings of the Old Covenant, among them the one-flesh union of Genesis and the blessing of procreation. The psalms praise the father of many sons.[47] While, as we have seen, the practice of "family purity" required considerable restraint in sexual relations, particularly on the part of the husband, this restraint was ordered to the enjoyment of the sexual union blessed by procreation. Joseph, on the contrary, was required to forego sexual relations altogether and yet to live in intimate physical proximity to Mary. Earlier testimony in Chapter Five of the experience of Bartolomeo de Dominici, in the presence of the beautiful Christ-filled Catherine of Siena, shows how sensual responses may be quieted. This would undoubtedly have been the case with St. Joseph, who was continually in the presence of Christ and the Blessed Virgin. But is it impossible to imagine that he was tempted, just as Jesus, himself, was tempted by Satan, but did not sin?[48] St. Joseph was also denied physical paternity, and Mary, as part of God's plan, conceived only one child. In a culture that praised many offspring, it is not inconceivable that at one level this constituted a suffering? Furthermore, the Holy Family enjoyed little status in society, residing in the insignificant town of Nazareth—as Nathaniel exclaimed, "Can anything good come out of Nazareth?" (Jn 1: 46). Joseph's modest profession as a carpenter did nothing to enhance Jesus' public image. "Is not this the Son of the carpenter, the Son of Mary?" (Mark 6:3; cf. Lk 4:22) Finally, Mary saw the death of her husband and later the ignominious death of her Son.

Looking at the sufferings of the Holy Family, we can see that they are divided into two categories, not necessarily separated from one another, firstly the vicissitudes of family life: a surprise pregnancy, rejection and birth in a stable, murderous threats against the life of the child, being forced to flee into exile at a moment's notice, leaving possessions and everything familiar behind, losing an only son at the age of twelve for three days with concomitant anxiety and, for Mary, widowhood. Secondly, although it was only recorded of Jesus that he "increased in wisdom and in stature, and in favor with God and man" (Lk 2: 52), Mary and Joseph, too, must have increased in wisdom and in virtue. Bearing the sufferings they underwent as a family would undoubtedly have caused them to exercise the natural virtues of justice, prudence, temperance and fortitude as well as the theological virtues of faith, hope and charity/love. In his encyclical, *Redemptoris mater*, John Paul II is eloquent on Mary's faith, making the words of Elizabeth, "Blessed is she who believed" (Lk 1: 45) the overarching theme of his exposition of the Blessed Virgin Mary. Living such faith in God's loving providence in the hidden life of Nazareth, during Jesus' public life and his crucifixion must have tested her faith, not to mention Joseph's, to the limits, which, in itself, is a suffering. All families undergo sufferings due to their particular circumstances. At the same time for man, who lives in a postlapsarian world, acquiring the natural virtues by itself entails suffering, since, as St. Paul says: "For I do not do the good I want but the evil I do not want is what I do" (Rm. 7:20). Even though Mary, conceived without original sin, was spared this inner disturbance, acquiring the virtues still required effort on her part.

There is a third kind of suffering that is also present to the Holy Family, because the extended family, which surrounded them, was afflicted by the legacy of what is now called family dysfunction, resulting often from the sins of previous generations.[49] The genealogies identify less than honorable characters such as Tamar, Ahaz, even David, who sired Solomon by the wife of the murdered Uriah (Mt. 1: 2-11). In the discussion of the nature of sin in the next chapter, St. John Paul II speaks of the "sin of the world," where the many personal sins coalesce and infect the environment. This makes living a life of charity much more difficult. Although it did not directly affect the communion of persons of the Holy Family itself, it was active in their relatives. For example, when Jesus preached in the synagogue at his home town of Nazareth, few put their faith in him (Lk 4: 25) and during his public life, his relatives were said not to believe in him (Jn 7:5). It is clear from the Genesis text that the first sin radically harmed the communion of persons between man and woman, causing a rupture between Adam and Eve and God, within the body-soul integrity of each and between each other. When the "sin of the world" is added to these personal disabilities in the communion of persons of the family, suffering inevitably results. As John Paul says, "Suffering cannot be divorced from the sin of the beginnings, from what St. John calls, 'the sin of the world' *from the sinful background* of the personal actions and social processes in human history" (SD 15).

CHAPTER 11

Sin, Conversion in Christ

Introduction

Reference has been made in the last chapter to ways the communion of persons in marriage suffers distortion. When Christ referred the Pharisees, who questioned him on divorce, back to "the beginning," he made it clear that such a disruption of the communion of persons in the family was not the norm (Matt 19:3-9). Christ had come precisely to show that the communion of persons could be restored, if not completely in this life, then in the resurrected state. Now, however the communion of persons is both a task and the fruit of sacramental grace. This chapter considers the effect of sin on the human family together with God's ever faithful mercy, which calls man not only to conversion but to a life of holiness. The restoration of the communion of persons in the family, in the manner of the Holy Family, passes by way of the Church's teaching on responsible parenthood. The chapter begins by discussing the nature of sin and sinful structures, especially as they affect the family. It moves to an analysis of conversion to sacramental love, with two examples of the distortion of the communion of persons and the differing levels of the grace of conversion. It ends with John Paul II's reflections on mercy in *Dives in Misericordia* as well as Pope Francis' call for accompaniment, discernment and integration. Mary, in the Holy Family, experienced the greatest mercy according to John Paul II.

The Holy Family differs from the ordinary Christian family, not only because there was no conjugal intercourse, but also because there was no sin as well as a plenitude of virtues. The Magisterium has not pronounced on the sanctification of St. Joseph. As we saw in Chapter Three, unlike Mary, who was immaculately conceived, there are various traditions on Joseph's sanctification. Was he sanctified in the womb like St. John the Baptist, as Dominican Basil Cole maintains, using the argument of fittingness, or was it at a later time? Whatever the final resolution (if any), from the time of his marriage to Mary until his death, St. Joseph lived constantly in the presence of Christ. In a similar way, through baptism, members of the Christian family are imbued with the presence of Christ. Nevertheless, despite the presence of Christ, on account of sin, it is the exceptional Christian family that even approximates the perfection of the Holy Family.

The Nature of Sin and the Family

In his Catechesis on the creed, which ran from August 27, 1986 to April 19, 1989, John Paul II began with an account of sin. "The 'mystery of iniquity,'" he says, "cannot be understood without reference to the mystery of redemption, to the paschal mystery of Jesus Christ."[1] Adam and Eve were created with original righteousness and holiness. This meant that they were free from the threefold concupiscence that, after the Fall, subjected them to inordinate desire for the pleasures of the flesh, covetousness of material goods and self-assertion that went beyond the limits of reason. John Paul II's analysis of the first sin is both succinct and profound. He notes that it did not arise in man's heart or conscience but from outside, from Satan, who had already placed God's goodness under suspicion. "They (the fallen angels) had already chosen themselves over God, instead of choosing themselves 'in God,' since they were only creatures."[2] By yielding to the temptation and disobeying God, man became Satan's accomplice. Although the original temptation came from outside and its effects are perceptible from outside, the pope notes that sin is most recognizable in the 'interior' of man, in the heart, citing *Gaudium et spes*, no. 13. Scripture confirms that sin became 'congenital' in human nature. The disobedience of the first sin, based on pride, also caused a break in the covenant between God and man, the covenant of creation. Consequently, sin opposes the objective order of human nature and of the world.

Here John Paul II introduces a discussion on the biblical phrase, "the sin of the world," found in St. John's gospel (Jn 1: 29). Sin is always the personal sin of a rational and free being but many personal sins create structures in society that make it difficult to avoid committing new personal sins. The 'sin of the world' is not to be identified with original sin. Rather the many personal sins coalesce and 'infect' the environment in which people live, so that the structures of various cultures and civilizations "bear a certain imprint of sin."[3] Here he cites the *Post-Synodal Apostolic Exhortation on Reconciliation and Penance* (1984) on the social dimension of sin. Every individual sin, from the relational nature of the human person, affects his solidarity with others and the society in which he lives. The 'sin of the world' encompasses both social sin and personal sins. In the *Exhortation on Penance*, John Paul II goes into more detail on social sin, arising from the 1982 Synod on the subject.[4]

Sin and the Civilization of Love

The pope comments that there was much talk of social sins at the Synod and he listed them as sins: against justice in interpersonal relations committed by individuals or the community; against the rights of the human person, including the unborn; against religious freedom; and against the common good of the city. He states, categorically, that it is wrong to impute personal sins to social sins because of the danger of watering down human responsibility.[5] Conversion is needed on an individual basis in order to change structures.[6] John Paul II charges, in fact, that "we are facing an enormous and dramatic clash between good and evil, death and life, the "culture of death" and the "culture of life" (EV no. 28). He attributes the roots of the "culture of death" to the rejection of

God by an all-pervasive secularism, which dominates contemporary culture and has spread its tentacles even within the Christian community. While he notes here the possibility of a "civilization of love" being opposed by an anti-civilization from current trends of positivism and utilitarianism, the following year, in addressing abortion, contraception and reproductive technologies, he gives a fuller analysis of what he now both calls the "culture of death " and the "civilization of love."

John Paul II takes up Pope Paul VI's phrase the "civilization of love," most notably in *Letter to Families* (1994) and in *Evangelism vitae* (1995). In *Letter to Families,* he refers to it after Section 12 on responsible fatherhood and motherhood, seeing the Church's teaching in *Humanae vitae* as intrinsic to a "civilization of love." He writes that the phrase is linked to the tradition of the family as "domestic Church" and has a particular relevance for our own time. In its most profound meaning it pertains to human culture and is connected to man, made in the image of God, shaping the world in accord with his lofty dignity. Since God is love, man is called to create a culture of love, so that at the heart of this civilization of love is the family.

> The family, in fact, depends for several reasons on the civilization of love and finds therein the reasons for its existence as family. And at the same time the family is the center and heart of the civilization of love (LF, no. 13).

Gift and the Civilization of Love

At the heart of a civilization of love is the concept of creation as gift. Philosopher Kenneth Schmitz in *The Gift: Creation* analyzes what creation as gift means. "*Creatio de nihilo* or *ex nihilo,* [creation out of nothing]" he says, "seems to fall outside common human experience, and consequently, outside of philosophic enquiry as such."[7] Creation from nothing is a Christian concept drawn from Scripture.[8] Scripture reveals that God creates freely out of his goodness, not out of necessity. That goodness is also reflected in the goodness of the creature. Schmitz continues that creation comes from God by way of agency which means he is the cause of production and material causality has its origin in him. Consequently, creation is not an affair of the creature until "after the fact." Turning to contemporary attitudes, Schmitz points to the modern exclusion of the Author of the gift and the treatment of creation as simply a *given fact.* These ideas, he says,

> Are a way of understanding what is before us, around us, present to us. They are burned deeply into the outlook of the so-called "advanced" societies.[9]

They are the starting point for the discourse of science, for technological advance and any generally "progressive" activity. How this eventually gives rise to the idea of the self-given of humanity itself is not the subject of this chapter or even of this book, except to say that the principle of human autonomy that resulted, is, in Schmitz's words, "shared by liberal and revolutionary ideologies alike."[10] While the scientific method has made many creative advances as part of man's call to "till the earth" (Gen 2:15), when it excludes the Creator as source of the gift, it deforms nature, man himself and his relationships, particularly in the family.

Conversion to a civilization of love, as a gift of the Trinitarian God, can only come about by a recommitment to the truth of the Gospel and a re-evangelization, especially, of the family, because, as John Paul states in *Letter to Families*:

> The family is placed at the center of the great struggle between good and evil, between life and death, between love and all that is opposed to love. To the family is entrusted the task of striving, first and foremost, to unleash the forces of good, the source of which is found in Christ, the redeemer of man (LF no. 23).

He goes on to say that "the family finds its fullest symbolic expression in the mystery of the Holy Family in which the divine bridegroom brings about the redemption of all families" (LF no. 23).

Conversion to Sacramental Love

The Sacrament of Creation

John Paul II continually states that redemption must always be measured against the creation of man "in the beginning." He does not hesitate to call the bodily union of Adam and Eve in original innocence a primordial sacrament.

> A primordial *sacrament* constituted, understood as a *sign that* efficaciously *transmits in the visible world the invisible mystery hidden in God from eternity.* And this is the mystery of Truth and Love, the mystery of divine life, in which man really participates (MW 19:4).

Creation, coming from the hand of God was endowed with holiness. Created in the grace of holiness, which belonged to the "sacrament of creation," man and woman were, indeed, its central part. After the Fall, the pope continues, when they lose the grace of holiness, *marriage never ceases to be the sacrament about which we read in Ephesians 5:22-33,* and which the author calls the "great mystery." In Atkinson's phrase, it is a secular reality before it is a sacrament of the New Covenant. Even as a secular reality it has been almost universally recognized as something sacred. In speaking of the bodily nature of man, John Paul II calls its likeness to the world of animals an analogy of "nature," but by being called the image of God, it is "raised to the level of the person and communion among persons (MW 14:6).

Sacrament: visible sign of invisible reality and efficacious sign of grace*

Primordial Sacrament	Prophets	Christ and Church	Sacrament
Made visible in man's genderdized body endowed with grace of original innocence	Sign expressed in spousal relation with people but God's loving initiative is grace, i.e. grace in God and covenant not marriage	Radical gift of God to Man (Israel/Church)	Indissolubility determined by Christ/Church union in redemption
Created in and for Christ Bore in souls fruit of election in Christ Supernatural efficacy	Marriage lost efficacy but remained site of God's design	Confers grace of participation in divine life	Sacramentality comes from Christ/Church union
From original innocence purpose (1) to prolong God's creation through procreation (2) extend fruit of election to descendants		Spousal form in continuity with original sacrament	Insistence on indissolubility opens to God's action
		Base of whole sacramental order	Ethos of redemption essential
		Determines indissolubility of marriage	Efficacious sign of God's saving power
		Takes on form of primordial sacrament	Remedy of concupiscence
		A new gracing, new creation and remission sin	Union in one flesh includes procreation and procreation comes from the Father
		New actuation of mystery	Redemption of the body points to resurrected state
		Church receives all fruitfulness from Christ as spouse	Spousal and redemptive dimensions linked in the sacrament
		Redemptive and spousal joined in sacramentality of Church and world	

*Source: John Paul II's *Theology of the Body*

It is through the lens of this beatified "beginning" that man's experience of sin must always be measured. In the second cycle of the *Catechesis*, the pope focuses on the historical state of sin, which entered the world through the very communion of the man and woman. Through this communion in the grace of original innocence, they imaged and actually began to participate in the communion of the Trinity. While sin affects every aspect of man and the world, it is John Paul II's specific contribution to show how it harms the communion of persons. While not neglecting the defects wrought in all man's nature by original sin, he rather stresses the specific effect brought about interiorly, which shatters their communion and happiness. His emphasis is always on the restoration of man's nature by the coming of the Redeemer, already foretold in Genesis 3.15 in what is called the protoevangelium. It is important to remember that neither man nor his body, which is the substratum of their communion, are evil, but sin arises in the heart. The choice of the Scripture passage of Matthew 5:27-28, which opens the discussion on concupiscence, is oriented to recovery of the spousal meaning of the body, not its condemnation. John Paul II brings the very compassion of Christ to man's suffering, calling his heart to conversion. In his Theology of the Body, the pope says that shame makes a specific contribution and "absolutely cannot be left out of consideration" (MW 11:3).

Shame

The historical state of sin is particularly characterized by shame. Here John Paul II makes use of his background in phenomenology to analyze the shame Adam and Eve and all humanity experience in the historical state of sin. He first analyzes shame in his philosophical book, *Love and Responsibility.* "It can be therefore said that the phenomenon of shame occurs when that which by reason of its essence or its purpose should be interior leaves the sphere of interiority of the person and becomes in some way exterior."[11] The topic particularly appeals to John Paul II, because it emphasizes that the truth of the person lies in the interior. For example, the person conceals the sexual parts of the body for fear of becoming a sexual object for another, or of treating another as a sexual object. Shame is intimately connected to the inviolability of the person. "In fact, this objective incommunicability (*alteri incommunicabilitas*) and inviolability of the person come to light precisely in the lived-experience of sexual shame."[12] These philosophical reflections enabled John Paul II to see a deep connection between immunity from shame, which was a fundamental character of man's creation in holiness, and the shame experienced in the historical state of sin. While man cannot cross the "boundary" between the two states, he can have an experience of what was lost. In this way the experience of shame confirms that there is a real continuity between the two states. Man can once again be called to holiness, which Christ, himself, confirms by his reference to "the beginning" on the indissolubility of marriage.

Conversion in Christian Families

Marc Cardinal Ouellet, following John Paul II, has analyzed the way conversion comes about in Christian families. The first sin was refusal of God, as Lord of the Covenant. This is most clearly seen in idolatry, which is compared to adultery in the Old Testament. God had established man and woman in spousal unity, so that the first sin not only broke their personal relationship with God but violated this unity. Original sin, itself, is measured from original justice, the state of grace bestowed on Adam and Eve. Christ, however, re-established the covenantal relationship with God "on a level well beyond original justice."[13] Therefore, Ouellet holds, the sin of the spouses must be measured, starting with the sacrament.[14] Although St. Thomas regarded the sacrament as the superior good, Ouellet charges that it has been "too strictly limited to the juridical indissolubility of the matrimonial contract." [15] The sacrament links the spouses to the nuptial union of Christ and the Church, so that their sin is first and foremost a sin against the sacrament.

The spouses' specific gift is a "community of life and love," which flows from their covenant of consent. With the sacrament they enter into a new relationship with God as both Creator and Redeemer. Their natural love is transformed by sacramental grace, the fruits of which are not simply a restitution of grace, or a remedy of concupiscence or generous procreation. They are, in fact, incorporated into the mission of Christ and the Church. *Familiaris consortio* speaks of the role of the Holy Spirit in bringing about a new communion of love. Building on its natural unity, the conjugal bond is now indissoluble because it participates in the indissoluble union of Christ and the Church.[16] Vatican Council II initiated a more Christocentric and personalist vision of marriage, in contrast to some traditional views that it was ordained mainly to the procreation and education of children. Christ's love, objectively speaking, enters conjugal love and subsumes it to his own spousal gift to the Church. As Ouellet says of this new perspective:

> This underlines the personal character of this grace, the dramatic interplay of the divine Persons who come to the spouses' encounter, who bless them with their Presence, and who commit them to serving and giving glory to God through dwelling in the temple of their divine communion.[17]

The human action of baptized spouses is transformed in Christ. Christ's love for the Church is now both the 'form' and the 'norm' for their love. Their sin lies in refusal of the covenant with God and the sacrament. It is expressed in neglect of the sacraments of Penance and the Eucharist, which enable them to live Gospel ethics, but above all to be an *ecclesia domestica* (domestic church). Conversion, therefore, means not only living ethically in accord with Christ, but also being in communion with the Spirit. As *Familiaris consortio* proclaims, they are called to be not just a saved community but also a saving community (FC 49). If they shirk this priestly duty, they deprive the Church of their ecclesial vocation.

The Kingdom of God

As "domestic Church," the spouses share in the mission of establishing the kingdom of God in the world. "The purpose of the vocation and mission of the apostles—and therefore of the Church—in the world is to establish God's kingdom in human history."[18] John Paul II, in the Catechesis on Jesus, Son and Savior, refers to the structure of the Kingdom of God in opposition to the structures of sin:

> Jesus of Nazareth proclaimed this kingdom from the beginning of his Messianic mission. "The time is fulfilled and the kingdom of God is at hand." (Mk 4:15). . . it is already present in his own Person.[19]

Christ's sovereignty now reigns for all time. There is a new creation. "Through Christ and in Christ all that is transient and ephemeral has been conquered, and he has established forever the true value of the human person and of everything created."[20] Through the Pascal mystery, Christ has canceled Satan's power in the world and in every human person. The structure of the kingdom is linked to the calling of the apostles and conferring on them of the power to forgive sin, reconciling all men to God.

The Christian family inherited from Israel the laws that had formed them into the People chosen to prepare for the coming of the Savior. Chief among these were the Ten Commandments given to Moses on Mt. Sinai. In the Sermon on the Mount, Christ gives a new law, which does not negate the old but brings it to fulfillment. John Paul II sees the encounter with the rich young man in the Gospel as a symbol of the new law centered on following Christ, which demanded more than the young man was willing to give.[21] Nevertheless, it is this new law which inaugurates the Kingdom. It can only be accomplished in and through Christ. This passage began his landmark encyclical, *Veritatis splendor* on the renewal of moral theology.[22] In taking the dialogue with the rich young man to a wholly new level, the encyclical responds to an "overall and systematic calling into question of the traditional moral doctrine on the basis of certain anthropological and ethical presuppositions" (VS 4).[23]

In his Catechesis on Human Love, John Paul II chooses Matthew's passage from the Sermon on the Mount:

> You have heard that it was said, "You shall not commit adultery." But I say to you: Whoever looks at a woman to desire her [in a reductive way] has already committed adultery with her *in his heart* (Mt 5:27-28)[24] (MW 24: 1).

The pope describes it as one of the passages in the Sermon on the Mount in which Jesus calls for a "*fundamental revision of the way of understanding and carrying out the moral law of the Old Covenant*" (MW 24:1). The old law is not abolished but brought to fulfillment and living the new law is a condition for the reign of the Kingdom. The old law against adultery was centered on external criteria. Intrinsic to the new law is a conversion of heart, which is the inner form of morality. The new law, the Pope points out, is given to the historical man of concupiscence, who is subject to the threefold lust that "comes from the world" as a consequence of original sin. As a result, the spousal meaning of the body is corrupted and man and woman lose the interior freedom of being a gift to each other. Christ's words bring a new ethos, the *ethos of the gospel*, which is deeply imbued with the mystery of creation "in the beginning" and yet is addressed to sinful man (MW 34: 2). Christ's words on adultery speak of the redemption of the body. The pope asks: "Should we *fear* the severity of these words or rather *have confidence* in their salvific content, in their power?" (MW 43: 7). These words are not so much a condemnation of the body as an appeal to the heart so that the full realization of the value of the body and sex may be put at the service of the communion of persons, which God intended from the 'beginning' and "is the deepest substratum of human ethics and culture" (MW 45: 3).

The Ethos of Redemption and Purity of Heart

The "new" ethos brought by Christ, the ethos of Redemption, especially of the body, John Paul II links to purity of heart. It does not imply a return to the 'beginning,' but the original ethos of creation is to be taken up anew by sinful man, imprinted first on his heart interiorly and then carried into his way of being and acting. It becomes a reality through self-mastery for self-gift. At stake is the body's spousal meaning, the perennial attraction of masculinity and femininity, through which man and woman realize communion in the image of the Trinity. The pope takes several passages of St. Paul to illuminate what is meant by "life in the Spirit," the life that is now made possible in the "kingdom." *"The Redemption of the Body* brings with it," he says, "the establishment in Christ and for Christ of a new *measure of the holiness of the body"* (MW, 56:4). Purity is both a virtue and a gift. Given to the sinful man, it is now assigned to man as a task. Awareness of sinfulness is, in fact, a necessary condition and starting point for aspiring to a life of virtue (MW, 49:7).

The task is not an easy one. As Jesus proclaims in the Gospel:

> If anyone would come after me, let him deny himself and take up his cross and follow me. For whoever would save his life will lose it and whoever loses his life for my sake will find it (Mt 16: 24-25).

Nevertheless, and here John Paul II refers to Paul Vl's encyclical, *Humanae vitae*, the possibility of fulfilling the demands of Christian morality have been given through the sacraments

The Interaction of Personal and "Structural" Sin

It would be naïve to suppose that ideal conditions exist or have ever existed for living out the demands of the Gospel. In our own day, the ubiquitous availability of contraception and a mindset that promotes them as the solution to "overpopulation," women's liberation and sexual freedom, militate against the narrow path to Christian virtue in the family. Sometimes it is easier to see both the challenges and the promise of Redemption in those who have lived in other historical periods. This chapter, therefore, takes the example of two families, which illustrate well the interaction of personal sin, structural sin and Redemption. They have been chosen, on the one hand, because they have left an account of their own experiences in an autobiography and, on the other, because they had and still have an effect on Christ's body, the Church, and its existence in society and history. They both, in their own way, reveal the contours of the communion of persons in the family, one by its absence, the other by its presence. Neither is free of the "sin of the world," the effects of original sin on family structures.[25] Lastly God's grace and mercy are shown, in one case, to overcome sin, shortly before death, and, in the other, to sanctify and bring about abundant fruits early in life.

In a bird's eye view of the way marriage and family were lived in the early Middle Ages, it was noted in Chapter Four, that a confluence of interests on the part of society and the Church facilitated the development of a theology of marriage and family. Also, in opposition to the Gnostic heresy of Albigensianism, which considered the body and everything associated with it, such as marriage and procreation, as evil, the Church fostered a spirituality of woman's body, especially maternal nursing. Both feudal society and the Church for their own reasons, according to Georges Duby, promoted indissoluble marriage. Since feudal society limited its interest to the eldest son and property rights, however, concubinage became widespread in society. Furthermore, an exception was given to the nobility to hire wet nurses, a practice that, eventually over the centuries and particularly in France, spread to every socioeconomic group in the cities. Parallel with this development came an emphasis on the spousal relation as one of companionship and intimacy at the ultimate expense of the child. Both practices served to weaken a true communion of persons in the family. The following narratives will illustrate the interaction of personal and "structural" sin and its effect on the person, family and society on the one hand, and on the other, the redeeming power of Christ in the "domestic church." These two families had and still have a profound effect on Western culture.

Charles Maurice de Talleyrand (1754-1838)

The first is Charles Maurice de Talleyrand, prince de Benevent. He has been described as "a man of surpassing talents and epic flaws [who] was admired as he was despised. . . He was also licentious—even in late *ancien regime* Paris, the city of the marquis de Sade and Laclos, marquise de Monteuil and vicomte de Valmont, his debaucheries earned him infamy and condemnation."[26] According to the American minister in Paris, "This man appears to me polished, cold, tricky, ambitious and bad."[27] Talleyrand was descended from one of the oldest French aristocratic families that was not well off but attended the court. As was the custom, he was sent to the suburbs to a wet nurse until the age of four.[28] Whether born with a club foot or suffering from a fall at the home of the wet nurse, he could not, as the eldest son, embark on a military career so the family destined him for the Church. In his autobiography, Talleyrand describes the effect this early abandonment by his family had on him. At the age of four his parents sent him to stay with his great grandmother in the family château in the country. There he experienced for the first time real family affection.[29] Often he felt bitterly the lack of affection in his own family, realizing that what one experiences in the earliest years has a profound effect on one's disposition and character in later life.[30]Talleyrand describes with precision his departure from his "grandmother," whom he left in tears at the age of eight years. After 17 days of coach travel, on the 17th day he was met at the station at 11:00am by an old retainer of his parents, who took him directly to the college. At exactly midday he was sitting at a table in the refectory, without having spent a single hour with his parents. Thereafter once a week he dined with his parents, immediately after the meal returning to the college. When he was twelve he came down with small pox and had to leave the college. He recalls how amazed he was at the little interest taken in his sickness, which could have been fatal, and this added to the memory of not seeing his parents on the journey to the college as well as other memories. It left him with a wounded heart.

Talleyrand both rationalizes his parents' behavior and takes some pride in the result. "Je me sentis isolé, sans soutien, toujours repoussé vers moi." (I feel myself isolated, without support, always pushed back towards myself.)[31] But he does not complain, believing it led him to reflect beyond his years.

He became resourceful and able to bear misfortune with indifference. He excused his parents by saying that they had to lead him to a profession for which he had no disposition, which they could not do if they saw him too much. All was for the sake of the prestige of the "Family."[32] At the age of fifteen he was sent to his uncle, who was attached to the archbishopric of Rheims, where he began his career in the Church, again not seeing his parents before departing. In the seminary he read not only theology but the latest books on the new philosophy, which later influenced the French revolution in which he was to take a major part. In 1780 he was put in charge of Church finances. Louis XVI "resisted promoting him up the Church hierarchy because of his lack of private virtue,"[33] but in 1788 did make him bishop of Autun. Ironically Talleyrand was the churchman, who, during the initial phase of the Revolution, administered the Oath of the king as constitutional monarch. Elected president of the Assembly in 1790, he presided at the Mass which declared July 14, in memory of the storming of the Bastille, a national holiday. Where once he had fiercely protected Church property and finances, now he proposed their nationalization. This was the first of several changes of allegiance from the Church to the Revolution, to Napoleon and back to a limited monarchy. Looking back at the end of his life, Talleyrand declared that he had no regrets about serving all the regimes. Just as for his parents, the ideal of family and name was paramount, regardless of pain to individual family members, so Talleyrand declared that he did everything for France, wishing above all to ensure stability and order after the horrors of the Revolution.[34] With such a history of betrayal in politics and also in his personal life through sexual licentiousness, Talleyrand still found mercy before his death.[35] He was reconciled with the Church and received the last sacraments. As we shall see later in the comparison with the life of St. Therese, Talleyrand suffered much from his family not being a true communion of persons.[36]

St. Therese of Lisieux (1873-1897)

It may seem strange to bracket Talleyrand with St. Thérese of Lisieux and her parents, Zélie and Louis Martin, now also canonized saints. The purpose is to show how similar life experiences engendered by "structures of sin" can produce strikingly different results. Distinguished psychologist, Paul Vitz, has shown how "Thérèse was able to use her childhood attachment traumas and pathological experiences of separation anxiety as a positive source of motivation in her search for and response to God."[37] Reference has already been made to the almost normative practice of sending infants to wet nurses in the countryside surrounding French cities. Although care was taken in choosing a wet nurse, believing that the child imbibed character with her milk, research on Attachment Theory only became a serious topic of study in the mid-20th century.[38] It was, therefore, "natural" that Zélie Martin should send her babies to wet nurses, especially as she ran a lace business in her home. Zélie loved each one of her nine children. In her correspondence, she says if she could just take care of the children and not send them to wet nurses, she would be so happy. "But it's quite necessary that their father and I work to earn money for their dowries."[39] In a footnote, the editor notes how Zélie came from an impoverished middle class family. To add to their income, her parents started a café on the ground floor. The rigidity and arrogance of Zélie's mother brought about its demise so that there was no dowry for her daughter, Zélie, to enter the convent. As the editor explains, this may be one of the reasons that drove Zélie not to depend on others financially even though the Martins were quite well off (CDL, fn 90, 36). Quite frequently she found herself "overwhelmed by work" (CDL 41) but when her husband wanted her to hire more workers and her brother urged her to close the business, she refused. The Martins lost two sons and a daughter to incompetent wet nurses.

Zélie determined to breastfeed her youngest, Thérèse, but her health did not allow it.[40] After two months the infant was sent to the country to a wet nurse for a year and a half. Her return began the second of the traumatic separations in Thérèse's childhood. The next was the death of her mother when she was four years old. Paul Vitz traces Thérèse's difficult path, in which she sought substitute mothers in her sisters, only to lose them as they entered the Carmelite convent.[41] At the same time she was granted profound spiritual experiences, including a vision of Mary which brought about a dramatic change and healing. Of particular importance on her journey is what is known as her Christmas Conversion, about which she is reported to have said, "Charity took possession of my heart, making me forget myself, and I have been happy ever since."[42] In her home, Therese was surrounded by love and devotion. As she wrote in a letter in 1897, "God gave me a father and mother more worthy of heaven than of earth: they asked the Lord to give them many children and to take them to himself" (CDL xvii). Experiencing both great human love as well as "abandonment" by beloved figures to whom she had become deeply attached, it is hardly surprising that Thérèse sought a Love that does not fail. As Vitz concludes:

> Thérèse . . . chose to transform her suffering and negative experiences into something positive. She accomplished this by seeking the love of God and practicing love toward others. One of Thérèse's important revelations is that her early lost loves were actually gifts rather than meaningless sources of pain because they strongly motivated her to seek God, and in the process, to love others.

Thérèse aspired to be "love at the heart of the Church." In a letter to her sister, on September 8, 1896, Thérèse wrote how she had, at last, found her vocation. After recounting a dream of Venerable Anne de Jesus, founder of the Carmelites in France, she speaks of the magnitude of her desires to be apostle, prophet, martyr, recognizing at the same time her weakness. Turning to 1 Corinthians 12 and 13, she reads there that not all can have these vocations, but, reading further, she learns that the most excellent way that leads to God is charity.

> I understood that the Church *had a heart and this heart was BURNING WITH LOVE. I understood that it was love alone* that made the Church's members act, that if *Love* ever became extinct, apostles would not preach the Gospel and martyrs would not shed their blood. I understood that LOVE COMPRISED ALL VOCATIONS, THAT LOVE WAS EVERYTHING, THAT IT EMBRACED ALL

> TIMES AND PLACES…IN A WORD THAT IT WAS ETERNAL (caps in original).[43]

Thérèse had found her vocation. She offered herself as a victim of love, fully aware of her weakness and nothingness. In fact, she rejoiced in her littleness. It was not enough for Thérèse to do good on earth through her little way of spiritual childhood but she declared she wanted to spend her heaven doing good on earth.[44] Her "little way" of spiritual childhood contrasts sharply with the autonomous self-sufficiency of modernity.

A Comparison

When we look at the two families, both of which are Christian, we find a great contrast. Talleyrand's parents only think of the prestige of their ancient family name, not the true well-being of their son or even of the Church. Parental love and affection seem not to exist. Ministry in the Church is primarily a means of advancement in society, unrelated to a vocation or virtue. Talleyrand has been nurtured by and separated from his nurse and his loving grandmother. This nurturing, such as it was, combined with the best education, allows him to make his way in society. He shows no loyalty to anyone other than himself, proud of his isolation and indifference, his autonomy. Entering a marriage with a divorced woman, he eventually divorces her also. Yet at the end of his life, mercy intervenes and he is reconciled to the Church. Neither personal sin nor the "structures of sin" have the last word. The possibility always exists of conversion to the kingdom of God.

Turning to the Martin family, here is a true "domestic Church," the fullest expression of which is the Holy Family. Such a human family, modeled on the Holy Family, is Christocentric and commits the spouses to glorifying God in their marriage. Christ's love must be the *norm* and *form* of their love. As a wedding gift, Louis gave to Zélie a medallion engraved with Sarah and Tobias as a symbol of the way they would receive all that was needed in their marriage from God. "They were called, through the Sacrament of Marriage, to be like the angel, Raphael in this biblical story, an angel in each other's life, radiating the face of Christ to each other" (CDF xxiii). They lived the *ethos* of Redemption, knowing that only in Christ could they become good as husband and wife, mother and father. Through their devotion to the Eucharist they were able to endure the loss of four of their children and later, for Louis, the loss of his wife and even of his mental capacity.

At the heart of the civilization of love, which is formed by the family as "domestic church," is the concept of mutual self-gift. Louis and Zélie were a "sincere gift" to each other, which comes across in the letters they wrote. Since Zélie wrote 120 to Louis' 16, we learn more about him. He was a caring and supportive husband. A devoted father to their children, he exercised a full partnership in their upbringing. He also had a deep relationship to God. "He was a man who lived in the world, but was totally immersed in Christ" (CDF xxvii). He sacrificed his own watch business, selling it in order to devote his financial expertise to Zélie's lace business. He also sent their eldest daughters to boarding school to free Zélie. When Zélie died, he moved the family away from his friends and family to be near hers. Zélie made her own sacrifices, giving all her energy to bearing and raising their children and making sure that they would have the dowries to enter religious life, which had been denied her. Through the culture of love in their home, they gave five daughters to the religious life and a saint to the Church, who is also a doctor of the Church. They were, indeed, both a saved and saving community.

Mercy was evident in both of these life stories in different ways. Mercy is a central theme of Jesus' preaching and, as was said earlier, mercy is a gift of the Trinitarian God for conversion. Here, mercy is expressed in the theological poem of Charles Peguy, *The Portal of the Mystery of Hope,* John Paul II's Encyclical Letter, *Dives in Misericordia,* and Pope Francis' prescription of accompanying those who are in situations that contradict sacramental love in the family.

Charles Péguy (1873-1914)

Charles Péguy, a contemporary of St. Thérèse, spent most of his life as an agnostic and socialist. In his mid-thirties, he moved towards the Catholic faith.

Because of his wife's opposition and his death at the age of 41 on the first day of the Battle of the Marnes in the first World War, he never formally rejoined the Church. Yet, his later poetry is full of Catholic themes. Experiencing the mercy of God, he devotes a section of his prose poem, *The Portal of the Mystery of Hope*[45] to a paean on the parable of the prodigal son. He treasures all three parables of the lost sheep, the lost coin and the lost child. Below are some excerpts:

> Throughout the thirteen and fourteen centuries that they've served, and throughout two thousand years and through centuries of centuries, they have been as young as on the first day. . . .
> These three parables (may God forgive us)
> Have held a special place in the heart.
> And may God forgive us as long as there are Christians,
> As long as, that is, eternally,
> Through the centuries of centuries there will be, for these three parables,
> A special place in the heart.
> And all three of them are parables of hope.[46]

But the last he loves best.

> *A man had two sons.* Of all God's parables
> This one has awakened the deepest echo.
> The most ancient echo
> The oldest, the newest echo
> The freshest echo. Believer or unbeliever.
> Known or unknown.
> A unique point of resonance.
> The only one the sinner has never been able to silence in his heart[47].

To be especially noted is that the parable of the prodigal son tells the story of the son returning to the bosom of the Father.

Dives in Misericordia

John Paul II was well aware that at the heart of the ethos of redemption is the mystery of the Father and his merciful love. He wrote the second encyclical of his pontificate on God's merciful love through Jesus Christ.[48] Israel, as the people of God, continually turned their back on God and his holiness, particularly through worshiping idols and adopting the licentious practices of their neighbors, which contravened chastity and faithful married love. Yet God never abandoned them. He always renewed his Covenant with them, placing mercy beyond justice. With the advent of his Son, and the Paschal Mystery of his death and resurrection, God's mercy was revealed in its fullness. The Cross on Calvary united justice with love so that the pope calls mercy "love's second name" (DM 7). Because of the strength of evil in the world, God's love must, in fact, be revealed in history as mercy. "It is precisely because sin exists in the world, which 'God so loved . . . that he gave his only Son', that God, who is love,' *cannot reveal himself otherwise* than as mercy" (DM 13). Just as God's mercy is infinite, so is his forgiveness. The Church constantly calls sinners to conversion, a conversion to holiness based on the Sermon on the Mount. To be authentic, conversion must become a "whole lifestyle" which "consists in the constant discovery and persevering practice of *love as a unifying and also elevating power* despite all difficulties of a psychological or social nature" (DM 14). This merciful love is especially necessary in the close relationships of the family. In no way does it mean indulging evil. In the paradigmatic parable of the prodigal son, repentance of evil brought reconciliation. Yet the father in the joy of his son's return not only forgave but celebrated the restoration, above all, of his son's lost dignity.

John Paul II refers to Mary as the one who received the greatest mercy in her preservation from sin, in her state of perfection and holiness. She is "the one who obtained mercy in a particular and exceptional way, as no other person has" (DM 9). In the Magnificat she exclaims "his mercy is on those who fear him from generation to generation," (Lk 4: 50) and "He has helped his servant Israel in remembrance of his mercy" (Lk 1: 54). The pope also notes that no one experienced his Cross the way Mary did. She is "the one who *has the deepest knowledge of God's mercy.* She knows its price" (DM 9). Sharing in the messianic mission of her Son, who was sent to bring good news to the poor, the blind, the oppressed and sinners, prepared her for a motherhood in grace. John Paul II cites Vatican Council II: "By her maternal charity, she takes care of the brethren of her Son who still journey on earth surrounded by dangers and difficulties, until they are led into their blessed home" (LG, 62).

Accompanying, Discerning, Integrating

The genius of Pope Francis is to show how the sinner needs to be accompanied in his return to a true communion of persons as "domestic church." Chapter Eight of *Amoris laetitia* (AL) is particularly concerned with man's frailty. "The Church must accompany with attention and care the weakest of her children, who show signs of a weakened and troubled love, by restoring in them hope and confidence, like the beacon of a lighthouse in a port or a torch carried among the people that has lost its way or who are in the midst of a storm" (AL 291). The danger in such accompaniment of those who have strayed, even with good intentions, is to seek resolution too quickly. The Law of Gradualism then becomes the Gradualism of the Law. In *Accompanying, Discerning, Integrating: A Handbook for the Pastoral Care of the Family According to* Amoris Laetitia, the authors avoid this error.[49]

In the section on "the itinerary of repentance," the authors cite Pope Francis in *Amoris Laetitia* that time is not important but the small steps are, in order to grow closer to the goal, which "always is life according to the promise made on the wedding day (cc. AL 271, 300, 305)." They emphasize "this ultimate goal is undeniable: the Church is called to support 'the way of grace and growth' and 'paths of sanctification which give glory to God' (AL 305)."[50] This calls for much patient accompaniment. "In the case of these divorced persons, it is a matter of recognizing that the indissoluble bond that has united them in matrimony is the only firm foundation to which they can return in order to rebuild their life, since this bond testifies to the truth of the love 'forever' and 'in spite of everything' that Jesus promised us."[51] The same patient accompaniment is in order for those who, often out of ignorance of Church teaching or from weakness, use contraception or resort to in vitro fertilization.

Summary

In this chapter we have seen how sin and the effects of the sin of our first parents make it difficult to live a true communion of persons both within and outside the family. Although every sin has its origin in the individual human heart, John Paul II emphasizes that an accumulation of personal sins can deform social structures. In spite of these defective structures, all have a vocation to love. Through sacramental grace Christ, by his death on the cross, has made it possible to work toward a "civilization of love," bringing about God's kingdom on earth, however imperfectly. Although weak human beings fail and fail often, even disastrously, God still calls them through his boundless mercy. Two examples have been given of how this mercy, on the one hand, called to repentance and conversion and, on the other, raised to sanctity in a true communion of persons.

EPILOGUE

THE INTRODUCTION TO THIS BOOK proposed the Holy Family with its union of the created reality of marriage and the eschatological perspective of grace and the presence of Christ, as not the ontological exception but a true model of the family as a communion of persons. In exploring this theme, two concepts have been primary, the family (a) as "domestic" Church, highlighting its intrinsic link to the Christ/Church union and (b) as a communion of persons modeled on the Trinity. While the Fathers of the Church (St. Augustine) spoke of the family as "domestic" Church, the concept remained undeveloped until Vatican Council II revived it. The Council also introduced a new understanding of the communion of persons, including the family, as an image of divine Trinitarian communion. Both of these developments opened up vistas for seeing the family in a new and more transcendent light. Paradoxically, the Christological and Trinitarian dimensions, far from overly spiritualizing the family, in fact, enhance its roots in creation from the Incarnation of Christ, so that it becomes more rather than less human.

The divine-human presence has been at the forefront in examining whether the Holy Family is or is not the "ontological exception. Two theologians, Cardinals Marc Ouellet and Angelo Scola, the former starting from the Trinitarian mystery (from above) and the latter from the human spousal union (from below) as the analogy of all reality, locate fecundity as an essential dimension both of the Trinitarian mystery and the human communion of persons. St. John Paul II, as we saw, grounds his anthropology in the Vatican II document, *Gaudium et spes*, specifically no 22 and 24, referring to Christ as the new Adam and man and woman's likeness to Trinitarian communion in their communion.

This is the path that has been followed in this book, examining the different aspects of being a communion of persons in the family and the Holy Family with special emphasis on the thought of John Paul II, introducing other theologians from time to time. Since the family is a created reality, reference has also been made to other disciplines such as philosophy and psychology.

The Communion of Persons and the Holy Family

Person

Chapter Two, after detailing new theological thinking expressed in Vatican Council II of the human family as an image of the Trinity, is devoted to showing how the Christian concept of person, unlike the autonomous individual of the Enlightenment, is fundamentally relational, first of all in a contingent relationship with the Creator and secondly dependent on each other for fulfillment. Each is created incommunicable as a "disinterested" gift. No one, not even God can will for the person, since "freedom of the gift" is necessary for a relationship of love. In looking at the relationships within the Holy Family, it was seen that Mary's personhood is revealed in three primary ways, (1) as virgin, which is the foundation of a communion of persons as the "sister" relation in the creation account of Genesis and the sign of every human person in the resurrected state; (2) through her faith, beginning with her *fiat* in the Annunciation, as sign of her "authentic subjectivity" in giving consent; and (3) her chastity, which signifies not only purity but total trust in God's loving designs. Joseph shared in both Mary's virginity and faith. Both, says John Paul II, go before us on our own pilgrimage of faith and are witnesses to the gift character of the human person.

Spousal Relation

The spousal relation, is, perhaps, the one in which the Holy Family without conjugal intercourse, is viewed the most as the "ontological exception." Both

John Paul II and Pope Benedict XVI forthrightly address the place of *eros* in the spousal relation, seeing it as first and foremost a desire for the good, the true and the beautiful. While *Eros* is ascending desire, the Christian virtue of *agape* is descending love. They are not in opposition but in a continuum. Recourse is had to St. Thomas' commentary on the natural inclinations to show how they are good in themselves when rightly ordered, and indeed a great help in fostering love. The person, however, must never become simply an object of pleasure in the sexual relation, but always treated as a "disinterested gift." Chastity in the spousal relation ensures freedom of the gift. Complete chastity, which pertained in the marriage of Mary and Joseph, is witness, on the one hand, to the eschatological state, and on the other, to consecrated virginity as a spousal relation with Christ at the center. (A wider meaning of chastity is proposed later in the book.) All other gestures of affection were available in their marriage as well as a deep spiritual closeness and friendship. Human spouses too are called to such friendship and some, through an impediment, may be called to live without conjugal intercourse.

Sexual difference is most visibly expressed in bodily conjugal union, since, as John Paul II says, the body is spousal, but it pertains in all spheres of life. While there is no marriage in the resurrected state, sexual difference remains and it is marked in that state, as John Paul II says, by "perfect intersubjectivity" (MW 68:4), especially between man and woman. Redemption in the historical state of sin makes possible the freedom of the gift but it is both a task and a gift of the Holy Spirit. John Paul II brings a new and fuller interpretation of Ephesians 5:21-33 by calling the mutual submission of the spouses an "experiencing of love." In other words the unity in difference is not abrogated but transformed in Christ. While Mary answered first and foremost to God in authentic subjectivity, she gave the headship to Joseph in their common life together in the Holy Family.

Paternity and Maternity

John Paul II recognizes that the woman has the more demanding part as the mother. As he says in *Mulieris dignitatem:*

> It is . . . necessary that the man be fully aware that in their shared parenthood, he owes a special debt to the woman. No program of "equal rights" between women and men is valid unless it takes that fact fully into account (MD 18).

By corollary, there can be no true communion of persons if both paternity and maternity are not fully taken into account. This concerns both physical and spiritual fruitfulness. While motherhood implies a "special openness to the new person" (MD 18) which translates into a more personal approach to the whole of reality, motherhood in the spiritual sphere "expresses a profound 'listening to the word of the living God" (MD 19). Mary uniquely combined both aspects as *Theotokos* (God bearer) yet the pope says that Mary's union with God determines in some way the dignity of all human beings. Mary's motherhood has traditionally been linked to her Ecclesial role, the essential symbol of the Church as mother. The education of children is a form of spiritual parenthood. We know nothing of Mary's activity outside the home in the hidden life of Nazareth but John Paul II is insistent that any public role for both men and women must enhance not detract from their role in the family.

An understanding of Joseph's role in salvation history as husband and father gradually developed along with devotion to the Holy Family. He only came to be honored as a young and more vigorous figure in the 16th century and became salient as protector of the Church only in the latter half of the 19th century. In his Apostolic Exhortation, *Redemptoris custos* John Paul II emphasizes especially Joseph's sacrifice, citing a discourse of Pope Paul VI: "His fatherhood is expressed concretely 'in his having made his life a service, a sacrifice to the mystery of the Incarnation and to the redemptive mission connected with it; in having used the legal authority which was his over the Holy Family in order to make a total gift of self, of his life and work; in having turned his human vocation to domestic love into a superhuman oblation of self, an oblation of his heart and all his abilities into love placed at the service of the Messiah growing up in his house'" (RC 8). His was a true servant leadership. Joseph, too, was called to be virgin and spouse. As John Paul II says, "There are really two kinds of love here, both of which *together* represent the mystery of the Church—virgin and spouse—as symbolized in the marriage of Mary and Joseph" (RC 20). Joseph also represents the union of the active and contemplative way of life (RC 27). The pope particularly stresses Joseph's silence that reveals his deep interior life. Joseph above all shared as no other human being did, except Mary, in the mystery of the Incarnation (RC 1), especially through the gift of his fatherhood.

It is the sharing in parenthood that John Paul II stresses above all. The communion of persons depends on the spouses having a subjective awareness of the transition to parenthood. The objective fact is not enough. Maternity and paternity occur through each other. The woman, especially, needs to be affirmed in her gift of motherhood. Here again the pope notes sexual difference with the mother having the more demanding part in the early years but both are involved in the child's education. The communion of persons plays a vital role in the mutual gift each is to the other. The child influences both the mother and father in the process of education. While the child is duty bound to honor his parents, the latter by a mature gift of their humanity are called to be worthy of such honor.

The Child

In Christianity there is a special emphasis on the child and childhood. Not only did Christ come as a child but he came to redeem us and make us adopted children of the Father. The child represents primal innocence and trust. With loving parents, this trust develops into a loving relationship with God, the Father. Here can be seen the great responsibility as well as opportunity of parents. The child is the fruit of the love of both the mother and father, but it is the mother who first awakens the smile of the child in loving embrace. If the mother for any reason fails to welcome the child, or there is disruption in the family, it can cause deep wounds. The child has a right to loving care but such care must be given freely. It is in the child's nature to respond to love with obedience and trust. Jesus' obedience to Mary and Joseph during the hidden years at Nazareth is recorded in the Gospel of Luke.

The relationship between love of God and love of a human father can be most clearly seen when human fatherhood is deficient. It has been shown that atheists disproportionately come from homes where there is an abusive or absent father. With regard to mothers, an unfortunate practice grew up of sending the children of the aristocracy, then of all urban classes, to wet nurses for up to two years or more. Church teaching did not endorse the practice doctrinally but often did not seek to prevent it. Once John Paul II saw the benefits of nursing on the mother's bond with the child and, therefore, on the communion of persons of the family, he spoke of the urgency of re-examining patterns of work in order to foster it. Just as disruption in the father child relationship has negative effects on the relationship with God the Father, it is proposed that the fracturing of the relationship with the mother affects the devotion to Mary and the Church. In the Holy Family, following Israelite custom, Mary breastfed Jesus. In fact it might be said that in nursing the infant Jesus she experienced a perfect fleshy union within the Holy Family.

The Significance of Bodily Presence

Since the human person is a union of body and soul, bodily presence is necessary for a communion of persons. Christ came in bodily form in the Incarnation and human spousal union is an analogy of the union with Christ and his Church. Through the baptized members he is present in the family as a "domestic church," in a way analogous to the Holy Family where Christ was present in his earthly life. The theological emphasis has moved from procreation to the consideration of fruitful conjugal love, which is comprised of total self-giving, openness to life and imaging the sacrament of Christ and the Church and divine Trinitarian communion. Christ's total self-giving on the Cross was life-giving. Encounter with Christ comes about through the sacraments and, especially through the gift of Christ's body in the Eucharist. In the same way human presence in the family is vital for a communion of persons, beginning in the fleshly unions of conjugal intercourse, gestation, birth and breastfeeding. Contraception prevents both the transmission of life and total self-giving. On the other hand, being present to signs of fertility in the body facilitates both life and communion.

Humanae Vitae, the Communion of Persons and the Holy Family

Having outlined the main features of a communion of persons and shown how it pertains in the Holy Family as a model for ordinary families, the task remains to propose that the Church's teaching on life and love in *Humanae vitae* helps to safeguard or restore the communion of persons in the family with a new understanding of marital chastity. It is important to acknowledge what John Paul II calls "anticipated signs of the gift" in the body, namely the fleshy communion of conjugal intercourse, gestation, birth and breastfeeding which make the family different from any other entity. It is also important to admit that certain distortions have occurred over the centuries in Church practice if not in doctrine, which have negatively affected the communion of persons. Such bodily unions are designed by the Creator to be a powerful bond of love. Nevertheless, the pleasure associated with conjugal union, especially, needs to be put at the service of both life and love.

Providentially at the end of the 19th century, science discovered the hormonal pattern of the woman's fertility cycle, which has enabled spouses both to achieve and space pregnancies. Various methods of natural family planning have been developed as a result. A period of abstinence is required if a pregnancy is to be avoided during the fertile time. While most couples find such abstinence difficult, it gives the opportunity to place the good of the person before immediate gratification and so grow in love and respect, which are at the heart of a communion of persons. Marital chastity, which is, in effect, honoring the good of sexual pleasure and at the same time respecting the person as a gift must be central to the love between the spouses. It is proposed that although conjugal intercourse was not present in the Holy Family, the nursing relationship between Mary and the infant Jesus was a perfect fleshy union.

While restraining lust or inordinate sexual desire as a result of original sin has been and continues to be the chief meaning of the virtue of purity, it has been proposed, that chastity has a much wider meaning. The chastity of Jesus first of all consisted in his abandonment and obedience to the Father's will as Son, so that the temptations, which he suffered at the beginning of his public life, attacked above all his filiation with the Father. In the same way spouses are called first and foremost to trust God's will in their family life. As John Paul II says:

> Through this sense of responsibility for love and life, God the Creator invites the spouses not to be passive operators, but rather "co-operators or almost interpreters" of his plan (GS 50). In fact they are called, out of respect for the objective moral order established by God, to an obligatory *discernment of the indications of God's will concerning their family.* Thus, in relation to physical, economic, psychological and social conditions, responsible parenthood will be able to be expressed "either by the deliberate and generous decision to raise a large family, or by the decision for serious moral reasons and with due respect for the moral law, to avoid for the time being, or even for an indeterminate period another birth" (HV 10).[1]

Such marital chastity is the key to living *Humanae vitae* as a way of life and is linked to the universal call to holiness.

Conversion to Holiness

Vatican Council II re-instituted the universal call to holiness beyond consecrated religious to all the laity according to their common baptism. While the married may not formally take vows of poverty, chastity and obedience, the spirit of the counsels inheres in their vow to love one another. The marriage of Mary and Joseph, as John Paul II says, is a perfect example of both types of holiness (MW 75:3). Such striving for holiness in the many vicissitudes of ordinary life involves suffering, which was also present in the Holy Family

The final chapter looks at humans in all their sinfulness. How can the Holy Family, where there is no sin, be a true model of the family as a communion of persons? The effects of the sin of Adam and Eve, indeed, make it hard to live a true communion of persons both within and outside the family. Although John Paul II insists that every sin begins in the individual, he recognizes that an accumulation of such sins deforms social structures. In spite of such distortion in society all are called to a vocation of love and holiness. In his great mercy, Christ has given the sacraments to restore human beings. Now they are recreated and can form a "civilization of love," inaugurating his kingdom, even if imperfectly.

Suggestions for Further Research

This book has touched on many issues of family life as a communion of persons, showing how it can image the Trinity and the Christ-Church union. There has been through the centuries much focus on marriage as sacrament and what it means, especially for the husband/wife union. More could be developed on the meaning of masculinity and femininity in themselves and their contribution to a communion of persons in marriage as well as in all walks of life. The definition of marriage as "fruitful conjugal love," comprising as it does both physical and spiritual fruitfulness, needs unpacking as it applies to both the gift of the child and intellectual, artistic and other creative gifts. At the same time, John Paul II finds crucially important the "sanctification of daily life," which need not involve "great things" (RC 24).

There needs to be more research on the theological import of the nursing mother. Fr. William Virtue has already made a significant contribution by pointing out that "Mary and Jesus, as mother and child, are the icon of the truth of human nature: the truth that we are created for love, for the communion of persons in a loving bond through embodied self-giving."[2] Virtue had already noted that "both maternal nursing and Eucharistic communion are for the formation of a bond; the first lays the foundation of human relationships, the second nurtures our relationship to God in Jesus Christ."[3] Above all, life and love, both natural and supernatural, are gifts from God and are to be transmitted in a *personal* way. Much of this theology was developed in the Middle Ages and then forgotten.

There also needs to be more research on the interface between paternity, maternity and the child, especially with regard to the stages of life. The life of the Holy Family is unveiled at specific moments of transition, from birth to adolescent independence to departure of Jesus from the home. All these instances provide fruitful models for transitions in Christian families. Above all the theological significance of the child and what John Paul II calls "mature humanity" needs to be explored.[4] John Paul II speaks of learning from St Joseph not only how to combine the contemplative and active life but "how to be servants of the 'economy of salvation'" (RC 32).

Conclusion

Emphasis on the Holy Family has been placed traditionally on its eschatological rather than earthly dimension, and applied particularly to the life of consecrated religious. Since the virginity of both Mary and Joseph--- not to mention Christ himself--- has been viewed as the model of spiritual fruitfulness for consecrated religious, the incarnational dimension of the Holy Family as a true family has been obscured. With Christ at the center, the Holy Family has long been considered an "earthly Trinity." Holy Christian families, modeled on the Holy Family, the "original domestic church," can now aspire to be "earthly Trinities" also.

This book has sought in a small way, drawing especially on the thought of John Paul II, to rectify this lacuna so that Christian families can truly see themselves as imaged in the Holy Family. Following John Paul II, who, throughout his vocation from priest to bishop to pope, sought to clarify the teaching of the Church laid out in Paul VI's encyclical, *Humanae vitae*, this book has striven to do the same.

END NOTES

Chapter 1

1. See Cormac Burke in Chapter 9 for erroneous views that developed from the 14th century on the meaning of "remedy for concupiscence."
2. Scola, *Nuptial Mystery*, 193.
3. Scola, *Nuptial Mystery*, 195.
4. Scola, *Nuptial Mystery*, 196.
5. Scola, *Nuptial Mystery*, 197.
6. Pope Leo XIII was particularly concerned with severing the marriage contract from the sacrament. He affirmed the teaching of previous popes that marriage was considered sacred even among unbelievers. Leo XIII, *Arcanum*.
7. "In the Latin Church, it is ordinarily understood that the spouses, as ministers of Christ's grace, mutually confer upon each other the sacrament of Matrimony by expressing their consent before the Church. In the Eastern liturgies the minister of this sacrament (which is called 'Crowning') is the priest or bishop who, after receiving the mutual consent of the spouses, successively crowns the bridegroom and the bride as a sign of the marriage covenant."
8. Chorpenning, Guidance, 41. "Before it became popular to speak of Jesus, Mary and Joseph as the Holy Family, they were referred to as the "earthly Trinity," an expression coined by Gerson." Chorpenning, "Holy Family," 85, fn 7.
9. Scola, *Nuptial Mystery*, 198.
10. See Atkinson, Foundations of the Family, 12.

11. Scola, *Nuptial Mystery*, 200.
12. Scola, *Nuptial Mystery*, 204.
13. The spouses as ministers of the sacrament are only instrumental causes of the sacrament, not secondary efficient causes.
14. Sanger advised, "Through sex mankind may attain great spiritual illumination which will transform the world, which will light up the only path to an earthly paradise." Sanger, *Pivot of Civilization*, 271.
15. McClory, *Turning Point.*
16. "In occasione dell-incontro di Roma dell'ano 1970, lo stesso P. Cafferel realizzo il bilancio dei primi 30 anni. Ricordo quello che credette di poter accreditare al Movimento come positive e annoto le mancanze che percepiva in quel momento: alcuni dissensi in seno alle équipes a proposito delle posizioni di contrasto riguaro all conduzione de Movimento, come anche de fronte alla Chiesa (nate dall'enciclica Humanae Vitae); l'anemia spirituael in un numero rilevante de coppie; la loro vita spirituale girava intorno all'impegno morale, ma mancava un vigoroso impegno teologale." Alberto e Constanza Alvarado, "Storia e Orientamenti," 3.
17. For example, a woman purposely sought out priests who told her to "follow her conscience." Personal communication, October 5, 2016.
18. Ouellet, *Divine Likeness*, 58.
19. Ouellet, *Divine Likeness*, 59
20. Ouellet, *Divine Likeness*, 60.
21. Ouellet, *Divine Likeness*, 39.
22. Ouellet, *Divine Likeness*, 53.
23. The same word exists in Thomistic Metaphysics but with a different meaning.
24. See John Paul II, *Man and Woman.*
25. John Paul II, *On the Family*, No. 15.
26. Secular historian Rudolf Binion surveys European literature of the 19th century and ascribes its anti-family theme to the introduction of contraception in the chapter "The Guilty Family, Ideology in the Bedroom, The Sublime and the Grotesque." Binion, *Past Impersonal*, 61-79.
27. *The Catechism of the Catholic Church* refers to the gradual revelation of the Trinity with the Father in the Old Testament, Jesus Christ in the New and the Holy Spirit in the time of the Church. (CCC 684) Although all

three were present from creation, the revelation of the Trinitarian persons occurred gradually. In the same way, it took several centuries to affirm the unity of humanity and divinity in the one nature of Christ. One might say also that the intrinsic value of celibacy had to be established to illuminate the value of periodic continence in marriage.

28. John Paul II Institute for Studies on Marriage & Family, *Academic Catalog 1995-1997*, 5.
29. John Paul II Institute for Studies on Marriage & Family, *Academic Catalog 1995-1997*, 15.
30. As one of the original lay S.T. L. students at the Institute, coming from 20 years of immersion in independent research into the topics of marriage, family and natural family planning, the opportunity to acquire a foundation in the theology of marriage and family was an enormous grace. A further grace was to work with Dr. Kenneth Schmitz on my doctoral topic of John Paul II's theology of the body. The dissertation served as the foundation of my book. Shivanandan, *Threshold of Love.*
31. Pontifical John Paul II Institute for Studies on Marriage & Family, *Academic Catalog 2005-2007*, 6.
32. "All God's action in human history at all times respects the free will of the human 'I.' And such was the case with the Annunciation at Nazareth" (MD, no. 4).
33. The theology of the Holy Family was a late development.
34. Since Mariology has been well developed over the ages, (see Hilda Graef *Mary: A History of Doctrine and Devotion*, London, Sheed & Ward, 1965) the emphasis will be more on Josephs role in salvation history. For without his participation there is no true communion of persons in the family.

Chapter 2

1. Both have taught at the John Paul II Institute for Studies on Marriage and Family, Roman Session and both are now Cardinals. Their principal works are: Ouellet, *Divine Likeness* and Scola, *The Nuptial Mystery.*
2. Shivanandan, *Threshold of Love*, xvii and 70-71.
3. Ouellet, *Divine Likeness*, 4, 5.

4. Ouellet, *Divine Likeness*, 6.
5. Ouellet, *Divine Likeness, 9.*
6. Ouellet, *Divine Likeness*, 14.
7. Ouellet, *Divine Likeness*, 24
8. Ouellet remarks that this exegesis has hardly received any attention in dogmatics. It is, however, central for John Paul II and others in an "adequate anthropology."
9. Ouellet, *Divine Likeness*, 27.
10. Ouellet, *Divine Likeness*, 28
11. Ouellet references here especially *Familiars Consortio*, *Letter to Families*, *Mulieris Dignitatem*, and *Man and Woman He Made Them.*
12. The initiation and receptivity of sexuality are features of the Trinity but not tied to sexuality as we understand it.
13. Ouellet, *Divine Likeness*, 33.
14. This will be discussed more fully in later chapters.
15. Scola, *Nuptial Mystery*, 3.
16. Scola, *Nuptial Mystery*, 7.
17. Scola, *Nuptial Mystery*, 9.
18. "In the event of the Incarnation a new, definitive relation between man and God is established. In fact, through the hypostatic union the person of Jesus constitutes the place of the encounter between God and humanity. This encounter can be read as a spousal union." Scola, *Nuptial Mystery,* 11.
19. Scola, *Nuptial Mystery*, 12.
20. Scola, *Nuptial Mystery* 34.
21. John Paul II is using sacrament here in a wider sense than is used in referring to one of the seven sacraments.
22. St. Paul's Letter to the Ephesians is addressed to the Christian community so that all could understand the depth of love married couples are called to.
23. Scola, *Nuptial Mystery*, 119.
24. As Ratzinger explains below.
25. John Paul II refers to the divine "we" in *Letter to Families*: "Before creating man, the Creator withdraws into himself in order to seek the pattern

and inspiration in the mystery of his being, which is already disclosed as the divine '*we*.'" Again he says: "The divine *we* is the eternal pattern of the human *we*, especially of that *we* formed by the man and woman created in the divine image and likeness. (LF 6). Joseph Atkinson, drawing on the work of H. Wheeler Robinson in 1907 and 1911 on the concept of corporate personality in the Israelite family cites three basic tenets, "organic unity, representative figure and the many/one oscillation. Corporate personality means that not only does the "one" represent the "many" but the "many" find their being in the "one." Atkinson, Domestic, 164- 170. Ancient Near Eastern scholar, Giorgio, Buccellati, calls the God of the Israelites unique in his relations with Man. God's covenant is a relation with one specific people through one specific man, Abraham. He concludes: "particularity is built into the very essence of the divine absolute . . . .Herein we can see one of the clearest anticipations of person as it will be elaborated in the early centuries of Christianity." Buccellati, Yahweh, 305. The particularity of God's call to Abraham finds its counterpart in the Annunciation to the Virgin of Nazareth. Just as the faith of Abraham in response to God's call initiated the Old Covenant, so Mary's response to the Angel's words initiated the New. (One might also say that this particularity was expressed in the New Covenant in one particular family, the Holy Family).

26. Ratzinger, "Retrieving the Tradition," 601-618 and 441.
27. Ratzinger, "Retrieving the Tradition," 441-442
28. Ratzinger, "Retrieving the Tradition," 443
29. Ratzinger, "Retrieving the Tradition," 444.
30. In the human family receptivity always precedes self-donation. Later chapters deal with all the relations in the family and the difference of the Christian view of the human person as relation and the autonomous individual of the enlightenment.
31. Ratzinger gives many examples from St. John's gospel. Ratzinger, "Retrieving the Tradition," 445-446.
32. Ratzinger, "Retrieving the Tradition," 449. The Greek view of the human person as a closed entity of form and matter is highly contested.

33. Ratzinger, "Retrieving the Tradition," 451.
34. Ratzinger, "Retrieving the Tradition," 453.
35. Koschorke, *Holy Family*, 140-141.
36. Wojtyla, *Love and Responsibility*, and *Man and Woman He Created Them*. (MW 133:4)
37. Scola, *Nuptial Mystery*, 5.
38. Wojtyla, "The Person," 219, 220.
39. Shivanandan, "Subjectivity," 257. This article gives a fuller account of the meaning of being a personal subject.
40. Wojtyla was first and foremost committed to a philosophy of being. Aquinas was not concerned with our modern pre-occupation with consciousness and self-consciousness. In *The Acting Person*, his major philosophical work on the nature of the human person and his acts, Wojtyla sought to integrate the Thomistic philosophy of being and the person with a philosophy of consciousness. Drawing on the pivotal role of potency and act in Aquinas, he posited that through his action man comes to the most complete comprehension of himself and that comes through experience. It was the phenomenological method that enabled him to have access to what he called lived experience but there is always a priority of being over act. Wojtyla totally rejects the idea that the person is constituted through consciousness. The roots of consciousness always lie in the suppositum of body- soul unity. Attention to conscious experience, however, is necessary to account for the personal subject in his or her uniqueness.
41. Although this does not correspond to the theological term "participation" meaning participating in being, there is a sense in which it means participating in the being of another analogously.
42. Shivanandan, "Subjectivity," 261, 262.
43. "Man turns back on God-Love, on the "Father." He in some sense casts him from his heart. At the same time, therefore, he detaches his heart and cuts it off, as it were, from that which "comes from the Father": in this way what is left in him "comes from the world." (MW 26:4)
44. In *Mulieris Dignitatem* John Paul also stresses that by her response, "Behold the handmaid of the Lord," Mary acknowledges her creatureliness in relation to God. (MD 5)

45. Joseph Chorpenning also posits the third millennium as an interpretive key to his work. Source: Joseph Chorpenning, "Holy Family," 78.
46. Ratzinger is referring to the collapse of devotion to Mary which in some quarters was regarded as exaggerated and obscuring. Ratzinger, "Marian Doctrine,"146-160.
47. Another characteristic of John Paul II is the extent to which he follows in his predecessor's footsteps, even to using the same language.
48. The question of St. Joseph's sanctification, which is an ongoing debate in the Church, will be addressed in the next chapter.
49. de la Potterie, *Mary*, 58-59.
50. Batut, "The Chastity of Jesus and the 'Refusal to Grasp,'" in *Communio* 24 (1997) 6.
51. Aquinas relates their temptation to the same kinds as the Angels' trial, namely, wanting happiness in their own way, not being dependent on God.
52. For a fuller discussion see Shivanandan, *Immaculate Conception*, 419-436; also see further discussion in Chapter 11.
53. John Paul II in a footnote lists some of the Fathers. In the encyclical letter *Dominum et Vivificantem* on the Holy Spirit the pope in reference to Adam and Eve speaks of "the same 'non-faith,' the same *'they have not believed'* which will be repeated in the Paschal Mystery." (D et V 33).
54. Ouellet, *Divine Likeness*, 184-5.
55. John Paul II continues to cite *Lumen Gentium* the Dogmatic Constitution on the Church. (LG 63)

Chapter 3

1. St. Justin, Trypho, 100; Tertullian, De Carne. Christ. 17; St. Irenaeus, Adv. Haer. III. 22.34.
2. Matthew 1:19. The Greek word for "just" or "righteous" differs in Old Testament usage to Greek. In Greek it referred to a man who fulfilled his civic duties. In the OT and NT it is not first and foremost related to virtue but how a person stands with God's Law. "The Messiah is called righteous because His whole nature and action are in conformity with the norm of the divine Will." *Theological Dictionary*, Vol. II, Ed. Gerhard

Kittel, 186. For Ubertino of Casale, "'Joseph is the apex, 'the happy conclusion of the Ancient law.'" Doze, *Shadow*, 13.

3. See for example Luke 2:39-42.
4. Luke 1: 26-35
5. In John's gospel, Fitzmeyer notes that he is only mentioned twice as a way to identify Jesus. "Jesus of Nazareth, son of Joseph" (1:45) and in the Bread of Life discourse "Is not this the son of Joseph, whose mother and father we know" (6.42). Fitzmeyer, *Matthew's Gospel*, 4.
6. Filas, *Joseph and Jesus,* 11.
7. Lienhard, *Joseph in Early Christianity*, 15, 16.
8. The Fathers devised various solutions to the differing genealogies, many settling on Jesus' dual role as king and priest. Augustine concludes that, although Mary and Joseph were not of the tribe of Levi, through Jesus' sacrifice of himself, he became the "eternal priest in the order of Melchisedek" and that is represented by descent through Nathan. Lienhard, *Joseph in Early Christianity,* 14, 15. Roy H. Schoeman, a Jewish convert to Catholicism, sees much significance in the two characteristics of the Messiah described in the OT, the one who suffers (cf Zechariah 12 and Isaiah 53) and the one who comes in glory. In the Gospels, Jesus is continually referred to as son of Joseph the carpenter of Nazareth, referencing his humanity. In his power He is called Son of David as the two blind men call him (Mt: 9:27-30) referencing his divinity. To solve the contradiction, the Talmudic rabbis propose two Messiahs, the one who suffers called Messiah ben Joseph and the one who comes in glory, Messiah ben David. Schoeman, "*Salvation is from the Jews,*" 118-122. When Pilate wrote the title, "Jesus of Nazareth, the King of the Jews" on the cross (John, 19:17) he did not realize that he was signifying both Messiah ben Joseph and Messiah ben David in the one Person of Jesus Christ at the moment both of his greatest humiliation and suffering and of his greatest glory before the Resurrection.
9. Fitzmeyer, *Matthew's Gospel*, 17, 18. In his infancy narrative Matthew is at pains to cite Old Testament prophecies, showing Jesus as their fulfillment (Isa 7-14 and Host 11:1).

10. Lienhard, *Joseph in Early Christianity,* 3. "Not only did Joseph not fit but he has to be absent," Ibid., 5.
11. The Protoevangelium also makes Joseph Mary's companion not spouse. Lienhard, *Joseph in Early Christianity,* 9.
12. Filas, *Joseph and Jesus,* 21.
13. "Et principem hujus mundi latuit Mariae virginitas and partus ipsius, similiter et mors domini; tria mysteria clamoris, quae in silentio Dei patrata sunt." Bertrand et Ponton, "Textes Patristiques," 147. (The texts are given in French, Greek and Latin); Joseph T. Leinhard also gives the principal passages from the Fathers of the Church at the end of *St. Joseph in Early Christianity.*
14. Filas, *Joseph and Jesus,* 25, 26.
15. Filas, *Joseph and Jesus,* 29.
16. Filas, *Joseph and Jesus,* 28, 29.
17. Jerome stressed Joseph's virginity, arguing from fittingness. In the Middle Ages this argument was common teaching in the west. Lienhard, *Joseph in Early Christianity,* 17.
18. Filas, *Joseph and Jesus,* 35.
19. Leinhard cites Ambrose's Commentary on Luke and On the Consecration of a Virgin. Lienhard, *Joseph in Early Christianity,* 20.
20. Leinhard cites Book 23 of Against Faustus the Manichee and On the Harmony of the Gospels. Lienhard, *Joseph in Early Christianity,* 23.
21. Lienhard, *Joseph in Early Christianity,* 24; Filas cites from De Nuptiis et Concupiscentia (1, 11) "*Omne itaque nuptiarum bonum impletum est in illis parentibus Christi, proles, fides, sacramentum. Prolem cognoscimus ipsum Dominum Jesus; fidem quia nullum adulterium; sacramentum quia nullum divortium. Solus ibi nuptialis concubitus no fuit.*" Lienhard, *Joseph in Early Christianity,* fn 51, 56.
22. Filas, *Joseph and Jesus,* 37, 38.
23. Filas, *Joseph and Jesus,* 38.
24. Augustine, "Sermons III," no. 21. Other sources in Augustine are *Against Faustus the Manichee, On the Harmony of the Gospels, On Marriage and Concupiscence* and *Against Julian.* Leinhard interprets Augustine as holding

that "In Christian faith, the heart of marriage is not carnal union but the kind of union Christ has with his members." Lienhard, *Joseph in Early Christianity*, 23.

25. Augustine, "Sermon 51," No. 23, 24. Leinhard asserts, "this argument—admittedly strange—depends on valuing chastity in marriage," and regarding spiritual begetting superior to physical. Ibid., 25. Augustine also states that "both the woman and the man may relieve their weakness with each other," Ibid., no. 22. Since the time of Augustine, the Church has developed a much greater appreciation of the role of conjugal intercourse in marriage. Popes John Paul II and Benedict have both affirmed the role of *eros* without mitigating the effects of concupiscence which can vitiate the total self-gift of the one-flesh union (MW no. 22:4).
26. Augustine, "Sermon 51," no. 30.
27. Atkinson, *Foundations of the Family,* 271.
28. Atkinson, *Foundations of the Family*, 271, 272.
29. Atkinson, *Foundations of the Family*, 277.
30. Atkinson, *Foundations of the Family,* 280. The following paragraphs in Atkinson cite other sources to show how continence in both celibacy and marriage is a gift of the Holy Spirit. The significance of "spiritual marriage" or marriage without consummation will be further discussed in Chapter 5.
31. Atkinson, *Foundations of the Family*, 275.
32. Filas, *Joseph and Jesus*, 61-62. Filas' main concern is the fatherhood of Joseph, which received less emphasis at the time, even though devotion to St. Joseph was beginning to be practiced. Nevertheless, since his fatherhood had been shown to depend on the marriage Filas gives the latter considerable attention.
33. See Gold, "Mary and Joseph."
34. Filas, *Joseph and Jesus*, 66.
35. According to Jewish custom, Mary was already pledged to Joseph as spouse by her betrothal. Cf contemporary Hindu custom.
36. Aquinas addresses Joseph's role as espoused virgin of Mary and whether there was a true marriage between Mary and Joseph in *Summa Theologica*, Tertia pars, q. 29, 1 and 2.

37. One might say this of any conception through *in vitro* and similar reproductive techniques.
38. Filas, *Joseph and Jesus*, 70. Among the texts of Aquinas that Filas cites are the following texts: *Summa Theologica*, 3, q. 29, a.2; IV Sent., d. 30, q. 2, a. 2, ad 4.
39. Filas, *Joseph and Jesus*, 87
40. Filas, *Joseph and Jesus*, 92, 93.
41. Filas, *Joseph and Jesus*, 94.
42. The marriage to Joseph was significant for the birth of Christ as divine and human.
43. Filas, *Joseph and Jesus*, 97.
44. Filas, *Joseph and Jesus*, 102. Contemporary theologians have examined this question of Joseph's participation in the Incarnation. Filas detects three options. Joseph was (1) a "condition" or (2) "cause removing obstacles" or (3) "cause in the moral order." God is the efficient cause and Joseph is a secondary cause. It was his holiness and cooperation with a virginal marriage that brought about the proper circumstances for the Savior's birth. Ibid., 141, 148.
45. This right also followed from his "true or interpretative consent" to the virginal marriage as "just man" eager to do God's Will. Filas, *Joseph and Jesus*, 74, 75.
46. He devoted much effort to refuting the apochrypha in order to establish Joseph's purity, Filas, *Joseph and Jesus,* 75. To him Joseph was a young man, sanctified in his mother's womb. Doze, *Shadow*, 15
47. Filas, *Joseph and Jesus*, 79-80
48. In the early church the saints were martyrs so that Joseph was not venerated as a saint. Lienhard, *Joseph in Early Christianity*, 23.

    5 Bernardine of Siena "had no doubt in particular that Joseph is in heaven, body and soul, for his role in the Incarnation was so great that he necessarily had to grace the eternal registers, in heaven as on earth." Doze, *Shadow*, 14.
49. The first chapel in honor of the saint was built in Toulouse in 1222 also by Franciscans. Doze, *Shadow,* 12.
50. Pope Pius IX in *Inclytum Patriarcham* has listed these as Gregory XV, May 8, 1621; Clement X, December 6, 1670, Clement XI, February 4,

1714 . In addition Benedict XIII decreed December 19, 1726 that Joseph be included in the litany of saints. He himself, on September 10, 1847, extended St. Joseph's feast to the whole Church.

51. This is promulgated in *Quemadmodum Dies* by Pius IX.
52. *Quamquam Pluries*, Encyclical of Pope Leo XIII.
53. Acta Benedicti PP. XV, "De Sacris Solemnibus Anni Quinquagesimi Ex Quo S. Joseph B.M.V., Num.8, 313-317.
54. Pius XI, Divini redemptoris cited in Filas, *Joseph and Jesus*, 116.
55. Filas, *Joseph and Jesus*, 116.
56. Pope Pius XI, *Divini redemptoris* on Atheistic Communism, no. 81.
57. Oblates of St. Joseph, *Le Voci - March 19, 1961.* It includes an excellent summary of papal pronouncements since the time of Pius IX, who called Vatican Council I. Called on June 29, 1898 and opened on December 8 1869 the Council was adjourned on October 20 1870 on the outbreak of the Franco-Prussian War. (online database)
58. Pope John XXIII, *Humanae salutis*, 703-709.
59. Pope Paul VI, *Address of Pope Paul VI, During Last General Meeting of the Second Vatican Council.*
60. The relevant section is no. 50 on Veneration of the Saints. Filas, *St. Joseph After Vatican II,* 40.
61. Filas, *St. Joseph After Vatican II,* 115. This followed a petition by the Directors of Research and Documentation Center of St. Joseph's Oratory, Montreal, January 1961. Filas gives a detailed record of earlier petitions on St. Joseph in both the 19th and 20th centuries. Ibid., 116, 117.
62. United States Conference of Catholic Bishops, *Vatican Approves.*
63. Doze, *Shadow*, 42.
64. Doze, *Shadow*, 43.
65. Chorpenning, "Mystery," 165.
66. In his second encyclical, *Dives in miserecordia*, John Paul II spells out his commitment to Vatican Council II's anthropocentrism, centered on its Christocentrism. He writes: "Since, therefore, in the present phase of the

Church's history, we put ourselves as our primary task *the implementation of the doctrine* of the great *Council*, we must act upon this principle with faith, with an open mind and with all our heart. (DM 1.)

67. As Chorpenning says; The guiding principle of John Paul II's thematization of these constituent elements of the mystery of the Holy Family is the personalist anthropology of *Gaudium et spes* that has had a decisive influence on his thought. Chorpenning, "Mystery," 165.

Chapter 4

1. Another word about sources used in this chapter. The author is professionally a theologian not an historian. Nevertheless, the theological development of the Holy Family cannot be understood without reference to historical developments in society, which Koschorke makes clear. The author has sought out recognized historians and/or cultural sociologists of the relevant period, insisting on at least two sources for each general statement made, sometimes from radically different perspectives. Notable sources consulted for the Middle Ages: *Christian Marriage: A Historical Study*, ed. Olsen; Noonan, *Contraception* and various works by Georges Duby and Caroline Walker Bynum.
2. Joseph Chorpenning, O.S.F.S. is currently assistant professor of Spanish and Theology, Allentown College of St. Francis de Sales.
3. Since 1992 an annual St. Joseph lecture has been given at St. Joseph's University, Philadelphia. Several of the lectures have been published by St. Joseph's University Press, edited by Joseph F. Chorpenning. In addition in 1996 on the 75th anniversary of the extension of the Feast of the Holy Family to the liturgical calendar of the Universal Church, St. Joseph's University together with the Wilmington-Philadelphia Province of the Oblates of St. Francis de Sales co-sponsored an exhibition and symposium, "The Holy Family as Prototype of the Civilization of Love: Images from the Viceregal Americas," later published and edited by Chorpenning as *The Holy Family in Art and Devotion.*

4. Koschorke, *Holy Family*, 138. Koschorke's testimony is valuable because he cannot deny the influence of the Holy Family on Western culture, yet he treats it reductively and from a negative viewpoint.
5. Koschorke, *Holy Family,* 187. Koschorke chose Freud as the lens through which to look at the Holy Family.
6. Chorpenning, "Guidance and Education." "The pattern which is observable throughout the history of devotion to the Holy Family is that it is always based on a strong, positive appreciation of the person and mission of St. Joseph in the mystery of the Incarnation." Ibid, 39.
7. Chorpenning, "Holy Family," Fn 7, 85.
8. Chorpenning notes that before Gerson, who initiated the term for the Holy Family, Trinity only referred to the heavenly trinity so that his use is implicit rather than explicit. He goes on to cite many pictorial renditions of the Holy Family together with the Heavenly Trinity above. Chorpenning, "Holy Family," Fn 7, 85.
9. Warner, *Albigensian Heresy*, 90. Albigensianism, also called Catharism from pure because of its emphasis on extreme asceticism, is a form of dualism. Warner says it is not true Gnosticism since the basis of Gnosticism is knowledge and that of the Cathars faith. In other words, it was spiritual not intellectual, esoteric rather than exoteric and closer to the Gnosticism of Marcion, 90. With regard to our sources, Noonan gives a lot of weight to the threat of Catharism, while Teresa Olsen Pierre devotes only one paragraph to the sect, virtually dismissing their influence. Pierre, "Marriage, Body and Sacrament,"246.
10. The elite of the sect eschewed marriage and sexuality altogether while the rank and file are said to have engaged in promiscuous sex. A form of androgyny prevailed. The perfecti (elite), who lived an extreme asceticism, encouraged a form of suicide (*endura*) since death was a desired goal. It is hardly necessary to enumerate the corresponding deformations of the nuptial mystery in our own day, androgyny, separation of procreation and sexuality, manipulation of both through technology, assisted suicide, confusion of the ontological orders of human and animal life. Warner, *Albengensian Heresy*, 65-87.

11. Duby in *Love and Marriage* describes the Church's response as removing guilt from the carnal. Duby, *Love and Marriage*, 17. See also Bynum, *Fragmentation,* 143.
12. Up to that time the Ave Maria had only been said on special feast days. Now it was required to be taught to every child over seven years along with the Our Father and the Creed. Noonan, *Contraception*, 192, 193.
13. Bynum, *Holy Feast,* 270. Christ's body was seen as female because *ecclesia* is female, nurturing her members through the Eucharist. Jesus's pain on the cross was also likened to a woman's birth pangs. Bynum, *Fragmentation*, 204-205.
14. Bernard of Clairvaux, *Sermons,* Ser. 9:6. At the time of Bernard iconography represented Christ feeding his people from his side like a nursing mother. Bynum, *Holy Feast*, 271.
15. Bernard of Clairvaux, *Sermons*, Ser. 9:7.
16. Bynum, *Holy Feast* 271, 272. Sister Prudence Allen, citing Bynum, points out that it was men who initiated the image of God as mother. Allen, *Jesus as Mother,* 140. "Although the most sophisticated use of the theme is Julian of Norwich's Trinitarian theology, there is no reason to assert, as some have done, that the theme of the motherhood of God is a 'feminine insight.'" Allen, *Concept of Woman,* 418. In the chapter, "Women Religious Develop Analogical Thinking," Allen discusses in detail how from analogy with human mothering to Mary as the perfect human mother Julian makes the transcendental move to Christ as our true mother, declaring that while Jesus is born from Mary, human beings are born into Jesus." Ibid., 415. She goes on to speak of the nurturing Christ. "The mother can give to her child to suck of her milk, but our precious Mother Jesus can feed us with himself, and does, most courteously and most tenderly, with the Blessed Sacrament, which is the precious food of true life." Ibid., 423.
17. It would be pertinent here to cite Donna Spivey Ellington: "Various historians have made much of the idea that the Dominican order promoted the cult of the Virgin's milk because lactation was viewed as part of the curse of original sin." Consequently, since Mary breastfed Jesus, she must have been subject to original sin. Ellington, *Sacred Body*, 58.

18. Duby, *Medieval Marriage*, 1-22. Other relevant works by Duby are *Love and Marriage* and *Women of the Twelfth Century.*
19. This is chronicled in Gies and Gies, *Marriage and Family,* 133-135, 145-150.
20. Gies, *Marriage and Family*, 150. In time the artisan class in the cities also hired wet nurses.
21. Gies, *Marriage and Family*, 150-151.
22. Etienne Gilson considers Bernard's "unique and definitive distinction is due to his method of reconciling personal, subjective experience with universal, objective teaching." Gilson, *Mystical Theology,* 14. In this the Cistercian abbot was a precursor of St. John Paul II.
23. Teresa Olsen Pierre comments: "Reflections on marital love multiplied among theologians in monastic and canonical orders, for whom marriage became a favorite metaphor for the nature of the love between God and humankind. Such reflections are a hallmark of the twelfth century development of the inner life of the Church." She goes on to say: "Monks were among the leading tweflth century spokesmen for the view that the body is important in the composition of the human person." She points to their meditation on Scripture which privileges images of the physical world in God's relation to his People. Bernard, especially, treats of the natural, psychological and spiritual levels. Olsen, *Christian Marriage*, 231, 232, 233.
24. Gilson, *Mystical Theology*, 178-181.
25. Teresa Olsen Pierre recounts how the monks "increasingly explored the interior dynamics of human love. The notion that true love for the divine begins with self-knowledge (i.e. properly ordered human love) permeated the age . . . . *Affectio maritalis,* marital affection, became ever more celebrated . . .and was promoted in scholastic and pastoral theology and law." Pierre, "Marriage, Body and Sacrament," 214.
26. The plays were usually performed around the feast of Corpus Christi in June, a feast established in 1311 and could have evolved from the procession in honor of the feast. The plays came to be performed on pageant wagons, which could move from town to town. http://www.english.cam.uk/medieval/mystery_plays.php.
27. Pilarz, "Medieval Stage," 11, 12, 13.

28. Scola, *Nuptial Mystery* "Appendix 2," 314-330. Scola says that "for him [Thomas], 'nature' always means creature.' In Thomas it is never possible to receive the category of *physis* and its derivatives in purely Aristotelian terms." Ibid., 315.
29. ST I-II, q.22, aa.1-3 and q. 26, aa 1-2).
30. Scola, *Nuptial Mystery*, 323.
31. Thomas distinguishes three types of love: *amor naturalis* which is a co-naturality with the object, *amor sensitivus* or pleasure in the good of the object and *amor intellectivus* or will, which involves choice for the object. *Amor naturalis*, because it is created by God has a built-in orientation to Him. Scola, "Appendix 2," 327, 328.
32. Pierre, "Marriage, Body, and Sacrament." Teresa Olsen Pierre comments how "the line of demarcation between 'ecclesiastical' and 'aristocratic' views of marriage...frequently blurred as a result of a shared desire to promote the stability of marriage and a Christian vison of conjugal union. Olsen, *Christian Marriage*, 214, and 158-169.
33. The recovery of the works of Plato and Aristotle provided the tools to advance a theology of Christian marriage in dialogue with philosophy that remains foundational to this day. Bonaventure represented the path of symbolism for accessing truth, prevalent in the early Middle Ages, while Aquinas applied the natural law arguments of Aristotle.
34. To this day arranged marriages approved by the Church take place in the Indian State of Kerala. Personal observation of Author.
35. "Consent was a requirement propounded by Roman Law and the Church Fathers, Gies and Gies, *Marriage and Famiy*, 137.
36. Augustine in discussing Joseph's fatherhood says the fact that there was no intercourse did not invalidate the marriage to Mary. "We know many brothers and sisters bearing much fruit in grace, who by mutual consent withhold from each other in the name of Christ the desire of the flesh but do not hold from each other their mutual love." Augustine, "Sermon 51," no. 21. Olsen notes the existence of such marriage in the time of Charlemagne. Olsen, *Christian Marriage*, 186-187. Spiritual marriage is discussed in greater detail in Chapter Five.

37. See Cahall, *Mystery of Marriage,* for a fuller discussion of the development of the theology of marriage. By the time of the Fourth Lateran Council of 1215, the canonical definition of marriage, while emphasizing the primacy of consent, acknowledged that in some sense consummation was proof of consent. Olsen, *Christian Marriage*, 229.
38. Pierre, "Marriage, Body and Sacrament," 219. We are not concerned here with the debates between Bonaventure and Aquinas on the sacramentality of marriage. Both agreed that grace flows from the sacrament although they disagreed on whether marriage is a sacrament from the beginning (Bonaventure) and whether it is a sacrament of the new order (Aquinas). For excellent discussions of this topic, see Miller, *Marriage,* 207-222 and Granados, "Bonaventure and Aquinas," 339-359. Later on we shall see how John Paul II successfully combines the two in his theology of the body.
39. F. Stan Parmisano quotes Eamon Duffy: "Any study of late medieval religion must begin with the liturgy, for within that great seasonal cycle of fast and festival, of ritual observance and symbolic gesture, lay Christians found the paradigms and stories which shaped their perception of the world and their place in it." Parmisano, "Spousal Love," Fn. 2, 786. We already saw the influence of the mystery plays on the Holy Family as a model for ordinary family life.
40. Parmisano gives a list of such authors. Parmisano, "Spousal Love," Fn. 1, 785, 786.
41. Parmisano, "Spousal Love," 787-794.
42. Parmisano, "Spousal Love," 794-95.
43. Parmisano, "Spousal Love," 799-801.
44. Parmisano, "Spousal Love," 803.
45. Olsen, *Christian Marriage,* 181.
46. Olsen, *Christian Marriage*, 182. He goes on to mention an Irish gospel commentary, which referred to the Holy Family as "the *ecclesia primitive*, the first or original church." The symbolism was more in ecclesiology than in the family as an institution per se, nevertheless, the "symbolism quite distinctive to Christianity, especially Catholic Christianity, became widespread. Just as the idea that each bishop is married to his church was to have far-ranging

juridical effects, the Holy Family presented a powerful image to society. . . . Indeed the Irish laid a special weight on the Holy Family in the history of salvation. One gloss on Luke 2:26 said of Mary, Joseph and Jesus, 'Through these three, the world was healed.'" The latter is reminiscent of John Paul II *Redemptoris custos*, no. 7 cited later in this chapter.

47. A 20th century medical researcher has pointed out that conjugal intercourse is only one reproductive relationship in the family. The other is birth and breastfeeding. All three activate the same neuro-hormonal and pleasure responses designed to initiate and strengthen a bond of love between the two subjects, in the case of intercourse the spouses, and in birth and breastfeeding the mother and child. (The husband plays a significant supportive role in the latter.) This will be more fully discussed in a later chapter.
48. Margaret R. Miles in an inter-disciplinary study has shown how, from being a powerful religious symbol of nurturance and care in art and culture in the Middle Ages, the breast was gradually eroticized or reduced to a simple anatomical object by medicine so that by 1750 images of the nursing Madonna had disappeared altogether. Her book has the provocative title of *A Complex Delight: The Secularization of the Breast, 1350-1750.* After 1750 Miles concludes from her research that there were no images of the Virgin with one bare breast for nursing. Miles, *Complex Delight*, 132.
49. Both the Church and secular authorities were implicated in this since the Bureau of Wet Nurses was set up in Paris and other major cities by which the police monitored payment to the wet nurses and the local village priest vouched for the character of the wet nurse. One reason given for the practice was to protect the marriage bed because it was believed the husband had to abstain while his wife nursed. "All of the French royal children going back at least to the future St. Louis at the beginning of the thirteenth century were suckled by hired women. . . . At social levels below the royal line the evidence of wet nursing in France goes back to the Middle Ages. The ordinance concerning the police of the realm, issued by King John on January 30, 1350 contains a title devoted to wet nurse." Sussman, *Selling Mothers' Milk,* 70. At the same time medical treatises encouraged wet nurses, usually of a lower social class, because it was believed that breast

milk as a transmutation of menstrual blood had a tendency towards corruption. MacLehose, "Nurturing Danger," 15. Also the mother was unable to produce breast milk immediately after birth. "There was thus an irresolvable impasse between the necessity of female nourishment of the child, and the danger in that nourishment," Ibid., 16. Whereas in the Levitical tradition of the Old Testament menstrual blood was considered spiritually unclean (there was no taboo attached to mother's milk) medieval medicine "stressed physical or material dangers," Ibid., 9. The "exception" for the nobility spread in the cities. In Florence in the 14th and 15th centuries it appears to have been not uncommon to send babies out to wet nurses in the country side. Fildes, *Breasts*, 50. France was particularly known for endorsing the use of wet nurses by all social classes in the cities. The mortality rate ranged from 18 percent for children nursed by their mothers, to 25 to 40 percent for those returned to their mothers and 65 to 85 percent for foundlings in the 18th century in four French cities.

50. Quattrin, "Milk of Christ," 48.
51. Miles, *Complex Delight*, 4, 131.
52. Miles, *Complex Delight*, 134, 135. Olsen Pierre sees the significance as primarily linked to ideas on the Incarnation, not women's bodies as such or the social impact on the mother-child relation. Olsen, *Christian Marriage*, 238-239.
53. In the latter half of the 20th century this symbolism was rediscovered. Two authors are notable, John Saward, in his review of Christ's life in the womb and what it teaches; *Redeemer in the Womb*; and William Virtue, in his comprehensive doctoral dissertation, *Mother and Infant,* Saward traces Christ's "revelation in the womb" from the Gospels through the Fathers, the Middle Ages, the Age of Baroque and in sacred art. Virtue writes: "Jesus Christ recapitulated human nature at the origins of human life in conception, birth and the nurturing in the bond formed with the infant nursed by his mother, all of which are renewed in the exemplar couplet in a transformation of nature by Grace, the New Covenant." Virtue, *Mother and Infant,* 365. Reiterating the analogy of the nursing mother with the Eucharist, he goes on to say: "Mary and Jesus as mother and child are

the icon of the truth of human nature: the truth that we are created for love, for the communion of persons in a loving bond through embodied self-giving." Ibid., 366, and "The image of the mother Mary holding her infant Jesus is deeply embedded in the psyche of Christians. After the image of the cross and crucified savior, this is the most popular icon . . . the icons [especially of the nursing Madonna] foster Eucharistic piety and have nurtured the mystical tradition of intimate communion of the lover and the beloved." Ibid., 367.

54. Ellington, *Sacred Body,* 31. "Mary's most potent appeal in the later Middle Ages, like that of the other saints, lay in her ability to serve as a sacred place to encounter the holy, a place where the purely human might come into contact with the divine." Ibid., 74.

55. Ellington, *Sacred Body*, 32. The author found abundant evidence that "people were using all of their senses to apprehend the holy; bodily metaphors abound in the arts and sciences. . . .Because of this emphasis on the concrete and the sacramental, Mary's bodily relation to Christ is at the heart of devotion surrounding her in this period." Ibid., 36, 37. Whereas some historians charge that Mariology became in some ways independent of Christology, Ellington claims that it is probably truer to say that Mary was approaching equity with Christ with regard to salvation. Ibid., 42-44.

56. It may be that decline in the bodily presence of nursing facilitated a more abstract mode of communication, just as in the 20th century, adoption of the more mechanical mode of bottle-feeding has facilitated the even more abstract mode of communication via the internet.

57. This is not the place to discuss the causes of the Protestant Reformation, from the immorality of the clergy to the abuse of indulgences, except to chronicle the changes that took place in the cult of the Holy Family. With Protestant rejection of devotion to Mary, the Holy Family as a model was seriously truncated, even abolished.

58. Ellington, *Sacred Body*, 143. Mary became a more distant figure, "silent, self-controlled and obedient." Ibid., 148.

59. Koschorke, *Holy Family*,134. The source for St. Joseph's great age were the Apochrypha in order to protect Mary's virginity. The Renaissance

challenged this view. Joseph had to be vigorous enough to support Mary and Jesus; if Joseph too old to generate, then Mary would seem to be an adulteress; it denies God's grace in endowing Joseph with the gift of virginity. Gracián, *Excellencies*, 114.

60. Wilson, "Images of St. Theresa," 26.
61. Wilson, "Images of St. Theresa," 32. In the Prologue to the account of her foundations, Theresa writes: "I begin in the name of the Lord, taking for my help His glorious Mother, whose habit I wear . . .and also my glorious father and lord, St. Joseph, in whose house I am, for he is patron of this monastery of discalced nuns, through whose prayer I have been constantly helped." St. Teresa of Avila, *Collected Works*, 97. Gerson was at the forefront with his reference to the "concord of love" between Jesus, Mary and Joseph. Wilson, "Images of St. Theresa," 84.
62. Gracián, *Excellencies.*
63. Gracián, *Excellencies*, 3.
64. Gracián's Summary was comprised of five books based on a biblical text: Joseph as (1) 'husband,' (2) father of Jesus, (3) 'just' (4) angels appeared to him and (5) angels spoke to him in dreams. Gracián, *Excellencies*, 24-27.
65. Gracián, *Excellencies*, 42.
66. Gracián, *Excellencies*, 52.53. Once St. Joseph is depicted as a young man in art, his face resembles Christ. Chorpenning says this "reflects the idea, widespread in the tradition of devotional writing on Joseph that this saint was a mirror of God the Father." Ibid., 148. El Greco was one of the first artists to glorify St Joseph following St. Theresa of Avila. Ibid., 115.
67. Chorpenning, "Guidance and Education," 38-52, 39. His sources are the Treatise on the Love of God, Book 7, Chapter 13 and sermons on the solemnity of St. Joseph.
68. Chorpenning, "Guidance and Education," 41.
69. Stopp, "Francois de Sales," 381-2.
70. Several commentators decry both the pessimism towards human nature of Cardinal Berulle, and St. John Eudes, and exaggerations in devotion to Mary. Graef, *Mary,* 31, 34, 36, 38-9.

71. Saward, "French School," 386. At his beatification in 1909, Pope Pius X called him "father, doctor, and apostle of the liturgical cult of the Hearts of Jesus and Mary." Thompson, *Berulle*, 21.
72. Berulle rooted the Marian mystery in Trinitarian relations. "O inclination of Jesus towards Mary, of Mary towards Jesus emanating from the eternal inclination of the Father towards the Son, of the Son towards the Father." Thompson, *Berulle.*
73. Saward, "French School," 54,58, 59. William Thompson comments: "The School's Trinitarianism brings out the loving, interpersonal reality of God, a love that ecstatically spills out into the world in Christ. Thompson, *Berulle*, 85.
74. Saward, "French School," 60, 61.
75. St. John Eudes was active in clergy reform in the seminaries. His new Congregation of Jesus and Mary, founded on the Feast of the Annunication, 1643, "took priestly formation and the missions as its work," both at home and abroad. Thompson, *Berulle*, 20.
76. Gauthier, "Holy Family."
77. Gauthier, "Holy Family," 68, 69.
78. Gauthier, "Holy Family," 69. The Oratory of St Joseph is a much loved pilgrimage site in Montreal.
79. Lallemont appropriated the Jewish tradition, finding in the ritual purification of the Old Testament a prelude for Mary and Christ who would come from this ancestry. Giorgio Buccellati would call this the "Catechumenate of the Old Testament." Buccellati, "Yahweh," 292-327.
80. Lallemant, *La Doctrine,* 17. He took Jesus Christ as model of humility, Mary for purity and Joseph for "la vie interieure." He practiced four meditations in honor of St. Joseph daily (1) the fidelity of Joseph's heart (2) his interior life, (3) Joseph as spouse of Mary; he liked to "*considerer les admirable connaissances qu'il avait eues de sa virginite et de sa maternite* and (4) St. Joseph's homage to Jesus. It was said of him, *Il voulut porter jusqu'au tombeau des marques de sa devotion envers Saint Josef,* Ibid., 21, and he asked the Virgin in prayer never to be separated from her or the humanity of Jesus. Ibid., 38.

81. It was confined to women and girls, as the men already had another fraternity. Gauthier, "Holy Family," 70.
82. Wilson, "Images of St. Theresa," 24-34.
83. Michael Gorman in his study of the use of covenant on the Old Testament concludes that it is not clearly transposed from God's love to that between the spouses. "Marriage as Covenant in the Catholic Tradition," in *Covenant Marriage in Comparative Perspective*, Ed. John Witte Jr. and Eliza Ellison (Grand Rapids, MI: W. B. Eerdmans, 2005) 70-91. In *The Documents of Vatican II* Ed Walter M. Abbott, SJ, no. 48 "The Church Today," the translation reads : It [marriage] is rooted in the conjugal covenant of irrevocable personal consent." The same word is translated "contract" in *Vatican Council II Vol. 1:The Concilial and Post Concilial Documents New Revised Edition* ed. Austin Flannery OP (Northport NY: Costello Pub. Co. 2005 5th printing; orig. 1975)
84. See Stanley Samuel Harakas, "Covenant Marriage from an Eastern Orthodox Perspective," in *Covenant Marriage in Comparative Perspective*, Ed. John Witte Jr. And Eliza Ellison (Grand Rapids, MI: W. B. Eerdmans, 2005) 92-152. In Ut Unum Sint, Encyclical Letter, May 25, 1995, John Paul II says "the Church must breathe with her two lungs," 54, of both the Eastern and Western Church.
85. Catholic theologian, Johann Adam Mohler, writing in the 19th century, whose most significant work is *Symbolism: Exposition of the Doctrinal Differences between Catholics and Protestants* sees the inevitably of the alignment of the state with Protestantism. With the abolition of papal authority and celibacy, which point to a transcendental realm, Mohler believes that the Protestant church in the early 19th century had "actually gone over to the state. Mohler, *Celibacy* 91. His defense of celibacy was written to respond to a public memorandum (Denkschrift) issued by a group of Freiburg professors in 1828 calling for the abolition of celibacy for the priesthood.
86. Kirsti Stjerna, *Women and the Reformation* (Malden, MA: Blackwell Publishing, 2009), 37. Luther's wife "Katherine von Bora Luther exemplifies the newly elevated vocation of mothers and the new calling of

Protestant pastors' spouses as domestic implementers of the faith through home and family." Ibid. 9. See also Max L. Stackhouse, "Covenant Marriage: Protestant Views and Contemporary Life in *Covenant Marriage,* Ed. Witte, 165-66.

87. James Turner Johnson, "Marriage as Covenant in Early Protestant Thought" in *Covenant Marriage Ed. Witte,* 133.
88. Johnson, "Marriage as Covenant" 146.
89. Johnson, "Marriage as Covenant," 150. Steinmetz cites Reinhold Niebuhr's comment that if all options are tainted by sin, "divine forgiveness will hallow and sanctify what is really unholy." This contradiction may well have led to the ready acceptance of contraception.
90. Duffy, *Stripping.* As Duffy writes: The attempt to obliterate the memory of traditional religion was not confined to the eradication of Catholic ritual and Catholic drama. Both the bishops and their Puritan critics were aware of the potent influence of what they called the "monuments of superstition," they physical remnants of Catholic cult which represented a symbolic focus for Catholic belief, a reminder of the community's Catholic past and its corporate investment in the old religion, and a concrete hope for its ultimate restoration." Ibid., 582.
91. Wandel, *Voracious Idols*, 196.
92. Wandel, *Voracious Idols*, 195-196.
93. It must be noted here that "by the early 17th century puritan theologians in particular were devoting sermons and large tracts of popular conduct books to the evils of non-breastfeeding mothers. Fildes, *Breasts, Bottles,* 98.
94. "The laity were no longer to be second to the clergy in piety or proximity to Christ," Wandel, *Voracious Idols,* 196.
95. See William J. Bouwsma, *John Calvin: a Sixteenth Century Portrait* (NY: Oxford University Press, 1988)131-148. This ambiguity can also be seen in belief in the resurrection but rejection of Christ's body on the cross.
96. John D'Emilio etc. *Intimate Matters,* 25.
97. D'Emilio, *Intimate Matters,* 4.
98. D'Emilio, *Intimate Matters,* 58.
99. D'Emilio, *Intimate Matters,* 73.

100. Gardella, *Innocent Ecstasy* etc.
101. Gardella, *Innocent Ecstasy*, 130.
102. Barger, *Eve's Revenge,* 153 is a good example. Ingrid Trobisch and her husband, Walter, were pioneers of Natural Family Planning.
103. Maritain, *Three Reformers,* 54, 55.
104. Maritain, *Three Reformers.* "So by curious chance," says Maritain, "the first move of rationalism is to disown reason, to do violence to its nature, to challenge the normal conditions of its activity. Ibid., 58.
105. Maritain, *Three Reformers,* 79.
106. Maritain, *Three Reformers,* 82.
107. A charge of "Bulverism" in which an argument is dismissed on grounds other than its own rational terms, might be laid on Karl Stern's analysis. But we have here an argument for splitting matter and spirit, which is exactly what Stern addresses in his explanation. See Lewis, "Bulverism," 271-277.
108. Stern, *Flight,* 84, 85.
109. Stern, *Flight,* 86.
110. Stern, *Flight,* 100. In the case of Descartes, without the ministrations of a wet nurse, he would not have survived but mostly it was a *choice* to send the infant to a wet nurse away from home.
111. Susan Bordo, also writes that "'the great Cartesian anxiety,' although manifestly expressed in epistemological terms, discloses itself as anxiety over *separation* from the organic female universe." Bordo, *Flight to Objectivity*, 5.
112. Stern, *Third Revolution*, 286.
113. John Paul II, *Fides et Ratio*, No. 32.
114. Stern, *Third Revolution*, 283.
115. Rousseau placed all the children as infants in an orphanage. Rousseau, *Contract,* 18. He was following in the footsteps of his own irresponsible father. Ibid., 10.
116. Maritain, *Three Reformers*, 115.
117. The answer came to him, writes Maurice Cranston, as a "sudden revelation." Jean Jacques Rousseau, *Contract*, trans. With intro. By Maurice Cranston (London, UK:, Penguin Books, Ltd., 1968) 15.

118. Maritain, *Three Reformers,* 134.

119. In *Emile,* Rousseau's treatise on education, he advises "Do you wish always to be well guided? Then always follow nature's indications," and "Everything that hinders and constrains nature is in bad taste." Rousseau, *Emile,* 363, 367. Allan Bloom notes in the introduction that Rousseau hates all books, especially the Bible, but allows *Robinson Crusoe* because the hero is "a solitary man in the state of nature, outside of civil society and unaffected by the deeds and opinions of men" Ibid., 7.

120. Rousseau, *Contract*, 26.

121. Rousseau, *Emile*, 357.

122. Maritain, *Three Reformers*, 141. In speaking of the education of Sophie, intended for Emile, Rousseau refers to woman being *made to please* and *to be subjugated* by men and their proper purpose is to *produce children.* He praises the customs of ancient Sparta, where after marriage, the girls are confined to their homes. "Such is the way of life that nature and reason prescribe for the fair sex." Rousseau, *Emile*, 366.

123. From Rousseau's *Emile,* cited by Ratner in *Child and Family,* 19: 98-100, 99.

124. Kukla, *Mass Hysteria*, 54.

125. Kukla cites Sussman, *Selling Mothers' Milk,* 52. The French Bureau of Wet Nurses shut down in 1876. By that time pasteurized milk was available. Rousseau gave a scathing diatribe against women who did not nurse their own children at the beginning of *Emile* which had a profound influence. Rousseau, *Emile*, 44-47.

126. Allen, *Concept of Woman*, 63.

127. Binion, *Past Impersonal*, 39.

128. Binion, *Past Impersonal*, 39, 40. In America, Smith surmises this may have been achieved by less intercourse, rather than *coitus interruptus*, as was more prevalent in France. In the 20th century abortion as a legal right is a *sine qua non* of feminist ideology.

129. Binion, *Past Impersonal*, 3.

130. Binion, *Past Impersonal*, 14. Pressure for contraception had already come from abandonment of breastfeeding. Peter Howie, professor of obstetrics

and gynecology, Scotland, details the reproductive life of the wife of the fourth Earl of Traquair in the 17th century, who employed a wet nurse. She produced a child every ten or eleventh months, resulting in seventeen children altogether. Her childbearing only ended with the death of her husband. In contrast the average family size of the Kung hunter-gatherer tribe of Africa is 4.4 children total. Peter Howie, "*Synopsis,*" 17-19.

131. Binion, *Past Impersonal,* 30.
132. Binion, *Past Impersonal,* 31.
133. Chorpenning, "Mystery," 140-166, 140.
134. Chorpenning, "Mystery," 141.
135. Chorpenning, "Mystery," 165.

Chapter 5

1. John Paul II, *Man and Woman,* 47: 1, fn 57.
2. According to Thomas Petri, OP, passions for Thomas Aquinas only exist in the sensitive appetite. For example, "For Aquinas the delight of sex is fundamentally a passion in the sensitive appetite that should be guided by reason." *Aquinas and the Theology of the Body,* 240 and 223. Antonio Lopez proposes that both *eros* and *agape* exist in the Trinity united by *logos.* Lopez, *Gift and the Unity of Being,* 65-70.
3. Atkinson, *Foundations of the Family,* 49.
4. Atkinson, *Foundations of the Family,* 49.
5. Atkinson, *Foundations of the Family,* 57.
6. Atkinson, *Foundations of the Family,* 65. "One of the most important elements which Christianity has inherited from Israel is the Old Testament's living, almost passionate, and certainly joyous confession of everyday secular values, understood not as self-contained, but as dynamic and proceeding directly from God." Schillebeeckx, *Marriage,* 7. "It is precisely this vision of the people of God which Christianity should strive to preserve and illuminate in the light of Christ." Ibid., 8.
7. Atkinson, Foundations of the Family, 321. The family was the "carrier of the covenant" in the Old Testament so that "there first needs to be a

recovery of the OT understanding of the family upon which the NT understanding is predicated."

8. Wenham, Leviticus, 17. Although pre-eminently present in worship, God is present at all times, "even in the mundane duties of life" 16.
9. Atkinson, *Foundations of the Family,* 137.
10. W. Kaiser interprets the ban on the husband engaging in sex with a woman in the ritually unclean state of *nidah* (the menstruant) as confirming that the wife's body belongs first and foremost to God. (Kaiser, 199) As Frank Gorman notes the instructions on impurity in Leviticus 11-16 "take the body seriously." They "suggest that the body is at the heart and practice of religion" (Gorman 69).
11. On the human level, part of *eros* is the desire to receive a perfection. Since God lacks nothing, he does not have *eros* in this sense.
12. Wojtyla, *Love and Responsibility,* 32.
13. Wojtyla, *Love and Responsibility,* 33
14. Wojtyla, *Love and Responsibility,* 34.
15. Pinckaers, "Natural Inclinations," 400-456.
16. One might ask if rejection of nursing by the upper classes did not have a hand in the rise of nominalism. When there is little experience of union and communion especially at the bodily level, keeping the commandments becomes rather a task of law not of love.
17. Pinckaers, "Natural Inclinations," 402-3.
18. Pinckaers, "Natural Inclinations," 403.
19. Pinckaers, "Natural Inclinations," 405.
20. Pinckaers, "Natural Inclinations," 439.
21. In *Soft Patriachs, New Men: How Christianity Shapes Fathers and Husbands,* W. Bradford Wilcox relates how the wives in Conservative Protestant families, who adhere to this Christian dynamic, report high levels of appreciation, affection and understanding and low levels of domestic violence. 198.
22. See Chapter 10 for a discussion of vows and life-long commitment in relation to freedom.
23. Wojtyla, *Love and Responsibility,* 117

24. *Wojtyla, Love and Responsibility,* 154. Both the egoism of the senses and of affection can mar and distort this transparency. Ibid.,140.
25. *Wojtyla, Love and Responsibility,* 155.
26. *Wojtyla, Love and Responsibility,* 156
27. The virtue of chastity is often confused with celibacy, which is the way the consecrated religious refrains from all sexual congress in order to give himself totally, body and soul, to Christ.
28. See the last section of this chapter.
29. *Wojtyla, Love and Responsibility,* 185-186.
30. *Wojtyla, Love and Responsibility,* 186
31. NFP couples find that in the periods of abstinence, this tenderness flourishes through different ways of expressing love than sexual union. See Shivanandan, *Crossing the Threshold of Love*, 264-267.
32. http://w2.vatican.va/content/francesco/en/homilies/2015/documents/papa-francesco_20150922_cuba-omelia-santiago.html.
33. In sacramental marriage, Christ is at the center through baptism and the Eucharist. In the marriage of Mary and Joseph, Christ is the center as the non-mediated gift of their union.
34. As we saw in the last chapter, this changed at the Reformation.
35. Earlier it was noted that John Paul II places St. Joseph's pilgrimage of faith closer to that of the pilgrim Church than of Mary.
36. Mary's freedom from original sin as a prevenient fruit of Christ's redemption had not yet been generally accepted.
37. Cole, "Mary's Virginity," 65-90, 71.
38. Cole, "Mary's Virginity," 73.
39. For the important role of the conjugal act in bonding the spouses, see Chapter seven.
40. Cole, "Mary's Virginity," 78.
41. Cole, "Mary's Virginity," 86.
42. Conner, *Celibate Love*, 56-67.
43. Cole, "Mary's Virginity," 90.
44. Melina, "Analogy," 274-279, 276.
45. Melina, "Analogy," 279.
46. Buccellati, "Prophetic," 43-99, 53.

47. Cramer, *Biblio-Theological Lexicon,* 184-5.
48. de la Potterie, *Mary,* 91-105. De la Potterie argues both from the meaning of the Greek and from the theological exegesis of several Fathers of the Church.
49. In formal Church documents, John Paul II is conservative in his presentation of modern scriptural exegesis, preferring to remain with well-proven interpretations. Prendergast, "Vision of Wholeness," 88.
50. Buccellati, "Prophetic," 86.
51. Buccellati, "Prophetic," 88.
52. Buccellati, "Prophetic," 99.
53. "The dignity of every human being and the vocation corresponding to that dignity find their definitive measure in union with God. Mary, the woman of the Bible, is the most complete expression of this dignity and vocation." John Paul II, Mulieris Dignitatem. (MD 5)
54. Elliott, *Spiritual Marriage,* 83.
55. See Cormac Murphy in Chapter 11 of this book.
56. Elliott, *Spiritual Marriage,* 141.
57. Wojtyla, *Love and Responsibility,* 94.
58. Elliott, *Spiritual Marriage,* 208. Possibly, women felt valued more for their sexual attraction than for their personhood.
59. Elliott, *Spiritual Marriage,* 264.
60. *Theological Dictionary,* ed. Kittel, Vol. II, 39-42.
61. For a fuller discussion, see Shivanandan, "Feminism and Marriage," 29, 11, especially 12.
63. A student in one of my classes on the theology of the body commented that that the husband needs to know the wife will surrender in order to totally give himself, and the wife can only surrender if she knows he will receive her totally.

Chapter 6

1. Wojtyla, "The Person," 248.
2. "As a person he 'exists for his own sake and reaches fulfillment precisely by sharing God's life'" (LF 9).
3. Scola, *Nuptial,* 131.

4. In *Mulieris Dignitatem* John Paul II is at pains to stress that generating in God does not have either masculine or feminine qualities as it is totally divine. "Thus even 'fatherhood' in God is completely divine and free of the 'masculine' bodily characteristics proper to human fatherhood" (MD 8).
5. Scola, *Nuptial,* 132-136. One must always remember that any analogy with the divine is more unlike than like yet love and fruitfulness are intrinsic to both. This also means that any separation of the act from its unitive and procreative dimensions as occurs in homosexual acts or in in vitro fertilization makes such acts unworthy of the dignity of the person made in the image of God in a communion of persons.
6. Ouellet, *Divine Likeness*, 103.
7. Ouellet, *Divine Likeness*, 110.
8. Ouellet, *Divine Likeness*, 111.
9. Ouellet, *Divine Likeness*, 112. See the many passages in the New Testament that underscore this statement, such as Mt. 12:46-50, Mk. 3:31-35, Lk. 8:19-21.
10. Ouellet, *Divine Likeness*, 123.
11. Two of these retreats were recorded, transcribed, translated and later published as Wojtyla, *Spiritual Exercises.*
12. The pope does not comment on this, but perhaps it was not lost on him that the passage follows both the reference to the significance of the child and the question the Pharisees ask about divorce.
13. Wojtyla, *Spiritual Exercises,* 50.
14. Wojtyla, *Spiritual Exercises,* 51.
15. Wojtyla, *Spiritual Exercises,* 55.
16. In the case of the rich young man in the gospel, his concept of adultery would simply mean not taking another man's wife. In the Old Testament concubines were permitted. Not so in the New Covenant, where Jesus says that even to "look" lustfully at another man's wife is to commit adultery with her (Luke 5: 27). The pope develops this advance of the New Covenant in the Wednesday Catechesis, *Man and Woman,* especially nos. 35—44.
17. Wojtyla, "Radiation," 336.

18. Wojtyla, "Radiation," 338.
19. Wojtyla, "Radiation," 340.
20. This negates any suggestion that the mother/child dyad can ever be sufficient in itself as a family form.
21. Wojtyla, "Radiation," 341.
22. Wojtyla, "Radiation," 327.
23. Wojtyla, "Radiation," 327.
24. Wojtyla, "Radiation," 354.
25. Wojtyla, "Radiation," 355.
26. We can see from the work of Johannes Pedersen, the continuity and discontinuity in the roles in the Holy Family of both Joseph and Mary, but especially of Joseph. A new house is formed by the man and the woman together. The man is the head; he supports the family through work. The woman's role is to bear the man children, especially sons, and so build up the father's house. Her husband is called *ba'al* which means master. Pedersen explains that the word, ba'al, implies a psychic relation, an intimate community which imposes certain limits on his power. Nevertheless the children as his own flesh and blood take precedence over his wife, even if she is usually selected from among his kindred. The wife is first and foremost a sexual being who provides her husband with children and totally belongs to him. There is a certain equality in the penalty for adultery but as long as a man does not violate another man's wife, he is free to have sex outside of marriage with other women and to take other wives. She acquires her place in the family through motherhood. Yet both mother and father share authority over their children and are usually spoken together. Pedersen, *Israel,* 62-63.
27. Berulle and the French School. Pierre, Cardinal de Berulle was renowned for his humility; Jean Jacques Olier and John Eudes also laid great stress on humility, although it was focused more on Jesus and Mary in the Holy Family than Joseph. Thompson, Glendon, and Muto, *Berulle*, 193, 232-242, 320.
28. See Chapter Two.
29. John Paul II *Redemptoris Custos* 1,5,7,8,14, 15, 28, 30, 32.

30. It was fitting for him to be guardian of the Church from being guardian of the Holy Family (RC no. 28).
31. Pedersen, *Israel*, 53. When the founder is a significant person, he gives his name and character to the house, as the House of David. In Israelite society it was the man as founding father who impressed his character on the house. When a young man leaves his father's house to form his own house, he still retains close ties to his father's house.
32. Statistics on fathers attending Sunday Mass and children's faith.
33. The translation of biblical excerpts comes from *New Oxford*, ed. May and Metzger.
34. *Gates of the Seasons*, ed. Knobel, 18.
35. *Gates of the Seasons*, ed. Knobel, 17.
36. *Gates of the Seasons*, ed. Knobel, 26; the references are to Exodus 20 and Deuteronomy 5.
37. Leo XIII, *Quamquam Pluries*, no. 5.
38. "*Non igitur seditiosorum hominum promissis confidant inopes, si sapiunt, sed exemplo patrocinioque beati Josephi, itemque maternae Ecclesiae caritate.*" Acta Benedicti PP. XV, "De Sacris Solemnibus Anni Quinquagesimi Ex Quo S. Joseph B.M.V.," August 2, 1920.
39. Pope Pius XI, *Divini redemptoris* on Atheistic Communism, no. 81.
40. Balthazar and Ratzinger, *Mary*, 33.
41. According to the Catechism of the Catholic Church: the deepening of faith in the virginal motherhood led the Church to confess Mary's real and perpetual virginity even in the act of giving birth to the Son of God made man. In fact Christ's birth "did not diminish His Mother's virginal integrity but sanctified it" (CCC #449).Cited in Calkins, "Virginal Conception," 31. John Paul II gave a discourse in Capra in May 1992 concerning Patristic teaching on the correlation between the *Virginias in partu*, and the Resurrection. Just as Christ was begotten from an intact womb, so his resurrection took place from an intact sepulcher. "There exists an intrinsic connection which corresponds to a precise plan of God: a connection which the Church, led by the Spirit, has discovered not created." The pope confirms that this belongs to the deposit of Faith. Ibid., 33, 34.

42. Saward's *Redeemer* is a useful summary through the centuries.
43. Bynum, *Fragmentation*, 182.
44. Bynum, *Fragmentation*, 205.
45. Bynum, *Fragmentation*, 210.
46. Bynum, "Woman as Body," 270. "Both men and women described Christ's body in its suffering and generativity as a birthing and lactating mother and may at some almost unconscious level have felt that woman's suffering was her way of fusing with Christ because Christ's suffering flesh was 'woman.'" Ibid., 60, 261.
47. Cole, *Mary's Virginity*, 74.
48. Cole, *Mary's Virginity*, 75.
49. Cole, *Mary's Virginity*, 75.
50. Virtue, *Mother and Infant*, 398.
51. John Paul II recommends obtaining assistance from qualified psychologists and psychotherapists for this crisis. Postpartum depression is not uncommon in mothers after giving birth not only due to hormonal changes but also due to changes in or, lack of social support for her new role. See Stephanie Balcheniuk, "Conceptualizing Postpartum Depression Through Attachmdnt Theory and a Catholic Understanding of Relationality and Motherhood" Unpublished Dissertation, Institute for the Psychological Sciences, Alexandria, VA 2017.
52. See chapter 2
53. John Paul II, Letter to Women, 3.
54. John Paul II, Letter to Women, 10.
55. John Paul II, Letter to Women,11
56. See *Letter to Families* numbers. 3,4,5,7,10,11,13,15,16,18,19,20.
57. Rahner, *Our Lady,* 6.
58. Rahner, *Our Lady,* 14.
59. Balthasar and Ratzinger, *Mary.* "The correspondence between Jesus' Incarnation by the power of the Spirit in Nazareth and the birth of the Church at Pentecost is unmistakable," Ibid, 57.
60. Balthazar and Ratzinger, *Mary*, 65-66. Von Balthasar cites "Scheeben's principle, (*Dogma.*V, n. 1819) that the mystery of Mary and the mystery

of the Church penetrate and illuminate each other perichoretically, that neither can be correctly situated without the other. 141

61. Von Balthazar comments that devotion to her is similar to that of all saints who cooperate in the work of the redemption.
62. Balthazar and Ratzinger, *Mary*, 141-143.
63. Balthazar and Ratzinger, *Mary*, 57.
64. Rahner, *Our Lady*, 116. We shall look at the implications of this in the next chapter.
65. Balthazar and Ratzinger, *Mary*, 16.
66. Balthazar and Ratzinger, *Mary*, 25.
67. Wojtyla, "Parenthood," 330. It is noteworthy that one of the key aspects of natural family planning is the ability it gives for the couple to know the peak time of fertility and to consciously achieve pregnancy together.
68. In *Letter to Families* John Paul II exclaims: "In God's plan the family is in many ways the first school of how to be human. Be human!" (LF no.15)
69. But that should not "impede the legitimate social advancement of women." (LF no. 16)
70. Kostenberger and Jones, *Biblical Foundation,* 94. John Paul II says that "the self-giving that inspires the love of husband and wife for each other must be practiced in the relations between brothers and sisters and the different generations living in the family (FC 37).
71. See also Kaufman, *Jewish Law,* especially Chapter 9, "Family Purity: The Jewish Refinement of Sexuality." Ibid., 195-212. This will be dealt with more in a later chapter.

Chapter 7

1. Vagaggini, *The Flesh,* 79. The citation is from *De Resurrectione Carnis,* Ibid., 6.
2. St. John of Damascus, *Divine Images,* 8.
3. John Paul II, *Image of God,* 63, 64 no. 64.
4. "The Child" cited in John Paul II, *Image of God,* 96 no. 86.
5. John Paul II, *Image of God,* 97 no.88.

6. John Paul II, *Image of God,* 89 no. 89. In other texts he speaks of the rights of the child, how the child teaches the adults in the family, and what adults owe the child.
7. The main sources for this section are Balthasar, *Unless you Become.* And Balthasar, "Jesus as Child," 625-634.
8. Balthasar, *Unless you Become,* 10.
9. Balthasar, *Unless you Become,* 11.
10. Balthasar, *Unless you Become,* 12.
11. See also Aquinas, *The Summa Theologiae* II-I. Q 89 art. 6.
12. Balthasar, *Unless you Become,* 17,18.
13. This insight is owed to Family Sociologist, Patrick Fagan, who was kind enough to review these chapters.
14. For example, Dr. Jesse Gill finds early attachment styles have a strong effect in marital discord and has developed therapeutic strategies for addressing them. See *Face to Face: Seven Keys to a Secure Marriage* (Nashville, TN: Westbow Press, 2015)
15. Balthasar, "Jesus as Child," 625-634, 626.
16. Balthasar, *Unless you Become,* 64. One might note here that the great gift a down-syndrome child or one with mental disabilities is to keep the innocence and simple joys of childhood present in the family.
17. David L Schindler, "'We Are Not Our Own': Childhood and the Integrity of the Human in a Technological Age," *Humanum,* Fall 2011 (www.humananumreview.com).
18. Schindler, David L, "'We Are Not Our Own,' 6.
19. Balthasar, *Unless you Become,* 17.
20. "When a child learns from its mother that it is "her treasure," it becomes aware not only of its "worth' but specifically of its uniqueness." Balthasar, *Theo-Drama,* 205.
21. Balthasar, *Theo-Drama,* 205.
22. Balthasar, *Unless you Become,* 31.
23. Balthasar, *Unless you Become,* 32.
24. "...And a part in the Redemption of the world." cited in John Paul II, *Image of God,* 65 no 66.

25. "Parents, children, relationships in family life." in John Paul II, *Image of God,* no. 67
26. "Parents, children, relationships in family life." in John Paul II, *Image of God,* no. 67.
27. The religious must obey the superior while the lay person is called to mutual submission in marriage as well as obedience to civil authorities.
28. Sales, "Becoming Children," 5-27.
29. It is clear from Mark 7:9-11 that Jesus enjoins the fourth commandment.
30. Sales, "Becoming Children," 5-27.
31. Sales, "Becoming Children," 26.
32. Miller, *Biblical Faith,* 8. Miller points out that in ancient Egyptian, Mesopotamian and Canaanite religions, father deities were less powerful than son, mother and daughter deities. *Biblical Faith,* 7.
33. Miller, *Biblical Faith,* 43.
34. Miller, *Biblical Faith,* 76.
35. Miller, *Biblical Faith,* 78, 79.
36. "Philip said to him, 'Lord, show us the Father, and we shall be satisfied.' Jesus said to him, 'Have I been with you so long, and yet you do not know me, Philip? He who has seem me has seen the Father'" (Jn 14:8-9).
37. Vitz, *Faith of the Fatherless,* 23.
38. Secure individuals arrive at their level of religiousness through a gradual socialization, in contrast to insecure individuals for whom religious affiliation is often motivated by an unmet emotional need for security, in this case, for the father. The former are more mature in their faith, less anxious. Those reporting insecure attachment tend to be disproportionately atheist. They reject God as creator and sustainer of the world with whom the believer has a personal relationship; in other words in Christianity, God the Father. What is at stake in the rupture of a child's attachment figure is basic trust, the trust proper to an infant, and at the heart of the childlikeness of the Gospel. For an account of the importance of basic trust in infancy, see three volumes by J. Bowlby, A*ttachment, Separation,* and *Attachment and Loss,* cited in Vitz, *Faith of the Fatherless,* fn 28.
39. Marshall, *The Many Sided Triangle,* 78-98.

40. Doze, *Shadow,* 98.
41. Doze, *Shadow,* 99.
42. Miller, *Biblical Faith,* 5.
43. It is for good reason that the Church opposes such technologies. Nevertheless the child conceived is still made in the image of God and called to the fullness of eternal life.
44. Saward, *Redeemer,* 6.
45. Saward, *Redeemer,* 12.
46. Virtue, *Mother and Infant,* 269, 270. Virtue states: "We must not lose sight of the fact that *the Church did present as her official moral teaching the obligation of maternal nursing* which was always stated as a primary instruction under the topic of parental duties" 300.
47. Virtue, *Mother and Infant,* 272.
48. Virtue, *Mother and Infant,* 279. As regards to this regression, John Paul II describes the historical situation of the family "as an interplay of light and darkness. This shows that history is not simply a fixed progression towards what is better, but rather an event of freedom, and even a struggle between freedoms that are in mutual conflict" (FC 6).
49. See Howie, "Synopsis," 7-22. His research was pivotal in international efforts to promote breastfeeding in developing countries. His research showed particularly the amenorrhea provided by exclusive breastfeeding which prevents more births than all contraceptive programs put together. In the U.S. the United States Breastfeeding Committee is an independent nonprofit coalition of 50 organizations promoting breastfeeding. It is important to note two contemporary books, Jessica Martucci, *Back to the Breast: Natural Motherhood and Breastfeeding in America* (Chicago, IL: University of Chicago Press, 2015) and Gabrielle Palmer, *The Politics of Breastfeeding: When Breasts are Bad for Business* (London, UK: Printer and Mart 2009). Palmer focuses on the global scene while Martucci concentrates on the US. Martucci notes that the medical profession and lactation consultants in the US regard breast milk more as a "product" administered through breastpumping and bottles rather than favoring its bonding between mother and child. She points out that La Leche League,

which supports natural mothering through breastfeeding, was founded by a group of Catholic mothers.

50. John Paul II, "Breast-Feeding: Science and Society," no. 4. Since by 1995, the pope had written his major encyclicals on women, Mary, and the laity, he did not incorporate these insights into any major document.
51. Newton, *Interrelationships*, 81-82.
52. For release of oxytocin in breastfeeding see, Lawrence, *Breastfeeding,* 197
53. Kippley, *Breastfeeding,* 47.
54. Kippley, *Breastfeeding,* 48.
55. This is evident in the homilies on the Song of Songs in John Paul II's Wednesday Catechesis and in Benedict's encyclical, *Deus caritas est.*
56. Miles, *Complex Delight*, 162.
57. Miles, *Complex Delight*, 137. Miles came to these insights largely from analyzing paintings of the Madonna. Ibid., 136.
58. Bloom, "Power of Breastfeeding."
59. This is not the case with bottle feeding. It is important to acknowledge that not every mother is able to breastfeed. Wet nurses in the past and bottle feeding in the present are often a necessity to save an infant's life.
60. http://archive.attachmentparenting.org/support/articles/artbonding.php
61. "The commandments represent the basic conditions for love of neighbor; at the same time they are proof of that love "(VS 13). The encyclical begins with the encounter of the rich young man with Jesus. Fr. William Virtue devotes chapter four of his dissertation, *Mother and Infant* to the serious obligation of mothers to breastfeed their infants as it is the "propaedeutic" to the moral life, 218,219. He repeats this admonition giving natural law reasons, 277,278, and citing *the gravity of this obligation,* " 277. He calls the Church's present practice towards the obligation to nurse as a "regression" in moral teaching 279,80, for "bottle feeding, like contraception, presents a barrier between the persons, though in a different way and not as serious as contraception, which breaks the bond and is an intrinsic evil," 276. Yet, he says "in making this judgment of the need for reform, we want to affirm the countless mothers who with loving devotion have

cared for their infants, even in hardship and heroic effort," 219. Virtue also says "breastfeeding may be a propaedeutic to the mystical life," 312.

62. Rudolf Binion in "The Guilty Family" and "Ideology in the Bedroom" chronicles what he calls a "European guilt trip" in the moral transition from "natural fertility" to "planned parenthood." In a survey of 19th century literature on the new mass practice of contraception, he writes: "the generalized adoption of contraceptive sex within marriage marked a dizzying and daring reversal of Europeans' attitudes toward their bodies and souls alike, a collective transgression of an age-old Christianized taboo that had carried over even into post-Christian mind-sets." A negative view in literature of marriage and family resulted.
63. Fr. Basil Cole, OP holds that if St. Joseph were sanctified in the womb it would have been easier for him. He considers it unseemly if St. Joseph had experienced temptation towards Mary.

Chapter 8

1. Corporate personality means that the many is found in the "one" and the "one" represents the many. Atkinson, *Biblical Foundations*, 169-170.
2. Atkinson, *Biblical Foundations*, 269. Atkinson argues that only if similar structures can be found both in the Church and the family can the term make sense. This Augustine does in addressing the role of the father in the family, comparing it to that of a bishop. In admonishing, exhorting, rebuking and exercising benevolent discipline, the father fulfills an ecclesial role in his family.
3. Atkinson, *Biblical Foundations*, 269.
4. Atkinson, *Biblical Foundations*, 269. Atkinson argues that only if similar structures can be found both in the Church and the family can the term make sense. This Augustine does in addressing the role of the father in the family, comparing it to that of a bishop. In admonishing, exhorting, rebuking and exercising benevolent discipline, the father fulfills an ecclesial role in his family.
5. Atkinson, Biblical Foundations, 282.

6. Ouellet, *Divine Likeness,* 39.
7. Ouellet, *Divine Likeness,* 43.
8. Balthazar, *Theo-Drama.* "In the acting area opened up by Christ, created conscious subjects can become persons of theological relevance, co-actors in the theo-drama. . . If man freely affirms and accepts the election, vocation and mission which God, in sovereign freedom, offers him, he has the greatest possible chance of becoming a person, of laying hold of his own substance, of grasping that most intimate idea of his own self---which otherwise would remain undiscoverable." 263.
9. Ouellet, *Divine Likeness,* 46.
10. Ouellet, *Divine Likeness,* 50.
11. This dissertation was completed in Rome, 1995.
12. Virtue, *Mother and Infant,* 329.
13. Fr. Virtue states that he drew the concept of presence and absence from the phenomenology of Fr. Robert Sokolowski, particularly from his treatment of the Mass and the Eucharist in which the sacrifice of the cross and the last supper are really present though seemingly absent. See *Christian Faith and Understanding: Studies in the Eucharist, Trinity and the Human Person* (Washington, DC: The Catholic University of America Press, 2006). For a more detailed theological account of the intersection of the divine and human, nature and grace in the Holy Family see Fr. Virtue's book, *Mother and Infant* especially the penultimate chapter, from which this comparison is drawn. In a personal communication with Fr. Sokolowski, he told the author that in the case of the Holy Family, it was more likely that presence and absence referred to the same and other, respectively (Academy of Catholic Theology Conference, May 24, 2017.
14. Virtue, 331.
15. We saw how this was true in the Old Covenant with adultery likened to idolatry. In the New Covenant from the earliest Days of the Church, divorce, and adultery have been considered grave sins. (CCC 2384)
16. Virtue, *Mother and Infant,* 352. Virtue recommends natural childbirth as a way of witnessing to the "new creation".
17. Virtue, *Mother and Infant,* page, 271 footnote 167.

18. Ouellet, *Divine Likeness*, 61.
19. "This mutual inward molding of husband wife, this determined effort to perfect each other, can in a very real sense, as the Roman Catechism teaches, be said to be the chief reason for marriage, provided matrimony be looked at not in the restricted sense as instituted for the proper conception and education of the child, but more widely as the blending of life as a whole and the mutual interchange and sharing thereof." Pope Pius XI, *Casti Connubii*, (CC) no. 24.
20. Anderson, "Political Reflections." "The discourse of *Humanae vitae* presupposes a certain social consensus which no longer exists. That former census included a confidence in human reason to find moral truths, an appreciation of procreation as a good of marriage and of marriage itself as a unique and stable institution." Ibid. 15.
21. Paul VI, *Good News.* "The whole being participates in this exchange of love, at the deepest levels of its own personal mystery, with all its dimensions--, emotional, sensual, sexual, and spiritual—thus forming ever more perfectly that image of God which the couple has the mission to make present and visible day by day as they live out the joys and trials of life—so true it is that there is more to love than love." Ibid. No. 6
22. Ouellet *Divine Likeness*, 62
23. Ouellet, *Divine Likeness*, 65.
24. Ouellet, *Divine Likeness*, 66.
25. Ouellet, *Divine Likeness*, 66.
26. Ouellet, *Divine Likeness*, 67.
27. Ouellet, *Divine Likeness*, 70.
28. Burke says it was not found in ecclesiastical writing before 1977. Burke, *Theology of Marriage*, 57.
29. "The matrimonial covenant by which a man and a woman establish between themselves a partnership of the whole of life, is by its nature ordered to the good of the spouses and the procreation and education of offspring." *Catechism*, 1601.
30. Burke, *Theology of Marriage*, 62.
31. Burke, *Theology of Marriage*, 66.

32. Burke, *Theology of Marriage*, 70
33. Burke, *Theology of Marriage*, 175. John Paul II speaks more of not reading the language of the body in truth. John Paul II, *Man and Woman*, 105, 1.
34. Fr. William Virtue devotes a chapter to touch in his dissertation *Mother and Infant* calling touch "above all the power of presence, interpersonal presence" 14. Again "*through touch our presence in the body becomes a way of self-giving* because touch enable the body to be a *medium of communication*"131. He notes how St. Thomas teaches that" *touch remains in eternal life; the risen body of glory in heaven will have the power of touch"132.*
35. This usually takes a lifetime. As Guardini points out our Lord's words ask us to upend our fallen human nature, honor women for themseves rather than lust after their beauty, embrace poverty rather than material goods, and show the other cheek.
36. Granados, "Order of Love," 208.
37. Granados, "Order of Love," 214.
38. Granados, "Order of Love," 222. This article covers much more than is presented here, whose emphasis is the body and love.
39. Granados, "Order of Love," 223.
40. Granados, "Order of Love," 225.
41. Lk 17:14. Jesus "touched" the bier of the widow of Naim's son before raising him from the dead. Again in Lk 8:43-48, touch was involved in healing the woman with "a flow of blood for twelve years."
42. Granados, "Order of Love," 220.
43. Granados, "Order of Love," 220.
44. Granados, "Order of Love," 224.
45. The pope also refers to Christ's presence in adoration and present in the heart through prayer (John Paul II, *Ecclesia de Eucharistia,* no. 25) and "making his presence in meal and sacrifice the promise of a humanity renewed by his love" (John Paul II, *Ecclesia de Eucharistia,* no. 20).
46. Ratner, "Nursing Couplet," 4-5. Infant attachment has a profound effect on all other later relationships in life including the conjugal relation.
47. Ratner, "Nursing Couplet," 3-11.

48. Virtue, *Mother and Infant,* fn 45, 230.
49. Ratner, "Nursing Couplet," 9. Psychologists Paul C. Vitz and Matthew McCall confirm the vital significance in human relations of what they call the "primal" or "interpersonal" gaze between mother and infant in an unpublished paper, "Psychology of the Body: A First Approximation" given at the Institute for the Psychological Sciences, April, 2012.
50. Buccellati, "Yahweh, the Trinity."
51. See St. John of Damascus, *Divine Images*; also the contribution of the patristic tradition in Vagaggini, *The Flesh,* 65-94.
52. It was said of Moses that he knew God "face to face" (Deut 34:10).
53. John Paul II, *Rosarium.*
54. John Paul II, *Rosarium,* no. 18.
55. Mary Timothy Prokes in *At the Interface: Theology and Virtual Reality* (Tucson, AZ: Fenestra Books, 2004) shows how bodily presence is being affected by the new communication technologies. She is particularly critical of what she calls "avatars," projections of various forms of the self in virtual reality. Avatars in pagan religions have also referred to divine-human mythical persons. "The real body," Prokes says, "is a fundamental aspect of Catholic faith" (122). Christ came in the flesh and he gives us his real body and blood to drink. As made in the image of God, we are physical realities as is Jesus himself. "There is need for renewed emphasis and clarification regarding the enduring reality of Christ's true bodiliness lest it be confused with 'avatars'" (125).
56. With the advent of bottle feeding on a mass scale, the fact that the child is attached to a substitute breast, that can be held by anyone, even by itself, seems to have escaped notice. At the very least, it has encouraged modes of reproductive behavior that bypass the natural processes of the body.
57. Norman Lamm, *A Hedge of Roses,* 45.
58. It is required that the *mikvah* be built directly into the ground and filled with rain or spring water. By being built into the ground, Aryeh Kaplan proposes that the natural water links it to Eden, to the mysterious account of the rivers of Eden, two of which, the Tigris and Euphrates, are well known from ancient times. Eden represents man's perfected state. When

man sinned and lost the integrity of Eden, God in time chose the Jewish people to recreate the state of Eden and thus to elevate all mankind. In order to accomplish this, he gave mankind the Torah. When a person immerses himself in the waters of *mikvah* he is also reestablishing a link with man's perfected state. John Paul II sees a link with man's perfected state in Eden through the experience of "original shame" (MW 12:1-2).

59. Wasserfall, 32.
60. Lamm describes it, because of its restraint, as "positively delightful and, ultimately, indispensable." Lamm, *Jewish Insights*, 15; See footnote 39 for more detail on the law of family purity (taharat hamishpacha) and the abstinence required.
61. Lamm, *Jewish Insights*, 54
62. Ibid. 65. Research has shown that couples who practice NFP simply as a healthy life-style choice, when their ideal family size is completed, choose sterilization. Not so those who are imbued with the religious significance of the communion of persons. Theresa Notare, Convocation of Catholic Leaders, Orlando, FL, July 3, 2017.
63. See Mary Shivanandan, *Crossing the Threshold* "Appendix" 275-281. For a more detailed account of the origin of the natural methods, see Mucharski, *History of the Biologic Control of Fertility.*
64. See the chapter, "Achieving Pregnancy" in Mary Shivanandan, *Challenge to Love* 73-89.
65. See especially the chapter, "Social Science and Contemporary Family Planning," in Shivanandan, *Crossing,* 234-251.
66. Shivanandan *Crossing*, 237.
67. This decline is due in part to the heavy promotion of contraceptive methods. See the appendix for current statistics for the United States.
68. Shivanandan, *Crossing,* 248. For further insight on NFP as an "innovation" see the article by Dr. Borkman, "Experiential Learning and the Professional in NFP" in the appendix.
69. For example the cervical mucus in the woman's body is designed solely to nourish and protect the sperm on its journey to the fallopian tube. It facilitates the penetration of the man's penis into the vagina, and his fertility is only actual when it is present The two main methods of NFP are

those that use cervical mucus as a single indicator of fertility such as the Billings Ovulation method or those that use multiple indicators, called the Symptothermal methods. It is important to mention also the program, TeenSTAR, established by Dr. Hanna Klaus and now active in several countries. The program, with the permission of parents, teaches adolescents to monitor their cycles in order to understand their gift of fertility in the context of chastity. Many studies show its effectiveness in either continuing a chaste life or discontinuing sexual activity. See www.teenstar.org.

70. John Paul II, in commenting on the difference between men and women at this deep level, says "In the whole perspective of his own history, man will not fail to confer a nuptial meaning on his own body" (MW 15:5).
71. John Kippley, *NFP: the Complete Approach* and *Battle Scarred: Justice Can be Elusive*
72. Sheila Kippley, *Breastfeeding and Natural Child Spacing.* The World Health Organization Los recognizes the child- spacing effect of exclusive breastfeeding for the first six months, which it recommends. See http://www.who.int/nutrition/topics/exclusive_breastfeeding/en/
73. A feminist researcher, Emily Martin, has found that the hostility goes even deeper. In a review of medical textbooks, she found words describing the reproductive system to be negative, especially in describing the "perilous" journey of the sperm through a "hostile" environment to "attack" the egg. On the other hand, a study by this author of NFP teaching manuals found words like "harmony," "gift," "unite," the "symphony of fertility." The "penetration" of the egg by the sperm is the strongest "attack" word used. To "meet" or "unite" are the preferred words. It can readily be seen that one use of words is problematic while the other is compatible with the person as gift and communion.

Chapter 9

1. Burke, *Marriage*, 181.
2. Burke, *Marriage*, 182.
3. Burke, *Marriage*, 182
4. See 1 Cor. 7:10 seq.

5. Burke, *Marriage*, 188.
6. Burke, *Marriage*, 206 and 209.
7. Burke. *Marriage*, 54
8. Burke, *Marriage*, 218.
9. Burke, *Marriage*, 239.
10. The following is taken from Guitton, *Eros,* 75-99.
11. Paul VI, Humanae vitae, no. 9. (hereafter in text as HV with no.)
12. See May, *Marriage.* "The man and the woman are not, for each other, replaceable and substitutable individuals but rather irreplaceable and non-substitutable persons (with the emphasis on 'persons')" 20.
13. "Pope to Two Groups," Dec. 3, 1979.
14. "Congress for the Family," Feb 2. 1981
15. "Participants to NFP," Dec. 17, 1990.
16. "Participants to NFP," Dec. 17, 1990.
17. "True contradiction." Dec. 16, 1992.
18. See Appendix on Female Use in the U.S. prepared by Patrick F. Fagan, Ph. D., Director, Marriage and Religion Research Institute, Washington, DC.
19. "Church must lead, "April 2, 1984.
20. "Pope calls spouses," Dec. 17, 1990.
21. For a fuller account of scientific developments of NFP, see Shivanandan, *Threshold of Love,* 275-281. Also see Mucharski, *Biologic Control* and Jackson, *Human Ecology.*
22. Prudence Allen has documented how Aristotelian science adopted by Aquinas, among others, believed that the man provided the seed and the woman only the material of generation, giving her a passive role. Also woman was in some sense a defective male. Philosophically this translated into man representing the soul as the form of the body and the woman the body, leading to polarities unfavorable to the woman. Allen, *Concept of Woman,* 84-97, 392.
23. Shivanandan, *Threshold of Love,* 279-80.
24. Michael Waldstein, translator and editor of the Catechesis, provides a long note in the Index outlining this relationship and its significance. John Paul II, *Man and Woman,* 683-4.

25. John Paul II, *Fides et Ratio*. Hereafter in text as FR and section no.
26. Emily Martin analyzed the language used by several leading medical textbooks on the reproductive system. She found a reductionist view of the woman's role as a "producer of eggs," which, when fertilized, "made babies." Menstruation is regarded as a failure of the system. By contrast the male reproductive system is depicted in glowing terms, as "the *remarkable* cellular transformation from spermatid to mature sperm." Cited in Shivanandan, "Body Narratives."
27. A more complete account may be found in Shivanandan, "Body Narratives,"166-193.
28. Hanna Klaus, personal communication, 6/27/2017. Although emphasis in this chapter has been on John and Sheila Kippley, they are by no means the only NFP pioneers. Drs. Lynn and John Billings, late founders of the Billings Ovulation Method, made an enormous contribution by developing a method of monitoring fertility through cervical mucus. Dr. Klaus was specifically asked by them to develop a program for adolescents, hence TeenSTAR. WOOMB International has teaching centers worldwide. There are two official web sites, www.billings.life and www.woombinternational.org. Numerous national locally affiliated web sites also dispense information on the Billings Ovulation Metthod. Dr. Thomas Hilgers founded the Creighton Model Fertility Care System. Theresa Notare, Assistant Director, NFP Programs, U.S. Conference of Catholic Bishops has been tireless in promoting NFP programs in the United States. The many other overseas programs must not be forgotten, an initial survey of which can be found in *Natural Family Planning: Development of National Programs*, ed. Claude Lanctot at al. (Washington, DC: IFFLP/FIDAF, 1984)
29. Shivanandan, *Natural Sex,* later abridged as *Challenge to Love* and in *Threshold of Love,* 261-267.
30. Marshall, *Love One Another.*
31. Marshall, *Love One Another,* 17.
32. Marshall, *Catholics*, 25.

33. Marshall, *Catholics,* 50. (Marshall was writing before the change in Canon Law, described earlier by Cormack Burke)
34. Marshall *Catholics,* xiv. Echoes of this language are evident in Kosnik et al., *Human Sexuality*, particularly in the "definition of sexuality." Ibid, 80-88. This study marked a decisive departure from received Catholic teaching on sexuality.
35. Kippley, *Birth Control,* 105-106. The second and much revised edition, incorporating *Familiaris consortio,* was republished as *Marriage Covenant.*
36. Kippley, *Birth Control,* 107.
37. For a full discussion of this see the first chapter of Shivanandan, *Threshold of Love*, 3-31, in section "The Experiential Foundation," and also Part II.
38. See Curran, *Loyal Dissent.*
39. Marshall records how the Archbishop of Westminster, Cardinal Heenan, who voted with the majority of the Birth Control Commission, told him, "It does not matter now what the pope says. It is too late. The people have made up their minds." Marshall, "Voyage of Discovery," 9.
40. Marshall, *Love One Another*, 25-26.
41. Marshall, "Voyage of Discovery," (Nov. 23, 2002) 8-9, 9. The full article is reproduced in the Appendix with permission of the publisher. The web site is http://www.thetablet.co.uk .
42. An experience of mercy can only follow an admission of sin.
43. See also, McClory, *Turning Point.* If contraception is not an evil then it is either neutral or a good and that opens the way for any act that separates the unitive and procreative dimensions of conjugal intercourse to be a good, such as *in vitro* fertilization.
44. Taking account of these goods in determining family size is not per se bad but the method to achieve them must be moral.
45. Riley, *Civilizing Sex*, 100.
46. Riley, *Civilizing Sex,* 100
47. "Go, take to yourself a wife of harlotry and have children of harlotry, for the land commits great harlotry by forsaking the Lord" (Hosea 1:2). John Paul II shows how Yahweh patiently led the Israelite people to the analogy of marriage to God's covenantal love for them, forgiving their

transgressions countless times. Finally he shows how Christ's words are not so much a condemnation as an appeal to conversion (MW 35-38).

48. The majority of couples have good intentions in separating the procreative and the unitive dimensions of conjugal union through contraception. Nevertheless, by adopting these methods, they open the door to the priority of sexual pleasure over the person and love with its many attendant evils.
49. Mersch, *Morality,* 95
50. Mersch, *Morality*, 235.
51. Mersch, *Morality*, 225.
52. Quay, *Christian Meaning*, 9.
53. Quay, *Christian Meaning*, 10.
54. Quay, *Christian Meaning*, 10.
55. Quay, *Christian Meaning*, 87.
56. Quay, *Christian Meaning*, 88. Quay draws attention to another aspect of the young man's struggle for self-control. Most cultures have a ritual the boy undergoes at puberty, which initiates him into manhood. Quay suggests that, in the Christian context, the painful struggle for self-mastery by the young man, substitutes for these rituals. (One might note here that *brahmacharya* or celibacy is a recognized stage in the life of a Hindu young man.) The young girl, on the other hand, must take control of her emotions. Quay concludes: "It is, then, of considerable importance to see that the state of virginity or the quasi-state of premarital chastity is always intended by God to aid us to grow in love of him and our fellowmen, 99.
57. Couples, who practice periodic continence for valid reasons, testify to this. See Shivanandan, *Natural Sex,* especially pp 87-104.
58. Montagu, *Touching,* 192.
59. Montagu, *Touching*, 248. The whole area of the relationship of touch to living a mature sexuality needs to be more fully explored.
60. According to another author, genital sex has to carry the weight of all men's touching needs. But even there, touch as a preliminary is often seen as a waste of time once the relationship has progressed to intercourse. Zilberfeld, *Male Sexuality*, 110-114.

61. Vanier, *Man and Woman* 60.
62. Vanier, *Man and Woman* 61.
63. Vanier, *Man and Woman,* 87-101.
64. Batut, "Chastity of Jesus," 5-13, 10.
65. Batut, "Chastity of Jesus," 10.
66. Batut, "Chastity of Jesus," 11.
67. Batut, "Chastity of Jesus," 7-8.
68. The U.S.Supreme Court in Obergefell v. Hodges, 135 S. Ct. 2071 (2015) legalized so-called same sex marriage.
69. The same is true of Mary as is recognized in the Tradition. According to St. Augustine in his work *On Holy Virginity*: "Blessed Mary intended to keep her vow of virginity in her heart, but she did not express that vow of virginity with her mouth; she subjected herself to the divine disposition, intending to keep herself a virgin unless God revealed otherwise to her. Therefore, committing her virginity to the divine disposition, she consented to carnal coupling, not seeking it but obeying the divine inspiration in either case (c. 3). Cited by Gold in "Marriage of Mary and Joseph," 103.
70. St. Justin Martyr contrasts the disobedience and death brought by Eve with Mary's conception of the Son of God by her obedience to the angel (*Tryph.* 100). For Tertullian, "Eve had believed the serpent; Mary believed Gabriel; the fault which the one committed by believing, the other by believing has blotted out." (*De Carn. Christ.* 17) Again St. Irenaeus: "So the knot of Eve's disobedience received the unhooking through the obedience of Mary; for what Eve, a virgin bound by incredulity, that Mary, a virgin, unloosed by faith." (*Adv Haer* v. 19). These excerpts have been taken from *"Extracts for the Times,"* compiled by Sister Eileen Breen, FMA.
71. He follows this with the reasons for recourse to the natural methods listed in *Humanae vitae,* 10. "Pope Calls Spouses," (17 December, 1990) 1 and 3.
72. "Pope Calls Spouses," (17 December, 1990) 3.

Chapter 10

1. In *Redemptoris custos* no. 7, St. John Paul II puts it succinctly: "while clearly affirming that Jesus was conceived by the Holy Spirit, and that virginity remained in tact in the marriage (CF. Mt 1:18-25: Lk 1:26-38), the evangelists refer to Joseph as Mary's husband and to Mary as his wife (CF. Mt. 1:16, 18-20, 24; Lk 1:27; 2:5).
2. [2] Keating emphasizes that the significance of the doctrine is not just purification from sin but communion with the Trinity. Keating, *Deification*, 346. In *The Glory of God's Grace: Deification According to Thomas Aquinas*, Daria Spezzano regards Thomas's thought on deification as more implicit than explicit, being particularly evident in his mature thought. Spezzano claims that Thomas equates salvation with deification by examining his teaching on grace, charity and wisdom. It is discernible throughout his works in his discussion of the supernatural end of life and the path to achieve it. "The perfection of the Imago Dei, because it is a progressive participation in the likeness of the Trinitarian Persons by charity and wisdom, is also a conformation 'to the image of the Son,' qua Son, and a participation in his Sonship" 334; Christ is both the cause and exemplar of the grace of adopted sonship of the Father. Through the sacraments and filial obedience, conformity with Christ's wisdom and charity comes about. As such, those infused with his light and love manifest God's glory. Spezzano concludes that "taken together, Thomas's mature teachings on grace, charity, and wisdom allow us to perceive an underlying theology of deification at work throughout the Summa Theologiae—profoundly Scriptural, Christological, and pneumatological in character—with extensive connections to his doctrines on the Trinity, image, moral life, Christ, and the sacraments."
3. Cited in Keating, *Deification*, 16. Keating cites Gal 4:4-6, Rm 8: 14-17,29:1 and 1 Jn 3:1-2. Keating, *Deification*, 117.
4. Keating, *Deification*, 116. Without engaging the controversy of the relation between nature and grace, it is worth citing Thomas Petri on Aquinas view. "God ordained human nature to attain the end of eternal life, not by its own strength but by the help of grace. (STI-II, q. 114, a. 2, ad 1)."

Petri, *Aquinas and the Theology of the Body,* 262. Because grace, according to Aquinas, does not effect a substantial change in the soul, there is no substantial difference between the soul of a believer and non-believer. Rather, grace, as a substantial quality heals and elevates nature as a free gift. Above all it recreates the relationship with God. Ibid. 263.

5. For a discussion of this development see both Mersch, *Whole Christ,* and Thomas Berg, "Christological Nexus," 83-103.
6. Mersch, *Morality and the Mystical Body,* 97.
7. Mersch, *Whole Christ,* 3.
8. He proposes that not only Christ pre-existed in relation to the Incarnation and creation but "there is in Christ a pre-existence of the Mystical Body in relation to all things that are created. The two are inseparable." It is a unity that descends from heaven. Mersch, *Whole Christ*, 23, 24.
9. John Paul II, *Redemptor hominis*, 10, here after in the text as RH with section no.
10. However, it must be kept in mind that the vows of the consecrated celibate perfect charity in a different way and both Mary and Joseph had vows of chastity.
11. John Paul II, *Novo millennio ineunte*, no. 30; afterwards in text as NMI and section no.
12. St. Joseph is constantly held out as the exemplar of the interior life (RC no. 26). In *Letter to Families,* prayer by the family, for the family and with the family is extolled as the path to increase the strength and unity of the family. (LF 4).
13. Mersch, *Whole Christ*, 5.
14. Mersch, *Morality,* 75.
15. Mersch, *Morality*, 239
16. Mersch, *Morality*, 206.
17. Mersch, *Morality*, 206-207.
18. Mersch, *Morality*, 210.
19. Mersch, *Morality*, 212.
20. Mersch, *Morality*, 210.
21. Mersch, *Morality*, 211.

22. Mersch, *Morality*, 212.
23. Mersch, *Morality*, 213.
24. Mersch, *Morality*, 224.
25. Mersch, *Morality*, 226. The measure of holiness is determined by charity regardless of one's state of life.
26. Aquinas, ST Pt. II-II, Q. 88 Art. 2 [Hereinafter as ST].
27. Aquinas, ST Pt. II-II Q. 88 Art. 6. Once a person makes a vow, he commits not only fruits of his action to God but his entire self since he has bound his future.
28. Aquinas, ST Pt. II-II, Q.186 Art. 6 (emphasis omitted).
29. Aquinas, ST Pt. II-II Q.186 Art. 6. In marriage this is expressed by the husband's surrender of himself to his wife and vice versa.
30. Balthasar, *Christian State,* 38, 39. See also Crawford, "Vows," 295, 296.
31. Aquinas, ST Pt. II-II Q. 186 Arts. 1 and 6.
32. Crawford, "Vows," 298.
33. Crawford, "Vows," 297.
34. Crawford, "Vows," 301.
35. Crawford, "Vows," 303.
36. Crawford, *Marriage*, 255
37. Crawford, *Marriage*, 292. It is noteworthy here that moderation in sex seems to lead to moderation in the use of material goods. As NFP user John Quesnell said, "NFP changed our financial attitudes. One of the immediate things we did was to cut our income in half, realizing we were becoming too dependent on material things. Cited in Mary Shivanandan, *Natural Sex,* (New York: Berkley Books, 1981, 159.
38. Some distinctions are in order. When a person makes public vows as a consecrated religious, it establishes him/her by a supernatural bond in a state of growing perfection (See ST Pt. II-II, Q. 88 Art.7). The bond is directly linked to Christ. Although it is an objective bond akin to a sacrament, the person may not subjectively live up to the bond. Private vows of consecration may approach the "bond" on the subjective order but not objectively and they do not take precedence over the marriage bond.

39. "Indeed, the Lord Jesus, when he prayed to the Father, 'that all may be one. . . as we are one' (Jn 17:21-22), opened up vistas closed to human reason, for he implied a certain likeness between the union of the divine Persons, and the unity of God's sons in truth and charity. This likeness reveals that man who is the only creature on earth that God willed for itself, cannot find himself, except through a sincere gift of himself." *Gadium et Spes*, 24.
40. John Paul II, *Vita consecrata*, no. 21. [here-in-after in text VC and no.]
41. In this understanding freedom is for self-gift, and this freedom is secured paradoxically by the vows. The English author, G. K. Chesterton speaks of the "self-respect that only goes with freedom" in relation to the vow. G. K. Chesterton, Superstition of Divorce, 95. Von Balthazar goes further. He points out that "true love want[s] to outlast time and, for this purpose, to rid itself of its most dangerous enemy, its own freedom of choice." Balthasar, *Christian State*, 39.
42. The Church reserves the right in extreme cases to dispense religious from their vows. Stockl, "Mary's Spousal," 170 n.476.
43. Stockl, "Mary's Spousal," 170 (quoting St. John Paul II's Address to Consecrated Women in Medellin, Columbia, July 5, 1986.)
44. Stockl, "Mary's Spousal,"169.
45. Stockl, "Mary's Spousal," 180.
46. A summary of "the largest survey to date on the impact of NFP on relationships and sexual satisfaction" is given in *Family Foundations* 43,6, May/June 2017, citing Unseld M., Rotzer E., Masel EK, and Manhart MD (2017), "Use of Natural Family Planning (NFP) and Its Effect on Couple Relationships and Sexual Satisfaction: A Multi-Country Survey of NFP Users from US and Europe," in *Frontier in Public Health* 5:42.
47. "Your wife shall be like a fruitful vine within your house; Your children will be like olive shoots around your table. Lo, thus shall the man be blessed who fears the Lord" (Psalm 128:3-4).
48. Joseph's temptations would have included the temptations of concupiscence as well as the temptation against filiation.

49. See Susan Jones, "The Dynamics of Intergenerational Behavior and Forgiveness Therapy" paper presented at the NACSW Convention, St. Louis MO, Oct. 2012. Abstract: "In this article the author presents an overview of various research themes regarding the dynamics of intergenerational behaviors. Intergenerational behaviors can be presented through ancestry lines as attitudes, beliefs, actions and habits. These intergenerational transmissions can present in a positive manner such as determination, hard work and success, or in a negative manner such as rage, greed and pride. This article will focus on how the negative intergenerational transmissions affect individuals and families. The social work field is committed to helping those suffering from issues such as addiction, depression, abuse (emotional, physical, sexual), fear, manipulation, violence and low self-esteem. In most cases, these behaviors are not only prevalent in the life of the individual, but in additional family members as well, and can be traced through intergenerational family lines."

Chapter 11

1. John Paul II, *Jesus*, Dec. 10, 1986.
2. John Paul II, *Jesus*, Sept 10, 1986.
3. John Paul II, *Jesus*, Nov. 5, 1986.
4. John Paul II, *Reconciliation*.
5. John Paul II, *Reconciliation*, no. 16.
6. In fact, the Catechism of the Catholic Church only speaks of "social sin" analogously in a brief paragraph (CCC no. 1869).
7. Schmitz, *Gift*, 13
8. According to Thomas Aquinas: When God creates, he produces things without motion. Now when motion is removed from action and passion, only relation remains . . . Hence creation in the creature is only a certain relation to the creator as to the principle of its being. Schmitz, *Gift*, 19.
9. Schmitz, *Gift*, 35.
10. Schmitz, *Gift*, 42.

11. Wojtyla, *Love and Responsibly*, 158.
12. Wojtyla, *Love and Responsibility*, 162.
13. Ouellet, *Divine Likeness*, 134.
14. Tracey Rowland and Connor Sweeney echo Ouellet in beginning with the sacraments in reflecting on marriage and family. "It is in the sacraments—most primordially in the sacrament of baptism—that all theological thinking must begin: in the experience of finding oneself caught up in the dramatic transformed relationship to God, in discovering oneself as a son or daughter; in discovering the Father." Rowland and Sweeney, "Elephants."
15. Ouellet, *Divine Likeness.*, 125.
16. Ouellet, *Divine Likeness*, 129.
17. Ouellet, *Divine Likeness*, 130.
18. John Paul II, *Jesus*, Nov. 4, 1987.
19. John Paul II, *Jesus*, Nov. 4, 1987.
20. John Paul II, *Jesus*, Nov. 4, 1987.
21. Frequently, to follow Jesus means not only to leave one's occupation and to sever one's bonds with the world, but also to renounce the condition of prosperity one may enjoy, and indeed to give one's goods to the poor. Not all are prepared to take this radical step. The rich young man was not prepared to do so, even though he had observed the law from his youth and was perhaps seeking seriously a way of perfection. John Paul II, *Jesus*, Oct. 29, 1987.
22. In the first occasion of reflecting on this passage in a retreat with university students, Bishop Wojtyla challenged the young men to a deeper religious life, instead of simply following their own inclinations in interpreting what God was calling them to do. "Maybe," he said, "this temptation to follow our inclinations and wishes to place ourselves 'beyond' Christ is found particularly in the field of sexual morality, because it is here that Christ makes demands on men." He goes on to say that the demands are greater than and different from the way men normally envisage. Wojtyla, *Way to Christ*, 55.
23. These presuppositions were especially related to rejection of the Church's teaching in *Humanae vitae* as an impossible ideal. Dominican, A. J.

DiNoia, particularly, finds significance in the day the encyclical was issued, the feast of the Transfiguration of Our Lord. The focus has moved from the young man to Jesus' reply to his question on the good. "There is only One who is good. If you wish to enter life keep the commandments" (Mt 19: 16-22). In other words, only by seeking the ultimate good can we become good. "Only in Christ can we discover and become enabled to seek the good through the keeping of the commandments." Our destiny is nothing less than communion with Father, Son, and Holy Spirit, a destiny made possible by Christ's passion and death. We must be transformed by grace so that we may enjoy this high destiny. The first truth here is the truth of God himself, as embodied in the person and teaching of Jesus. If we want to live in the truth, we must be conformed to the Truth who is Christ himself. Just as Christ is the perfect image of God, so we are called to be conformed to that image and the Transfiguration shows us that the conformation "gives us entry into the Trinitarian family." The conformation is not a denial of our uniqueness but its full flowering. DiNoia states that it is as persons that we must embrace the Trinitarian communion offered as our greatest happiness and good and he calls the family "in a true sense an image of Trinitarian communion itself." DiNoia, *Veritatis splendor*, 1-10.

24. The translator, Michael Waldstein, in a footnote, explains the Pope's understanding of the difference between sexual desire ordered to the good of the person and concupiscent desire, which is simply focused one's own pleasure. "It does not matter whether the person one desires in this reductive way is one's spouse or not, because the reduction is in both cases contrary to the full dignity and beauty of the person." John Paul II, *Man and Woman*, Introduction by Michael Waldstein, 43.
25. In each case, there was a resort to wet-nurses which was considered normal family custom at the time, but it disrupted the mother-child relation at a critical moment of development. As we saw earlier, St. Thomas Aquinas regarded it as a mother's moral duty to nurse her child.
26. Furstenberg, *Spoke French,* 67.
27. Furstenberg, *Spoke French*, 67.

28. Talleyrand comments that too much tenderness would have been considered pedantry and ridiculous. "Des soins trop multiplier auraient paru de la pédanterie; une tendresse trop exprimée aurait paru quelque chose de nouveau et par consequent ridicule." Talleyrand, *Mémoires*, loc 409.
29. Talleyrand says of his "grandmother" "C'est la première personne de ma famille qui m'ait témoigne de l'affection, et c'est la première aussi qui m'ait fait gouter bonheur d'aimer." Talleyrand, *Mémoires*, loc 422.
30. "Les premiers objets, qui frappent les yeux et le coeur de enfance determinent souvent ses dispositions, et donnent au charactère les penchants que nous suivron dans le cours de notre vie." Talleyrand, *Mémoires*, loc 435.
31. Talleyrand, *Mémoires*, loc 509.
32. "Cette crainte est une preuve de tendresse dont je me plais a leur savoir gré." (This fear is a proof of tenderness which it pleases me to know.") Talleyrand, *Mémoires*, loc 521.
33. Furstenberg, *Spoke French*, 68.
34. The Duc de Broglie writes in the preface, "C'est toujours la France et elle doit etre servie avec un souci egal de sa security presente et de sa grandeur a venir." Talleyrand, *Mémoires*, loc 339.
35. Talleyrand, *Mémoires*, loc 509. Given his many separations from attachment figures in childhood, it is not surprising that Tallyerand lived a life of promiscuity and later divorced after marrying. Attachment theory researchers link early bonding experiences to adult ability to form romantic attachments. Bohacik, "Becoming a Bride," 100.
36. This analysis of Talleyrand has been drawn by the author, herself, from the thesis of this book on the communion of persons and the family.
37. Vitz, "Thérèse," 571. The study of St. Therese by Marc Foley, O.C.D., confirms all of Dr. Vitz's findings.
38. Andrew Sodergren has detailed the theories of the main researchers, especially Bowlby and Ainsworth, in his doctoral dissertation for the Institute of Psychological Sciences, Arlington, VA, "Attachment and Morality: A Catholic Perspective, a Theoretical Dissertation, 2009.
39. Martin, *Deeper Love*, 31. Hereafter references to the correspondence will be in the text as CDL with number.

40. Zelie wrote: "if God gives me the grace of being able to nurse my child, it will be nothing but a pleasure to raise her . . . As for me I am crazy about children." When it didn't work out she consoled herself with the thought that God wanted it that way." Martin, *Deeper Love*, 89. She bore with great fortitude the loss of her babies.
41. In *Context of Holiness*, Marc Foley, O.C.D. details the same separation traumas.
42. Vitz, "Thérèse," 70.
43. Thérèse, *Story*, 194.
44. Thérèse, *Story*, 208.
45. Péguy, *Mystery of Hope.*
46. Péguy, *Mystery of Hope*, 91.
47. Péguy, *Mystery of Hope*, 94..
48. John Paul II, *Dives in Misericordia.* [hereinafter in text as DM]
49. Granados, *Accompanying*
50. Granados, Accompaniment 70.
51. Granados, Accompaniment 71

Epilogue

1. L'Osservatore Romano, "Pope Calls Spouses to a Sense of Responsibility."
2. Virtue *Mother and Infant* 367.
3. Virtue *Mother and Infant* 331.
4. John, Paul II. *Letter to Families* no. 16

BIBLIOGRAPHY

1977. *The New Oxford Annotated Bible with Apocrypha.* Revised Standard Version ed. New York Oxford University Press.

1979. "Pope to Two Groups of International Researchers." *L'Osservatore Romano (Weekly Edition)*, December 3.

1981. "Address to the First Congress for the Family of America and Europe Jan 15, 1981 " *L'Osservatore Romano* Feb. 2, 1981.

1983. *Gates of the Seasons: A Guide to the Jewish Year.* New York: Central Conference of American Rabbis.

1984. "Church must lead couples to the truth about themselves and their love." *L'Osservatore Romano* April 2, 1984.

1990. "Papal Audience to Participants to NFP Course in Rome." *L'Osservatore Romano* Dec. 17, 1990.

1990. "Pope calls spouses to a sense of responsibility for love and for life." *L'Osservatore Romano* Dec. 17, 1990.

1991. Theological Dictionary of the New Testament. edited by Gerhard Kittel. Grand Rapids, MI: Wm B. Eerdmans Publishing Co. Original edition, 1964.

1992. "A true contradiction cannot exist between divine laws of transmitting life and of fostering love." Dec. 16, 1992.

1994. *Catechism of the Catholic Church.* Mahwah, NJ: Paulist Press.

1995-1997. Academic Catalog. edited by John Paul II Institute for Studies on Marriage and Family. Washington, DC.

1999. *Women and Water: Menstruation in Jewish Life and Law,* Edited by Shulamit Reinharz, *Brandeis Series on Jewish Women.* Hannover, NH: Brandeis University Press.

2004. *Harvesting Luther's Reflections on Theology, Ethics, and the Church,* Grand Rapids, MI: William B. Eerdmans Publishing Co. Theology.

2005. *Covenant Marriage in Comparative Perspective,* Grand Rapids, MI: William B. Eerdmans Publishing Company

2005. *On Marriage and Family: Classic and Contemporary Texts,* Lanham, MD: Rowman & Littlefield Publishers, Inc.

2005-2007. Academic Catalog. edited by Pontifical John Paul II Institute for Studies on Marriage and Family at The Catholic University of America. Washington, DC.

2009. "Storia e Oreintamenti del Movimento negli Ultimi Anni" Equipes Notre-Dame Roma.

Allen, Sister Prudence. 1982. *Jesus as Mother: Studies in the Spirituality of the High Middle Ages*. Los Angeles, CA: University of California Press.

Allen, Sister Prudence. 2002. *The Concept of Woman: Volume II The Early Humanist Reformation, 1250- 1500*. Vol. 2. Grand Rapids MI: William B. Eerdmans Publishing Company.

Alvarado, Alberto e Constanza. 2009. Storia e Orientamenti del Movimento negli Ultimi Anni. Roma.

Anderson, Carl. 1993. "Political Reflections on *Humanae Vitae*." Theological and Pastoral Congress on the 25th Anniversary of Humana Vitae, Rome, November 24-26, 1993.

Aquinas, St. Thomas. 2007. *Summa Theologica*: New Advent. CD-Rom, Philosophy/theology.

Atkinson, Joseph C. 2004. Summer Institute for Priests, St. Michael's Parish, Long Branch, NJ, June 27 - July 2, 2004.

Atkinson, Joseph C. 2013. *Biblical and Theological Foundations of the Family:The Domestic Church*. Washington, DC: The Catholic University of America Press.

Augustine, St. "Sermon 51: The Harmony between the Evangelists Matthew and Luke Concerning the Lord's Genalogy." In *Sermons III (51-94) on the New Testament*, 19-49.

Augustine, St. 1990. "Sermons III (51-94) on the New Testament." In *The Works of St. Augustine: A Translation for the 21st Century*, edited by John E. Rotelle. Brooklyn, NY: New City Press.

Avila, St. Teresa of. 1985. *The Collected Works of St. Teresa of Avila*. Translated by O.C.D. and Otilio Rodrigues Kieran Kavanaugh, O.C.D. Vol. 3. Washington, D.C. ICS Publications.

Badinter, Elisabeth. 1982. *Mother Love: Myth and Reality, Motherhood in Modern History*: Macmillan Publishing Company.

Ballantine, Samuel E. 1999. *The Torah's Vision of Worship*. Minneapolis, MN: Fortress Press.

Balthasar, Hans Urs von 1991. *Unless You Become Like this Child.* San Francisco: Ignatius Press.

Balthasar, Hans Urs von. 1992. *Theo-Drama: Theological Dramatic Theory, Vol. 3: Dramatis Personae: Persons in Christ* Vol. III. San Francisco: Ignatius Press.

Balthasar, Hans Urs von. 1995. "Jesus as Child and His Praise of the Child." in *Communio* 22 (4, Winter):625-634.

Balthasar, Hans Urs von. 2002. *The Christian State of Life*. San Francisco: Ignatius Press.

Balthasar, Hans Urs von and Joseph Cardinal Ratzinger. 1997. *Mary: The Church at the Source*. San Francisco: Ignatius Press. Mariology.

Barger, Lilian Calles. 2003. *Eve's Revenge*. First ed. Grand Rapids, MI: Brazos Press. spirituality, anthropology.

Batut, Jean-Pierre. 1997. "The Chastity of Jesus and the Refusal to Grasp." in *Communio* 24:5-13.

Berg, Thomas. 2014. "Freedom and the Moral Law: Proceedings from the 36th Annual Convention of the Fellowship of Catholic Scholars, September 27-28, 2013." in *Freedom and the Moral Law*, edited by Elizabeth C. Shaw, 83-103. Philadelphia, PA: Fellowship of Catholic Scholars.

Binion, Rudolph. 2005. "The Guilty Family, Ideology in the Bedroom, The Sublime and the Grotesque, Notes." in *Past Impersonal, Group Process in Human History*, 14-45, 61-79, 150-160. Dekalb: Northern Illinois University Press.

Binion, Rudolph. 2005. *Past Impersonal: Group Process in Human History*. First ed. Dekalb, IL: Northern Illinois University Press.

Bishops, United States Conference of Catholic. 2013. Vatican Approves Inclusion Of St. Joseph's Name In Main Eucharistic Prayers.

Bloom, Mayra. 1985."The Romance and Power of Breastfeeding."40-50.

Bohacik, Jill. 2015. Becoming a Bride. Arlington, VA. Doctoral Dissertation.

Bordo, Susan. 1987. *The Flight to Objectivity: Essays on Cartesianism and Culture*. Edited by Robert C. Neville, *SUNY Series in Philosophy*. Albany: State University of New York Press.

Bouwsma, William J. 1988. *John Calvin: A Sixteenth Century Portrait.* First ed. New York: Oxford University Press. history, biography.

Buccellati, Giorgio. 2006. "The Prophetic Dimension of Joseph." in *Communio: International Catholic Review* 33 (1):43-99.

Buccellati, Giorgio. 2007. "Yahweh, the Trinity: the Old Testament Catechumenate: Part Two." in *Communio: International Catholic Review* 34 (2):292-327.

Burke, Cormac. 2015. *The Theology of Marriage: Personalism, Doctrine and Canon Law.* Washington, D.C.: The Catholic University Press. Theology.

Bynum, Caroline Walker. 1987. "Woman as Body and as Food." in *Holy Feast and Holy Fast*, 260-276. Los Angeles: University of California Press.

Bynum, Caroline Walker. 1988. *Holy Feast and Holy Fast: The Religious Significance of Food to Medieval Women* Berkeley, CA: University of California Press.

Bynum, Caroline Walker. 1991. *Fragmentation and Redemption: Essays on Gender and the Human Body in Medieval Religion.* New York: Zone Books.

Cahall, Perry. 2016. *The Mystery of Marriage: a Theology of the Body and Sacrament* Mundelein, IL: Hillenbrand Books.

Calkins, Arthur B. 2005. "The Virginal Conception and Birth of Jesus Christ as Received and Handed on by the Catholic Church." in *The Virgin Mary and the Theology of the Body*, edited by Donald H. Calloway. Stockbridge, MA: Marian Press.

Calloway, Donald H., ed. 2005. *The Virgin Mary and the Theology of the Body.* Stockbridge, MA: Marian Press.

Canty, Aaron. 2011. *Light & Glory: The Transfiguration in Early Franciscan and Dominican Theology.* First ed. Washington, DC: The Catholic University of America Press. Theological and Scriptural exegesis.

Chesterton, G.K. 1920. "The Story of the Vow." in *The Superstition of Divorce*, 83-101. New York: John Lane Co.

Chorpenning, Joseph F. 1995. "The Holy Family as icon and model of the civilization of love: John Paul II's *Letter to Families*." in *Communio* 22:77-98.

Chorpenning, Joseph F. 1998. "The Guidance and Education of His Divine Infancy: The Holy Family's Mission in St. Francis de Sales " In *The Holy Family in Art and Devotion* Philadelphia, PA: St. Joseph's University Press

Chorpenning, Joseph F., ed. 1998. *The Holy Family in Art and Devotion.* Philadelphia, PA: St. Joseph's University Press.

Chorpenning, Joseph F. 2001. "John Paul II's Theology of the Mystery of the Holy Family." in *Communio* 28 (1):140-166.

Clairvaux, St. Bernard of. 1971. *Bernard of Clairvaux: Sermons on the Song of Songs Volume 1.* Translated by O.S.C.O. and Irene M. Edmonds Kilian Walsh. Vol. I, *Cistercian Fathers Series.* Kalamazoo, MI: Cistercian Publications, Inc.

Cole, Basil B. 2005. "Mary's Virginity, the Theology of the Body and St. Thomas Aquinas." in *The Virgin Mary and the Theology of the Body*, edited by Donald H. Calloway, 65-90. Stockbridge, MA: Marian Press.

Conner, Paul. 1979. *Celibate Love* Huntington, IN: Our Sunday Visitor.

Cramer, Hermann. 1895. *Biblio-Theological Lexicon of New Testament Greek with Supplement.* Translated by William Urwick. New York: Charles Scribner's Sons.

Crawford, David 2005. "Love, Action, and Vows as 'Inner Form' of the Moral Life."in *Communio: International Catholic Review* 32 (2): 295-312.

Crawford, David S. 2004. *Marriage and the Sequela Christi: A Study of Marriage as a "State of Perfection."* First, Signed ed, *Light of Henri de Lubac's Theology of Nature and Grace*

Rome: Lateran University Press.

Curran, Charles. 2006. *Loyal Dissent: Memoirs of a Catholic Theologian* Washington, D.C.: Georgetown University Press.

Damascus, St. John of. 1994. *On the Divine Images: Three Apologies Against Those Who Attack the Divine Images.* Translated by David Anderson. Crestwood, NY: St. Vladimir's Seminary Press.

de la Potterie, Ignace. 1995. *Mary in the Mystery of the Covenant.* Translated by SM Bertrand Busby. Bombay: St. Pauls.

D'Emilio, John, and Estelle B. Freedman. 1988. *Intimate Matters: A History of Sexuality in America.* New York: Harper & Row. History of Sexuality

Dillon, Mary Margaret. 1988. "Breastfeeding: A Family Affair." in *Family Enrichment Features.*

Dinoia, J.A. and Romanus Cessario, ed. 1999. *The Splendor of the Truth: Veritatis Splendor and the Renewal of Moral Theology.* First ed. Princeton, NJ: Scepter Publishers.

Doze, Andrew. 1992. *Saint Joseph: Shadow of the Father.* Translated by RJM Florestine Audett. New York: Alba House.

Dubois, Abbe J. A. 1924. *Hindu Manners, Customs and Ceremonies.* 3rd ed. Oxford: Clarendon Press. Original edition, 1897.

Duby, Georges. 1978. *Medieval Marriage: Two Models from Twelfth Century France* Translated by Elborg Forster. Baltimore: The Johns Hopkins University Press.

Duby, Georges. 1988. *Love and Marriage in the Middle Ages* Chicago, IL: The University of Chicago Press.

Duby, Georges. 1998. *Women of the Twelfth Century.* Vol. 3: Eve and the Church. Chicago, IL: University of Chicago Press.

Duffy, Eamon. 1993. *The Stripping of the Altars: Traditional Religion in England, 1400-1580* New Haven, CT: Yale University Press.

Ellington, Donna Spivey. 2001. *From Sacred Body to Angelic Soul: Understanding Mary in Late Medieval and Early Modern Europe.* First ed. United States of America: Catholic University of America Press. History.

Elliott, Dyan. 1993. *Spiritual Marriage: Sexual Abstinence in Medieval Wedlock* New Jersey: Princeton University Press.

English, University of Cambridge Faculty of. 2002. "Mystery plays: a brief insight and link to prose." http://www.english.cam.ac.uk/medieval/mystery_plays.php.

Eyer, Diane E. 1992. *Mother-Infant Bonding: A Scientific Fiction.* London Yale University Press.

Filas, Francis L. 1952. *Joseph and Jesus: A Theological Study of Their Relationship.* Milwaukee The Bruce Publishing Company.

Filas, Francis L. 1969. *St. Joseph After Vatican II: Conciliar Implications Regarding St. Joseph and his Inclusion in the Roman Canon.* Staten Island, NY: Alba House.

Fildes, V. 1986. *Breasts, Bottles and Babies: A History of Infant Feeding.* Edinburgh: Edinburgh University Press.

Fitzmyer, S.J., Joseph A. 1997. *Saint Joseph in Matthew's Gospel* Philadelphia, P.A. St Joseph University Press.

Foley, Marc, O.C.D. 2008. *The Context of Holiness: Psychological and Spiritual Reflection on the Life of St. Thérèse of Lisieux* Washington, D.C.: ICS Publications Original edition, 1949.

Fonrobert, Charlotte Elisheva 1999. "Yalta's Ruse: Resistance versus Rabbinic Menstrual Authority in Talmudic Literature " In *Women and Water: Menstruation in Jewish Life and Law*, edited by Rahel R. Wasserfall. Hannover, NH: Brandeis University Press.

Furstenberg, Francois 2014. *When the United States Spoke French: Five Refugees Who Shaped a Nation.* New York, NY: The Penguin Press.

Gardella, Peter. 1985. *Innocent Ecstasy: How Christianity Gave America an Ethic of Sexual Pleasure.* New York: Oxford University Press. History of Sexuality.

Garrigues, O.P., Jean-Miguel 2014. "The Jewishness of the Apostles and Its Implications for the Apostolic Church." *Nova et Vetera* 12 (1).

Gauthier, Roland. 1998. "Devotion to the Holy Family in Seventeenth-Century Canada." in *The Holy Family in Art and Devotion*, edited by Joseph F. Chorpenning. Philadelphia, PA: St. Joseph's University Press.

Gies, Frances and Joseph. 1989. *Marriage and Family in the Middle Ages.* Second ed. New York: Perennial Library.

Gill, Jesse. 2015. *Face to Face: Seven Keys to a Secure Marriage.* Nashville, TN: Westbow Press.

Gilson, Etienne. 1990. *The Mystical Theology of Saint Bernard.* Translated by A.H.C. Downes. Kalamazoo: Cistercian Publications.

Gold, Penny S. 1982. "The Marriage of Mary and Joseph in the Twelfth-Century Ideology of Marriage." in *Sexual Practices in the Medieval Church* edited by Vernan L Bullough and James Brundage. Buffalo, New York: Prometheus Books.

Goman, Michael. 2005. "Marriage as Covenant in the Catholic Tradition." in *Covenant Marriage in Comparative Perspective*, edited by John Witte and Elizabeth Ellison, 70-91. Grand Rapids, MI: W.B Eerdmans.

Gorman, Frank H. 1997. *Leviticus: Divine Presence and Community: A Commentary on the Book of Leviticus.* Grand Rapids: MI: William B. Eerdmans Publishing Co.

Gorman, Michael J. 1865. *Abortion and the Early Church: Christian, Jewish and Pagan Attitudes in the Greco-Roman World* New York, NY: Paulist Press.

Grabowski, John S. 2003. *Sex and Virtue: An Introduction to Sexual Ethics.* First ed. Washington DC: The Catholic University of America Press.

Gracián, Jerónimo. 1993. *Just Man, Husband of Mary, Guardian of Christ: An Anthology of Readings from Jerónimo Gracián's Summary of Excellencies of St. Joseph (1957).* Translated by Michael L. McGrath. Edited by Joseph F. Chorpenning. Philadelphia, PA: St. Joseph's University Press. Theological.

Graef, Hilda. 1990. *Mary: A History of Doctrine and Devotion* London: Sheed & Ward.

Granados, José. 2012. "The Body, the Family and the Order of Love: The Interpretive Key to Vatican II." in *Communio* 39 (1, Spring-Summer):201-226.

Granados, José. 2012. "Bonaventure and Aquinas on Marriage Between Creation and Redemption." in *Anthropotes* 28:339-359.

Guitton, Jean. 1981. *Eros and Agape in Christian Married Love.* San Francisco: Ignatius Press.

Howie, Peter. 1986. "Synopsis of Research on Breastfeeding and Fertility." in *Breastfeeding and Natural Family Planning: Selected Papers from the Fourth National and International Symposium on Natural Family Planning, Chevy Chase, MD, November 1985*, edited by Mary Shivanandan, 7-21. Bethesda, MD: KM Associates.

II, John Paul. 1979. *Redeemer of Man (Redemptor Hominis).* Washington, DC: United States Catholic Conference. First Encyclical Letter.

II, John Paul. 1981. *On Human Work (Laborem Exercens): On the Ninetieth Anniversary of Rerum Novarum.* Boston: St. Paul Books & Media. Encyclical Letter.

II, John Paul. 1981. On the Family (*Familiaris Consortio*). Washington, DC: United States Catholic Conference.

II, John Paul. 1984. "On the Christian Meaning of Human Suffering: *Salvifici Doloris*," in *Apostolic Letter*.

II, John Paul. 1988. "On the Dignity and Vocation of Women (*Mulieris Dignitatem*), Apostolic Letter, Aug. 15, 1988." in *Origins* 18 (17).

II, John Paul. 1988. *The Vocation and the Mission of the Lay Faithful in the Church and in the World, Christifideles Laici*. Washington, DC: United States Catholic Conference. Apostolic Exhortation on the Laity.

II, John Paul. 1989. *Guardian of the Redeemer (Redemptoris Custos), Apostolic Exhortation of the Supreme Pontiff on the Person and Mission of Saint Joseph in the Life of Christ and of the Church*. Boston: St. Paul Books & Media. Apostolic exhortation.

II, John Paul. 1993. *The Splendor of Truth (Veritatis Splendor)*. Boston St. Paul Books and Media; Origins vol. 23, No. 18. Encyclical Letter.

II, John Paul. 1995. "Address of His Holiness John Paul II to the Participants in the 'Breast-feeding: Science and Society,' Study Sessions Organized by the Pontifical Academy of Sciences." *Natural Family Planning Diocesan Activity Report* 6 (2):7-8.

II, John Paul. 1995. *The Gospel of Life*. Boston, MA: Pauline Books and Media. Encyclical

II, John Paul. 1995. "Letter to Women" (in preparation for Beijing Conference) released July 10, 1995.

II, John Paul. 1996. *Jesus Son and Savior: A Catechesis on the Creed*. Vol. Two. Boston MA: Pauline Books and Media. Catechetical.

II, John Paul. 1998. "Apostolic Letter." in *Dies Domini* given May 31st, 1998.

II, John Paul. 1998. *On the Relationship Between Faith and Reason (Fides et ratio)*. Boston, MA: Pauline Books and Media. Encyclical

II, John Paul. 2002. *On the Most Holy Rosary: Rosarium Virginias Mariae*. Boston, MA: Pauline Books and Media. Apostolic Letter.

II, John Paul. 2003. *Novo Millennio Ineunte*. Boston, MA: Pauline Books and Media. Apostolic Letter.

II, John Paul. 2003. *On the Eucharist in its Relationship to the Church: Encyclical Letter Ecclesia de Eucharistia* Boston, MA: Daughters of St. Paul. Encyclical

II, John Paul. 2003. *Reconciliation and Penance in the Mission of the Church Today*. Boston, MA: Pauline Books and Media. Apostolic Exhortation

II, John Paul. 2006. *Man and Woman He Created Them: A Theology of the Body*. Translated by Michael Waldstein. Boston: Pauline Books and Media

II, John Paul. 2012. *The Consecrated Life (Vita Consecrata)*. Washington, DC: United States Conference of Catholic Bishops.

II, John Paul. *In the Image of God, Marriage and Family: A Vocation -- Texts from John Paul II (October 1978-June 1980)*. Vatican City: Committee for the Family. texts on marriage.

II, John Paul. 1980. *On the Mercy of God (Dives in Misericordia)*. Boston: St. Paul Books & Media. encyclical letter.

II, John Paul. 1986. *The Holy Spirit in the Life of the Church and the World (Dominum et Vivicantem)*. Boston: St. Paul Books & Media. Encyclical Letter.

II, John Paul. 1987. *Mother of the Redeemer (Redemptoris mater), Encyclical Letter of John Paul II on the Blessed Virgin Mary in the Life of the Pilgrim Church*. Boston, MA: St. Paul Books & Media.

II, John Paul. 1994. Letter to Families.

II, John Paul. 1994. Tertio Millennio Adveniente.

II, Vatican. *Pastoral Constitution on the Church in the Modern World (Gaudium et Spes): Promulgated by Paul VI, Dec. 7, 1965*. Translated by N.C.W.C., *Documents of Vatican II*. Boston: St. Paul Editions.

IX, Pope Pius. 1870. *Quemadmodum Dies*

IX, Pope Pius. 1871. *Inclytum Patriarcham*

Jackson, M.D., Robert. 1990. *Human Ecology: A Physician's Advice for Human Life*. Petersham, MA: St. Bede's Publications. growth and development.

Jones, Susan. 2012. "The Dynamics of Intergenerational Behavior and Forgiveness Therapy." NACSW Convention, St. Louis, MO, Oct. 2012.

Joseph, Oblates of St. Le Voci. 1961. in "Le Voci for the protection of St. Joseph on the Second Vatican Council." Apostolic letter of Pope John XXIII.

Kaiser, Walter. 1991. *Toward an Old Testament Ethics*. Grand Rapids, MI: Zondervan Publishing House.

Kaplan, Aryeh. 1994. *Waters of Eden: The Mystery of the Mikvah* New York, NY: New Conference of Synagogue Youth/Union of Orthodox Jewish Congregations of America

Karen, Robert. 1994. *Becoming Attached: Unfolding the Mystery of the Infant-Mother Bond and Its Impact on Later Life.* New York Warner Books

Kaufman, Michael. 1996. *Love, Marriage, and Family in Jewish Law and Tradition.* Northvale, NJ: Jason Aronson Inc. Theology

Keating, Daniel A. 2007. *Deification and Grace.* Naples, FL: Sapientia Press.

Kippley, John. 1986. *Birth Control and the Marriage Covenant* 2ed. Collegeville, MN: Liturgical Pres.

Kippley, John. 2005. *Sex and the Marriage Covenant: a Basis for Morality* San Francisco Ignatius Press.

Kippley, Sheila. 2005. *Breastfeeding and Catholic Motherhood: God's Plan for You and Your Baby.* Manchester, NH: Sophia Institute Press. motherhood.

Klaus, Hanna. 2013. "The Body is Not a Mere Tool for the Expression of Feelings: How to Counter Dualism." in *Fellowship of Catholic Scholars Quarterly* 3 (4 Fall/Winter).

Koschorke, Albrecht. 2003. *The Holy Family and its Legacy: Religious Imagination from the Gosepls to Star Wars.* Translated by Thomas Dunlap. New York: Columbia University Press.

Kosnik, Anthony, William Carroll, Agnes Cunningham, Ronald Modras, and James Schulte. 1977. *Human Sexuality: New Directions in American Catholic Thought.* First ed. New York: Paulist Press. Moral theology, dissident.

Kostenberger, Andreas J. and David W. Jones. 2004. *God, Marriage and Family: Rebuilding the Biblical Foundation.* Wheaton, IL: Crossway Books.

Ktjerna, Kirsi. 2009. *Women and the Reformation.* Malden, MA: Blackwell Publishing.

Kukla, Rebecca. 2005. *Mass Hysteria: Medicine, Culture, and Mothers' Bodies.* Lanham, MD: Rowman & Littlefield Publishers, Inc.

Lallemant, P. Louis 1887. *La Doctrine Spirituelle precede de sa vie* Paris: Librairie Victor Lacoffre.

Lawrence, Ruth A. 1985. *Breastfeeding: A Guide for the Medical Profession.* Second ed. St. Louis: C.V. Mosby Co. Medical guide.

Lewis, C. S. 1970. "'Bulverism'." in *God in the Dock: Essays on Theology and Ethics*, edited by Walter Hooper, 271-277. Grand Rapids, Michigan William B. Eerdmans Publishing Company.

Lewis, Mark. 2015. *The Biology of Desire: Why Addiction is Not a Disease* New York, NY: Public Affairs.

Lienhard, Joseph T. S.J. 1999. *St. Joseph in early Christianity: Devotion and Theology: A Study and an Anthology of Patristic Texts.* Philadelphia, PA: Saint Joseph's University Press.

López, Antonio. 2014. *Gift and the Unity of Being.* Eugene, OR: Cascade Books. Theology.

Maccoby, Hyam. 1999. *Ritual and Morality:The Ritual Purity System and its Place in Judaism.* New York Cambridge University Press.

MacLehose, William F. 1996. "Nurturing Danger, High Medieval Medicine and the Problem(s) of the Child." In *Medieval Mothering*, edited by John Carmi and Bonnie Wheeler Parsons. New York: Garland Publishing, Inc.

Maddocks, Fiona. 2003. *Hildegard of Bingen: The Woman of Her Age.* New York, NY: Image Books/ Doubleday. Biography.

Maritain, Jacques. 1929. *Three Reformers: Luther-Descartes-Rousseau.* New York: Charles Scribner's Sons.

Marshall, Audrey and McDonald, Margaret. 2001. *The Many Sided Triangle: Adoption in Australia.* First ed. Carlton South, Victoria, Australia: Melbourne University Press. psychology, anthropology, adoption.

Marshall, John. 1965. *Catholics, Marriage and Contraception.* Baltimore, Maryland Helicon.

Marshall, John. 1995. *Love One Another: Psychological Aspects of Natural Family Planning.* First ed. London: Sheed and Ward.

Marshall, John. 2002. "My Voyage of Discovery: How Vatican II challenged the Church." in *The Tablet.*

Martin, Zelie and Louis Martin. 2011. *A Call to a Deeper Love: The Family Correspondence of the Parents of Saint Therese of the Child Jesus, 1864-1885* Translated by Ann Hess. New York: Alba House.

Martucci, Jessica. 2015. *Back to the Breast: Natural Motherhood and Breastfeeding in America*. Chicago, IL: University of Chicago Press.

May, William E. 1995. *Marriage: The Rock on Which the Family is Built*. First and second ed. San Francisco: Ignatius Press.

McClory, Robert. 1995. *Turning Point: The Inside Story of the Papal Birth Control Commission and How Humanae Vitae Changed the Life of Patty Crowley and the Future of the Church*. New York, NY: The Crossroads Publishing Company.

Melina, Livio. 2011. "The Analogy of Love." in *Josephinum Journal of Theology* 18 (2):274-279.

Mersch, SJ, Emile. 1938. *The Whole Christ: The Historical Development of the Doctrine of the Mystical Body in Scripture and Tradition*. Translated by SJ John R. Kelly. Milwaukee: Bruce Publishing Company.

Mersch, SJ, Emile. 1939. *Morality and the Mystical Body*. Translated by SJ Damiel F. Ryan. New York: P.J Kennedy and Sons Publishers.

Miles, Margaret R. 2008. *A Complex Delight: The Secularization of the Breast 1350-1750*. Berkeley, CA: University of California Press.

Milgrom, Jacob. 1991. *Leviticus 4-16, Anchor Bible* New York: Doubleday.

Miller, John W. 1989. *Biblical Fatih and Fathering: Why We Call God "Father"*. Mahwah NJ: Paulist Press.

Miller, Paula Jean. 1995. *Marriage: The Sacrament of Divine-Human Communion*. First ed. 2 vols. Vol. I: A Commentary on St. Bonaventure's Breviloquium. Quincy, IL: Franciscan Press.

Mohler, Johann Adam. 2007. *The Spirit of Celibacy: An examination of the Denkschrift fur die Aufhebung des den katholischen Geistlichen vorgeschriebenen Zolibates (Memorandum on the Abolition of the Celibacy Requirement for Catholic Priests)*. Translated by Cyprian Blamires. Chicago, IL: Hillebrand Books.

Montagu, Ashley. 1972. *Touching: The Human Significance of the Skin*. New York: Perennial Library, Harper & Row. physiological, psychological.

Mucharski, Jan. 1982. *History of the Biologic Control of Human Fertility*. Oak Ridge, NJ: Married Life Information.

Newman, John Henry. Extracts for the Times: Mary--The Second Eve From the Writings of John Henry Newman.

Newton, Niles. 1973. "Interrelationships between Sexual Responsiveness, Birth and Breastfeeding." in *Contemporary Sexual Behavior: Critical Issues in the 1970's*, edited by Joseph; Money Zubin, John, 77-99. Baltimore, MD: The Johns Hopkins University Press.

Nofziger, Margaret. 1979. *A Cooperative Method of Natural Birth Control*. Third ed. Summertown, TN: The Book Publishing Co.

Noonan, John T. 1986. *Contraception: A History of Its Treatment by the Catholic Theologians and Canonists*. Cambridge, MA: Harvard University Press.

Nyssa, Gregory of. 1966. "On Virginity." in *Saint Gregory of Nyssa Ascetical Works*. Washington, DC: The Catholic University of America Press.

O'Brien, John A. 2004. *Saints of the American Wilderness: The Brave Lives and Holy Deaths of eight North American Martyrs*. Manchester, NH: Sophia Institute Press.

of Lisieux, St. Therese. 1996. *Story of a Soul*. Translated by O.C.D. John Clarke. third ed. Washington DC: ICS Publications. autobiographical.

Olsen, Glenn W., ed. 2001. *Christian Marriage: A Historical Study*. New York, NY: The Crossroad Publishing Company.

Ouellet, Marc Cardinal. 2006. *Divine Likeness: Toward a Trinitarian Anthropology of the Family*. Translated by Philip Milligan and Linda M. Cicone. Edited by David L. Schindler, *Ressourcement: Retrieval and Renewal in Catholic Thought*. Grand Rapids, MI: William B. Eerdmans.

Palmer, Gabrielle. 2009. *The Politics of Breastfeeding: When Breasts Are Bad for Business*. Third revised ed. London UK: Pinter & Martin.

Parmisano, F. S. "Spousal Love in the Medieval Rite of Marriage." in *Nova et Vetera* 3 (4):785-806.

Parmisano, Stan. 2009. *The Craft of Love: Love and Intimacy in Christian Marriage*. Antioch, CA: Solas Press.

Pedersen, Johannes. 1959. *Israel: Its Life and Culture* 2vols. Vol. I-II. London: Oxford University Press. Original edition, 1926. Reprint, 1959.

Pegis, Anton C, ed. 1945. *Basic Writings of Saint Thomas Aquinas*. First ed. Two vols. Vol. Two. New York: Random House.

Peguy, Charles. 1996. *The Portal of the Mystery of Hope*. Translated by David Louis Schindler Jr. Edited by David L. Schindler, *Retrieval and Ressourcement in Catholic Thought*. Grand Rapids, MI: William B. Eerdmans.

Pierre, Terese Olsen 2001. "Marriage, Body and Sacrament in the Age of Hugh of St. Victor." in *Christian Marriage: A Historical Study*, edited by Glenn W. Olson. New York: Crossroad Publishing Company.

Pilarz, Scott R., S.J. 1996. "The Holy Family on the Medieval Stage." in *The Holy Family in Art and Devotion*, edited by Joseph F. Chorpenning. Philadelphia: St. Joseph's University Press.

Pinckaers, Servais. 1995. "Natural Inclinations at the Source of Freedom and Morality." in *The Sources of Christian Ethics*, 400-456. Washington DC: The Catholic University of America Press

Pinckaers, Servais. 1995. *The Sources of Christian Ethics*. Translated by O.P. Sr. Mary Thomas Noble. Third ed. Washington, DC: The Catholic University of America Press.

Podles, Leon J. 1998. "The Destiny of Men: Patriarchy or Crime." in *Defending the Family: Source Book*. Steubenville, OH: Catholic Social Science Press.

Ponton, Bertrand-Guy-M et G. 1955. "Textes Patristiques sur Saint Joseph." in *Cahiers de Joséphologie*

Prendergast, Terence. 1993. "A Vision of Wholeness: A Reflection on the Use of Scripture in a Cross-Section of Papal Writings." in *The Thought of John Paul II: A Collection of Essays and Studies*, edited by S.J. John M. McDermott, 69-91. Rome: Editrice Pontificia Universita Gregoriana.

Quattrin, Patricia Ann. 1996. "The Milk of Christ: Herzeloyde as Spiritual Symbol in Wolfram Von Eschenbach's Parsifal." in *Medieval Mothering* edited by John Carmi Parsons and Bonnie Wheeler. New York: Garland Publishing Company.

Quay, Paul. 1985. *The Christian Meaning of Human Sexuality.* Evanston, IL: Credo House.

Rahner, Hugo. 2004. *Our Lady and the Church.* Translated by Sebastian Bullough. Bethesda, MD: Zaccheus Press.

Ratner, Herbert, ed. *Child and Family: The Nursing Mother Historical Insights from Art and Theology, Reprint Booklet Series.* Oak Park, IL: National Commission on Human Life, Reproduction and Rhythm.

Ratzinger, Cardinal Joseph. 1992. "Retrieving the Tradition: Concerning the Notion of Person in Theology." in *Communio: International Catholic Review* 19 (Winter 1992):601-618.

Ratzinger, Cardinal Joseph. 2003. "Thoughts on the Place of Marian Doctrine and Piety in Faith and Theology as a Whole." in *Communio: International Catholic Review* 30 (1):146-160.

Rawson, Beryl 1986. "Wet-Nursing at Rome: A Study in Social Relations." In *The Family in Ancient Rome* edited by Beryl Rawson, 201-229. Cornell, NY: Cornell University Press.

Riley, Patrick. 2000. *Civilizing Sex: On Chastity and the Common Good.* Edinburgh: T & T Clark.

Rousseau, Jean- Jacques. 1968. *The Social Contract.* Translated by Maurice Cranston. New York: Penguin Books.

Rousseau, Jean- Jacques. 1979. *Emile or On Education.* Translated by Allan Bloom. New York: Basic Books, Inc.

Rowland, Tracey and Conor Sweeney 2015. "The Elephants at the Synod: Logos, Ethos and Sacramentality." in *Anthropotes*

Sales, Michel. 1995. "The honor of becoming children: What it means to honor one's father and mother." in *Communio* 22 (1, Spring):5-27.

Sanger, Margaret. 1969. *The Pivot of Civilization.* Elmsford, NY: Maxwell Reprint Co.

Saward, John. 1986. "Berulle and the French School." in *The Study of Spirituality*, edited by Cheslyn; Geoffrey Wainwright and Edward Yarnold S.J. Jones, 386. New York: Oxford University Press.

Saward, John. 1993. *Redeemer in the Womb: Jesus Living in Mary.* San Francisco: Ignatius Press.

Saward, John. 1998. "'The Earthly Home of the Eternal Father:' The Holy Family in the Spirituality of the French School." in *The Holy Family in Art and Devotion*, edited by Joseph F. Chorpenning. Philadelphia, PA: St. Joseph's University Press.

Schillebeeckx, Edward. 1965. *Marriage, Human Reality and Saving Mystery: I--Marriage in the Old and New Testaments and II--Marriage in the History of the Church.* Translated by N.D. Smith. Vol. 1 & 2. New York: Sheed and Ward.

Schindler, David L. 2011. "'We Are Not Our Own': Childhood and the Integrity of the Human in a Technological Age." in *Humanum.*

Schindler, David L. Fall 2008. "The Embodied Person as Gift and the Cultural Task in America: Status Quaestionis " *Communio* 35 (3, Fall):397-431.

Schmitz, Kenneth L. 1982. *The Gift: Creation* Milwaukee: Marquette University Press.

Schoeman, Roy H. 2003. *"Salvation is from the Jews" (John 4:22): the Role of Judaism in Salvation History from Abraham to the Second Coming.* San Francisco: Ignatius Press.

Scola, Angelo. 2005. "Appendix 2, Affection in the Light of Several Articles of Saint Thomas Aquinas's De Passionibus: A Reading of the Summa Theologiae 1-II, q.22, aa, 1-3, and q.26, aa. 1-2." in *The Nuptial Mystery*, 314-330. Grand Rapids MI: William B. Eerdmans Publishing Co.

Scola, Angelo. 2005. *The Nuptial Mystery.* Grand Rapids, MI: William B. Eerdmans Publishing Company.

Shivanandan, Mary. 1979. *Natural Sex.* Author's, hardcover and trade paperback ed. New York: Rawson, Wade Publishers, Inc.

Shivanandan, Mary. 1988. *Challenge to Love.* Bethesda MD: KM Associates.

Shivanandan, Mary. 1996. "Feminism and Marriage: A Reflection on Ephesians 5:21-33." In *Diakonia* XXIX (1).

Shivanandan, Mary. 1999. *Crossing the Threshold of Love: A New Vision of Marriage.* First, author's copy ed. Edinburgh: T&T Clarke.

Shivanandan, Mary. 2000. "Body Narratives: Language of Truth?" *LOGOS* 3 (3):166-193.

Shivanandan, Mary. 2001. "Subjectivity and the Order of Love." in *Fides Quaerens Intellectum* I (2).

Shivanandan, Mary. 2004. "Mary's Immaculate Conception and Theological Anthropology." in *Anthropotes* 20 (2):419-436.

Sodergren, Andrew J. 2009. *Attachment and Morality: A Catholic Perspective.* Washington DC: The Institute for the Psychological Sciences. theoretical dissertation.

Spezzano, Daria. 2015. *The Glory of God's Grace: Deification According to Thomas Aquinas* Naples, FL: Sapientia Press.

Steinmetz, David C. 1986. *Luther in Context* Bloomington, IN: Indiana University Press.

Steinmetz, David C. 2004. *Harvesting Martin Luther's Reflections on Theology, Ethics, and the Church.* Grand Rapids, MI: William B. Eerdmans Publishing Company

Stern, Karl. 1954. *The Third Revolution: Psychiatry and Religion.* New York: Harcourt, Brace and Company. Psychiatry, religion.

Stern, Karl. 1985. *The Flight from Woman.* New York: Paragon House.

Stjerna, Kirsi. 1988. *Women and the Reformation.* Malden, MA: Blackwell Publishing.

Stockl, Fidelis. 2003. *Mary: Model and Mother of Consecrated Life: A Marian Synthesis of the Theology of Consecrated Life Based on the Teachings of John Paul II.* Quezon City, Phillipines: ICLA Publications.

Stockl, Fidelis. 2003. "Mary's Spousal Consecration (Consecration as a Covenant of Spousal Love)." in *Mary, Model and Mother of Consecrated Life*, 165-198. Quezon City, Phillipines: ICLA Publishers.

Stopp, Elizabeth. 1986. "Francois de Sales." in *The Study of Spirituality*, edited by Geoffrey Wainwright Cheslyn Jones, and Edward Yarnold, S.J. , 381-382. New York: Oxford University Press.

Sussman, George D. 1982. *Selling Mother's Milk: The Wet-Nursing Business in France 1715- 1914.* First ed. Chicago: University of Illinois Press. history.

Talleyrand-Périgord, Charles Maurice de 1891. "Mémoires du prince de Talleyrand." in, ed Calmann Lévy. Paris: La Librairie Nouvelle.

Thomas Petri, OP. 2015. *Aquinas and the Theology of the Body.* Edited by Matthew Levering and Thomas JosephWhite, *Thomistic Ressourcement Series.* Washington DC: The Catholic University of America Press. Theological.

Thompson, William A., Lowell M. Glendon, Susan A. Muto. 1989. *Berulle and the French School.* New Jersey: Paulist Press.

Vagaggini, C. 1969. *The Flesh: Instrument of Salvation: A Theology of the Human Body.* Staten Island NY: Society of St. Paul.

Vanier, Jean. 1989. *Man and Woman He Made Them.* Mahwah, NJ: Paulist Press.

Vaux, Roland de. 1977. *Ancient Israel: Its Life and Institutions.* Translated by John McHugh. Grand Rapids, Michigan: William B. Eerdmans Publishing Company. Original edition, 1926. Reprint, 1977.

VI, Pope Paul. 1964. Dogmatic Constitution on the Church (Lumen Gentium). November 21, 1964.

VI, Pope Paul. 1965. Address of Pope Paul VI, During Last General Meeting of the Second Vatican Council.

VI, Pope Paul. 1968. *Of Human Life: Humanae vitae.* Boston, MA: Pauline Books and Media. Encyclical Letter.

VI, Pope Paul. 1969. "Discourse (March 19, 1969)." In *Insegnamenti*, 1268. Vatican

VI, Pope Paul. 1974. *Good News for Married Love: Address of Pope Paul VI to the Teams of Our Lady (Equipes Notre-Dame).* Translated by Randall Blackall. Collegeville, MN: The Liturgical Press.

Virtue, William D. 1995. *Mother and Infant: The Moral Theology of Embodied Self-Giving Motherhood In Light of the Exemplar Couplet Mary and Jesus Christ.* Rome: Pontificiam Universitatem S. Thomae. Dissertation.

Vitz, Paul C. 2013. *Faith of the Fatherless: The Psychology of Atheism* San Francisco: Ignatius Press.

Vitz, Paul C. and Christina P. Lynch. 2007. "Thérèse of Lisieux from the Perspective of Attachment Theory and Separation Anxiety." in *The International Journal for the Psychology of Religion* 17 (1):19.

Wandel, Lee Palmer. 1995. *Voracious Idols and Violent Hands: Iconoclasm in Reformation Zurich, Strasbourg, and Basel.* First ed. New York: Cambridge University Press. history.

Warner, H.J. 1922. *The Albigensian Heresy* New York: Russell and Russell. Reprint, 1987.

Wenham, Gordon J. 1979. *The Book of Leviticus.* Grand Rapids, MI: William B. Eerdman's

Wilcox, Bradford W. 2004. *Soft Patriarchs, New Men: How Christianity Shapes Fathers and Husbands.* Chicago IL: University of Chiago Press. Theology.

Wilson, Christopher C. 1998. "'Living Among Jesus, Mary and Joseph:' Images of St. Theresa of Avila with the Holy Family in Spanish Colonial Art." in *The Holy Family in Art and Devotion*, edited by Joseph F. Chorpenning. Philadelphia, PA: St. Joseph's University Press.

Wojtyla, Karol. 1984. *The Way to Christ: Spiritual Exercises* Translated by Leslie Wearney. New York: Harper & Row. Spiritual exercises.

Wojtyla, Karol. 1987. *The Collected Plays and Writings on Theater.* Translated by Boleslaw Taborski. Berkeley, CA: University of California Press.

Wojtyla, Karol. 1987. "Radiation of Fatherhood." in *The Collected Plays and Writings on Theater*, 336. Berkeley, CA: University of California Press.

Wojtyla, Karol. 1993. "Parenthood as a Community of Persons." in *Person and Community: Selected Essays*, 329-342. New York: Peter Lang.

Wojtyla, Karol. 1993. "The Person: Subject and Community." in *Person and Community: Selected Essays*, 219-261. New York: Peter Lang.

Wojtyla, Karol. 2013. *Love and Responsibility.* Translated by Grzegorz Ignatik with endnotes and foreword. Boston, MA: Pauline Books & Media.

XI, Pope Pius. 1930. *Encyclical Letter of Pope Pius XI on Christian Marriage (Casti Connubii).* Official Vatican Text ed. Boston: St. Paul Books and Media.

XI, Pope Pius. 1937. Divini redemptoris: Encyclical on Atheistic Communism.

XIII, Leo. 1886. "*Arcanum*, Encyclical of Pope Leo XIII on Christian Marriage, February 10, 1980." in *The Papal Encyclicals, 1878-1903*, edited by Claudia Carlen. Wilmington, NC: McGrath Pub. Co.

XIII, Pope Leo. 1889. Quamquam Pluries: Encyclical of Pope Leo XIII on Devotion to St. Joseph.

XV, Benedicti PP. 1920. "De Sacris Solemnibus Anni Quinquagesimi Ex Quo S. Joseph B.M.V." in *Acta Apostolicae Sedis: Commentarium Officiale*, 313-317. Romae: Typis Polyglottis Vaticanis.

XVI, Benedict. 2006. Deus Caritas Est.

XXIII, Pope John. 1961. "Humanae salutis." in *The Documents of Vatican II*, 703-709. Chicago: Association Press & Follett Publishing Company.

Zilberfeld, Bernie. 1978. *Male Sexuality, a Guide to Sexual Fulfillment* Boston, MA: Little, Brown and Company.

Zola, Emile. 1900. *Fruitfulness (Fecondite)*. Translated by Ernest Alfred Vizetelly. First ed. New York: Doubleday, Page and Co. Novel.

APPENDIX

Statistics on NFP Use in the United States, 2014 prepared by Patrick Fagan.

Final Meeting on Natural Family Planning: Natural Methods Respect the Divine Gift of Procreation, *L'Osservatore Romano,* English Edition, January 13, 1993.

Thomasina Smith Borkman, "Experiential Learning and the Professional in NFP," in *Natural Family Planning: Development of National Programs,* ed. Claude A. Lanctot et al. (Washington, DC: IFFLP/FIDAF, 1984) Reprinted with permission of Dr. Thomasina Borkman.

John Marshall, "My Voyage of Discovery: How Vatican II changed the Church: 7," *The Tablet,* 23 November 2002. Reprinted with permission of *The Tablet,* www.thetablet.co.uk.

John Marshall, *Love One Another: Psychological Aspects of Natural Family Planning,* (London, Sheed & Ward, 1995) reviewed by Mary Shivanandan. Reprinted with permission of the Diocesan Development Program for NFP, USCCB.

Rates of NFP Use in the United States

Patrick Fagan, Ph.D. Director,
The Marriage and Religion Research Initiative at
The Catholic University of America

Rates of Use

NFP: "In the 2002 NSFG (Cycle 6) there were 7,635 women in the sample, 2,250 of whom were Catholic (29.5%).1 In 2002, the 3 most frequent methods of contraception among all US women (in order of frequency) were oral hormonal contraception (i.e., the birth control pill), male sterilization, and condoms. Only 15 women between the ages of 15-44 (or 0.2% of the sample) listed natural family planning (NFP) as their current method of family planning."[1]

Female use in US:

- Only 2% of at-risk Catholic women rely on natural family planning; the proportion is the same even among those women who attend church once a month or more."

http://www.guttmacher.org/pubs/fb_contr_use.html#5

6. Jones RK and Dreweke J, ***Countering Conventional Wisdom: New Evidence on Religion and Contraceptive Use***, New York: Guttmacher Institute, 2011.

"The overall findings from the 2002 NSFG indicate that US Roman Catholic women between the ages of 15-44 have patterns of use of contraceptive methods similar to those of US women in general.... However, of note is the fact that most of the women who use modern methods of NFP (mucus and temperature) are Roman Catholic. When the 15 users of NFP in the data set are extrapolated to the total number of women in the US, about 124,000 currently use NFP as their primary method of family planning."[2]

"The findings also show that Roman Catholic women were more likely (90-187%) to have used NFP if they attend church services frequently, believe that their Roman Catholic faith is very important, and are orthodox in their sexual ethics."[3]

"The use of NFP among Roman Catholic couples has been declining since the 1950s when there was a high frequency of use among married Roman Catholic couples of about 54%. The use of NFP has declined and leveled off to around 2-3% among married couples since 1988."[4]

1 J. Ohlendorf, and R. J. Fehring, "The Influence of Religiosity on Contraceptive Use among Roman Catholic Women in the United States," The Linacre Quarterly 74 No. (2007): 135.
2 J. Ohlendorf, and R. J. Fehring, "The Influence of Religiosity on Contraceptive Use among Roman Catholic Women in the United States," The Linacre Quarterly 74 No. 2 (2007): 140.
3 J. Ohlendorf, and R. J. Fehring, "The Influence of Religiosity on Contraceptive Use among Roman Catholic Women in the United States," The Linacre Quarterly 74 No. 2 (2007): 141.
4 J. Ohlendorf, and R. J. Fehring, "The Influence of Religiosity on Contraceptive Use among Roman Catholic Women in the United States," The Linacre Quarterly 74 No. 2 (2007): 141.

L'OSSERVATORE ROMANO

English Edition January 13 1993

Final declaration of meeting on family planning: Natural methods respect divine gift of procreation

The following is the Final Declaration of the summit meeting on the natural methods of regulating fertility held in Rome from 9-11 December under the auspices of the Pontifical Council for the Family.

Gathered to study the latest developments in the natural methods of regulating fertility, as 45 scientific experts, social workers and moralists, we wish to speak to the women and men of the world.

The regulation of human fertility is a delicate matter involving serious choices and decisions. Many problems have arisen in this important area of human experience. We confidently propose the authentic way for the true humanization of God's wonderful gift of procreation. It allows the achievement of "natural family planning".

We want to emphasize that the natural methods imply a specific life-style and ethical behaviour, which appeals to the responsibility of spouses, and which is based on unconditional respect for the dignity of the person, the true nature of marriage and the primary and fundamental value of life — and the appreciation of sexuality as a gift of God.

Over the past 60 years, the study of the symptoms which accompany the cycle of a woman's fertility has revolutionized knowledge of them and has allowed people to decide responsibly about the natural spacing of childbirths. Having moved far beyond the calendar method, "rhythm", the modern methods are reliable and precise ways of trying to achieve or postpone pregnancy. *These natural methods rest on a sound scientific foundation.* Today, rapid advances in scientific research and technology are enhancing the use of these methods. But public opinion about natural methods is often deficient and sometimes erroneous.

Therefore, we affirm the value of the natural regulation of fertility.

— The natural methods are easy to teach and understand. They can be used in any social context and do not require literacy.

— The *health of mothers and infants* is furthered through spacing childbirth in a natural way which harms neither the mother nor her baby. Natural methods do not harm the *health of couples.*

— The freedom and rights of the wife and husband are respected through these methods which centre around the woman and are based on the integrity of her body.

— Because they indicate the time of fertility, the *natural* methods can help couples *to achieve pregnancy.* These methods have brought joy to couples facing problems of apparent infertility.

— The natural methods can develop *a deeper interpersonal relationship* between a wife and husband, based on communication, shared decisions and mutual respect. The use of these methods reinforces marriage and hence strengthens family life.

— The natural methods promote a positive attitude to the child and maintain reverence for human life at all stages of development.

— The natural methods are compatible with all cultures and all religions.

— Development of *sexual responsibility,* understood as chastity before marriage and fidelity in marriage, is fostered by knowledge of our fertility. The teaching of natural family planning is therefore of primary importance in preserving reproductive health, including the prevention of AIDS and other sexually transmitted diseases.

— These methods do not place a financial burden on families; hence they are welcomed by many women and men in developing countries.

Recommendations

In the light of the benefits of natural methods and firmly believing that every woman has the right to understand her fertility:

1. We recommend that the Church significantly increase efforts to teach the religious and human values contained in her tradition, specifically in *Humanae vitae* and *Familiaris consortio,* in the catechesis of Pope John Paul II "on human love in the divine plan" and in other magisterial documents.

2. We recommend that the natural methods should be available to all couples everywhere. We call on governments and private organizations to positively assist and support couples in this task.

3. We recommend that the natural methods should be taught in all medical faculties. We call on the medical profession to study and promote the scientific methods of natural family planning as responsible parenthood and to make them available to women and men.

4. We recommend that the natural methods be gradually taught to young women and men before they enter married life.

5. We support breast-feeding for the good of the family, the child and the mother and as a way of spacing childbirths and we encourage public policy which will enable mothers to breast-feed their children.

6. We recommend that there be more multidisciplinary research to assist couples to achieve responsible parenthood through natural means.

7. We recommend that the natural methods receive appropriate funds for research and promotion of the regulation of human fertility.

8. We recommend that national associations be established in all countries, so that promoters of the different natural methods can collaborate, support one another and exchange information.

We ask pastors to give effective attention to the pastoral directives formulated in *Humanae vitae* and *Familiaris consortio* and to give concrete support to initiatives for research and teaching the natural methods.

Coming together from different nations, cultures and religious traditions, we express our gratitude to the Catholic Church which has strongly encouraged responsible parenthood through the use of natural methods of regulating fertility. In 1993, the Church celebrates the 25th anniversary of the Encyclical *Humanae vitae.* As we remember the prophetic teaching of Pope Paul VI, we thank Pope John Paul II for his teaching in *Familiaris consortio* and for his continuing support and encouragement. We also thank Cardinal Alfonso López Trujillo and the Pontifical Council for the Family for making this meeting in Rome possible.

As we look to the future in hope and confidence, we thank all those couples throughout the world who have chosen the natural methods as the authentic alternative and the dedicated teachers who help and inspire them.

[Sr Catherine Bernard, *India;* Dr John Billings, *Australia;* Dr Lyn Billings, *Australia;* Dr Anna Cappella, *Italy;* Mons. Ignacio Carrasco de Paula, *Spain;* Fr Lino Ciccone, C.M., *Italy;* Mr William N. Corey, *USA;* Prof. Sergio Cortesi, *Italy;* Fr Georges Marie Martin Cottier, O.P., *Switzerland;* Dr Achille Dedè, *Italy;* Dr André Devos, *Belgium;* Prof. Joaquín Fernández-Crehuet, *Spain;* Dr Anna Flynn, *Great Britain;* Prof. Dr Günther Freundl, *Germany;* Rev. Prof. Ramón García de Haro, *Spain;* Prof. Enrique Gómez García, *Spain;* Dr Elena Giacchi, *Italy;* Rev. Dr William Gibbons, *USA;* Dr Hanna Goszczynska, *Poland;* Dr François Guy, *France;* Dr Michele Guy, *France;* Dr Thomas Hilgers, *USA;* Fr Bonifacio Hönings, O.C.D., *Netherlands;* Dr Stefan Horvath, *Slovakia;* Fr Henryk Hoser, S.A.C., *Rwanda;* Dr Victoria Jennings, *Georgetown University;* Sr Francesca Kearns, C.C.V.I., *Guatemala;* Dr Hanna Klaus, *USA;* Dr Miriam Labbok, *Georgetown University;* Dr Claude Lanctot, *USA;* Mme. Angela De Malherbe, *France;* Dr Salvatore Mancuso, *Italy;* Fr Daniel McCaffrey, *USA;* Bishop James McHugh, *USA;* Dr Miroslav Mikolasik, *Slovakia;* Mr Kinji Nishimura, *Japan;* Dr Alfredo Pérez, *Chile;* Dr Wanda Poltawski, *Poland;* Fr Pedro Richards, C.P., *Uruguay;* Dr Josef Rötzer, *Austria;* Fr Denis L. St. Marie, *USA;* Prof. Janet E. Smith, *USA;* Dr H. William Taylor, *USA;* Dr Romana Wilhelm, *Austria;* Mrs Mercedes Arzu Wilson, *USA.*

Experiential Learning and the Professional in NFP

THOMASINA SMITH BORKMAN

Thomasina Smith Borkman, Ph.D., associate professor of sociology, George Mason University, Fairfax, VA, USA; leading expert in self-help groups

NFP services are growing beyond their original part-time volunteer-based beginnings. The expansion of high-quality NFP services to more people and countries is the challenge now. This paper invites you to consider some directions NFP services can take and their implications.

Certain assumptions which, in fact, are value judgments, underlie this sociological analysis. These are: NFP should be made available at low cost to many interested people in many countries within a reasonable time period; the services should be of high quality, accountable and respectful of the diverse values of the people involved; and finally, the methods should be grounded in biomedical science.

In sociological terms, NFP is a social innovation and like any innovation needs to become known and respected. As part of this process of expansion, NFP leaders need to promote the acceptance and credibility of NFP among established leaders and institutions. Three orientations have provided the primary leadership in developing NFP services up to now: (1) NFP teachers and users with experiential knowledge of NFP, (2) the medical profession, and (3) religious groups, especially Catholics. NFP services currently combine these orientations in a variety of mixtures in different programs and countries. Each of these orientations offers both advantages and disadvantages to service delivery. The experiential is not presently given legitimacy while the religious and medical are.

The paradox of NFP is that services cannot expand to a large number of places without existing institutional networks, but if essential features of the experiential component are lost, only a few people in any locality will be reached. Furthermore, if these NFP programs are designed according to the conventional professional or medical model, the services would be so expensive and ineffective that the advantage of the network would be lost.

New kinds of programs and nonprofessional occupations need to be designed that enable experiential experts to play their irreplaceable role in the institutional context.

This paper raises this challenge for NFP and institutional leaders.

Natural Family Planning services are a relatively new social innovation having been created during the past 25-30 years. During this time, several kinds of groups—with medical, religious, and experienced-user orientations—have evolved their own approaches to teaching NFP to women or couples. Many of these efforts have been ad hoc, part-time, and volunteer-based. Many have been too informal and irregular to be entitled service programs. Some groups are free-standing and independent, whereas others operate inside such institutionalized delivery systems as medical care systems or Catholic marriage and family programs.

Dr. Claude Lanctôt (1982) recently summarized the status of these NFP services.

It appears clear that NFP has achieved

a new status of respectability and credibility. Yet it is still very close to its grass-roots origins being still in many places method specific, women oriented, and mostly by peer instructors. The challenge of the next decade will be to expand the movement into offering quality services to a much larger number of potential clients.

The challenge of expanding high-quality NFP services to more people and places is accepted here as the issue of interest. This congress is an important occasion, and I invite you to consider some major directions that the development of NFP services is likely to take based on the history of these services and the apparently available options. The implications of following these directions will be spelled out. This sociological analysis suggests that there are major pitfalls to expansion if NFP services are simply modeled after existing medical, educational, or religious delivery systems. Some suggestions are offered to avoid these pitfalls.

Certain assumptions have been made that were used as criteria in conducting this sociological analysis. These assumptions are also, in fact, several value judgments. Current sociology recognizes that certain value judgments are necessarily involved in sociology and any scientific work (Gouldner 1962, 1968; Foss 1977). Often these value judgments are implicit, not explicit. Certain explicit value judgments underlie this analysis, and they represent the criteria or parameters in terms of which the analysis was conducted.

There are three basic assumptions:

First, NFP should be made available to many interested people in many countries within a reasonable period of time. This assumption focuses on the idea that the capacity for wide diffusion of services should guide the direction of their development.

Second, the NFP services that are developed should be low-cost, high-quality, accountable to their constituencies, and respectful of the values of the people involved. Once NFP services come into the public domain, whether they are mandated by church, medical, or government policy, the services can no longer be solely a part-time, volunteer activity. Moreover, publicly authorized services have to be accountable and have external means to measure quality. Also, publicly authorized services cannot usually be restricted and available to persons of certain religious or ethical value positions while excluding persons with other values.

Third, the methods should continue to be grounded both in biomedical science and in the experiential knowledge (Borkman 1976, 1979, 1980) of successful users. This assumption refers to the knowledge base of NFP services and to what kind of expertise is needed to direct NFP programs. Two kinds of knowledge are distinguished here. Both seem essential for effective NFP services: (1) the *application* of biomedical research findings on human reproduction and fertility, and (2) experiential knowledge gained by practicing NFP or teaching NFP to users.

1. The essential biomedical scientific knowledge is *applied* information taken from research findings. It is important to encourage biomedical research on reproduction and refinement of the methods, but as a separate activity from NFP service programs. Medical professionals per se are not necessary to provide NFP services. The applied research material is neither highly technical nor extremely complex. It has been well demonstrated that nonliterates and educated people alike from many cultural backgrounds can be taught the applied biomedical knowledge and can use it effectively in practicing NFP. Therefore, neither the teaching of NFP nor the directing of programs needs to be controlled by physicians or other health professionals on the basis of technical or specialized knowledge. The physician or other medical professional is needed on a consultant basis, however, for problematic medical conditions and to review the applied biomedical knowledge base of NFP services.

2. The essential kind of knowledge for an effective NFP program is experiential knowledge of NFP. This refers to trusted information gained by personal, lived experience (Borkman 1976, 1979, 1980) that many teacher users and long-term NFP users obtain through their practice of NFP. The experiential knowledge of NFP in-

cludes the practical application of the biomedical information to everyday life plus the emotional and relational aspects of the abstinence, sexuality, and communication between the partners. The necessity of experiential knowledge is recognized by many NFP service programs that require teachers to be users.

Elements in a Publicly Accountable NFP Program

From a sociological perspective, NFP is a social innovation, and, like any innovation, it needs to become known and respected. Social innovation refers to ideas or practices that are new to the involved individuals or organizations; it does not mean new in the sense of never previously occurring throughout human history (Borkman 1979). What is needed to translate this social innovation into respected and effective program services that can be diffused to many people and countries? The services need to become regular programs, have quality control and accountability standards, develop new NFP occupations, and become accepted by relevant leaders and institutions. Some people call this professionalizing an NFP program.

As can be seen, the term "professional" is problematic because it has many meanings and is used in different ways by people. Some of what people discuss under the term "professional" I will discuss under the headings of: regular program, quality control, and accountability standards and NFP occupations. There is another meaning to the term "professionalize" that is a danger for NFP programs. I will discuss it later.

Since NFP is changing from a local option to a service mandated by public policy in some countries, NFP services will need to be *regular programs* that are publicly accountable and have some means of showing the quality of their services. Regular programs are defined here as legally and financially responsible services that are regularly available and have a continuous, identifiable presence in the community. A regular program is contrasted with a part-time, ad hoc "fold-up" group that may rely only on volunteer effort. A program administrator who is publicly responsible and accountable is another ingredient of a regular program; the administrator function represents the program to the relevant communities. A regular program may rely on part-time, unpaid volunteer effort for most of its service provision, but the identifiable, continuous presence is provided by the administrator.

A second necessary element is the *conceptualization* of the NFP program in terms of its nature (an educational approach, a religious or a medical one); the values attached to it; what groups (medical, experienced user, or religious) will control it; how it is viewed in relation to other family planning methods; and how the program articulates with other local health, family planning, marriage and family, and educational services.

Third, the functions of NFP teacher, supervisor of teachers, and program administrator need to develop into identifiable occupations. Occupations are job positions that define responsibilities, duties, and privileges, and that have selection criteria, standards for training, experience, performance, and ideologies. Ideology refers to the set of ideas that occupational members develop about the nature of their work, its linkages with other occupations, ethical standards, what the occupation contributes to its clients and to society, and so forth (Freidson 1973).

These issues pertain to the fact that in many places the spread of NFP services is hindered by the lack of trained, committed NFP instructors. These instructors would be trained to work regularly in NFP programs and have the "occupational qualities" of confidence, commitment to follow program guidelines and procedures, willingness to submit to administrative control for the good of providing regular services, and familiarity with paper work, terminology, and organizational practices of agencies so that they could operate as "professional" as contrasted with "amateur." I am deliberately using descriptive terms about what is needed for occupational performance rather than using the terminology of professionals. Some of what is meant by "professionalizing" NFP is to call for the above qualities in contrast with the qualities found among many current instructors, who are not systematically or uniformly trained or tested in any way to identify the level of their knowledge and skills; who are unpaid volunteers whose commitment to NFP lies in their zeal about its values (and are thus effective teachers); who may not be occupationally committed to providing services in an NFP program by submitting to its administrative procedures; who may not be familiar with the practices and "culture" of agencies.

Fourth, external quality control and accountability standards for NFP programs need to be developed and agreed upon. These standards are mainly for outsiders—the relevant local communities who give the legitimacy to a program that is vital for its diffusion. These program elements include such aspects as standards of follow-up, confidentiality requirements, record-keeping requirements, guidelines for supervising teachers, and so forth. There are major dangers in defining and implementing quality and accountability standards. The most frequent error in developed countries with high educational levels is to equate standardization, the written form, or activities done by a professional group as prima facie evidence of quality and accountability.

Fifth, obtaining acceptance from the relevant leaders and institutions is critical for obtaining funds, for attracting clients, and for becoming a regular program. All of the preceding four elements contribute to the legitimating of NFP programs.

Three Orientations Found in Current NFP Services

Three orientations have provided primary leadership in developing NFP services up to now: (1) NFP teachers and users with experiential knowledge of NFP; (2) the medical profession; and (3) religious groups, especially Catholics. NFP services currently combine these orientations in a variety of mixtures in different programs and countries. There are experientialists with strong religious orientations leading voluntary associations like John Kippley's Couple to Couple League. There are other experientially controlled voluntary associations that are moderate in medical and in religious orientation, such as Serena Canada. Physicians who often have religious values have led some groups, either voluntary associations of primarily experiential users like the World Organization of the Ovulation Method Billings (WOOMB) or more medically based clinics with some emphasis on research, like Dr. Roetzer in Austria. Religiously oriented programs are often within the context of Catholic marriage and family programs like Ireland's, but these programs have strong input from health professionals and experiential users who teach NFP.

The three orientations are important because each seems to contribute something vital to the philosophy and knowledge of NFP as it is currently constituted. It seems that effective NFP services combine some aspects of all three orientations. As discussed earlier, the biomedical, scientific grounding of NFP methods is absolutely critical, and their appropriate application ensures that NFP is reliable and effective as a family planning method. Similarly, the experiential knowledge for teaching NFP to newcomers and for informing issues of NFP service delivery seems critical from past history. The extreme case would be using males without personal experience of NFP who learned it from books and lectures as teachers; one would expect many dropouts and unsuccessful users. The religious dimension as world view is seen here as key in providing a value framework within which NFP is interpreted. Values are often articulated in NFP by religious groups, but this need not be the case. In this paper, religion is being defined in two senses: first, as the world view in which human values guide choices and behavior; and second, as an institutional entity which encompasses a network of organizations, occupations, and administration. Many secular or nonsectarian value-oriented groups, however, also could and do provide a value framework within which NFP can be interpreted. For example, the feminist health movement and alternative living groups like Summertown (Shivanandan 1979) are examples of value-oriented groups.

Each of the three orientations also

represents a direction that NFP can develop as service programs. What are the major strengths and weaknesses of each orientation as a form of service delivery for NFP? Strengths and weaknesses were identified relative to the value judgments that were the criteria for analysis.

The strength of the religious orientation lies in its clear and continuous articulation of the human and religious values of NFP. Religious institutions could also facilitiate the expansion of NFP services by designing programs linked with their existing institutional networks (as is being done by the U.S. Catholic Diocesan Development Plan). The weaknesses of the religious orientation are that: (1) some religious groups are intolerant of value systems other than their own; (2) some religious groups would not offer services to persons with value systems different from theirs; (3) some religious services impose their marriage or family services as a condition of participation in NFP; (4) some religious power structures and organizations do not legitimize experiential user knowledge and may not be respectful of it or incorporate it appropriately into their service program; and (5) religiously based services would be unacceptable to some persons in some localities.

The strengths of the experiential learning include the following: (1) experiential users as the teachers of NFP can be very effective and suitable in many cultural contexts; (2) experiential knowledge as a major basis for a new *occupation* of NFP teacher and teacher-supervisor would be effective; (3) the experiential approach incorporates human and religious values and is sensitive to local cultural contexts; (4) an experiential approach stimulates users to become volunteers to teach or help with NFP services, thus lowering the cost; and (5) NFP would be viewed as an educational approach compatible with a variety of functional areas. The weaknesses of the experiential approach are these: (1) in some contexts experiential users are intolerant of other value systems and do not respect diverse value systems; (2) there is a lack of models of experientially based human service occupations; (3) there is a lack of models of experientially based publicly accountable regular programs; (4) it would be difficult to develop external quality and accountability standards for local programs that were suitable for application in a variety of places; and (5) experiential knowledge is not socially legitimated in the modern world, and it may be difficult to incorporate it faithfully into institutionalized medical or Western religious service programs. Overall, the experiential orientation results in great value diversity of NFP programs, but serious conflict can arise in the struggle to develop regular programs with new occupations, quality, and accountability standards and to obtain legitimacy for NFP programs. The resulting NFP services, however, would likely be low-cost, contain many volunteer users, and be widely available to many people.

The strengths of the medical orientation are also several. They include the following: (1) updating NFP methods would be facilitated by the relatively close links of biomedical researchers and clinicians providing services; (2) existing models of quality and accountability can be relatively easily applied to NFP; (3) existing models of how to develop regular programs and their elements are easily applied to a new area like NFP; (4) the prestige and power of the medical profession would increase the credibility and respectability of NFP; and (5) the rapid expansion of NFP services would be facilitated by incorporating NFP programs into existing medical care delivery systems.

The weaknesses of the medical orientation lie especially in the related dangers of *professionalization* and of *medicalization.* These processes would be likely to make NFP services expensive, to limit severely their availability to a few people, and to threaten value diversity and the human and religious values attached to NFP.

Medicalization refers to the social-political process of defining a phenomenon as a disease or within the medical pathology system under the jurisdiction of the medical system to be controlled by physicians (Conrad and Schneider 1980, Zola 1977). An often-quoted example of medicalization is the recent change in the

United States from defining alcoholism as a crime under the criminal justice system to the current concept of alcoholism as a disease that is treatable within the medical treatment system. I selected this illustration of medicalization because there are important parallels, to which I will return, between the treatment of alcoholism and the provision of NFP services.

Contraceptives are already medicalized, and fertility is regarded within a pathology orientation by the medical profession. This approach is antithetical to the values of NFP, where fertility is viewed as a natural life process not to be artificially suppressed. There is already an example of the medicalization of NFP—those health personnel who redefine NFP and label it from within their medical orientation "fertility awareness with a barrier method."

Sociological analysts of cases of medicalization point out that when the medical profession takes over a condition, they conceptualize it to fit their world view (Conrad and Schneider 1980). The world view of scientific medicine contains the tendency to strip conditions of their human and religious value connotations and to replace these with technical connotations. Eric Cassell, himself an M.D., is one of many who argue that medicine is inherently moral but knowledge of this fact is denied with the belief that

> the physician does not make ethical decisions, he only makes technical decisions. Such concern for morality is not a generalization of expertise but an accepted part of the physician's role, and is so recognized by the society, though largely in a covert manner. But he and the patient protect themselves from the awesome implications of that responsibility by hiding behind the belief that doctors only make technical decisions. (Cassell 1973: 57).

If NFP were to become the territory of the regular medical establishment—with the exception of those physicians who support NFP for its value orientation, such as Roetzer, Billings, and Hilgers—it is quite predictable that many of the human and religious values attached to NFP would be stripped away in favor of redefining it in technical terms. Concurrently, the value diversity of NFP among different cultural and religious groups could be diminished. The medicalization of NFP would likely be accompanied by its professionalization, since the two seem to occur together.

Sociologists define the term "to professionalize" as the process through which occupational groups attempt upward social mobility, that is, to increase their prestige, remuneration, autonomy from clients, and control over their work territory (Wilensky 1964). In the professionalizing process, occupations usually emulate prestigious, autonomous professions like the medical profession (Freidson 1970; Starr 1982). Although the ideologies of professionalizing occupations often center around altruistic ethics of service, objectivity and impartiality, and a client service orientation, sociological analyses of these occupational groups reveal that their behaviors are often contradictory to their ideologies (Gerstl and Jacobs 1976). Occupational groups often restrict recruitment by imposing standards of formal education and training that serve to limit the number in the occupation. Restrictive recruitment or standards of training also lead to exclusivity in who is allowed into the occupation. Part-time or volunteer workers may be discouraged from obtaining training in attempts to uphold uniform and high salary levels. Many standards supposedly instituted to establish and maintain quality control lead to expensive training and certification mechanisms that are never demonstrated to accomplish their objective. Thus, in a variety of ways, the occupational groups are self-serving at the expense of service to clients and client interests.

The professionalization of NFP has pitfalls that could lead to serious problems. Two particular dangers are (1) diminishing the experiential-user knowledge since it is not easily codified in written form and is not respected in professional models of occupations; and (2) discouraging the training and utilization of part-time and volunteer experiential users as NFP teachers or participants in programs. Maximizing the use of volunteers in NFP programs can keep costs down and enthusiasm high, which is important to motivating couples, whereas the professionalizing of NFP occupations would drive costs up and dampen zeal.

Having considered some strengths and weaknesses of the three orientations as service delivery systems, what can we conclude? The paradox of NFP is that services cannot expand to a large number of places without using existing institutional networks (medical or religious), but if these networks lose the experiential component of NFP, then only a few people in each locality will be reached. Furthermore, if these NFP programs and occupations are designed according to the conventional professional or medical models, the services could be so expensive and ineffective that the advantage of the network would be lost. The temptation would be to professionalize NFP occupations if conventional models are followed. Similarly, the current model of the medical profession, if applied to NFP programs, could medicalize NFP and distort its integrity. New kinds of programs and nonprofessional occupations need to be designed that enable experiential experts to play their irreplaceable role in NFP and that preserve the values attached to NFP.

Suggested Recommendations

I have considered some of the potential advantages and disadvantages of following the extremes of each of the three orientations (religious, medical, or experiential) as a model of NFP programs and services. The approach will need to be novel in order to retain the combination of needed ingredients from all three orientations: the religious respect for human values, the applied biomedical knowledge of fertility awareness and reproduction, and the experiential learning of translating the biomedical knowledge to everyday life within the value framework of the involved individuals. Exactly how to accomplish this in any pragmatic situation is impossible to say; indeed, the important message is probably to maintain the spirit of the strengths from the three orientations, not to rigidly or systematically apply some formula in a standardized manner.

The following recommendations suggest how NFP services can make a successful transition from part-time, "fold-up," volunteer services to regular programs staffed with trained instructors, whether paid or unpaid.

1. Invite persons who have a commitment in each of the orientations to help in planning and development. It is important to have adequate representation of the three orientations, not just tokenism. Careful attention should be paid to choosing an experiential expert who will not be intimidated by the authority of health personnel or religious representatives.

2. Prepare a straightforward and explicit outline of values and criteria regarding NFP programs similar to mine at the beginning of this presentation (or in even more detail). The first step to awareness is to become cognizant of the values and criteria for a program within which one wishes to operate.

3. Invite a sympathetic but independent outside observer to help assess whether the approach is consistent with its own values if a group is in doubt about its direction or process. There are probably many experienced persons who would provide free consultation in exchange for helping to develop a novel value-oriented service program for NFP.

4. Try developing two solutions to any problem you face rather than one. As appropriate, select contrasting types of solutions: for example, if appropriate, an inexpensive rickshaw solution and a more expensive limousine solution if you have funds; or a solution depending totally on volunteer staff along with a solution depending on paid staff and minimum volunteer help. This approach may reduce attachment to a single solution, and it may open up more possibilities.

5. Look for other areas of human services that face similar problems and examine the ways they conceptualized issues and the solutions at which they arrived. For example, the alcoholism treatment field has agencies termed "social model" or "social-experiential model" (Borkman 1982) programs that faced similar dilem-

mas. The experiential knowledge of the recovering alcoholic from Alcoholics Anonymous was not legitimized in professionally based programs; the mutual self-help form of service giving had limitations since it was a "fold-up service" and a regular program was needed; the recovering alcoholic—an experiential expert—was not necessarily trained "occupationally" or in how to submit to an administrative program; and linkages with medical care and other social services had to be made.

The social experiential model alcoholism programs have developed an administrative and organizational structure that satisfies local legal, financial, and public accountability requirements (not without some controversy), but not at the expense of the experiential orientation. Experiential expertise informs basic policy-making and is paramount in staff services to program participants. Scrutiny is made of any proposed practice for its implications for the values of the agency. There are many other parallels that could be useful to persons developing NFP programs.

6. Adapt a model based on apprenticeship and service in developing NFP *occupations* such as instructor, trainer of instructors, and administrator, not a professional occupation based on formal education. The latter can quickly lead to concern about status, prestige, and other areas of self-interest. Training that emphasizes on-the-job apprenticeship and minimizes special training facilities or formal schooling is much more in keeping with the experiential learning that is the strength of current NFP instructors and is in keeping with fostering many volunteer instructors.

Consider new technologies that could be exploited for didactic training in the applied biomedical aspects. An example is the use of video cassettes for training sessions. Training could be designed to be as low-cost as possible and to make it widely available in many places.

7. Adopt an "NFP Impact Statement." I am suggesting a new kind of systematic analysis of selected consequences of any proposed procedure, policy, or practice on the client, the program, or values. The idea for this came from "Environmental Impact Statements" (EIS) that are required by U.S. law in certain physical development situations (Finsterbusch, Llewellyn, and Wolf 1983). The EIS is a formal analysis of the probable physical and social consequences of developing a new project such as a dam, highway, or nuclear power plant. The EIS can be used by policy-makers as a rational basis for weighing the positive and negative consequences of proposed projects. The requirement to think out potential consequences seems to be a valuable exercise.

A few ideas of the kinds of guidelines that could be used for the NFP Impact Statement will be mentioned for illustration; many others could be added depending on the values and objectives of the persons developing the program. Will the change (a) limit or increase access to training or services? (b) treat volunteer and paid staff alike or differently? (c) increase, decrease, or maintain the same level of costs to the NFP clientele or program? (d) increase, decrease, or have no impact on client involvement and participation in the learning process and receiving services? (e) decrease or increase client autonomy in the use of the method? (f) increase, decrease, or maintain the amount and quality of client volunteering in the program or in instruction? (g) increase, decrease, or maintain current levels of social distance between the NFP occupation and clientele?

In conclusion, it seems likely that it will be especially difficult to incorporate and legitimize the experiential-user role in new occupations and programs since the experiential user is not accepted as a vital part of service giving in current medical care or religious delivery systems. The task before you now in the expansion of NFP is the challenge of developing new NFP occupations and programs that fit within existing medical care or religious delivery systems without compromising the integrity of NFP.

References

Borkman, Thomasina.
1976 Experiential Knowledge: A New Concept for the Analysis of Self-Help Groups. *Social Service Review* 50:445-56.

1979 A Social Science Perspective of Research Issues for Natural Family Planning. *International Review of Natural Family Planning* 3:331-55.

1980 "A Social-Experiential Perspective of Natural Family Planning." Paper presented at the Second International Congress of the International Federation for Family Life Promotion, Navan, Ireland, Sept. 24.

1982 *A Social-Experiential Model in Programs for Alcoholism Recovery: A Research Report on a New Treatment Design.* Washington: National Institute for Alcohol Abuse and Alcoholism. DHHS Publication No. (ADM) 83-1259.

Cassell, Eric J.
1973 Making and Escaping Moral Decisions. *Hastings Center Studies* 1, No. 2:53-62.

Conrad, Peter, and Joseph W. Schneider.
1980 *Deviance and Medicalization: From Badness to Sickness.* St. Louis: C.V. Mosby.

Finsterbusch, Kurt, Lynn Llewellyn and C.P. Wolf, eds.
1983 *Social Imipact Assessment Methods.* Beverly Hills, CA: Sage Publications.

Foss, Dennis C.
1977 *The Value Controversy in Sociology.* San Francisco: Jossey-Bass.

Friedson, Eliot.
1970 *Profession of Medicine.* New York: Dodd, Mead & Co.

Friedson, Eliot, ed.
1973 *The Professions and Their Prospects.* Beverly Hills: Sage.

Gerstl, Joel and Glenn Jacobs, eds.
1976 *Professions for the People: The Politics of Skill.* New York: Schenkman.

Gouldner, Alvin W.
1962 Anti-Minotaur: The Myth of a Value-Free Sociology. *Social Problems* 3:103-16.

1968 The Sociologist as Partisan: Sociology and The Welfare State. *American Sociologist* 3:103-16.

Illich, Ivan et al., eds.
1977 *Disabling Professions.* London: Marion Boyars.

Lanctôt, Claude A.
1982 "Natural Family Planning: An Overview." Paper presented at the German Agency for Technical Cooperation Workshop on Current Approaches to Population Problems, Wachtberg-Niederbachen, Oct. 28.

Shivanandan, Mary.
1979 *Natural Sex.* New York: Rawson Wade, 13-15.

Starr, Paul.
1982 *The Social Transformation of American Medicine.* New York: Basic Books.

Wilensky, Harold L.
1964 The Professionalization of Everyone? *American Journal of Sociology,* LXX:137-58.

Zola, Irving K.
1977 "Healthism and Disabling Medicalization" In *Disabling Professions,* edited by Ivan Illich et al. London: Marion Boyars.

Comments

Stephen Burke

Stephen Burke, A.C.S.W., assistant director of Catholic Social Services, Diocese of Providence, R.I., USA; director of NFP of Rhode Island

Before reacting to several points in Mrs. Doyle's excellent paper, I would like to say a little about my own work. My wife Sheila and I direct Natural Family Planning of Rhode Island, a program of Catholic social services in Rhode Island. The program, begun in November 1977, is sponsored by the Catholic Church, and we are directly accountable to it. It is funded through Catholic Social Services, and we also receive Title X monies from the United States government for the education and training of NFP teachers in the public sector. I am also secretary of the committee for standards for New England Natural Family Planning, Inc., an organization representing the NFP interest of the six northeastern states. Nine of the 11 dioceses in the New England region are members of our regional association.

Mrs. Doyle has given us several models of natural family planning national development, from top down to bottom up. I personally favor development from

8 THE TABLET 23 November 2002

How Vatican II changed the Church: 7

JOHN MARSHALL

My voyage of discovery

As the council met in Rome, the papal commission on birth control was concluding that the ban on contraception should be lifted.

MY appointment to the Pontifical Commission on Population, Family and Birth set up by Pope John XXIII in 1963 was for me a voyage of discovery. At the outset, like so many of my colleagues on the commission, I accepted the traditional teaching that contraception is intrinsically evil. But the inexorable unfolding of the scientific evidence and theological argument showed me otherwise, and gradually I came to believe that the traditional ban on artificial birth control could not be upheld. Unlike some of my colleagues, it was no "Road to Damascus" experience of blinding revelation that made me change my opinion in this way. Rather, it was as though the traditional teaching was contained in a corroding cistern; one leak in the argument was plugged only for another to develop, until it became obvious to most of us that nothing but a new cistern would suffice.

The Second Vatican Council was in session. Its theological commission was engaged in a bitterly fought battle between those who wished to restate the traditional view that procreation is the primary end of marriage, love being only secondary, and those who wished to do away with such a hierarchy of ends. A compromise was reached in paragraph 50 of the council's pastoral constitution on the Church in the modern world, *Gaudium et Spes*, where it is stated that the whole meaning of family life is to enlarge God's family "while not making the other purposes of matrimony of less account".

As this battle continued, Pope John XXIII suddenly announced that the question of birth control was to be removed from the council's agenda and given to a special body which came to be known as the birth control commission. Action was needed because international agencies, such as the United Nations and the World Health Organisation, had decided to become involved in a major way with the population question, which until that time had been avoided out of deference to Roman Catholic sensitivities. One task of the birth control commission: to advise the Holy See on how it should respond.

There was some criticism of the decision to remove the question from the council, the highest teaching authority in the Church. But many welcomed the move, since the birth control commission contained both laity and clergy, and hence was felt to be better equipped to deal with the subject than a solely clerical group.

The original commission consisted of three priests and three laymen (of which I was one) with backgrounds in sociology, economics, medicine and international diplomacy. My qualification was that as medical adviser to

Britain's Catholic Marriage Advisory Council, I had carried out and published extensive research into natural family planning.

We first met in a hotel in the woods outside Louvain in Belgium and quickly identified two tasks: thoroughly to assess the growing body of demographic, economic, sociological and psychological evidence related to population growth; and to prepare a clear explanation of the Church's teaching on birth control. It was hoped that the latter would at least gain respect for the Church's position. These tasks required wider skills than we possessed and so we recommended enlargement of our numbers. Pope John accepted the recommendation and added demographers and theologians, among others, bringing the total to 18.

The enlarged commission met at Domus Mariae in Rome in 1964 and soon reached what proved to be the first turning point in its existence. Canon Pierre de Locht, who had done much work with family movements in Belgium, made a powerful presentation. In essence he said that the Church's view of marriage had been distorted by the teaching that procreation is the primary end of marriage and sexual intercourse: this did not accord either with the scientific evidence or with the experience of married couples. The need was to start again from scratch. The Redemptorist theologian, Fr Bernard Häring, said, "But you are raising questions of fundamental theology", to which De Locht replied, "Yes, I suppose I am". (It must be remembered that up to this point the remit of the commission was to prepare a coherent account of the traditional teaching.) It was decided that we should take a break to allow time for private reflection and discussion. When we resumed, we concluded that unless we addressed fundamental questions, a coherent presentation of the teaching on contraception could not be achieved.

The Swiss Dominican, Henri de Reidmatten, secretary-general to the commission, presented an interim report to Pope Paul VI, who, on succeeding Pope John, had confirmed the existence of the commission and its work. The outcome was awaited with some trepidation, but Pope Paul's response was that the discussion should continue in a serious and responsible fashion wherever it led. At the same time he again enlarged the commission to some 64 members, to include different cultures – the original six members were all Europeans – cardinals and bishops, theologians, scientists and, most important, married people.

We met in 1965 at the Spanish College in Rome. Among many significant contributions was the dossier presented by the American couple, Pat and Patty Crowley: the women among us were playing a significant part. The Crowleys had conducted a survey among members of the Christian Family Movement in the United States which revealed something of the suffering experienced by married people in trying to observe the Church's ban on contraception. Attempts were made by some observers to dismiss this evidence by nostrums such as, "The Church is not a democracy", or "Morality is not determined by surveys". This was to miss the point, for the survey had been carried out among loyal Catholics who were often the backbone of their parishes; the previously hidden evidence of the damaging effect of the teaching on marriage could no longer be ignored. Instead of operating with intellectual constructs divorced from reality, the theology of marriage had to reflect living experience. This was not situation ethics; it was ethics grounded in reality.

During this session it was decided that the theologians should meet by themselves as a group, maintaining the interdisciplinary nature of the commission's work by having John Barret, professor of sociology at Notre Dame University, in attendance. The aim was to examine the history and theological basis of the teaching on birth control in depth. This the theologians did over a period of two weeks, most reaching the conclusion that the intrinsic evil of contraception could not be demonstrated and should not be sustained; a minority agreed that the intrinsic evil of contraception could not be demonstrated but thought the teaching should nevertheless be sustained because of the authority the Church had invested in it.

This was the second turning point in the life of the commission. The conclusions of the

THE TABLET 23 November 2002 — 9

theologians were thoroughly debated in plenary session, and most members of the commission agreed with the majority view. It was a time of great crisis. The debates were always scholarly, calm and courteous, but many commission members had invested greatly in the traditional teaching and they could not conceal their personal anguish.

Everyone was conscious of the tremendous significance of the conclusion of the majority. It was as though infallibility were being challenged. In fact it was not. The mistake had been to adopt a description of a natural phenomenon, sexual intercourse, as primarily procreative which did not accord with the scientific evidence (the majority of acts of intercourse do not have procreative potential) nor with the experience of couples. The Church is not infallible about natural phenomena.

I was scandalised by the view of the minority that although the validity of the teaching could not be demonstrated, it should be sustained because otherwise the authority of the Church and its authority as an infallible guide would be threatened. I thought it was wrong to put authority before truth. My final decision was much influenced by revolt against such an argument for maintaining the status quo.

The third and final turning point in the life of the commission was the presentation of the conclusions to a session of all the member bishops. Karol Wojtyla, later Pope John Paul II, had been named as one of them but he never once attended because, it was said, the Polish authorities would not give him a visa. In keeping with the interdisciplinary nature of the commission, individual bishops had taken part in specialist groups throughout and were seemingly in accord with the developments. But how would the bishops as a body react? In the event, the majority agreed with the majority conclusion.

Three years after the first meeting of the original six, in 1966, a final report was presented to Paul VI. This has never been published officially, but an authentic account appeared in *The Tablet* and the *National Catholic Reporter* of Kansas City.

The commission had now concluded its work and was disbanded. There followed 18 months of silence during which the Congregation for the Doctrine of the Faith (CDF) was feverishly active. Because the commission had been established to advise the Holy See on its stance in relation to the international organisations, its verdict should have been the responsibility of the Secretary of State, not the CDF. Cardinal Ottaviani, prefect of the CDF, was a member of the commission but said little; he was no doubt biding his time, as experienced bureaucrats do.

The CDF set up a highly secret group, composed entirely of hand-picked clergy, to produce a new report. This was reportedly so conservative that even the CDF found it unacceptable. So a second group, again entirely clerical, was convened and reported in due course, with what influence is unclear; the belief is that a draft of the 1968 encyclical *Humanae Vitae* was prepared for Paul VI by the French Jesuit, Gustave Martelet. As we know, the encyclical, though eloquent on the role of love in marriage, rejected our commission's line, and upheld the traditional teaching that contraception is intrinsically wrong.

What might have happened if the question of contraception had not been removed from the council? It is unlikely that the theological commission, composed as it was of clergy, would have been able to conduct a similarly wide-ranging, in-depth review. They might not have been able to get further than revising the previous doctrine that procreation was the primary end of marriage. On the other hand, if the conclusions had been those of the council, they could not have been strangled at birth by the CDF.

YET there has been change. During the long wait for the encyclical, Cardinal Heenan, with great prescience, said to me, "It does not matter now what the Pope says. It is too late. The people have made up their minds." Cardinal Heenan was a member of the commission and insisted throughout that both sides of the argument be presented fairly and squarely. I have no doubt that initially he accepted the traditional teaching; but in the final session he voted with the majority to change it.

Catholics as a whole did not accept the encyclical's teaching, and this non-acceptance differed from times past when someone who disagreed might argue: "I know the Church says this is wrong, but what else can I do in the circumstances? The Lord will understand." Now, however, the judgement of many was: "The teaching reaffirmed in *Humanae Vitae* is wrong. I cannot accept it as the word of God."

To have the Pope saying that contraception is intrinsically evil and his followers saying it is not, and acting accordingly, greatly weakens the witness of the Church in every field. It is ironic to recall that Paul VI was so powerfully motivated by a concern to uphold the Church's authority. Instead, it seems to me, he showed that the Church needs to re-evaluate the origin and nature and exercise of its authority on moral questions.

The story of the birth control commission and its aftermath illustrates the achievements and the shortcomings of the Second Vatican Council. There remains much unfinished business.

Dr John Marshall is emeritus professor of neurology at the University of London.

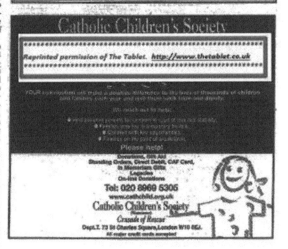

Readers' Reviews

John Marshall's *Love One Another: Psychological Aspects of Natural Family Planning,* (London: Sheed & Ward, 1995).

Mary Shivanandan, S.T.D.

We all know that books and articles are important vehicles through which we can spread the NFP message. Sadly, we also know that bad publications keep blocking the light of truth the world so desperately needs. In order to fight the good fight, NFP promoters need to keep track of not only the good resources but also those that are seriously flawed. In the following review one of those "problem" books is reviewed. Our reviewer, Mary Shivanandan, has graciously provided a careful examination of John Marshall's book, **Love One Another.** *Because we expect opponents of the Church's teachings on responsible parenthood to use this text against us, we suggest that you keep the following as an important reference.*

This book holds out the promise of being a major contribution to understanding the Church's teaching on responsible parenthood. Written by a distinguished medical researcher in natural family planning (NFP), Dr. John Marshall, it is based on correspondence with 10,000 NFP users in the British Isles and Ireland. Dr. Marshall, Emeritus Professor of Neurology, University of London, confirms through this correspondence that natural family planning is a reliable method of birth control that can be and is used by numerous ordinary couples. (The couples in his correspondence are primarily what we would call blue-collar.) He cites statistics as well as testimonies to show that many couples find the method both effective and beneficial to their marriage. For example he includes such quotes from women as:

> Most months I am quite sure of myself and see the temperature due to ovulation quite clearly. There is the odd time when I am in doubt, but play it safe and take one or two more temperatures... I must say my husband and I find this form of family planning most satisfactory. (p. 28)

and

> The temperature method has helped my husband and myself to be happier in our sexual relationship than we have been at any time previously in our 19 years of marriage, and consequently the whole of our relationship is more loving. (p. 29)

Marshall also confirms and highlights some of the challenges NFP couples experience such as: sex on a schedule with too much intercourse crammed into one week; the problem of expressing love in the fertile phase; the woman's heightened desire in the fertile phase and lack of desire in the post-ovulatory phase; as well as the importance of the husband's cooperation. It is not that NFP practitioners are not aware of these challenges, but Dr. Marshall shows how critical the psychological aspect is. Much attention has been paid to perfecting the physiological aspects of the method and an equal effort expended on a new theological exposition of the Church's teaching but the psychological aspects have, indeed, been neglected.[1] Here the book provides a most valuable service.

Given all this why, then, is the book a major disappointment and likely to damage rather than assist the cause of natural family planning? The last chapter provides the answer. Dr. Marshall, because of negative experiences by a number of the couples, recommends that the Church change its teaching on contraception.

The Author's Ambivalence towards NFP

In order to assess the weight of Dr. Marshall's case, it is important to examine first his own long-standing ambivalence towards the Church's teaching which is evident throughout the book. The author was one of the original six members of the Papal Birth Control Commission established in 1964 to consider the question of family planning which was being promoted by international agencies. Because the issue was seen to cover so many disciplines, the original commission, consisting of two physicians, two sociologists, an economist, and a secretary was expanded. Theologians were among those added and they concluded that from the point of view of natural law, contraception could not be classified as an "intrinsic evil." Dr. Marshall accepted this theological evaluation as is evident in the last chapter on "The Ethics of Contraception." Yet he continued to devote enormous amounts of time to natural family planning through the Catholic Marriage Advisory Council in England, personally answering every one of the 10,000 letters from NFP users over the years himself.

Dr. Marshall's ambivalence towards NFP appears throughout his work. For example, while describing as spurious the inseparability of the unitive and procreative aspects of sexual intercourse because not every act of intercourse is procreative, he also applauds the linking of the unitive and procreative since to separate them has resulted in trivializing sex. Again while he admits that NFP affects the whole person, he cannot see it as a "way of life." Not only is Dr. Marshall ambivalent but he is biased towards the negative and this is evident in the method he employs to present his material.

NFP Method

But first a look at the particular natural method of NFP taught by correspondence. It is referred to throughout the book as the BBT (Basal Body Temperature) method. Dr. Marshall says that it includes mucus but he does not appear to trust the mucus sign, especially in the preovulatory phase. In fact he gives an erroneous definition of Peak mucus, describing it as "the day on which the mucus is experienced as maximally slippery and lubricative"(p. 15) instead of the last day of fertile-type mucus before the change.[2] As a result an undue number of couples appear to confine intercourse to the post-ovulatory phase. Certainly negative comments come conspicuously from such couples.

> My own experience of the intimate side of marriage has yet to be fully satisfactory, and I put this down to the fact that we must remain virtually aloof for the greater part of the month, and then have to pack a whole month's love-making into the last eight days or so. (p. 62)

> One knows that there is just this one week in the month when one can live a normal married life and things always seem to be conspiring to threaten it. (p. 69)

Presentation of Material

Throughout the book, Dr. Marshall gives the negative experiences either equal or greater weight than the positive experiences. This he does despite the fact that he showed otherwise in a summary of a prospective study he had conducted from 1965-68 on the psychological aspects of the BBT method. In that study only 8 to 9% of both men and women felt that the BBT method "had hindered" their marriage, while about 74 to 75% felt it "had helped." As many as 69% of men and 61% of women appreciated intercourse more after the abstinence phase while only 9% of men and 13% of women appreciated it less. When it comes to specific aspects such as effect on spontaneity, the majority—more than 50 percent said it did not affect, while less than a third said that it did. Again three quarters of women and two-thirds of men found the method satisfactory while only 22 percent of men and 17 percent of women did not. In any case, these statistics are interpreted by the majority of NFP users in the study *(about three quarters)* who found the method satisfactory and helpful to their marriages. With regard to the letters on which the book is based, Dr. Marshall's method was to extract comments, place them on cards and file in categories. Unlike the prospective study, such a method could not provide any percentages between satisfied and dissatisfied users. Yet he dismisses the significance of percentages and instead gives equal weight to both negative and positive comments. (p. 34)

A further bias in his presentation can be seen from the relative space devoted to negative and positive comments. Negative comments are generally longer with more pages devoted to them. This is particularly noticeable in the chapter on "spiritual aspects." Only one page is devoted to positive comments and five to negative. By placing the negative after the positive in almost all cases, it tends to negate or diminish the impact of the positive comments.

Dr. Marshall's method of extracting comments also means that it is not possible to assess the context in which they were written nor evaluate the general adjustment of the couple's marriage. There seems to have been no follow-up when the couples were having difficulty with their sexual relationship *(see page 37-38)*. While the NFP teacher's role is not to tell the couple how to behave during the abstinence phase, as he says (p. 96), it is appropriate to refer couples who are having sexual or psychological difficulties for additional counseling, just as it would be to refer them for a medical diagnosis if there were an unusual physical discharge.

Inadequacy of Concepts

Nowhere in the book does Dr. Marshall cite other psychosocial studies, such as those by Robert Jonas, Sr. Peter McCusker, Grace Boys, Denise Desmarteaux, Gunter Freundl, Notker Klann, and Thomasina Borkman and Mary Shivanandan. An important aspect of these studies, limited though they may be, is the development of concepts related to the practice of natural family planning. His analysis does not even match that of the primarily descriptive McCusker study in 1976. While some of the testimonies he cites refer to stages in integrating NFP into the couple's relationship, Dr. Marshall makes no attempt to examine this phenomenon. The same couple, as Klann shows, may experience NFP as negative at one phase of their life and positive at another.[3]

Borkman and Shivanandan found two distinct stages; one the primarily physiological and the other the psychological and relational. Couples who remain at the physiological stage tend to have more negative experiences than those who have reached the relational transformative stage. At the transformative stage, couples often view NFP as a "way of life."[4] One woman in the book referred to this:

> Actually, I still think of it as family planning, when it's really our WAY OF LIFE! Something now, quite naturally integrated into our happy relaxed relationship. (p.29)

Dr. Marshall clearly does not see it as a "way of life." (p. 57) Yet the transformative potential of NFP is one of its greatest assets.

Dr. Marshall's limited approach can best be seen in the chapter on spiritual aspects. The quotes refer mainly to the couples' attitudes towards Church teaching, building up to his own ultimate rejection of that teaching. Three women appear to enjoy spiritual benefits over and beyond obeying the Church's teaching but most of the others are still at the rule stage of religion/spirituality with the majority chafing at the restrictions.

(pp. 84-90) Part of Dr. Marshall's problem may be due to his view of difficulties with abstinence as always a negative experience. Dr. Thomasina Borkman, professor of sociology, George Mason University, faced with her own negative views of sexual abstinence when she first studied the experiences of NFP couples, found herself impelled to rethink her position. How could couples both say that abstinence was difficult and yet describe it as benefiting their marriages? The dictionary gave her the answer, ascribing two meanings to the word, "difficult," one a challenge and the second deprivation. In Dr. Marshall's 1965-68 study about 8-9% found NFP unequivocally a deprivation, the same percentage as the couples in the Shivanandan/ Borkman study. Not to make this distinction is seriously to misinterpret the experiences of NFP couples. Every worthwhile venture poses some challenges. While these may not be welcomed at the time, the rewards can outweigh the difficulty of the effort. One has only to think of the struggle involved in mastering any sport.

> *Dr. Marshall's book, with its overemphasis on negative experiences. . .is likely to discourage couples from ever trying this method. . . .*

Experiential Learning

Dr. Marshall places strong stress on experience together with scientific observation as the ultimate arbiter of the validity of the Church's teaching on responsible parenthood. (p. 118) Yet there is no evidence that he understands the process of experiential learning. Experience is, indeed, important in the integration of NFP into the couple's relationship, but it is a dynamic not a static process. In its medical aspects, NFP involves what is called "head knowledge," i.e., the couples must learn the basics of the method and charting. But in its psychological aspect it calls for behavior modification and this involves experiential learning. Dr. Borkman, one of the leading experiential experts nationally and internationally[5], describes experiential learning as a process that involves the whole person, spiritual, psychological and physical. It proceeds by way of trial and error with many falls along the way. For example, there are two ways of looking at the tendency of couples to caress each other to orgasm during the abstinence phase, (1) as part of the process of sexual mastery and (2) as a fixed condition. In the one case the couple is striving for sexual integration and in the other they have settled for a spurious abstinence.[6]

While the basics of NFP can be taught by correspondence, it is much more difficult to teach couples how to integrate it into their marital relationship. A surprising number have succeeded, which says much for the potential of the method itself, but sociological research shows that certain conditions facilitate the integration. One of these is witness by other couples. Sharing their personal story of struggle and reward acts as a spur to couples going through a similar experience. The couple's frame of reference is also important. For example, one couple quoted in the book sees sexual intercourse as a gift from God that should not be restricted, while another is "sufficiently realistic to think that the perfect sexuality described in novels does not exist in reality." Obviously such attitudes affect their experience of a method that requires periods of abstinence. On this score Dr. Marshall's book, with its overemphasis on negative experiences and an inadequate theological framework, is likely to discourage couples from even trying the method let alone persevering if they run into difficulties.

Ethics of Contraception

Dr. Marshall is not a theologian, let alone a moral theologian. His justification for attempting an ethical appraisal of the Church's teaching is based on his "scientific" understanding of the nature of sexual intercourse and the experience of couples. The first part of this review has shown the danger of basing theology on experience without a full understanding of the nature of experience and experiential learning. It is equally hazardous to base moral theology on a limited physical understanding of sexual intercourse. That, indeed is biologism or physicalism.

First of all it is incorrect to say that the Church did not recognize as early as the 1930s that not every act of intercourse is physically open to generation.[7] Pius XI did describe contraception as "intrinsically against nature" because it deprives sexual intercourse of its "natural power."[8] His condemnation was set within the living tradition of the Church from earliest times. Dr. Marshall finds fault with this argument from "against nature," citing several meanings of "nature." First let it be said that NFP proponents do not reject artificial aids for determining the fertile period. Contraception is opposed not because it makes use of science but because it is against (contra) life (conception).

Both Paul VI and John Paul II uphold their predecessor's view of the law of nature as in essence divinely ordered since God is the author of nature and God has linked the generation of life to sexual intercourse.[9] The third meaning of nature as according to human reason and will is developed both by Paul VI in *Humanae vitae* and John Paul II, especially in *Love and Responsibility*.[10] Their arguments are very different from the limited interpretation of Dr. Marshall.

Reason and will belong to man's spiritual nature and love can only exist when they dominate the physical and psychological drives. Contraception makes the domination of the sexual drive in the service of life and love irrelevant. It elevates the physical side of marriage at the expense of the spiritual. It is physicalist in its truest sense.

Far from neglecting love in the marital relationship, as Dr. Marshall charges, Pius XI in *Casti connubii (On Christian Marriage)* gave a greater recognition to love in the marital relationship than any of his predecessors.[11] Paul VI further developed the role of love and John Paul II categorically states that it is love that coordinates the two meanings of marital intercourse, the unitive and procreative.[12] But love is an act of reason and will first, then it finds its expression in sexual intercourse. Periods of abstinence help to ensure the primacy of agapic over erotic love. It facilitates self-mastery. Sexual intercourse is a sign of total self-giving. A person can only make a complete gift of self if he is in full possession of himself including his sexual drive. Dr. Marshall has ignored these more profound insights into the place of love and sexual intercourse in marriage.

Conclusion

Other inadequacies of Dr. Marshall's book could be noted, such as: his neglect of breastfeeding; the role of NFP in achieving pregnancy and in encouraging an openness to children; his superficial historical review of the birth control movement "to safeguard the health of the mother;" and the complete absence of any negative effects of contraception on the woman, the couple's relationship, or society.

But most of all, it is regrettable that a man of Dr. Marshall's stature and apparent dedication to natural family planning should fail so signally to understand much less promote the Church's teaching on responsible parenthood. The testimonies themselves provide invaluable information on the practice of NFP. No serious NFP advocate can afford to overlook the very real struggles and difficulties of some couples in its practice. In this aspect Dr. Marshall has made a substantial contribution. The danger is that his interpretation and conclusions will be accepted as gospel truth and further undermine the credibility of NFP especially among those who could do most to promote it such as pastors and doctors. ■

Mary Shivanandan, STD, is a well know NFP author and is currently teaching at the John Paul II Institute on the Family in Washington, D.C.

End Notes:

1 Louis P. LaBarber, "Psychosocial Aspects of NFP Instruction: A National Survey," *International Review of Natural Family Planning* 14 (1) (Spring 1990): 34-53.

2 Professor Erik Odeblad, renowned expert on cervical mucus, says that "it is very important to know that the quantity of mucus is usually not at its maximum on the Peak Day. The quantity and also the stretchiness are greater on the day preceding the Peak." "The Discovery of Different Types of Cervical Mucus and the Billings Ovulation Method,"*Bulletin of the Natural Family Planning Council of Victoria* 21 (3) (September 1994): 3-34.

3 Notker Klann et al. "Psychological Aspects of NFP Practice," *International Journal of Fertility* Supplement (May 1988): 65-69.

4 Thomasina Borkman and Mary Shivanandan, "The Impact of Natural Family Planning on Selected Aspects of the Couple Relationship," *International Review of Natural Family Planning* 8 (1) (Spring 1984): 58-66.

5 Dr. Borkman, professor of Sociology, George Mason University, has studied the process of experiential learning in natural family planning as well as other areas where behavioral change is implicated such as recovery from an addiction. As applied to NFP see especially: "A Social-Science Perspective of Research Issues for Natural Family Planning," *International Review of Natural Family Planning* 3 (4) (Winter 1979): 331-355.

6 See John Harvey, "Expressing Marital Love during the Fertile Phase," *International Review of Natural Family Planning* 4 (4) (Winter 1980): 279-296.

7 Ramón García de Haro. *Marriage and the Family in the Documents of the Magisterium: Course in the Theology of Marriage*, (San Francisco: Ignatius Press, 1993), 133. See also *Humanae vitae*, no. 11.

8 Ibid., 131.

9 *Humanae vitae*, no. 12, and *Familiaris consortio*, no. 33.

10 *Humane vitae*, no. 9, and Karol Wojtyla, *Love and Responsibility* (San Francisco: Ignatius Press, 1993), 21-24.

11 Pius XI, *On Christian Marriage* (Boston, MA: St. Paul Books & Media, n.d.), 14.

12 See especially Paul VI's *"Address to the Teams of Our Lady,"* 1970, in *Good News for Married Love* (Collegeville, MN: The Liturgical Press, 1974) and De Haro, *Marriage and the Family*, 342.

LIST OF ARTICLES CITED

Conjugal Spirituality and the Gift of Reverence," ***Nova et Vetera***, 10:2 (2012)

"An Anthropology of Love: ***Caritas in Veriitate,***" in Proceedings of "Human Fertility—Where Faith and Science Meet" Conference, July 15-17, 2010 (Washington, DC: USCCB, 2011)

"Reflections on ***Humanae Vitae*** in the Light of ***Fides et Ratio; Nova et Vetera***,6:4, (2008)

"John Paul II: The Redemption of the Body and the Call to Holiness," ***Faith & Reason*** 31: 1 (Spring 2006)

"The Immaculate Conception and Theological Anthropology," in ***The Immaculate Conception in the Life of the Church,*** Ed. Donald H. Calloway (Stockbridge, MA: Marian Press 2004)

"Body Narratives: Language of Truth?," ***Logos*** 3: 3 (Summer, 2000), 166-193.

"Feminism and Marriage: a Reflection on Ephesians 5:21-33," *Diakonia* 29, 1, 1996.

Made in the USA
Columbia, SC
17 April 2018